THE CHARTIST LEGACY

MERLIN PRESS

THE CHARTIST LEGACY

Edited by Owen Ashton, Robert Fyson and
Stephen Roberts

With a Foreword by Asa Briggs

MERLIN PRESS
1999

First published in 1999
By the Merlin Press Ltd
2 Rendlesham Mews, Rendlesham
Nr. Woodbridge, Suffolk
IP12 2SZ

ISBN   085036 486 8 (Hbk)
ISBN   085036 484 1 (Pbk)

Typesetting by Julie Rainford
Cover designed by Louis Mackay

The image of Feargus O'Connor taken from a photo
reproduced by kind permission of Nottingham City
Council Leisure and Community Services, Nottingham
Central Library and the *Nottingham Evening Post*

Printed in Finland by WSOY

CONTENTS

ACKNOWLEDGEMENTS

The editors would like to thank the Lipman-Miliband Trust, the Scouloudi Foundation and the Royal Historical Society for their generous financial support; the University of Birmingham for the use of conference facilities, which enabled a number of chapters to be aired; and Dorothy Thompson and Pat Eve for advice and encouragement in the preparation of this book.

NOTES ON CONTRIBUTORS

OWEN ASHTON is a Reader in Modern British Social History at Staffordshire University. Among his publications are: *W.E. Adams, Chartist, Radical and Journalist* (Bewick Press, 1991); with Robert Fyson and Stephen Roberts, *The Chartist Movement: A New Annotated* Bibliography (Mansell, 1995) and *The Duty of Discontent: Essays for Dorothy Thompson* (Mansell, 1995); and with Stephen Roberts, *The Victorian Working Class Writer* (Mansell, 1999)

JAMIE L. BRONSTEIN is an Assistant Professor in the History Department of New Mexico State University and author of *Land Reform and Working-Class Experience in Britain and the United States, 1800-1862* (Stanford University Press, 1999). She is currently working on a comparative study of workplace accidents and injured workers in Britain and the United States before 1880.

ROBERT FYSON, formerly Senior Lecturer in History, is now an Honorary Research Associate at Staffordshire University. For many years his main research interest has been Chartism in North Staffordshire, and he recently completed his Ph.D. thesis on that subject. He has co-edited two previous books with Owen Ashton and Stephen Roberts. He has also contributed to John Rule (ed.), *British Trade Unionism 1750-1850: The Formative Years* (Longman, 1988) and James Epstein and Dorothy Thompson (eds.), *The Chartist Experience,* (Macmillan, 1982).

ROBERT G. HALL is an Assistant Professor of History at Ball State University in Muncie, Indiana. He has published essays on William Aitken and on the 1818 strike wave in the cotton district and has edited with Stephen Roberts, *William Aitken: The Writings of a Nineteenth Century Working Man* (Tameside Libraries, 1996). At present he is completing a manuscript on collective identities in nineteenth-century Lancashire.

JOAN HUGMAN is Lecturer in History at the University of Northumbria at Newcastle-upon-Tyne, where she completed her Ph.D. thesis on 'Joseph Cowen of Newcastle and Radical Liberalism'. In 1996, she contributed a chapter on 'Joseph Cowen and the Blaydon Co-operative Society' in B. Lancaster and P. Maguire (eds.) *Towards The Co-operative Commonwealth* (The Co-operative College, Loughborough); and co-authored an article 'Letters from America: George Julian Harney, Boston, U.S.A., and Newcastle-upon-Tyne, England, 1863-1888' in *Proceedings of the Massachusetts Historical Society,* Vol. CVII. Currently, she is engaged in writing the official history of the University of Northumbria.

KELLY J. MAYS is Assistant Professor of English at New Mexico State University, and author of *The Instructors' Guide to the Norton Introduction to Literature* (7th edition) and of 'The Disease of Reading and Victorian Periodicals' in John O. Jordan and Robert L. Patten (eds.) *Literature in the Marketplace: Nineteenth-Century British Publishing and Reading Practices* (Cambridge, 1995). She is currently completing a book project, which analyses representations of reading and literacy in texts ranging from Walter Scott's *Waverley* and working-class autobiographies such as W.E. Adams' *Memoirs of a Social Atom* to the records of several mutual improvement societies established by working-class men in late-nineteenth-century West Yorkshire.

PAUL A. PICKERING is a postdoctoral fellow in the Research School of Social Sciences, The Australian National University, Canberra. He is author of *Chartism and the Chartists in Manchester and Salford* (Macmillan, 1995), and several articles on nineteenth-century radicalism. He is currently writing, with Alex Tyrrell, a social history of the campaign against the Corn Laws to be published by Leicester University Press.

TIMOTHY RANDALL is a part-time Lecturer in English at Havering College of Further and Higher Education, and a part-time care worker at a home for the elderly. He has published articles on John Doherty and Ebenezer Elliott. At present he is completing a book on Chartist verse and fiction.

STEPHEN ROBERTS is Head of History and Law at Hagley R.C. High School, Worcestershire, and a Fellow of the University of Birmingham. He is author of *Radical Politicians and Poets in Early Victorian Britain* (Edwin Mellen, 1993) and other studies of Chartist leaders, and co-editor, with Dorothy Thompson, of *Images of Chartism* (Merlin Press, 1998).

ANTONY TAYLOR is Lecturer in History at Sheffield Hallam University. He is author of a number of books and articles on post-Chartist radicalism. His most recent work is *'Down with the Crown': British Anti-Monarchism and Debates about Royalty from 1790*, (Forthcoming, Reaktion Books, 1999).

MILES TAYLOR is Lecturer in Modern History at King's College, University of London. He is the author of several articles and *The Decline of British Radicalism 1847-1860* (Oxford, 1995). He is currently completing a biography of the last Chartist leader, Ernest Jones.

FOREWORD

ASA BRIGGS

Chartism has inspired a remarkable volume of research since G.D.H. Cole published *Chartist Portraits* in 1941. 'Inspired' is the right verb – for behind much of the work there has been feeling as well as thought. Chartism is also a subject which wins the sympathy of reviewers almost as much as of authors, sometimes more, and its study encourages a re-examination not only of history from below, but of history from above.

I am glad to be able to write a foreword to a collection of essays on Chartism by scholars of a different generation from my own. They are characterised both by a deep commitment to the subject and thorough research, and they cover many themes, a greater variety, indeed, than any previous volume on Chartism.

Cole's volume of profiles, which I bought when they came out in 1941, the year when I graduated from Cambridge University, were not the product of such research, and his wife, Margaret, did not even choose to mention them when she wrote Douglas's *Life* in 1971. Nor did she mention, for that matter, the volume of essays on labour history which John Saville and I prepared for her husband's seventieth birthday, which he did not live quite long enough to celebrate, or the other volume of *Chartist Studies*, which I edited alone and which appeared a year later.

No one did more than Cole to stimulate the study of 'labour movements,' the title of a paper which he introduced into Modern Greats (Philosophy, Politics and Economics) in Oxford University: a paper which I taught throughout most of my years in Oxford from 1945 to 1955. There had been no labour history in Cambridge, nor was there in most universities before the War. And this in itself puts into perspective the burst of work on the subject since 1959. The founding of the Society for the Study of Labour History in 1959, of which I was first President, was a landmark date, a by-product of the Briggs/Saville volume. It fostered collective as well as individual research.

In 1965, when I wrote an introduction to a new print of Cole's *Chartist Portraits*, the Society was well established, and so, too, were Chartist studies. I called it 'one of the most readable and interesting' of Cole's many books on labour history. And before that (1963) Edward Thompson's *The Making of the English Working Class* had appeared, 'a long and exciting prelude,' as I described it, to the story of Chartism. It has had a bigger influence on research on labour movements than Cole himself had.

As far as Chartism was concerned, Cole's 'introductory study,' as he called his own introduction to *Chartist Portraits*, began with a sentence which might have come straight out of Thomas Carlyle's *Chartism* (1840), a work that he did not mention in his text. 'Hunger and hatred – these were the forces that made Chartism a mass movement of the British working class'. An inadequate analysis, it was a good beginning. At the time I wrote my own introduction I preferred Max Beer's 'the victory of the vanquished'. Cole's comments, however, are worth quoting. They looked to the future.

There was a 'vast amount of work that still needs to be done,' he concluded, 'before anyone can hope to produce a really satisfactory history of Chartism'. 'There is room for a dozen local studies in Chartism and for a dozen biographies, on a larger scale than mine, of outstanding Chartist leaders. It is one of the most curious gaps in biographical writing that there is no Life of Feargus O'Connor – surely the most influential figure in nineteenth century England who has been left lacking such a monument. But then ... social history is in its infancy: there are no academic endowments for it, and few to care whether it is written or not'. (He is writing *before* G.M. Trevelyan published his best seller, *English Social History*, which defined social history in a way that I sharply criticised as 'history with the politics left out'. For me it was better defined as economic history with the politics put in).

Cole did not live to see the boom in social history of the 1960s and 1970s, but he was right to refer to local studies, an area I discussed with him in the 1950s, as well as to biographies. *Chartist Studies* pushed research on the subject into what the Chartists called 'the localities,' and this meant examining grass roots as well as leadership. With newspapers as a main source – and with the invaluable help of the *Northern Star*, which was to push research back to O'Connor – the interpretation of Chartism was, in my view, transformed. My reasons for pushing research in a local direction evolved not out of my interest in labour's rank-and-file, but in local history. I had published my *History of Birmingham* [from 1865 to 1938] in 1951, and two long and heavily researched articles on Thomas Attwood and local reform politics in the *Cambridge Historical Journal* three years earlier. (These were my substitute for a doctorate which was not then a necessary qualification for academic historians). Thanks to Cole, I was appointed Reader in Recent Social and Economic History in Oxford in 1950 – he wanted to save me from returning to Cambridge where I was approached about a Readership – and now had time to devote myself to labour history and to supervise the first of a huge number of postgraduate students in the subject, to whose own work I owe a great debt.

In one of my articles on Attwood I quoted a remark by G.J. Holyoake in *Sixty Years of an Agitator's Life* (1892) that 'Londoners are the lapidaries of the nation: they polish the diamond found in the counties, and sometimes, if no one challenges them, they take credit for the jewel'. As a Yorkshireman, I read what Holyoake (with Birmingham credentials) had to say with deep feeling. It was not merely that I wished to encourage local studies of Chartism. I believed that we needed a new social history of England with local experience at its base and not just put in as illustration. I thought of it ambitiously as far more than the history of the labour movement. It had to be 'total history,' a term I used without having read Braudel. I was already moving from economic and social into cultural history, although the term was not then used, and was very sympathetic myself to 'the culture of Chartism,' its language, its imagery, and its use of memory and myth.

To me, local Chartist studies were not a substitute for studies of
Chartism in its international setting. In 1948 I was invited to Paris
as a young historian to take part in the celebrations of the centenary
of the revolutions of 1848, and I spent time before I went
researching on comparative social history and on Chartist links
with European revolutionaries. I also wrote an article in 1950, in
the very first number of the *British Journal of Sociology*, on 'Social
Structure in Birmingham and Lyons, 1825-1848,' and I was glad
when years later in 1978, Eva Haraszti, who was to marry A.J.P.
Taylor, produced for the Hungarian Academy of Sciences her book
on Chartism, which included an appendix 'Hungarian Papers on
Chartism and England'. Hungary had figured so prominently in the
politics of the New Left that it has an important place in twentieth
century British history.

I had been interested to read in T.F. Tout's introduction to Mark
Hovell's much criticised *The Chartist Movement* (1925 edn) – and I
was among his sharpest critics – how Hovell, sadly killed during
the First World War, went from Manchester to Leipzig to study
Kulturgeschichte just before the War broke out and that it was there
that he first read Max Beer. Already, however, he had given
Workers' Education Association classes on Chartism. WEA people
who followed in his wake included Hugh Gaitskell who wrote a
pamphlet (without carrying out any research) in 1929. I
occasionally discussed Chartism with Gaitskell when he was one of
the Leeds MPs and I was Professor of History at the University,
after leaving Oxford, from 1955 to 1961. I did a lot of writing in
Leeds – and the decision to start a Labour History Society was
taken in my rooms there – but I now regret that I did not carry out
more research on Leeds Chartism, which has its own place,
different from that of Birmingham, in the 1830s and 1840s. I did
enough research on Samuel Smiles, however, and on Joshua
Hobson, to appreciate their particular angles on Chartism. The
essay on Chartism in Leeds in *Chartist Studies* was written by John
Harrison, then in the Adult Education Department in Leeds, along
with Edward Thompson. I managed with some difficulty to get
them both to give lectures to history undergraduates as well as to
WEA and other adult education classes.

The proofs of *Chartist Studies* were read by Maurice Hutt, one of my colleagues in the School of History at Leeds, and he accompanied me to Sussex University in 1961, with John Harrison to follow. There was a special subject on Chartism at Sussex from the start and the very last academic contribution I made at Sussex in 1975 was to take a seminar on Chartism. I had given the first years before and many people who were subsequently to write learnedly and, I'm glad to say, imaginatively on Chartism were either staff members of it or postgraduate students, first under my supervision and then under that of John Harrison. One of them was Tom Kemnitz, one of a long line of Americans who were as interested in Chartism as Europeans (or Australians, the latest of them represented in this volume). Hovell did not live long enough to mention Rosenblatt, Slosson or Faulkner; Tout, a born historiographer, did. In my preface to *Chartist Studies*, the only book that I mentioned was A.R. Schoyen's study of G.J. Harney, *The Chartist Challenge* (1958). It had appeared too late to have been read by me or the other contributors when they wrote their pieces, but it had a considerable influence on me. When I returned to Oxford from Sussex in 1976, 'Labour Movements' had sadly disappeared.

I was asked by the hard working editors of this volume to give this foreword an autobiographical twist. I am reluctant to be autobiographical since I am still heavily involved in historical writing, and look to future projects rather than past publications. Yet I understand the importance of trying to get right the recent historiography of Chartism. While I did little work as an undergraduate in Cambridge on Chartism – I spent two years on medieval history and one on modern – I did learn about historiography. I have never forgotten what I learned, and Chartism did figure as a climax in my special subject on 'Utilitarianism and Tory Democracy,' beautifully supervised by R.J. White, who has been dismissed by some labour historians.

Within this context past and present converged in an active present when last year, 1998, I produced a very short 'pocket history' of Chartism in 20,000 words. Writing on this scale was a challenge and I had to leave out more than I put in. Some discarded sections

seemed to me – even as general editor – to be fundamental. What
had to be put in was a narrative, for I knew that despite Dorothy
Thompson and all her collaborators, we still lack one. The essays in
this volume will be essential reading for the historian who finally
succeeds in producing a full narrative. Where it must begin and end
is still an open question.

Lewes, 1999

THE SIX POINTS: CHARTISM AND THE REFORM OF PARLIAMENT

Miles Taylor

At the heart of the Chartist movement, as every schoolchild knows, was the demand for the six points of the 'People's Charter': manhood suffrage, equal electoral districts, vote by ballot, annual parliaments, payment of MPs, and abolition of the property qualification. This is not, of course, strictly accurate. Although the phrase 'the six points' became widely used from around 1840 onwards - in speeches, advertising handbills, anti-Chartist tracts, banners and flags - only one of the key texts of Chartism ever put forward a list of six points, namely, the last Chartist petition, presented to Parliament in April, 1848. But this was the exception, not the rule. The original 'People's Charter,' drawn up and published by the London Working Men's Association in May 1838, actually contained nine points, which incorporated the six points *inter alia* within a set of reforms to the machinery of elections. The 'national petition' agreed to by the meeting of the Birmingham Political Union in August, 1838, which subsequently became the first Chartist petition presented to Parliament in July of the following year, called for only five points (it excluded equal electoral districts). And the second Chartist petition, which went to the House of Commons in May 1842, in fact called for eight points (ie: in addition to the six points, it demanded repeal of the Union between Britain and Ireland, and required that MPs seek approval of their conduct by their constituents at frequent intervals).[1] Clearly, either someone could not count properly, or Chartist ideas about parliamentary reform were rather more complex than appears at first sight.

The specific demands of the Charter - whether they be five points, eight or nine, or even six - have been surprisingly neglected by historians. The Chartist call for the reform of the representative and electoral system comes a long way down the list of historians' interests in the movement. Chartist attitudes towards the constitution seldom receive coverage beyond the perennial problem of physical versus moral force. There are two main reasons for this neglect. First, the Charter itself tends to be seen, even by historians

sympathetic to the movement, as embodying a rather unrealistic set
of demands. It is thought to have served primarily as a rallying-cry:
a simple, comprehensible plea behind which a disparate army of
followers up and down the country could unite.[2] The actual content
of the Charter mattered less than its symbolic function. Secondly,
the Charter has been passed over by historians, because, on the face
of it, it is a rather familiar document, one which encapsulates
radical reform demands dating back sixty years to the days of John
Wilkes and Major John Cartwright.[3] In other words, the points of
the Charter are historically uninteresting because they were too
impractical or too unoriginal.

Both these premises, this chapter argues, are misleading and
unhelpful. The 'People's Charter' of 1838 and the three national
petitions which followed were the outcome of a very specific
critique of the workings of the House of Commons, a critique
which developed in the aftermath of the 1832 Reform Act. Nearly
all the points of the Charter were discussed inside and outside
parliament in the years between 1832 and the beginning of
Chartism in 1837. The Chartists continued and developed the
widespread view that the main problem with the reformed
parliament and the electoral system on which it was based was that
its members were not sufficiently responsive to their constituents.
The result was that they passed unpopular legislation such as the
1834 Poor Law Amendment Act. The remedy was to make MPs
more accountable, and to a large extent the points of the Charter
were designed with this in mind. Moreover, Chartists had their own
idea of how a people's representative should behave. From the
workings of the Chartist General Convention of the Industrious
Classes in 1839, and from the subsequent involvement of many
Chartists in parliamentary and municipal elections, it becomes clear
that the Chartists believed MPs should be delegates not simply
representatives. Arguably, the greatest threat posed by the Chartists
in constitutional terms, was not universal suffrage, but the
mandatory theory of representation.

The rest of this chapter falls into three main sections. First, I
bring out the significant differences between the Charter and the
so-called 'radical tradition' of parliamentary reform which
stretched back to the 1770s. I emphasise how the points of the
Charter, and particularly the concerns of the L.W.M.A., can only

really be understood in the light of the debate which raged in the radical press over the operation of the reformed parliament and, especially, the new electoral system after 1832. The Charter, in other words, had less to do with the older concerns of successive generations of Whigs and radical reformers than is usually supposed. Secondly, I describe the Chartist idea of delegation evident in the proceedings of the 1839 Convention. Finally I consider Chartist involvement in parliamentary and municipal elections through the 1840s and 1850s.

I

On the face of it, as many historians have suggested, the demands of the Charter seem to be in line with the radical reform programme which first emerged in Britain during the early decades of the reign of George III. The Chartists themselves claimed descent from the demands put forward by Whig reformers such as Charles James Fox and the Duke of Richmond in 1780,[4] and it is certainly the case that all of the Chartists' six points had been called for at one time or another during the preceding sixty years. But whilst some items on the reform agenda remained constant - principally, the insistence on annual parliaments and manhood suffrage - the reasoning behind their inclusion and the result they were designed to achieve changed a great deal. The Chartists invented a tradition of radical reform which helped to legitimise their own campaign, but on closer inspection, what they wanted from parliamentary reform, and what their Hanoverian predecessors had wanted, turn out to be poles apart.

The preoccupation of radical reformers and Foxite Whigs, from the 1770s through to the revival of the reform movement after 1815, can be summed up in one phrase: the influence of the Crown. The reform of the House of Commons was believed to be the best antidote to the growth of kingly and executive power associated with George III and several of his prime ministers: in particular, Lord North, Pitt the younger and the Duke of Portland. Before the accession of George III in 1760, reformers argued, parliamentary elections had been frequent, prime ministers of the day such as Harley, Walpole and the elder Pitt had worked hard at earning the confidence of the Commons (admittedly, through extensive patronage), and the monarchy in the shape of the first two Georges had for the most part kept out of British politics, remaining more concerned with their dynastic and strategic interests in Hanover. After 1760, however, Parliament seemed to have lost effective control over the affairs of the nation, as George III and his ministers - the 'double cabinet' in Burke's famous phrase - began to govern without consultation. Parliament fell into abeyance: elections became infrequent, absenteeism from the Commons was rife, and corrupt nomination boroughs ensured a steady stream of pliant MPs ready to do the bidding of the King's ministers. Reformers pointed to the consequences of this growth of the influence of the crown: the war with America and the spread of territorial dominion in Asia, the extension of the civil list, the growth of the military establishment during the Napoleonic wars, and an unremitting increase in indirect taxation and the national debt to pay for it all.[5] This is the wider political context in which the parliamentary reform agenda developed in modern Britain. Of course the demand for parliamentary reform also reflected the growth of urban population and the needs of an industrialising society, but what gave the reform agenda its cutting edge and appeal throughout the Hanoverian era was its focus on the system of 'old corruption' or 'the Thing' as Cobbett called it, centred on the monarchy.

Parliamentary reform in the reign of George III, in short, aimed at rejuvenating the House of Commons, an institution which many reformers felt (and which electoral statistics of the 1780s onwards certainly suggest)[6] had become moribund and ineffectual. An active Parliament would constrain the actions of the Crown, the policies of which had led the country into such disastrous and expensive military entanglements. In so doing, the original powers of the Commons would be restored: namely, its control over taxation, and its control over the army. Reasserting the sovereignty of Parliament in the face of what historians now call the 'fiscal-military state' led reformers to concentrate on three reforms of Parliament in particular: shortening the duration of parliament, extending the suffrage to all males liable for the militia, and curbing the power of the nomination boroughs. Annual parliaments were the priority for many reformers, including Major John Cartwright in 1776 and Christopher Wyvill's Yorkshire Association in 1779, on the grounds that regularity of election would make the House of

Commons less likely to countenance excessive government expenditure and taxation.[7] Cartwright also linked the suffrage to the question of national defence, arguing that all those who were liable for the militia should also be entitled to the vote. Associating citizenship with the bearing of arms was a common theme in late 18th century reform arguments. It is no coincidence that many late 18th century parliamentary reformers were military men of one sort or another: Cartwright, the Duke of Richmond and Henry Flood, to name but a few. The Duke of Richmond was so concerned with ensuring the armed forces were able to vote that he made special provisions for them in his bill of 1780.[8]

But by far the most important parliamentary reform called for throughout the period was the ending of the corruption of the small nomination boroughs. Reformers tended to favour two remedies for ridding the parliament of placemen. First, they recommended the bolstering of the electoral power of the counties, and in some cases of London. In the proposals of Wilkes in 1776, Charles Grey in 1797 and Thomas Brand in 1810, small boroughs would have been disfranchised, and their representation transferred to the counties and to the metropolis.[9] Other reformers, such as Flood in 1790 and Burdett in 1809, proposed dividing the counties up into equal districts and introducing household suffrage in them.[10] What is significant about all these schemes is that it was not unrepresented, urban England which was seen as the virtuous part of the polity, but, rather, the county electorate. County electors, whether they be freeholders, or as reformers intended, copyholders, leaseholders and householders, were thought to be more independent and immune to influence and bribery than their town counterparts. The second remedy looked to by parliamentary reformers as a means of curing Parliament of corruption was a residential suffrage. The great problem with the small nomination boroughs was not only that their electorates were numerically tiny, they were also malleable and artificial. Non-resident voters who owned property in the constituency - for example, county magnates, or men who, although living elsewhere, belonged to one of the corporations - could vote. Moreover, those who had no connection with the borough, but who bought up property on the eve of elections, often effectively purchased a seat in parliament. Enfranchising resident householders in the boroughs was seen as the means of ending this subservience to carpetbagging, outside influence. Virtually all technical discussions of manhood suffrage in this period (not unlike discussions of strict settlement in the poor law) were centred around the question of establishing residence, protecting the local interests of the constituency, and warding off outsiders (usually from London, or, earlier in George III's reign, from Scotland). The rights of man effectively meant the rights of householders.

So, parliamentary reformers of the Hanoverian era were no strangers to many of the demands that the Chartists were to make their own. But these earlier schemes, all of which incorporated four, five or all six points of what became known as the 'People's Charter,' had a rather different end in view to that of the Chartists. They were all preoccupied with limiting the influence of the Crown. Annual parliaments would subject the king's ministers to regular scrutiny. Equalising the representation, whether in the form of electoral districts in the counties or transferring seats from small boroughs to the counties and to London, would neutralise executive influence in the Commons. And household suffrage would establish a fixed and local electorate which would weaken courtly and plutocratic influence. All these demands reflected a pronounced dislike of executive power and a rather exaggerated sense of the importance of the House of Commons. Invigorated by reform, the Commons would resume its traditional role of protecting the people from the encroachments of the Crown. Few reformers, it should be noted, entertained a dim view of the operations of the Commons itself. The Commons was the solution, not the problem. Jeremy Bentham, who had a pretty dim view of MPs, along with the rest of mankind, was almost alone in insisting that the operations of the Commons might be in need of reform as well. In his *Plan of Parliamentary Reform* (1817) he proposed, in addition to annual parliaments, universal suffrage (male and female) and the ballot, what he called 'universal constancy of attendance' by MPs, by which all of them would deposit £400 at the beginning of the parliamentary session, and receive back £2 for every day they attended.[11] That way absenteeism could be avoided. As with most of his writings during his lifetime, Bentham's plan had little impact at the time, but it resurfaced in the 1830s as the parliamentary reform agenda swung away from a critique of 'old corruption' and crown influence and instead homed in on the workings of the

House of Commons. Here lies the context for understanding the contents of the 'People's Charter'.

II

The 'People's Charter' embodied a very different set of demands from this earlier radical tradition of parliamentary reform. In the twenty years or so which intervened between the end of the Napoleonic wars in 1815, and the beginning of Chartism, the radical clamour over the crown and 'old corruption' had become much more muted. Amidst the backlash against Jacobinism, the monarchy itself enjoyed new popularity, to the extent that the rather dubious claims of Queen Caroline, the estranged wife of George IV, became a *cause celebre* for radicals and Whigs alike during 1820-21.[12] And although attitudes towards Queen Victoria were to change somewhat in the 1840s, her accession in 1837 and coronation in 1838 were characterised by a grudging respect even in radical circles (not least because her succession ended the prospects of the despotic Ernest Augustus, George III's fifth son). In the summer of 1837 the L.W.M.A., for example, noted in its address on the elections that 'we are now at the commencement of a new reign and from promises of youthful unbiased feelings, as well as from the education given to our Queen, great expectations have been generated'.[13] 'Old corruption' too was becoming a thing of the past. The economical reforms begun by Pitt the younger, and continued by the Liverpool ministries of the 1820s, cut the costs of government in areas such as bureaucracy, colonial administration, the military establishment and the civil list, although without making any inroads on the tax burden, which in real terms increased in peacetime.[14] And, most important of all, the long-cherished desire of the radical reformers and Foxite Whigs - the rejuvenation of Parliament - was largely achieved with the passing of the Reform Bill in the summer of 1832. Not that the 1832 Reform Act implemented any of the earlier reform schemes in total, but it did address most of their central concerns. The nomination boroughs were reduced, the large metropolitan areas and the counties were strengthened at the expense of the small boroughs, and, perhaps most significantly, the principle of residence was established as the essential prerequisite for entitlement to vote.[15] Much is often made of how the 1832 Reform Act continued a long, unfair aristocratic convention of a property-owning franchise. But this is not really true. Under the terms of the new electoral registration system introduced by the Reform Act, unless would-be-voters could prove they had been resident for at least twelve months and paid all their local taxes, no matter how grand their property - be it castle or cottage, ten-pounder or tenement - they would not be placed on the electoral register. Thus, the 1832 Reform Act removed one scourge - the non-resident voter - from the constitution, only to replace it with another: an arbitrary and complicated registration system, the reform of which became one of the abiding concerns of reformers down to the 1918 Representation of the People Act.

The effect of the Reform Act was therefore to resuscitate the House of Commons. During the 1830s parliamentary elections became more frequent making the Septennial Act something of an irrelevance: the number of uncontested seats dropped to an all-time low, electoral turn-out rose to an average of 70%, the proceedings of Parliament became more widely reported, a greater proportion of MPs than ever before contributed to parliamentary debates, and public petitioning of Parliament increased massively (from around 4,000 petitions presented per annum in the late 1820s, to a post-1832 average of around 25,000 per annum, peaking at over 35,000 in 1843).[16] At the same time the members of the reformed House of Commons were returned under a new electoral system, two features of which were to prove particularly controversial during the 1830s.[17] First and foremost, the requirement that electors prove their qualification to vote by virtue of at least a year's residence, and by prompt payment of local rates, was felt to be too great an obstacle to the simple right of exercising the vote, and, in the election of December 1832, it seems to have encouraged a lower turn-out than was expected. Secondly, the management of the new registration system gave considerable power to non-elected parochial officials, who were now responsible for all aspects of the machinery of elections. Moreover, making a published register of all voters the basis of the electoral process opened the door to local party committees who from the 1835 election onwards began to systematically canvass names and addresses on the register, helping to secure the qualifications of their own supporters during the annual visits of the revising barristers who adjudicated on the content of the register, whilst challenging and often removing the names of their opponents' supporters. As is well-known, early Victorian elections turned not so much on events in the polling booth as in the chambers of the revising barrister. What is less known, is how central this new system was to the Chartist critique of the reformed Parliament.

Radical scrutiny of the constitution after 1832 focused on the activities of the reformed House of Commons. Of no movement was this truer than Chartism. The sense of betrayal and dashed hopes expressed by the Chartists in the aftermath of 1832 has been described by all its main historians. As the first Chartist petition said of the reformed Parliament, '[t]he fruit which looked so fair to the eye has turned to dust and ashes when gathered.'[18] The acquiescence of the Commons in a series of measures earned it widespread unpopularity: the limited nature of the Factory Act of 1833, the restrictions on press freedom which remained in spite of the reduction of the stamp duty in August, 1836, the arrest and transportation of the six Dorchester labourers in 1834, and above all the Poor Law Amendment Act, passed in the same year, but revealed in its full force to the manufacturing districts as the new Poor Law Commissioners moved northwards during 1837. All of these issues fuelled the take-off of Chartism during 1838. The reformed Parliament was roundly condemned. Initially, in the mid-1830s, radical critics chided the reformed Parliament for not doing its work properly. MPs were criticised for not attending on vital divisions, or for betraying the pledges and promises which they had given to their constituents at the time of their election. In 1837, the newspaper, the *Constitutional*, for example, compiled a 'registry' of the voting behaviour of MPs, drawing up a 'black-list' of those who had violated their promises, or who had defaulted in attendance.[19] There was also much criticism of the dismissive way in which the reformed Parliament handled the great volume of petitions now being sent up to Westminster. Alarmed at the huge increase in petitioning, most in evidence during the anti-slavery campaign of 1832-3, the Commons had introduced restrictions on the debating time which could be set aside for petitions. Such restrictions enraged radicals, who valued petitioning as the only legitimate means by which the voice of non-electors could be heard. Bronterre O'Brien, for example, referred to the new rules on petitioning as 'one of the worst acts of the reformed parliament'.[20] In these ways, radicals - soon to be Chartists - associated the evils of Whig legislation with the new innovations and personnel of the reformed Parliament, rather than with the persistence of 'old Corruption'.

Inevitably such criticism not only focused on the new procedures of Parliament, but also on the new electoral system which had put MPs into the House of Commons in the first place. In the spring of 1836, radicals in Parliament made further attempts to alter the ratepaying clauses of the 1832 Reform Act. At the end of April, Thomas Duncombe, the radical MP for Finsbury, failed to persuade Parliament to enfranchise compound householders (those £10 householders whose rates were paid by their landlords) and during June, the Commons moved slowly on other minor changes to the registration of voters.[21] In June, the London Working Men's Association was formed, and one of its first tasks was to set up a sub-committee to enquire into the state of the franchise. Many of its findings were incorporated into one of the L.W.M.A.'s first publications, *The Rotten House of Commons* (1836) which complained of the way in which Parliament ignored our 'humble petitions,' and pointed out how owing to the unequal distribution of seats only 1/5 of males over 21 had the right to vote. Moreover, the tract emphasised, this proportion was even lower because of the system of registration and the plurality of votes.[22] Over the next eighteen months, the L.W.M.A.'s critique of the electoral system gathered pace, as Parliament continued to refuse to move on the issue of the ratepaying clauses, or, indeed, on any other aspect of parliamentary reform. In June, 1837, Lord John Russell, the leader of the Whigs in the Commons, indicated in a speech in Stroud that there would be no further adjustments by the government to the provisions of the Reform Act (although interestingly, he did not rule out possible reform of the House of Lords).[23] At the same time the L.W.M.A., in consultation with six MPs, began to draw up what it called a 'petition for universal suffrage'. By the following February it was nearly ready and was announced in outline to a meeting at the 'Crown and Anchor' in the Strand, a meeting held shortly after the Commons had voted down Thomas Duncombe's attempt to drop the ratepaying clauses of the Reform Act.[24] In May 1838, the 'petition for universal suffrage,' now known as the

'People's Charter' was published in full. From first to last it was an indictment of the new voting system introduced in 1832.

Over one-half of the 'People's Charter' (13 pages out of 22) was devoted to proposed reforms in the registration of voters, the selection of election officials, and the actual means of taking votes.[25] The famous six points were submerged within a much more detailed and far-reaching scheme for overhauling and simplifying the machinery of elections newly established six years earlier. In fact, so submerged were the six points that, when the 'People's Charter' was republished in penny editions in 1842, and 1845, the six points, dispersed as they were in the rest of the text, had to be printed in bold type.[26] What, then, did the 'People's Charter' demand? First on the list was universal manhood suffrage - all sane males over 21 not convicted of a felony (felony to include breaking of electoral laws). Manhood suffrage was recommended not, as might be expected on the grounds of natural rights, but because it was 'simpler' and 'cheaper...than the present expensive machinery'. Voters would need to prove three months' residence, for which they would receive an election 'certificate,' and they would be prosecuted if they registered in more than one constituency. The kingdom was to be divided into 300 equal electoral districts each returning one MP only. Elections would be held every June, on the completion of the parliamentary year, which was to run from the third week in June to the first week of the following June. MPs were to receive an annual salary (daily wages were considered but ruled out) of £500 and at the end of every parliament details of their rate of attendance would be published. Considerable attention was focused on the procedure to be followed at elections. The 'People's Charter' provided for the election by manhood suffrage of the returning officer and the deputy returning officer, and their special duties in calling elections, arranging the nomination of candidates and taking the votes by secret ballot were spelled out in great detail. Of particular significance here were two reforms. First, the new procedure for nomination required that any candidate needed to secure the signatures of 100 electors. Having done this his name would be posted on a board with those of any other candidates, and only when the returning officer decided an election was necessary would these candidates be able to address the voters. There was to be no canvassing of electors. Indeed, what the 'People's Charter' called 'going from house to house' in order to solicit votes was to be made a criminal offence. The second, notable, feature of the proposed reform of election proceedings was the suggested taking of votes by ballot. Appended to the 'People's Charter' was a diagram showing a newly-designed ballot box, which automatically counted up the votes for the different candidates; rendering tellers completely unnecessary.

The 'People's Charter' was a remarkable document. In later versions some of its demands were revised.[27] But the basic text, with its focus on reforming the whole electoral system, remained unchanged over the next decade and, it has to be said, has remained largely unread by many historians of the movement ever since. It is remarkable not so much for its call for universal suffrage, on which the modern gaze inevitably falls, but for its extensive onslaught on the new voting system of 1832. In fact on the question of the suffrage the Charter seems somewhat moderate. In an age of great internal migration and rising crime rates enfranchising all resident non-offending males over 21 was not as far-reaching as it sounded, quite apart from the fact that it excluded women, many of whom were prominent in the early stages of Chartism.[28] There is not room here to go into the lengthy discussions which surrounded the Chartist definition of universal suffrage, suffice it to say that for many it did not go far enough. But the 'People's Charter' was a truly revolutionary document in the changes it recommended for the machinery of elections. Had it been enacted the size of the Commons would have been halved (or even reduced by 2/3), whilst the parliamentary calendar would have been extended by six months. Scope for partisanship at election time would have been severely limited, as all canvassing of voters and party manipulation of the electoral register would have become illegal. Indeed, the whole 'rough music' of elections would have disappeared overnight, as the nomination and presentation of candidates would have become a routine piece of administration, carried out by the returning officers. MPs might have become much more accountable. Subject to regular election, with their attendance record known to all, a greater transparency might have characterised parliamentary proceedings. Finally, the whole system would have been underwritten by the penal armoury of the courts, rather than by the Commons, notoriously ineffectual (as we know to this day) in prosecuting its own. Terms of imprisonment could be given for what might be seen as minor offences of bribery and corruption. No wonder the 'People's Charter' closed with a note to the effect that all existing statutes relating to registration, nomination and sittings of the House of Commons, would need to be repealed. These were unprecedented demands, some of which would have nipped in the bud the management of elections by political parties. The 'People's Charter' thus needs to be seen, not so much as the last shot in the radical attack on 'old Corruption,' as the opening sally in the long campaign to clean up electoral procedure, and extend the franchise by reforming the registration system.

III

The Chartist contribution to the question of parliamentary reform is not only to be found in the 'People's Charter'. Between February and September 1839 the Chartists organised their own 'people's parliament' or the General Convention of the Industrious Classes, to give it its full title, to which delegates were elected by a range of district associations up and down the country. Similar conventions were held again in London and Birmingham during the 1840s, and the National Charter Association, also constituted by elected delegates, was formed in 1840 and functioned intermittently until 1860.[29] The main purpose of these conventions was to prepare for, put pressure on MPs and monitor Parliament's reception of the Chartist petitions, as well as to administer the collection of the 'national rent' used to fund the lecture tours of Chartist 'missionaries'. Many of the proceedings of these conventions were dominated by debates between militants and moderates over the question of physical force - the so-called 'ulterior measures'. But the conventions also provide further evidence of how the Chartists sought to make the representative and the election system more accountable. The procedural aspects of the first Convention in 1839 were natural extensions of the democratic demands made in the 'People's Charter' a year earlier.

The plan for a Chartist Convention surfaced during the summer of 1838. Various radicals and Chartists, including Attwood and O'Brien, claimed the idea of a 'people's parliament' as their own, but, as we know, the tradition of anti-parliaments had a long pedigree going back to the 17th century.[30] Attwood suggested that 49 towns send delegates, and although this number was never strictly adhered to, it is a rough approximation of the size of the Convention.[31] From October, 1838, onwards, the first delegates began to be selected at public meetings, which often followed in the wake of visits by London-based Chartist speakers, such as O'Brien, Feargus O'Connor, and Henry Vincent. Initially, the election of delegates was something of a formality, with a cursory show of hands at a large meeting sufficient to secure a place at the Convention. The Convention itself, when it commenced business at the beginning of February 1839, accepted the credentials of any delegate who appeared with either a petition for the Charter, or a contribution to the national rent. Initially, some delegates appeared without either petition or rent, and their authenticity had to be confirmed by two other delegates.[32] However, during the course of 1839, amidst complaints from the localities that outsiders were being foisted upon them by unfamiliar organisations, the rules for the nomination of candidates for the Convention were tightened up. Election remained by show of hands, but ten days' notice had to be given for such elections and the meeting had to be truly public and not organised by 'Societies or Public Bodies of any description'.[33] Once election had taken place, constituents had to abide by the decisions of the Convention. As Attwood explained in a letter published at the beginning of December, 1838, 'they must be obeyed in all things under the law so long as they discharge their duty'. Should the constituencies be dissatisfied with their delegate, their complaints could be expressed at a public meeting. The constituencies would defray all the expenses of their delegate.[34]

Additional rules governed the internal procedure of the Convention. In the light of the Chartist complaints about the workings of the reformed House of Commons after 1832, they make interesting reading. All officers of the Convention, from the chairman and the treasurer, down to the doorkeeper, would be subject to regular election. Indeed the chief officers would be elected on a daily basis. As in Parliament, written notice of all motions for debate had to be given in advance, and no motion on an issue relating to public money could be discussed on the same day as it was presented. Speaking in debate was to be within strict time limits: twenty minutes if presenting a motion, and ten minutes otherwise, and a pair of sand-glasses were invested in by the Convention to ensure this regulation. Finally, it was intended that the debates of the Convention be transparent. Visitors, including women and children, were allowed to watch the proceedings. A register of attendance would be published weekly. There would be no official record of proceedings; instead the newspapers would be expected to carry full coverage, although within a fortnight of the start of the Convention, an argument flared up over whether someone should be paid to make a report for distribution to the press.[35]

The 1839 Convention was not of course intended to be a real parliament. It was a form of pressure from without, designed to impress upon the House of Commons the urgency and legitimacy of the demands contained in the 'People's Charter'. Nor, as it turned out, was it a particularly representative or democratic assembly. Moderates and militants vied with one another by fair means, and foul, for control over the direction of the Convention. And it succumbed to the same problems of absenteeism of which Chartists had been so critical when commentating on the real House of Commons in the 1830s. Enforcing better attendance was one of the most constantly debated issues in the 1839 Convention's short life.[36] But the Convention does reveal something of the Chartist idea of representation, demonstrating what they believed to be the respective duties of delegates and their constituents. Superficially, the most striking feature of the Convention was its omnipotence. Its decisions needed no further ratification, and the constituent body was bound to obey and give the delegates undivided and unquestioning support. Does this mean that the Chartists preferred a Jacobin-style system, in which all power was concentrated in a single assembly? This was an accusation that was sometimes made at the time, but can be rejected if we bear in mind that as in the case of the Political Unions of the early 1830s, the Chartist Convention faced legal limitations. It could not correspond, organise nationally or subdivide, so delegates were bound to insist that they be left alone to make their decisions, because any more intimate or direct relationship with their constituents would have been illegal. A closer look reveals that constituents had the right to discharge their delegate - or 'cashier' him, as Attwood put it - if he did not fulfil his duties. Moreover, through the publication of attendance sheets constituents had the means to monitor his behaviour. More perplexing is the manner of election preferred by the Convention. The show of hands was after all a rather inaccurate gauge of public opinion, and, as both Chartists and liberal opponents such as Edward Baines Jr. pointed out, it hardly amounted to the principle of universal suffrage championed in the 'People's Charter'.[37] But delegates to the Convention insisted that they had been elected by universal suffrage. For example, Peter Bussey, the West Riding delegate told a meeting that he was 'the representative of 300,000 of the working classes in the north of England...men of cool heads and strong arms'.[38] Here it can be suggested that for the Chartists, choice by public acclamation, however inexact, was deemed to be an improvement on the cumbersome new machinery of elections introduced in 1832. Overall, the rules and procedures for the Convention do provide further evidence of how the Chartists sought accountable representation.

IV

There is one other area in which the specific constitutional demands of the Charter were attempted in practice, or put to the test in some way: parliamentary and municipal elections. Between 1839 and 1848 eighteen different Chartist candidates contested seats at parliamentary elections, going all the way to the final poll. Some of these men, such as the redoubtable Henry Vincent and Peter McDouall stood more than once, and one most famously, Feargus O'Connor, as Stephen Roberts describes elsewhere in this volume, secured election to Parliament. But many more Chartists - it is difficult to determine how many more - fought parliamentary election campaigns up to the point of the nomination of candidates, only to withdraw at the traditional show of hands, claiming a moral victory if they secured the majority by public acclaim. These so-called 'hustings candidates' often stood in constituencies and against opponents where they would gain maximum publicity for the Charter, for example: Robert Lowery at Edinburgh in 1841 (against Macaulay, the Whig Secretary of State for War), or George Julian Harney (against Lord Palmerston) at Tiverton in 1847.[39] There was a co-ordinated Chartist campaign of such candidates in

1841 in Scotland, considered to be more fertile election ground as the property qualification for MPs did not apply there.[40] Chartists used these occasions to highlight the absurdities of the present electoral system. They made a great show of arriving in the constituency only a day or so before the nomination, and thereby not conducting any canvass. Some, such as Ernest Jones at Halifax in 1847, or W.P. Roberts in Blackburn the same year, did issue an address to electors, and some, such as Peter McDouall, considered conducting a canvass, but most relied on the simple effects of their nomination speech.[41] Invariably, when the show of hands was taken, it was dominated by non-electors, and Chartist candidates 'won'. Their opponents, as was the convention, insisted on going to the poll, and at that point Chartist candidates withdrew. In part, this was a politics of intimidation. At Nottingham in 1847, for example, O'Connor taunted his opponents for not appearing in public, but transacting their business of the canvass in hiding in their hotels. But it should also be seen as evidence that the Chartists actually thought the whole process of open elections was ridiculous and required reform. As the *Northern Star* observed, and this was only days after O'Connor had been successful, '[o]n the nomination day many thousands elect a member, on the next day a few hundreds unseat him'.[42]

Municipal elections afford an even better site of investigation for Chartist attitudes towards the representative process, not least because Chartists were more successful in local government elections from the late 1830s through to the 1850s. Although it varied from place to place, the early Victorian municipal electorate was not quite as restrictive as the new parliamentary electorate created in 1832. Some towns had open vestries in which effectively all parishioners had the vote, and could, if they chose, vote by ballot. Newer boroughs, incorporated under the terms of the Municipal Corporations Act, had more restrictive conditions: longer residential requirements for voters, and high property qualifications for councillors. But the municipal electorate, in marked contrast to the parliamentary electorate, continued to expand through the 1840s and 1850s, helped on by the implementation of the Small Tenements Rating Act of 1850 in many towns, through which tenement dwellers gained the vote.[43] By the late 1840s Chartists and ex-Chartists sat on the town councils of Birmingham, Bolton, Bradford, Leeds, Manchester, Rochdale and Sheffield, to name only the better-documented examples. They secured control of the Police Commission in Salford, and, behind the eccentric leadership of Isaac Ironside, ran the Highway Commission in Sheffield.[44] Municipal Chartism threw up a host of local political figures: for example, Robert Carter, Abel Heywood, Joshua Hobson, Thomas Livsey, James Moir and William Newton, who remained faithful to the principles of the Charter after the 1840s and attempted their implementation when and wherever possible - in the council chamber, in local constituency associations, and, in the 1860s in the revived reform agitation which culminated in the campaigns of the Reform League. The attempted democratisation of municipal politics owed much to the influence of Chartists. It was Chartists who insisted on greater accountability, for example, allowing the public into meetings, outlawing all canvassing during municipal elections (as was attempted in Aberdeen),[45] requiring those elected to give regular accounts of their activities to their constituents and resigning if called on to do so by their constituents,[46] as well as pressing for further extension of the municipal suffrage - all of these demands can be seen as very real attempts by Chartists in local government to put into practice the representative principles embodied in the original 'People's Charter'.

V

The Charter then was much more than a restatement of traditional radical concerns, and much more than a flag of convenience under which various forms of protest could be mobilised. The 'People's Charter' contained a simple diagnosis of the nation's ills - the lack of accountability in the reformed parliament, and proposed a rather more complex remedy - rid the Commons of absenteeism, and rid the electoral system of fixers, partisan officials and the early Victorian equivalent of spin-doctors. These were the issues which dominate the pages of the document drawn up by the L.W.M.A. in 1838. The six points of legend, and notably the call for universal suffrage were there, but they were not paramount in the way in which they were to become during the course of the 1840s. Without doubt, the prioritising of the reform of the machinery of election reflects the more moderate, Benthamite stance of the L.W.M.A. and some of the MPs who helped draw up the Charter, as well as the constitutionalist strategy preferred by some members of the 1839 Convention. John Frost, the Newport Chartist and 1839 delegate, for example, was himself a former election returning officer and so knew only too well the evils of which the Charter complained.[47] We can see the influence of the Irish MPs in the Charter too, through the insistence on election certificates, a scheme which only operated in Ireland (until 1850).[48] And the old Benthamite idea of keeping a record of parliamentary attendance resurfaced in the Charter. So it may be the case that in describing the constitutional ideas of the Chartists this chapter has erred on the side of looking at the more moderate, 'moral reform' wing. But this was the same document which was to be returned to again and again during the 1840s by all wings of the movement. It was after all the implementation of the L.W.M.A.'s 'People's Charter' for which the final Chartist petition called in 1848.

Chartism was a major threat to the British state, in the physical sense that the British ruling class was at times during the late 1830s and 1840s virtually in a state of siege as the people of this country protested, struck and armed against the establishment. Chartism was also a major threat to the British state inasmuch as it turned the idea of the constitution upside down, and contested the Whigs' claim that the 1832 Reform Act was a natural evolution in accordance with past practice or present-day common sense. The 'People's Charter' challenged early Victorian ideas about representative government, and it is perhaps this challenge which is one of the Chartists' great legacies. When Parliament returned to the question of parliamentary reform in 1866 the greatest fear of the governing classes was that a working-class electorate would not return representatives, but delegates elected solely to do the bidding of their constituents.[49] The ideas of the 'People's Charter' were alive and well nearly thirty years on.

NOTES

[1] For the text of the 1848 petition: *Times*, 6 April 1848 p. 5. For the 1838 Charter: *The People's Charter; being the Outline of an Act to Provide for the Just*

Representation of the People of Great Britain in the Commons House of Parliament, L.W.M.A., London, Henry Hetherington, 1838. For the Birmingham resolution of August, 1838: *Northern Star*, 11 August, 1838, p. 6. For the text of the 1842 petition: Report of the Select Committee on Public Petitions, 2 May, 1842, p. 399. Although the 1838 'People's Charter' was reprinted in full as an appendix to some of the early histories of the movement (namely Gammage [1854], Lovett [1876] and Rosenblatt [1916]), most modern histories of Chartism, from Hovell onwards, cite the petition agreed at the Crown and Anchor meeting of February 1838 as the definitive statement of the '6 points': See Mark Hovell, *The Chartist Movement*, Manchester, Manchester University Press, 1918, pp 69–74; Dorothy Thompson, *The Early Chartists*, London, Macmillan, 1971, pp. 64–6.

[2] Asa Briggs, 'The local background of Chartism' in Briggs (ed.), *Chartist Studies*, London, Macmillan, 1959, p. 25; Dorothy Thompson, *The Chartists: Popular Politics in the Industrial Revolution*, London, Temple Smith, 1984, pp. 58-60.

[3] Alexander Paul, *The History of Reform: A Record of the Struggle for the Representation of the People in Parliament*, London, George Routledge, 1884; Simon Maccoby, *The English Radical Tradition*, London, Adam & Charles Black, 1952; John W. Derry, *The Radical Tradition: Tom Paine to Lloyd George*, London, Macmillan, 1967, pp. 157–8. The continuity between the Hanoverian agenda of parliamentary reform and that of the Chartists is of course one of the central claims of Gareth Stedman Jones' influential 'Rethinking Chartism' in his *Languages of Class: Studies in English Working-Class History, 1832–1982*, Cambridge, Cambridge University Press, 1983, ch. 3. In some of my own earlier work I have followed this interpretation, but as this chapter makes clear, I now believe that the emphasis on continuity as far as parliamentary reform is concerned is undue.

[4] *The People's Charter*, pp. 8–9. In 1839 the *Western Vindicator* reprinted Richmond's 1780 bill in full: 13 April, 1839, p. 2.

[5] G. S. Veitch, *The Genesis of Parliamentary Reform*, London, Constable, 1913, p. 50; A. S. Foord, *His Majesty's Opposition, 1714–1830*, Oxford, Clarendon Press, 1964, pp. 348–9; John Cannon, *Parliamentary Reform, 1640–1832*, Cambridge, Cambridge University Press, 1973, pp. 72–5; John Brewer, 'English radicalism in the age of George III,' in J.G.A. Pocock (ed.), *Three British Revolutions: 1641, 1688, 1776*, Princeton, Princeton University Press, 1980, pp. 323–67; J.R. Dinwiddy, *Radicalism and Reform in Britain, 1780-1850*, London, Hambledon Press, 1992, chs 4, 6; Philip Harling, *The Waning of 'Old Corruption': The Politics of Economical Reform, 1779–1846*, Oxford, Clarendon Press, 1996, pp. 97–101.

[6] Frank O'Gorman, *Voters, Patrons and Parties: The Unreformed Electorate of Hanoverian England, 1734–1832*, Oxford, Clarendon Press, 1989, p. 108.

[7] [John Cartwright], *Take Your Choice*, London, J. Almon, 1776, pp. xiv–xv; John W. Osborne, *John Cartwright*, Cambridge, Cambridge University Press, 1972, ch. 2; Ian R. Christie, *Wilkes, Wyvill and Reform: The Parliamentary Reform Movement in British Politics, 1760–1785*, London, Macmillan, 1962, p.70.

[8] *An Authentic Copy of the Duke of Richmond's Bill, for a Parliamentary Reform*, London, J. Stockdale, 1783, pp. 33–41. For Richmond and parliamentary reform

see A. G. Olson, *The Radical Duke: The Career and Correspondence of Charles Lennox, 3rd Duke of Richmond*, Oxford, Clarendon Press, 1961.

[9] Peter D. G. Thomas, *John Wilkes: A Friend to Liberty*, Oxford, Clarendon Press, 1996, pp. 180–1; E. A. Smith, *Lord Grey, 1764–1845*, Oxford, Clarendon Press, 1990, p. 66. For Brand's scheme, see *Parliamentary Debates*, vol. 17, 21 May, 1810, cols. 126–9.

[10] For Flood's scheme, see W. Flood, *Memoirs of the Life and Correspondence of the Right Hon. Henry Flood MP, etc*, London, Dublin, 1838, p. 386. For Burdett's, see *The Plan of Reform Proposed by Sir Francis Burdett, etc*, London, Bone & Hone, 1809, p. 18; M. W. Patterson, *Sir Francis Burdett and his Times (1770–1844)*, London, Macmillan, 2 vols. 1931, vol. i, pp. 234–5.

[11] Bentham, *Plan of Parliamentary Reform* (1817), reprinted in *The Collected Works of Jeremy Bentham*, ed. J. Bowring, Edinburgh, William Tate, 1843, vol. iii, p. 545.

[12] Thomas W. Laqueur, 'The Queen Caroline Affair: Politics as Art in the Reign of George IV,' *Journal of Modern History*, 54 (1982); E.A. Smith, *The Queen on Trial: The Affair of Queen Caroline*, Stroud, Sutton, 1993, pp 417-66.

[13] *Address of the L.W.M.A. to the Radical Reformers of Great Britain on the Forthcoming Elections*, London, Henry Hetherington, 1837, p.12; Dorothy Thompson, *Queen Victoria: Gender and Power*, London, Virago, 1990, pp. 23–9.

[14] Harling, *Waning of 'Old Corruption,'* ch. 6; Philip Harling & Peter Mandler, 'From 'fiscal-military' state to laissez-faire state, 1760-1850,' *Journal of British Studies*, 32 (1993), 44–70.

[15] Jonathan Parry, *The Rise and Fall of Liberal Government in Victorian Britain*, London, Yale University Press, chs. 2–3; L.G. Mitchell, 'Foxite Politics and the Great Reform Bill,' *English Historical Review*, 108, (1993), pp. 338–64.

[16] Parry, *Rise and Fall of Liberal Government*, ch. 3; John Phillips, *The Great Reform Bill in the Boroughs, English Electoral Behaviour, 1818–41*, Oxford, Clarendon Press, 1992; Colin Leys, 'Petitioning of Parliament in the Nineteenth and Twentieth Centuries,' *Political Studies*, 3, (1955), pp. 45–64.

[17] For an excellent recent discussion, on which much of this paragraph is based, see Philip Salmon, 'Electoral Reform at Work: Local Politics and National Politics, 1732-1841,' unpublished DPhil thesis, University of Oxford, 1997, ch 1.

[18] For the text of the 1839 petition, see the Supplement to the Votes and Proceedings of the House of Commons, 1839, p. 875.

[19] *Constitutional*, 20 October, 1837, p. 3, 28 October, 1837, p. 3.

[20] *London Mercury*, 7 May 1837, p. 268. On the background to the changes in petitioning procedure, see Leys, 'Petitioning'.

[21] *Hansard*, 33, (29 April, 1836), cols. 472-3; Salmon, 'Electoral Reform at Work,' p. 127.

[22] L.W.M.A, 'Minute-book,' 21 August, 1836, British Library, Add. Ms. 37, 773; *The Rotten House of Commons, being an Appeal to the Nation on the Course to be Pursued in the Approaching Crisis*, L.W.M.A., London, Henry Hetherington, 1836, p. 6. For the history of the L.W.M.A. see George Howell, *A History of the Working Men's Association from 1836 to 1850*, ed. D.J. Rowe, Frank Graham,

Newcastle, 1972; *Life and Struggles of William Lovett, etc*, 3rd edn., London, MacGibbon & Kee, chs. 7–8.

[23] John Prest, *Lord John Russell*, London, Constable, 1972, pp. 120, 123, 145.

[24] *Hansard*, xl (5 February, 1838), cols. 794, 807–9.

[25] Unless otherwise indicated all references in this paragraph are to *The People's Charter*, L.W.M.A., London, Henry Hetherington, 1838.

[26] *People's Charter*, London, Henry Hetherington, 1842; *The People's Charter*, London, James Watson, 1845.

[27] The principal changes came in the 1842 edition, whereby the penalties for electoral corruption were increased, and provisions were made to ensure that voting papers were distributed to workhouses.

[28] Dorothy Thompson, 'Women and Nineteenth-Century Radical Politics: A Lost Dimension,' in her *Outsiders: Class, Gender and Nation*, London, Verso, 1993, pp. 88–91. For Chartist arguments (albeit limited) for the enfranchisement of women, see Jutta Schwarzkopf, *Women in the Chartist Movement*, London, Macmillan, 1993, pp. 60–2.

[29] J. R. Clinton, 'The National Charter Association and its role in the Chartist Movement, 1840-1858,' unpublished MPhil thesis, University of Southampton, 1980.

[30] T.M. Parsinnen, 'Association, Convention and Anti-Parliament in British Radical Politics, 1771-1848,' *English Historical Review*, 88, (1973), 504-33; Kenneth Judge, 'Early Chartist Organisation and the Convention of 1839,' *International Review of Social History*, 20, (1975), 370-97; T.M. Kemnitz, 'The Chartist Convention of 1839,' *Albion*, 10, (1978), 152-70.

[31] 49 delegates was deemed the legal maximum. The London Corresponding Society of the 1790s had been proscribed for having 50 delegates. For a good discussion of the legal limitations on the summoning of a convention, see the *Charter*, 27 January, 1839, p. 13.

[32] *Chartist*, 9 February, 1839, p. 3.

[33] James Knight (Dumfries) to the Convention, 2 February, 1839, British Library, Add. Ms., 34, 245A; *Rules and Regulations of the General Convention of the Industrious Classes*, n.d., British Library, Add. Ms. 34, 245B, p. 6. Accused of being a 'travelling demagogue' Henry Vincent chose not to stand as delegate for Bath, and recommended instead that Chartists there elect a 'townsman': Henry Vincent to John Miniken, Miniken-Vincent collection, National Museum of Labour History, Manchester, VIN/1/1/11.

[34] *Rules*, p. 6; *London Dispatch*, 2 December, 1838, p. 922.

[35] *Rules*, pp. 10–12; *Chartist*, 2 March, 1839, p. 2.

[36] 'Notice book of the First General Convention of the Industrious Classes,' British Library, Add. Ms. 34, 245B, fols. 244–5, 249, 250, 258.

[37] *Northern Star*, 27 October, 1838, p. 4; *London Dispatch*, 11 November, 1838, p. 898.

[38] *London Dispatch*, 17 February, 1839, p. 1011.

[39] Brian Harrison & Patricia Hollis (eds.), *Robert Lowery: Radical and Chartist*, London, Europa, 1979, p. 181; A.R. Schoyen, *The Chartist Challenge: A Portrait of George Julian Harney*, London, Heinemann, pp. 150–2.

[40] H.E. Witmer, *The Property Qualifications of Members of Parliament*, New York, Columbia University Press, 1943, pp. 40–2.

[41] J.A. Jowitt, 'A Crossroads in Halifax Politics,' *Transactions of the Halifax Antiquarian Society*, (1973–4), 19–36; Raymond Challinor, *A Radical Lawyer in Victorian England: W.P. Roberts and the Struggle for Workers' Rights*, London, I.B. Tauris, 1990, pp. 157–8; *McDouall's Chartist & Republican Journal*, 17 July, 1841, p. 122; William Dorling, *Henry Vincent: A Biographical Sketch*, London, James Clarke, 1879, pp. 33–5.

[42] *Northern Star*, 7 August, 1847, p. 4.

[43] B. Keith-Lucas, *The English Local Government Franchise: A Short History*, Oxford, Clarendon Press, 1952, pp. 68–70; Salmon, 'Electoral Reform at Work,' ch. 7. See also my 'Interests, Parties and the State: The Urban Electorate, c. 1820–67' in J. Lawrence and M Taylor (eds.), *Party, State and Society: Electoral Behaviour in Britain since 1820*, Aldershot, Scolar Press, 1997, p. 61.

[44] E.P. Hennock, *Fit and Proper Persons: Ideal and Reality in Nineteenth-Century Urban Government*, London, Edward Arnold, 1973, pp. 197-8; John Garrard, *Leadership and Power in Victorian Industrial Towns, 1830-80*, Manchester, Manchester University Press, 1983, pp. 114–15, 128–9, 168; Adrian Elliott, 'Municipal Government in Bradford in the mid-nineteenth century' in D. Fraser (ed.), *Municipal Reform and the Industrial City*, Leicester, Leicester University Press, 1982, p. 149; J.F.C. Harrison, 'Chartism in Leeds,' in Briggs (ed.), *Chartist Studies*, pp. 85–93; Paul Pickering, *Chartism and the Chartists in Manchester and Salford*, London, Macmillan, 1995, ch. 4; Brian Barber, 'Sheffield Borough Council, 1843–1893' in Clyde Binfield et al (eds.), *The History of the City of Sheffield, 1843-1993. Volume 1: Politics*, Sheffield, Sheffield Academic Press, 1993, pp. 29–32.

[45] James A Ross, *Record of Municipal Affairs in Aberdeen since the Passing of the Burgh Reform Act in 1833*, Aberdeen, D. Wyllie, 1889, p. 100.

[46] Pickering, *Chartism and the Chartists*, p. 80.

[47] David Williams, *John Frost: A Study in Chartism*, Cardiff, University of Wales Press Board, 1939, p. 90.

[48] K. Theodore Hoppen, *Elections, Politics and Society in Ireland, 1832-1885*, Oxford, Clarendon Press, 1984, pp. 5–6.

[49] Eg: Robert Lowe, *Hansard*, clxxxii, (13 March, 1866), cols. 141–2; Walter Bagehot, *The English Constitution*, London, Chapman & Hall, 1867, p. 181.

'A SMALL DROP OF INK' :
TYNESIDE CHARTISM AND THE *Northern Liberator*

Joan Hugman

As the newspaper and periodical section of the new annotated bibliography of Chartism[1] shows, with its mammoth one hundred and twenty three entries, an energetic, propagandist press was of crucial importance to the movement. Some radical periodicals had a very short shelf life, unable to compete with the respectable press once the stamp duty had been reduced, making 'the rich man's paper cheaper and the poor man's paper dearer'.[2] However, the operation of the Six Acts and the residual fear of coercive legislation that continued, long after repeal, served to galvanise concerted opposition, and as this spirit of defiance became harnessed to the new print technology a greatly expanded, more resilient cheap press began to emerge.[3] The dialectic force of Chartism rested as much upon this burgeoning print culture as it did upon the radical mass platform and the symbiotic relationship between the local Chartist press and the wider movement has indeed been universally acknowledged by historians ever since R.G. Gammage penned his travelogue history in 1854.[4] In the intervening years historians have come to know a great deal about the workings of the movement's premier newspaper, the *Northern Star:* its journalistic style and in-house wrangling, its subscription base and, more recently, its correspondents.[5] Quite naturally, given its unusual longevity, its pages have been carefully studied in a bid to chart the many twists and turns of the national campaign. Other Chartist newspapers have also come under some scrutiny but in the main these have tended to be more generalised and cursory.- a litany of the 'also ran'. Only rarely have they been given more sustained treatment, as in A. Temple Patterson's study of the *Leicester Mercury*[6] or Alexander Wilson's critical appraisal of the Scottish Chartist press, the *True Scotsman, The Scottish Patriot* and the enormously successful *Chartist Circular*.[7]

Oddly enough, the linguistic turn of over a decade ago,[8] with its much vaunted back to basics, trail-blazing agenda, did not immediately send academics scurrying to the outer reaches of the Chartist press to read between the lines. Instead, the opportunity to

24

arrive at a better understanding of both form and function was lost sight of in the combative broth and froth of theoretical discourse. Some of the more interesting critical work on the Chartist press has been left to literary and cultural historians,[9] and this is unfortunate. While they have undoubtedly thrown considerable light upon the literary dimension of the Chartist press, they cannot fully address the political or socio-economic questions that remain unresolved.

The *Northern Liberator* has long been accorded premier league ranking. As Dorothy Thompson observed, the *Northern Liberator* was 'the longest-lived and liveliest'[10] of them all, and references to the paper have featured as at least a footnote in almost all of the significant Chartist texts. Some valuable work on the paper and its editor, Augustus Hardin Beaumont, was brought together in the 1960s[11] but since then, apart from Ian Haywood's scholarly critique of its literary merits and peculiarities in his anthology of Chartist fiction, no comprehensive survey of the newspaper's history has been undertaken.

The aim here is certainly not to challenge the unique status which has been duly accorded to the *Northern Star*; in a sense, the objective is altogether more serious. Arguably, without access to a propagandist press, at a local level where so much of the activity was organised and carried out, there would not have been a movement at all. As so much of this journalistic activity was small scale and independent in every sense of the word, there is an urgent need to move the agenda forward and foster an energetic and wide-ranging programme of individual critical press studies. One of the greatest problems in embarking on this study proved to be the paucity of detailed comparative material. Reading nineteenth century newspapers is labour intensive and Chartist periodicals are just as capable of providing distractions from weightier concerns as any other; a 'saxony flushing mattress' can become, albeit momentarily, more intriguing than a chronicle of missionary meetings. Thus far it has been impossible to study more than a small sample of other papers and, therefore, some of the findings presented here must be qualified by the understanding that they may require modification as and when other press studies become available.

This is not the forum to elaborate upon the strength of north east Chartism in any detail and it is, in any case, well documented elsewhere. For the purposes of the argument advanced here it is important to note that Radicalism in the north east had remarkably strong roots, traceable first of all from the emergence of Tyneside's carboniferous capital in the early eighteenth century. According to Levine and Wrightson, in their pioneering study of the Whickham coalfield,[12] it is then and in that corner of the national landscape that industrial society was born. And as Malcolm Chase's revisionist work on agrarian radicalism has shown, late eighteenth century Tyneside was also the place where Thomas Spence spent his formative years, drawing upon an existing radical tradition as well as making a profound and lasting contribution to it.[13] Spence made full use of Newcastle's relatively sophisticated publishing facilities and his rush to print his controversial lecture on agrarian reform led to his expulsion from the city's prestigious Literary and Philosophical Society in 1775.

Whether this nascent dissenting polity would have developed into such a powerful lobby for reform without the prior existence of an unusually rich printing culture is, however, a moot point, and one which certainly warrants further exploration; the connection seems irresistible. By 1790 Newcastle was a veritable publishing hothouse, with some 'twenty printers, twelve booksellers and stationers, thirteen bookbinders and three engravers'[14] including Thomas Bewick; at a time when most towns struggled to support a single newspaper, Newcastle published three and was also home to ten periodicals. Rapid industrialisation on the Tyne seems to have acted as the crucial accelerator. The mass journalism which Aled Jones identifies as 'an essential if problematic part of a 'speeded up' society' was well established in Newcastle some decades before commentators were predicting that newspapers would eventually become 'the whole press': the primary means by which new ideas 'instantly conceived, instantly written, instantly understood' would be accessed by an increasingly large and literate public.[15]

In the 1820s and 1830s northeast communities enthusiastically embraced the radical agenda and it has now been firmly established that the Northern Political Union (NPU) played a key role in the passage of the 1832 Reform Act. Press activity proved to be a singularly potent force. The forty strong NPU Council, who had agitated so aggressively during the May crisis, were backed by a vast army of committed reformers who purchased between them an estimated 20,000 copies of the *Black Dwarf* at the time of the Peterloo Massacre, and upwards of 2,400 unstamped newspapers 'at Newcastle Quayside on Saturday evenings in 1830'.[16] As elsewhere, the local press always had the edge when it came to wielding influence; the editors and proprietors were fully conversant with shifting commercial concerns, religious sensibilities and the popularity or otherwise of the town's oligarchy, and they knew exactly how to promote their own agenda persuasively. Their very survival depended upon it, if they were to please their readers and retain stable advertising revenues.

The monthly *Newcastle Magazine*, which began publication in 1830, was to all intents and purposes a respectable journal with all the standard features that presupposes - poems, local historical anecdotes and scholarly treatises on flora and fauna - but its flagship motto '*Be Just and Fear Not*' unequivocally paraded the paper's actual progressive sympathies. In February 1831, the editors began a lengthy serialised exposition upon the prospects for parliamentary reform by boldly stating that they were not prepared to enter into any discussion of whether such a measure was necessary. To engage in such an exercise would, they claimed, be 'almost an insult to the good sense of our countrymen' and the editorial frankly warned that

> if there should be any attempt to ...give as little instead
> of as much as possible, in proportion will be the popular
> disappointment - in proportion will be the danger of the
> empire.[17]

Like many other newspapers and magazines at that time the *Newcastle Magazine* did not survive long, but the publishing sector in the city remained buoyant and in the years before the *Northern Liberator* finally made its dramatic appearance there were a number of attempts to provide the region with a more progressive journal.

One of the more notable of these was the *Newcastle Standard* which was launched in January 1837 as a stamped weekly, costing fourpence-halfpenny, by Dr. Charles Larkin, a stalwart former member of the NPU and prominent local Irish nationalist. Almost immediately, the *Standard* embarked upon a concerted campaign for electoral and church reform. The editorial columns sarcastically denounced the notoriously corrupt electoral practices and called upon every man 'who is not a slave or a tyrant' to sign a petition in favour of the secret ballot.[18] By March the paper was carrying an open letter to the 'Mechanics and Labouring Men,' which trumpeted the view that 'the will of the people is the sovereign power'. Inevitably, the *Standard* met with concerted opposition from the rest of the Newcastle press, especially the *Newcastle Journal* which attacked it for its 'Popish bias' as well as its 'intemperate' opinions.[19] Unfortunately for Larkin, his publishing venture was heavily dependent upon the good will of his Roman Catholic sponsors, who hoped he would help them to promote the disestablishment cause. When he persisted in publishing material of which they strongly disapproved, they instituted a determined campaign to have the paper banned among the region's loyal Catholic communities. Larkin's vitriolic editorial availed him little, and the paper ignominiously collapsed through lack of funds.

In essence, what is being suggested here is that the success which the *Northern Liberator* enjoyed in the three years between 1837 and 1840 rested to a large extent upon a deeply rooted radical tradition, and drew strength from an established regional print culture which was sophisticated enough to support and sustain it. But these advantages alone cannot be held to account for the *Liberator*'s robust circulation and role as the organisational arm of northeast Chartism. Even though the draconian provisions of the Six Acts had been virtually removed from the statute book, the ruthless prosecution of over 700 newspaper proprietors and agents between 1830 and 1836 lingered on in the public mind,[20] and the possibility of a new wave of repressive legislation remained a constant source of anxiety and resentment. The *Liberator*'s editors had to give a radical lead to its readers while, at the same time, avoiding any blatant infringement of the ascribed legislative boundaries. In this respect, the intellectual agility of its editors must be regarded as a decisive factor.

The *Northern Liberator* was launched on 21 October, 1837, just a few weeks ahead of the *Northern Star,* as a stamped weekly newspaper in a large format of four pages and, like the *Standard*, priced at fourpence-halfpenny per copy. Although nationally there were a number of radical papers in circulation at that time, the explicit statement of aims proclaimed on the front page anticipated the Charter on every count apart from the payment of members, and this must be recognised as a distinctive initiative. In addition, the editorial called for the introduction of a free national unsectarian education system, the abolition of the Combination Acts and, predictably, the 'entire emancipation of the press'. Initially the paper was jointly owned by an Anglo- American radical, Augustus Hardin Beaumont (1798-1838)[21] and his brother Arthur, but after Augustus died suddenly in January 1838 the paper was bought for the princely sum of £500 by Robert Blakey (1795-1878), a wealthy furrier and Mayor of Morpeth in Northumberland, who published it and edited it jointly with Thomas Doubleday (1790-1870).[22] With the appointment of an Irish radical activist, Thomas Ainge Devyr, as roving reporter in the spring of 1838 the *Liberator*'s editorial team was complete and remained stable until 2 May 1840, when the paper was forced to merge with the London *Champion*. When the *Liberator* eventually sank under the weight of its financial losses on 19 December, 1840, as a direct result of Blakey's prosecution for sedition, its advertising portfolio and goodwill were bought out by a new journal, 'unconnected with politics'. The *Liberator*'s successor, the *Great Northern Advertiser and Commercial Herald,* was a four page advertising freesheet. For the editors this was a satisfactory outcome: the *Liberator*'s radical credentials had not been bought out by a political rival. For the local Chartist movement, the loss was immeasurable.

By 20 January 1838, the *Liberator* boasted not just an average weekly circulation of 4,000 copies but of outselling the other five local papers, including the *Newcastle Courant* which had been founded more than a century before, in 1711. Competition among the various city titles was fierce and again this must have impacted upon the commercial as well as the political decisions made by the editors over time. From the outset it is evident that the editors intended that the *Liberator* would compete for readers, operating as a local newspaper as well as a political instructor, and this made sound commercial sense. But the decision to target a local readership did not mean that they intended the circulation to be limited to the north east region. Both Beaumont and Blakey were ambitious men, all too eager to achieve national recognition, and establishing the *Liberator*'s radical credentials and role in the wider movement was an essential part of their own bid for power. By the end of May 1840, the *Liberator* had agents in 112 towns across the country,[23] and this compares favourably with the geographical reaches of the rest of the Chartist press, apart from the *Northern Star*. To understand how this was accomplished requires a closer examination of the role of the editors themselves, and then of the form and function of the paper.

The life and career of Augustus Beaumont was carefully documented some years ago in a series of articles by William H. Maehl Jnr, and this section of this study owes much to his work. It also draws upon the serialised biography printed in the *Northern Liberator* as an obituary tribute in the weeks immediately following his death. With his brother's assistance, Beaumont bought and produced the paper for just a little over two months and as a foreign national (he had American roots and had lived and worked in Jamaica for most of his life) his connection with the north east and the region's radical community had been all too brief. His legacy, though, outlived him, and his revolutionary fervour was constantly referred to at meetings well into the 1840s, when toasts to his memory were repeatedly called for.

Beaumont had worked his way into Jamaican politics, gaining a seat in the Colonial Assembly in Kingston in 1829 after several failed attempts, and his vigorous campaign to remove the Jewish disabilities legislation brought him a measure of status and respect. He opposed British proposals to abolish slavery, arguing that appropriate legislation would be best designed and implemented by an independent Jamaica, but his determination to end the flogging of slaves aroused a groundswell of establishment hostility and, in the acrimonious backlash which followed, he was accused of inciting a slave rebellion and resigned. In the meanwhile Arthur had become actively involved in the European republican movement and, in 1830, Augustus was persuaded to travel with him to Paris and then on to Brussels 'to give their aid in the revolution then progressing to depose the King (Charles X), by the grace of God set over the Belgians by the order of the despot of Vienna'. A remarkable account (anonymous, but reliably attributable to Augustus)[24] of their Belgian adventure still survives in which he lambasts the aristocracy for being 'craven in the face of the enemy, concerned only with their own comfort. The working classes were the defenders of liberty'. By then his political colours were transparently revolutionary: according to his own definition the patriot was the 'successful rebel'; the rebel the 'unsuccessful patriot,'[25] and it was this hot-headed approach to politics which earned him the reputation of being something of a maverick in radical circles. Nevertheless his contact with the leading lights of radical society, both at home and abroad, proved invaluable and he was always able to call upon the good offices of men such as Feargus O'Connor, William Cobbett and J.R.Stephens to address meetings once he began to establish himself in the north. Such contacts with the radical hierarchy were to prove a valuable asset when the *Liberator* was being set up.[26] In any case, Beaumont was always more than just a volatile political adventurer. He was a clever politician and his journalistic skills were excellent. His first newspaper venture, *The Trifler* (1822-3), had flourished only briefly, killed off by a libellous lawsuit,[27] but was soon replaced in 1826 by what became the *Jamaica Courant and Public Advertiser.* After he left Jamaica for London in 1836 he used the revenue from the sale of the *Advertiser* to launch *The Radical*, which was 'devoted to democracy,'[28] and his reputation as a political journalist grew apace. On his travels around the country he had been 'impressed by what he perceived to be the more revolutionary quality of the men in the north' [29]and, when he was subsequently invited to contest a Newcastle seat for the Working Men's Association in July 1837, Beaumont made plans to relaunch the *Radical* under a new title, the *Northern Liberator.*

Initially, the *Northern Liberator* was published in a fairly low key format, with a plain unpretentious mast head, and a few appropriately stirring lines of Byron's verse as preface to the editorial column:

> Words are things and a small drop of ink
> Falling like dew upon a thought produces
> That which makes thousands, perhaps millions think.[30]

By the second week of publication the mast head had been reset in an oversized and grandiose Gothic typeface and the symbolism of the title was now emphatically reinforced by a line from

Herodotus *'We should advance the multitude'.*[31] In recent years the iconography of newspapers has attracted a good deal of academic interest and there is some justification for taking the choice of title seriously. As Aled Jones notes, 'the emblems and mottoes crystallised a title's identity and provided the reader with immediate identifiers'.[32] In this instance, title and motto asserted the intention to be proactive, to be the agent of change rather than a mere chronicler of events. With strident editorials proclaiming 'The Coming Revolution,' in which 'five hundred thousand democrats in arms' would be mustered from Yorkshire, Lancashire, Northumberland and Scotland,[33] and extensive coverage of radical meetings, the political objectives of the paper dominated the majority of its four pages. Even the advertisement columns included exhortations to buy the *Political Mirror* and Henry Hetherington's tracts and pamphlets.[34] Within weeks the *Liberator* was being circulated extensively by agents in twenty towns, mostly in northern England but also in London, Glasgow and Edinburgh.[35]

Beaumont was a shrewd businessman, fully alive to the need to ensure the paper's commercial viability. He published two editions of the paper: the first, printed on Friday afternoons, was sent out of the region early to ensure that readers elsewhere received their copy at the same time as the local edition hit the streets. More interesting, though, was the appointment in December 1837 of 'one of the ablest London reporters' specifically to 'furnish the latest parliamentary intelligence up to the adjournment of the House on Thursday in time for publication the ensuing Saturday'.[36] As Beaumont's editorial stressed, this would provide more immediate news coverage than that available to any of his competitors, and probably helps to explain the excellent circulation rates. Typically enough, Beaumont's all-consuming passion for action was not satisfied by the demands of setting up a new newspaper, even on this enterprising basis. Spurred on by the gathering crisis in Canada, he sold the *Liberator* and embarked on a lecture tour at the beginning of January 1838 to publicise the cause and raise a force of 500 men to support the rebels.[37] As it turned out, he never lived to see the fruits of his fund-raising tour. He succumbed to a virulent fever and was dead before the month was out.

Robert Blakey took over the reins of a newspaper that had quickly established itself as a pugnacious and fearless defender of democracy, and already gained the loyalties of a large and growing readership. He could easily, it seems, have cruised along in the wake of Beaumont's popularity and tinkered with it very little. Blakey, however, was an extremely astute and able politician. In his *Memoirs* he acknowledged Beaumont's generous spirit and enthusiasm but, as the *Liberator*'s lengthy obituary repeatedly observed (and here we can detect the hand of Blakey), he judged him to have been politically naive and wanting in judgement; 'guided more by impulse than by reason'.[38] A self-made man of a deeply religious and philosophical turn of mind, Blakey had served a commensurate political and journalistic apprenticeship, almost all of it local. He was finely tuned to the subtleties of local radicalism and, more importantly, capable of presenting an irrefutably rational analysis of the political situation. His weapon was not passion and bluster but a firm unflappable logic. The annals of the later careers of Chartists always make interesting reading but none more so than Blakey's, who ended up as Professor of Logic and Metaphysics at Queen's College, Belfast in 1849 and was awarded a pension from the Civil List. This prestigious academic appointment was no mean feat for someone who had been convicted of seditious activity and bound over to keep the peace for three years less than a decade before.

Blakey was an experienced writer and journalist long before he took over the running of the paper. In the 1820s he had written for a number of stamped and unstamped papers including Wooler's *Black Dwarf*, the *Newcastle Magazine* and the *Tyne Mercury*,[39] as well as working on philosophical treatises of his own. In due course several of his philosophical studies had been published: a study of *Free Will* in 1831 and a *History of Moral Science* in 1834. At the same time he enjoyed a lively correspondence with such radical luminaries as William Godwin, J. Horne Tooke, Thomas Paine, and John Thelwall.[40] William Cobbett had been an important ally from the early 1830s and had stayed with Blakey when he travelled to Northumberland in 1832. He called upon Blakey's assistance in getting up a petition about the Reform Bill that same year and, in return, responded warmly to a request for help in setting up a radical newspaper in 1835.[41] Cobbett generously offered to release his own assistant, Mr Gutsell, from work on the *Register*, in order that Blakey could benefit from expert assistance, and urged him to inform himself on church reform before parliament reconvened: '...remember...I expect great things from you, and that you shall have every little assistance which it is in my power to give you'.[42]

Although the planned journal did not materialise, Cobbett proved to be a seminal influence. The following year Blakey was elected Mayor of the new reformed corporation of Morpeth, and it is a measure of his uncompromising, sturdy radicalism that he still felt compelled in November, 1837, to expose publicly the 'cruelty and inhumanity' of the Poor Law Amendment Act, in an open letter printed in Larkin's *Newcastle Standard.*[43] The letter gave full details of individual cases of hardship together with the financial statement of the Morpeth Union, castigating his fellow members with charges of brutality and drunkenness: 'Is this not a starvation scale?' he railed, drawing attention to the availability of revenues to relieve the poor and the unwillingness of the Morpeth Union to assist. The *Standard*'s readers were urged to give their votes only to those who would commit themselves to an immediate repeal of the despised legislation.[44]

Intellectually Blakey was more than capable of taking up the challenge of running the *Liberator* and he also had the local standing and the money to fight off the combined attacks of his political and commercial rivals. His fellow editor, Thomas Doubleday, was a poet and dramatist as well as secretary of the NPU. His well connected family had a soap manufactory on the Tyne and Doubleday had been pressed into the business much against his own wish to pursue a literary career. So much more at ease in print than on the political platform, Doubleday's romanticism was the perfect foil for Blakey's cool dialectics. They managed the paper between them and, apart from Devyr's reports of NPU activities and the parliamentary reports from London, together they produced all of the editorial and news items.

Whereas under Beaumont's editorship the *Liberator*'s manifesto for reform had been characterised by a commitment to a broad spectrum of radical causes, the new editorial tactics were markedly different. By the end of March, 1838, the focus of the *Northern Liberator* had shifted detectably. Given Blakey's deep seated opposition to the New Poor Law of 1834, and Doubleday's interest in population theory, it was probably inevitable that they would try to provoke local radicals into an anti-Poor Law campaign. As the application of logic was Blakey's instinctive *modus operandi* that meant a sustained attack upon the capitalist system. The economic analysis consistently advanced by the editors to drive home the claims for radical reform became central to the agenda of north east Chartists at that time: the Poor Law Amendment Act was presented as a vicious piece of class legislation aimed at protecting the privileges of the wealthy and powerful; and, by extension of the same logic, reform of the capitalist system was the only means of recasting a more egalitarian and just society. The centrality of the anti-Poor Law campaign has been played down in the past, notably by D. J. Rowe,[45] who had difficulty reconciling the existence of a high-waged buoyant industrial sector with the platform rhetoric of key speakers at local rallies. Such wages were not, of course, available to the majority of the region's workers and, just as Rowe signally underestimated the *Liberator*'s national readership,[46] he also failed to appreciate the way that north east Chartists were being expertly tutored to articulate a wider, national agenda. The strength of north east Chartism ought to be located in their expressed solidarity with distressed and dispossessed communities and individuals elsewhere, and their commitment to reforms that would benefit the working classes as a whole.

With the constant threat of prosecution and punitive fines hanging over them, Blakey and Doubleday took refuge in a highly intellectualised form of satire which drew heavily upon classical literature. The decision to resort to comic parody was far from accidental. Blakey's experience of working on *Black Dwarf* served him well. Wooler had deployed Pope's adage

> Satire's my weapon, but I'm too discreet
> To run a muck and tilt at all I meet,
> I only wear it in a land of Hectors,
> Thieves, Supercargoes, Sharpers and directors.[47]

to great effect and the *Liberator*'s editorial team became adept at dressing up scurrilous and libellous copy as bona fide comic novelties. Both editors had an extensive classical and literary repertoire upon which they could draw. While none of the caustic humour escaped the readers who could readily pick up on the all too familiar register of the in-house joke, the authorities clearly found it extremely difficult to prove libel or slander in a court of law. The Treasury, banks and, more controversially, Jewish moneylenders became the natural targets of their increasingly biting and scornful caricature. Just occasionally, illustrative material was used to lend the message a more graphic and accessible impact. The publication of an engraving featuring the 'Tree of Taxation' is a prime example of the creative tactics deployed by the editors. Borrowing from Spence's imaginative Upas Tree, it first appeared in the *Liberator* on 13 October, 1838, but was subsequently sold at a handsome profit as a handbill for distribution at meetings for 6/- per hundred. Lancashire and Yorkshire alone took more than 40,000 copies.[48] It was cheap to produce and, not surprisingly, the editors went on to publish other material which began life in serialised form in the paper. One of the most potent of these extended satires was *The Political Tale of a Tub*, loosely based on Swift's famous political squib published in 1704 (which itself parodied Hobbes' *Leviathan*). In this version the Tory dies of dropsy, the Liberal becomes dotty and imbecilic and, appropriately enough, the radical inherits everything! From 1840 it was made available as a separate volume.[49]

More revealing, though, was *The Political Pilgrim's Progress* which was given a lengthy serialisation beginning in January 1839, but eventually published as a 90 page tract costing 6d per copy. As a parody of Bunyan's original work, it is crude and clumsy but it nonetheless effectively delivered a moral tale with a political message. The publications' side of the business was essential, generating much needed revenue, and *The Political Pilgrim's Progress* was probably the biggest moneyspinner, with more than 6,000 copies sold by January 1840. It was, claimed the New Year editorial, being 'reprinted in New York and circulating extensively in the United States'.[50]

The virulent anti-Semitism of this piece, and the later *Northern Lights* collection of short articles is extremely unpleasant.[51] Had Beaumont survived it is highly unlikely that north east Chartism and the *Liberator* would have been associated with it, given that so much of his early career had been devoted to stamping out racism and anti-Semitism in Jamaica. Anti-Semitism has been identified with radicalism in the past, of course, but it has not yet been subjected to any systematic examination by mainstream Chartist historians. W.D.Rubinstein has drawn attention to what he calls the 'dark side of populism,' claiming that anti-Semitism was 'an important and possibly pervasive feature of English radicalism,' not just in the 1830s but 'arguably much later,'[52] and it is his contention that there has been a marked unwillingness to deal with the anti-Semitic element of Chartist rationale, or its wider implications. Whether, as he suggests, a deliberate 'bowdlerisation' of the evidence[53] has been undertaken is surely stretching the extent of our collective embarrassment beyond reasonable boundaries, but, as matters stand, it is difficult to rebut the charge; a response based on a measured and rigorous scholarly enquiry would certainly seem to be long overdue. Rubinstein attributes much of the anti-Semitism in British radicalism to Cobbett's attack upon the financial system, citing his xenophobic hatred of Jews and his extensive influence upon the Chartist press.[54] As far as the *Liberator*'s wholly prejudiced attitudes are concerned, this would explain a good deal. As noted earlier on, Cobbett and Blakey were very close, with Blakey cast in the role of pupil/disciple and heavily dependent upon Cobbett for advice and counsel; this would help to explain why in this respect Blakey's usual calm rationality should have completely deserted him.

By 1839 the *Liberator* was being published in three separate editions and had even introduced home deliveries for subscribers as an added incentive.[55] Robert Lowery's appointment as missionary lecturer and subscription agent contributed a great deal to the efficient management of the paper and, with an estimated 7,000 membership of the NPU,[56] a regular stable income was virtually assured. While it is difficult to offer any precise statement of the paper's circulation rates after 1838, the indications are that they were extremely healthy. The editors were predictably ebullient, claiming that the paper was even taken at the Treasury 'because although they don't like us, they think it just as well to know what we say...even the Jews read the *Northern Liberator*'.[57] More persuasive than Blakey's bullish editorial, or even the published list of 112 agents, is the attempt by the proprietors of the Whiggish *Gateshead Observer* to sponsor a rival newspaper. Lampooned as a 'kind of second rate, private asylum for the weak minded, idiotic and foolish part of mankind'[58] the *Observer* had every reason to resent its rival's continuing success; it was, in fact, struggling to match half of the *Liberator*'s output. The discovery that Dr John Taylor had been offered £300 to act as editor of a new paper caused a furore[59] and stung the Editors into relaunching the *Liberator* in a new extended format. The revamped version had 48 columns of letter press which brought it more into line with the *Northern Star*, although it did not finally appear in its modified form until 13 July 1839. The much vaunted extension of news which the editors made so much of was in reality something of an exaggeration. The smaller page format easily accounted for the need to produce extra pages.

Given Doubleday's and Blakey's skilful management of the paper, which had a healthy advertising base throughout its circulation, it probably would have served the local Chartist movement for much longer than a few brief years, had the authorities not moved so punitively against Blakey and Bell, the *Liberator*'s printer, for publishing a paper on the 'National Right of Resistance to Constituted Authorities.' Fighting the case cost Blakey dearly and, by his own account, after he was 'bound over to keep the peace for 3 years in the sum of £500 he was forced to sell the paper at a considerable loss'.[60] By that stage, he had already sunk some £1,800 of his money into keeping the *Liberator* afloat and he simply did not have the necessary resources to absorb such a crippling fine.

The cost to the NPU and local Chartism is more difficult to measure. Movement and newspaper had essentially been a joint enterprise, each dependent upon the other, ideologically and financially. The demise of the paper came hard on the heels of the arrests of key personnel and the internecine conflict over David Urquhart's Russophobic evangelism.[61] Whatever its undoubted strength, outside of Yorkshire and Lancashire the *Northern Star* could not, and did not, fulfil the same vital function as the more successful Chartist papers in their own town centres and regions. It is tempting to speculate on what might have happened if the paper had survived. At the very least, the loss of its own propagandist organ helps to explain the doldrums phase of north east Chartism which set in after 1840.

This brings us to the thorny question of northeast Chartism and the persistent ambiguities as to its physical force character. Reprints of public speeches are not always the best means of deciding the issue one way or the other. Platform speakers were wholly constrained by the legal niceties of the times and had less recourse to more subtle means of making their position clear. Devyr's *Odd Book of the Nineteenth Century* has been largely ridiculed as the romantic ravings of a man tilting at his own claim to fame, particularly as he ascribes a starring role to himself in the supposed rising of the northern towns. According to his account, Devyr was taken to task for firing muskets from the windows of the *Liberator*'s offices as a salute to the passing crowds on their way to the Town Moor, but, more crucially, he contends that they were all closely involved in the procurement of firearms. The offices were, he claimed, the centre of gravity for the movement, the place where the entire NPU Council could be rapidly assembled, and he and his compatriots used the rooms above to make shells.[62] Some evidence drawn from the pages of the *Liberator* would appear to offer a more reliable guide.

During Beaumont's period as editor there were abundant references to an armed struggle '*if need be*'. As he told a crowd at a meeting assembled in defence of the Glasgow spinners, 'We abhor Civil War; but if we cannot obtain freedom without it, then welcome the barricades'.[63] As far as 1838 is concerned there does not appear to be any concrete evidence that violent means had become official NPU Council policy, or that the majority of local radicals favoured a physical force solution. With the Charter published in May, the mood of the people seemed to be relatively optimistic: a determined and implacable insistence upon the necessity for reform, and a show of strength would win the day. Numbers were not a problem. A massive demonstration on the Town Moor on Coronation Day raised an estimated 80,000 strong crowd.[64] And, as late in the year as November, the editors were exhorting everyone to 'be peaceful in your actions but invincible in your determination'.[65] The tide, though, was beginning to turn. Harney's speech to a Christmas Day gathering sounded a more aggressive, less placatory note: '...they were met with their feet on God's own earth, with God's own sky for their canopy... would they take the oath to live free or die?'

The arrest of J.R.Stephens served as a vital energiser and at a moonlight meeting in Winlaton in early January the assembly pledged support for O'Connor and Stephens 'to the death if necessary'.[66] We can, of course, dismiss much of this as just so much hot air, indicative merely of the whiff of cannon allegedly fired, or just the heat of the moment. Much less easy to discount is the sudden replacement of the *Liberator's* prefatory lines from Byron by an extract from *Blackstone's Commentaries on the Law of England*, which unequivocally confirmed the right to bear arms:

> the subjects of England are entitled first to the regular administration and free course of justice in the courts of law; next to the right of petitioning the King and Parliament for a redress of grievances; and lastly to the right of having arms for self preservation and defence.[67]

From that point onwards the right to bear arms became a mantra for the local movement and a permanent preface to every editorial column thereafter. On 12 January 1839, readers were given detailed advice on making ball and buckshot cartridges, 'moveable barricades are recommended in street fighting....hand grenades can be cast by any workman of the thousands of the NPU employed in iron foundries'. This was indeed a new departure. The new 'Hymn of the Northern Political Union,' published on 16 February was combative, cast in terms of a just war in which God would defend the patriots. 'The Radical's Song,' published in the next issue, went one step further:

> be peril in the path, be death upon the way,
> when Liberty's the prize, what to the brave are they?
> The steel is in my hand, before me is my foe;
> and for freedom God himself shall help to strike the blow.[68]

The constitutional requirement to bear arms only in self defence was not construed as any kind of obstacle since, as the editorial of 16 March insisted, the gentry were actively arming themselves; even the Duke of Newcastle was said to have fortified his residence with 'several pieces of brass cannon'. The National Convention declaration which asserted the right of the people to have warlike weapons was formally endorsed by the *Liberator* on 20 April, although the editors were careful to add their own assurance that the people would 'never have to use these arms'. The Six Points of the Charter effectively became seven as the right to bear arms became an important addendum. An 'Open Letter to the Upper and Middle Classes' published on the 18 May 1839, was an uncompromising and threatening challenge:

> we warn you to reflect that in taking up arms to defend the present system...you are counting all the fearful consequences that may arise from the resentment of men driven to despair,

The potent symbolism of banners and flags should not be underestimated either.[69] All too frequently they were adorned with martial lines lifted directly from biblical or classical texts. Legitimisation was everything, and those who marched beneath banners emblazoned with such slogans as *'War in each breast and Freedom on each brow,'* or *'It is better to die by the sword than perish with hunger,'* emphatically expressed their collective resistance. Even the advertising pages were pressed into service to hammer home the new physical force rhetoric; an advertisement for stomach pills entitled *PHYSICAL FORCE* made play with the new rationale, claiming that their miraculous little pills were as 'weapons at their service which allay irritation ..in these turbulent times' and which 'have for many years been highly celebrated as a sure and efficient force'.[70] The extended metaphors resonate with the 'culture of mutuality'[71] and, interestingly enough, can be traced back to Wooler's creative advertising tactics. Once more, this indicates just how closely Blakey's vision of the *Northern Liberator* adhered to the *Black Dwarf's* tried and tested earlier formula. It was no accident that the editors chose this opportune moment to reprint a separate volume of *The Political Pilgrim's Progress,* illustrated with woodcuts, chronicling the eventual resort to violent means as Radical (as Pilgrim) struggles to reach the City of Reform.[72] As January 1840 dawned the *Liberator* was still carrying fulsome reports of dangerously seditious activities - most notably at Seghill Colliery where the 'Sacred Week' was kept in riotous fashion with an exhibition of pikes and the firing of guns.[73]

Frost's trial, extensively covered by the *Liberator* throughout January, acted as a catalyst and a front page appeal by Charles Attwood called upon all Chartists to exercise due caution, to protest peacefully 'as anything else might precipitate great trouble for Frost'.[74] Blakey's response was to turn his attention once more to the excesses of the capitalist system and launch a sustained attack upon the Jewish financial interests which he held fully accountable for the trade protection policy. From early spring until July 1840, the paper carried a series of anti-Semitic articles which, among other matters, accused the Jewish people of sexual deviance, indulging in human sacrifices and other unspeakable atrocities. Editorials continued to denounce the financial institutions who benefited from the tide of bankruptcies and bad debts, and forced vast numbers into a humiliating and degrading dependency upon the Poor Law. Banks were, the paper claimed, 'simply large pawnbrokers'.[75]

This economic agenda was also an intensely personal issue for Blakey, as he wrestled with the financial implications of his impending prosecution and contemplated the impact this would have upon the paper's viability. From the beginning of May the paper was published as the *Liberator and Champion*, but even this eleventh-hour rescue package was not enough to save it. A change of management, with Blakey's brother-in law, Henry Gibb, as the new proprietor had already brought unwelcome efficiency measures to bear upon the *Liberator*'s nervous workforce, sparking off a bad tempered dispute about working practices and supervisory roles. The disgruntled workers' grievances soon became notorious as they circulated a handbill in *Cleave's Gazette of Varieties* complaining of 'petty tyranny' and questioning the *Liberator*'s supposed advocacy of radical principles and commitment to support the working classes.[76] The dispute was eventually settled, partly because the Northern Typographical Union upbraided the workers for leaving their employment without giving the required two weeks notice, but also because some private mediation took place which reinstated key members of staff. A public apology by one of the men, William Inglis, who claimed that his employers had been maliciously misrepresented to him, marked the end of an affair which cast the paper's management and editorial team in a very dubious light.[77]

Unfortunately, internal dissension was also undermining the activities of the NPU. Riven by dispute over Urquhartism and the Anti-Corn Law League,[78] and unnerved by the possibility that the

Council had been infiltrated by spies, meetings had declined into a bitter and vitriolic exchange of abuse. The working class members deeply resented what they perceived to be Larkin's and Attwood's determination to prioritize their own commercial agenda. As it became apparent that the uneasy class alliance was no longer tenable, tempers finally exploded and 'the illiterate middle class popinjays' stormed out of the meeting, leaving the NPU in total disarray. A damning editorial on 28 April carried a full report and rejected the activities of the Anti-Corn Law Leaguers. Conflict was in fact endemic throughout the movement as a whole and the major reorganisation of the NPU's Council undertaken in May 1840 subsequently acted as a template for the new organisational structure adopted by the National Charter Association.[79] These structural changes were accompanied by a lecture programme aimed at educating local Chartists in the precepts of electoral reform, the distribution of 12,000 tracts and the collection of door to door subscriptions. The implementation of all these measures would seem to suggest that, although the movement was weakened, it was still capable of seizing the initiative and pressing the campaign forward. The *Liberator* had always acted as the movement's organisational muscle, co-ordinating activities and presenting the impression that there was a single united ideological voice. As the paper tottered towards collapse at the close of 1840, the foundations of the local movement were seriously undermined and a lengthy period was to elapse before north east Chartism was able to reassert its radical convictions with anything approaching its earlier self-confidence.

This study of the *Liberator* has revealed the centrality of press support to the vigour and confidence of north east Chartism. The success of both newspaper and movement were indivisible; both rested heavily upon the existence of an unusually sophisticated and buoyant print culture and the dynamism of an indigenous radical tradition. While Beaumont's legacy as architect of the *Liberator*'s early achievements must be acknowledged, in the longer term Blakey's formidable intellect served the paper better. With Doubleday's assistance he produced a paper that could realise several related objectives at one and the same time. The *Liberator* operated as a political organ and a local newspaper, catering for a national as well as a local constituency of readers. The satirical edge of much of the reportage and articles gave the paper a distinctive, modern personality which, in many respects, anticipated the mixed formula of news and entertainment expected of newspapers later in the century - and, crucially, enabled the paper to escape prosecution for so long. Most telling of all, evidence from the pages of the *Liberator* supports the view that an economic analysis lay at the heart of northeast Chartism and the reform principles the movement espoused. The editorials and satirical works were a potent vehicle for exposing the stark inequalities of the political system and an understanding of this sharpened popular perceptions of the class divide. During 1839 physical force gradually became accepted, albeit briefly, as a realistic if last-resort alternative to the established protocol of constitutional pressure.

NOTES

I am grateful to Ian Haywood for his advice and comments on an early draft of this chapter.

[1] O.R.Ashton, R.Fyson, S.Roberts (eds), *The Chartist Movement: A New Annotated Bibliography,* London, Mansell, 1995, pp 64-70.

[2] *Northern Star,* 2 June, 1838, as cited by D.Read : *Press and People, 1790-1850: Opinion in Three English Cities,* London, Edward Arnold, 1961, p97.

[3] K.Gilmartin, *Print Politics: The Press and Radical Opposition in Early Nineteenth Century England,* Cambridge, Cambridge University Press, 1996, provides the most recent discussion but see also P.Hollis, *The Pauper Press: A Study in Working-Class Radicalism of the 1830s,* Oxford University Press, 1970. J.Stevenson: *Popular Disturbances in England 1700-1870,* London, Longman, 1979, p219 provides a useful discussion of the residual impact of coercive legislation.

[4] R.G.Gammage, *History of the Chartist Movement,* London, Merlin 1969; *Reminiscences of a Chartist*, reptd. by the Society for the Study of Labour History, Manchester, 1983 with an Introduction and annotations by W.H.Maehl.

[5] S.Roberts, 'Who Wrote to the *Northern Star*?' in O.Ashton, R.Fyson, S.Roberts (eds), *The Duty of Discontent,* London, Mansell, 1995, pp 55-70

[6] A.Temple Patterson, *Radical Leicester: A History of Leicester, 1780-1850,* Leicester, Leicester University Press, 1954.

[7] A.Wilson, *The Chartist Movement in Scotland,* Manchester, Manchester University Press, 1970; see also A.Briggs (ed), *Chartist Studies,* London and Basingstoke, Macmillan, 1959, Chapter VIII.

[8] The debate was sparked off by a seminal article by G.S.Jones 'Rethinking Chartism,' *Languages of Class: Studies in English Working Class History,1832-1982,* Cambridge, Cambridge University Press, 1983 who called for a new analysis of 'what Chartists actually said or wrote'. Aside from the theoretical discussion much of the new work has devolved upon the concept of 'populism'. See for example P.Joyce, *Visions of the People: Industrial England and the Question of Class 1840-1914,* Cambridge, Cambridge University Press, 1991.

[9] For instance I.Haywood, *The Literature of Struggle: An Anthology of Chartist Fiction,* Aldershot, Scolar Press, 1995.

[10] D.Thompson, *The Chartists: Popular Politics in the Industrial Revolution,* London and New York, Temple Smith, 1984, p54.

[11] W.H.Maehl, 'Chartist disturbances in Northeastern England, 1839,' *International Review of Social History,* Vol. VIII, No 3, 1963; 'Augustus Hardin Beaumont : Anglo-American Radical (1798-1838),' *International Review of Social History,* Vol. XIV, 1969, pp 237-251.

[12] D.Levine & K.Wrightson, *The Making of an Industrial Society: Whickham 1560-1765,* Oxford, Oxford University Press, 1991.

[13] M.Chase, *The People's Farm: English Agrarian Radicalism 1775-1840,* Oxford, Oxford University Press, 1988

[14] As cited by A.Myers in his review of J.Brewer: *The Pleasures of the Imagination,* in *Northern Review:A Journal of Regional and Cultural Affairs,* Volume 6, Spring 1998, p111.

[15] Aled Jones, *Powers of the Press: Newspapers, Power and the Public in Nineteenth Century England,* Aldershot, Scolar Press, 1996, p4.

[16] D.Ridley, 'The Spital Fields Demonstration and the Parliamentary Reform Crisis in Newcastle upon Tyne, May 1832' in *North East Labour History Society Bulletin,* No 27,1992.

[17] *Newcastle Magazine,* February 1831, Vol XI, pp71-77.

[18] *Newcastle Standard,* 4 February, 1837.

[19] *Newcastle Standard,* 21 January, 1837

[20] Read, *Press and People,* p97.

[21] For biographical material see *Northern Liberator* 29 April 1838; 5 May 1838. See also study of Beaumont's life and career by W.H.Maehl, *'Augustus Hardin Beaumont'.*

[22] Biographies of both Blakey and Doubleday appear in R.Welford, *Men of Mark 'Twixt Tyne and Tweed,* Newcastle upon Tyne, 1892 and J.O.Baylen & N.J.Gossman (eds), *Biographical Dictionary of Modern British Radicals Since 1770,* Brighton, Harvester Press, Vol II, 1984.

[23] *Northern Liberator,* 23 May 1840.

[24] Anon, *Adventures of Two Americans in the Siege of Brussels,* Cornhill, Edmund H.Beaumont 1830.

[25] *Ibid.,* Appendix.

[26] Maehl, *'Augustus Hardin Beaumont'* p248.

[27] *Ibid.,* p239.

[28] *Ibid.,* p240.

[29] *Ibid.,* p 246.

[30] *Northern Liberator,* 3 February, 1838.

[31] *Northern Liberator,* 28 October, 1837.

[32] Jones, *Powers of the Press.,*p34.

[33] *Northern Liberator,* 18 November, 1837.

[34] *Northern Liberator,* 21 October, 1837.

[35] A list of agents was carried on the back page of each edition; as cited here, 16 December, 1837.

[36] *Ibid.*

[37] *Ibid.,* 27 January, 1838; see also R.Blakey, *Memoirs of Dr.Robert Blakey,* London, Rev. H. Miller, 1879, p108.

[38] *Ibid.; Northern Liberator,* 5.May, 1938.

[39] Blakey, *Memoirs,.* p 27.

[40] *Ibid.* especially p 89.

[41] There are extensive references to Blakey's friendship with Cobbett in his *Memoirs* but see p 53f .

[42] *Ibid.,* p61.

[43] *Newcastle Standard,* 18 March, 1837. This Address and a succeeding article were also privately printed for circulation by the Standard Office, Newcastle upon Tyne, 27 March 1837.

[44] *Ibid.,* 18 March 1837.

[45] D.J.Rowe, 'Some Aspects of Chartism on Tyneside,' *International Review of Social History* Vol.XVI, 1971, especially pp18-21.See also T.J.Nossiter, *Influence, Opinion and Political Idiom in Reformed England: Case Studies from the North East 1832-74,* Brighton, Harvester Press, 1975, p153

[46] *Ibid.,* p18.

[47] Gilmartin, *Print Politics,* has a lengthy discussion of Wooler's tactics but see illustration p36 which shows that the cited quotation was used as a motto on the title page of Volume One, 1817.

[48] *Northern Liberator,* 4 January 1840.

[49] *The Political Tale of a Tub,* Newcastle upon Tyne, *Northern Liberator,* 1840.

[50] *Northern Liberator,* 4 January 1840. See also Ian Haywood, *Chartist Fiction,* Vol.2 (forthcoming) which includes a lengthy study of the *Political Pilgrim's Progress.*

[51] *The Northern Lights,* Newcastle upon Tyne, 1838 brought together a collection of 42 short articles from previous editions of the *Liberator.* No 34, from *Northern Liberator,* 10 November, 1838, 'Important Medical Consultation' carries a particularly nasty caricature of a Jewish doctor.

[52] W.D.Rubinstein (ed), *Elites and the Wealthy in Modern British History,* Brighton, Harvester Press, 1987. see authored article 'British Radicalism and the 'Dark Side' of Populism'.pp 339 - 373.

[53] *Ibid.,* p 365.

[54] *Ibid.,* p 350.

[55] *Northern Liberator,* 21 April, 1838.

[56] *Northern Liberator,* 20 April, 1839.

[57] *Northern Liberator,* 5 January, 1839.

[58] *Ibid.* The *Observer's* circulation was 1,875 per week.

[59] *Northern Liberator,* 19 January, 1839.

[60] Blakey, *Memoirs,* p103.

[61] J. H. Gleason, *The Genesis of Russophobia in Great Britain : A Study of the Interaction of Public   Opinion,* Cambridge, Harvard University Press, 1950, pp 260-1. A section of the NPU, including the influential Charles Attwood, subscribed to Urquhart's Russophobic foreign policy and organised a series of parliamentary petitions. As Gleason suggests the motivation was primarily economic but they also, it seems, relished the opportunity to air their hostility to Palmerston. See also R.Shannon, 'David Urquhart and the Foreign Affairs Committees,' pp239-261, in P.Hollis (ed), *Pressure From Without in early Victorian England,* London, Edward Arnold, 1974.

[62] T.A.Devyr, *The Odd Book of the Nineteenth Century or Chivalry in Modern Days,* New York, 1882, pp 159-204.

[63] *Northern Liberator,* 2 December, 1837.

[64] *Northern Liberator,* 2 June, 1838.

[65] *Northern Liberator,* 24 November, 1838.

[66] *Northern Liberator,* 5 January, 1839.

[67] *Ibid.*

[68] *Northern Liberator,* 28 February, 1839.

[69] Paul A.Pickering, 'Class without Words:Symbolic Communication in the Chartist Movement,' *Past & Present,* No 112, August 1986, p153 fn.

[70] *Northern Liberator,* 4 January, 1840.

[71] Paul A.Pickering, 'Chartism and the 'Trade of Agitation' in Early Victorian Britain,' *History,* Vol.76, No 247, June 1991, p222; p224.

[72] In this parodied version of Bunyan's classic moral fable, published separately in 1839, *Radical* encounters an emasculated *Moral Force,* overcomes a series of obstacles (e.g. *Bribery,Debt, Treachery* and kills *Political Apollyon (*owner of the *City of Plunder*) in order to reach the *City of Reform* 'in triumph and unhurt,' p 89.

[73] *Ibid.*

[74] *Ibid.*

[75] *Northern Liberator,* various, especially 25 April; 15 May, 6 June; 4 July.

[76] The dispute was aired publicly in the pages of the *Liberator,* notably 16 May and 23 May, 1840, and in pamphlet form: *The Workmen of the Liberator and their Employers: To the Printers of Newcastle, The Working Classes and the Public Generally,* 12 May, 1840.

[77] *Northern Liberator,* 13 June, 1840.

[78] *Northern Liberator,* 28 March, 1840.

[79] E.Yeo, 'Some Practices and Problems of Chartist Democracy,'p365, in J.Epstein & D.Thompson(eds), *The Chartist Experience: Studies in Working Class Radicalism and Culture, 1830-1860,* London, Macmillan, 1982.

ORATORS AND ORATORY IN THE CHARTIST MOVEMENT, 1840-1848

Owen Ashton

It must be borne in mind that down to about this period, with the single exception of the time of the Consolidated Trades' Union, even the more enlightened of the working class had been but little accustomed to public speaking. The platform had been almost exclusively occupied by the upper and middle classes, and it could hardly be expected that the working men, deprived in a great measure of educational advantages, would become Ciceros in a day. But the dawn of the Chartist movement was quite an era in working class oratory. It gave to the humblest the opportunity of raising his voice in public meeting, and that opportunity was not disregarded, but, on the other hand, was embraced with avidity.

(Extract from R.G. Gammage, *The History of the Chartist Movement, from its Commencement down to the Present Time,* London, 1854, p.24)

Gammage's opinion on platform oratory might well be viewed, of course, as predictable: he was himself by this time a leading Chartist orator and keenly interested in advancing the whole business and art of popular communication. Significantly, however, even unsympathetic middle class contemporaries were also commenting on Chartist speakers in favourable terms. In 1839, when the fifty or so delegates to the first Chartist Convention gathered to debate in their rooms off Fleet Street, London, an experienced and acute observer who gained access, the French writer Flora Tristan, was particularly impressed by their oratorical talents.[1] Nine years later Matthew Arnold attended the last great Convention of 1848 and was equally struck by the ability of the speakers, but thought he would not like to be governed by them.[2] Convention membership was not necessarily synonymous with prowess on the radical rostrum. Leading Chartists like William Lovett and Henry Hetherington, for example, were not particularly

48

vocal.[3] Yet the overwhelming majority of Convention delegates were Ciceros in the making. They were in fact part of a whole galaxy of itinerant orators or lecturers thrown up by the growing organisational strength of Chartism as a working class movement. Some were prominent nationally, others served on a regional basis, still more worked within a local district. Between them, they helped to mobilize communities within and across geographical regions which were politically, industrially and culturally diverse.[4] Indeed, David Jones is probably correct in his judgement that the travelling orator - an amateur or paid professional – 'produced infinitely better results than tracts or conventions.'[5]

According to Edward Royle, by organisation, publication and by oratory, Chartism flourished.[6] Both the formation and functioning of the National Charter Association, and the place of the *Northern Star*, have been accorded proper historical attention in recent years.[7] Yet the important question of the role and contribution of the third agency, oratory, has to a certain extent been overlooked. Important advances in our understanding of the role of the spoken word have been made, for example, through biographical studies of leading Chartist figures. While Michael Edwards has explored the pull of the Rev J.R. Stephens' oratory in terms of his use of the language of romantic Christian violence, James Epstein's analysis of Feargus O'Connor's leadership has left us in no doubt that the Irishman by his presence, manner of presentation, racy and vivid language, and remarkable versatility, was unrivalled as the consummate performer in platform oratory.[8] Complementing these works are the interpretations of a number of historians who have become more critically aware, yet at the same time ideologically divided, over the Chartist use of language and communication, both verbal and non-verbal. Controversially, Gareth Stedman Jones has pioneered one particular approach -'the linguistic turn' - by his study of Chartist language - what they 'actually said or wrote' - from carefully selected articles and reports of speeches.[9] Such a narrow focus takes little or no account of either the socio-economic context in which the speeches occurred, or the face-to-face interaction between the speaker and audience. The net effect, advanced by the interpretations of Patrick Joyce and James Vernon,[10] has been to suggest that Chartist language and consciousness were more 'populist' than class-based in character.

These views have been fundamentally challenged by, for example, James Epstein and Paul Pickering,[11] who argue that the study of the spoken word should include the visual, oral and symbolic elements surrounding the platform, and not simply a reliance on the printed word. Thus, the pictorial representation of banners and flags, the donning of red caps of liberty by members of the audience, and the appearance of 'gentleman' speakers like Feargus O'Connor, dressed in working men's clothes and with rolled-up shirt sleeves, are taken to be statements of either class appropriation or oppression, or both. As to the anatomy of Chartist speech-making itself, Martha Vicinus has looked at the complex relationship between the strategies and styles of those followers who cohered around the views of the rationalist William Lovett, the 'live free or die' stance of Julian Harney and the ambivalent rhetoric of constitutional intimidation practised by O'Connor during 1838-1839.[12] For 1848, John Belchem has also shown how both Dr Peter Murray McDouall's and Feargus O'Connor's thrilling oratory skilfully pushed the language of constitutional action once more to its legal limits, on the by now moribund mass platform. Their speeches were, it is reiterated, in the best tradition of 'gentlemanly' leadership, the rhetoric of mutual flattery, the platform ploy of self-sacrifice for the cause, and the complete identification of leaders and led.[13] The most recent research however, has begun to look at the role and content of oratory in the intervening nine years, a period when the formation of the National Charter Association (founded July 1840) necessitated the whole business of lecturing to be made more systematic and professionalized on an unprecedented scale.[14] In this phase itinerant orators drawn increasingly from the regional and local ranks, served what Philip Howell has called 'a commission in the democracy';[15] for their part Chartist audiences up and down the country hungered eagerly for what these speakers had to say; in turn the latter became outstanding communicators and personalities; and Chartism remained a national movement based upon both the magic of the voice and the power of the pen.

This chapter makes no claims to be the definitive work on Chartist oratory. Rather, its aims are more modest: to establish a tentative typology of Chartist speakers; to make clearer some of the arts of speech-making in the 'movement culture' of the new National Charter Association; to explore the texture of Chartist oratory, paying particular attention, wherever possible, to the importance of dialect or language difference, as for example, was practised in Wales; and to examine the styles of the different speakers, the difficulties they encountered, and the achievements they secured in strengthening resolve and integrating the movement when criss-crossing the country on exhausting lecturing tours. Such aims must, of course, take into consideration how orators projected themselves in terms of personal dress codes, level of preparation, type of delivery, and their use of theatrical and rhetorical devices; they must also touch on those aspects of a speech that made listening and watching by the audience such a benumbing experience - the orator's body language, the role of gesture and gesticulation, voice tone, the ability to participate, the effect of visual aids and any special talents a speaker might have, such as the power of mimicry.

It is difficult to capture the appeal of stirring speeches once they are translated into unimpassioned print. Methodological problems abound. Paul Pickering has shown in his work on the visual spectacle of the public meeting, how newspaper articles not only reflected political bias and editorial selection but also the practical difficulties facing the reporter on the spot. Accuracy in reporting was hampered by, for example, extraneous noise, unclear articulation by the speaker, variables in accent and dialect and, on occasions, by the general hurly-burly.[16]

Autobiographies can also be double-edged source material. Those of national orators like Thomas Cooper, Robert Gammage and Robert Lowery[17] are patently very useful for their graphic descriptions of platform speakers, but we need to be extremely mindful of their hostility to O'Connorites, a patronising view of dialect and, in Lowery's case, of his early departure from the mainstream movement in 1842. Another important eye-witness, the radical Samuel Bamford, did not rate platform oratory as a mnemonic force, believing that its appeal to the emotions and passions created only transient enthusiasm and prevented the building up of a firmly grounded rational support.[18] By contrast, a number of significant activists including W.E. Adams, William Aitken, Robert Crowe, William Farish and Ben Wilson[19] - all respecters of accuracy in their individual accounts - were in no doubt that speech-making was absolutely vital to communicating radical ideas and sustaining Chartism. Given such predilections, like those of the *Northern Star*'s own reporters, they provide, as eye-witnesses, some important clues both to the context surrounding the speech, the presentation of self by the orators and the interactive relationship involving speaker and audience. Careful checks can also be made by comparing their views to those more soberly revealed in private papers and government files. The former take us behind the scenes and reveal some personality clashes and attempts at character assassination; the latter yield important information about the authorities' own fears concerning the powerful hold Chartist orators had over whole districts.

Chartist orators who came into the movement were broadly speaking of three types. The first of these were men of social standing: they were either drawn to the tradition of the role of the 'gentleman' radical of the platform or were learned, professional people who turned political orators. They included national leaders like Feargus O'Connor, Bronterre O'Brien and Dr Peter McDouall; regional men of influence such as Rev J.R. Stephens, W.P. Roberts, Augustus Beaumont and Dr John Taylor; and local visionaries such as the draper, George Binns at Sunderland, the Newcastle surgeon, Dr Charles Larkin and William Penn Gaskell, the politically disillusioned aristocrat in Cheltenham Spa.[20]

Two of the most striking features which turned orators from this group into personality figures, idolised on a grand scale, were a distinct command of language and flamboyant platform appearance. As the products of either a public school education, or university studies or Methodist training, they imbibed the benefits of a learned culture which in turn controlled the terms of literacy criticism and set the rules of public speaking. In their school debating societies, legal training classes at university, or pulpit activities in Dissenting chapels, they came to acquire, regardless of accent, those linguistic skills necessary for the 'correct' or 'received' pronunciation of English. In the new capitalist society of the 1830s such speech patterns expressed and encoded critical differences about class and power. What contemporary codifiers had done, according to Dick Leith, was to cultivate a code of linguistic terms which were different from those in use amongst the vast majority of the population. In effect, while the working population spoke in the vernacular or dialect, only the educated few spoke 'correctly' and correct English speech was both the natural tongue of power and part of the alibi for cultural conquest.[21]

The move from professional barrister or surgeon, however, to the Chartist platform and a practised lecturing role was far from automatic. Indeed, it could be quite a daunting experience. For Bronterre O'Brien, a young barrister and later known as the schoolmaster of Chartism, the early years were difficult ones as he struggled to overcome a weakness of being too hesitant in his delivery.[22] In the case of Peter McDouall, this young surgeon turned Chartist was known in 1838 to be nervous and stuttering to the extent that his speeches were punctuated with embarrassing pauses.[23] Yet the 'little Doctor,' as he was popularly known, became, like O'Connor and the rest of this well-educated group, a skilful, accomplished and stimulating orator. In their speeches, pronunciation and social standing were closely allied. The ex-surgeon, Dr John Taylor, became renowned for what Harney referred to as his 'lava-like eloquence that set on fire all combustible matter in his path'.[24] The effects of this linguistic power were rapidly apparent as J.H. Burland recalled shortly before the beginning of Chartism in Barnsley. At a meeting addressed by the 'Lion of Freedom' himself:

> In a graceful manner and in emphatic language, he told the radicals of Barnsley that he had sold off his horses and dogs, greatly reduced his establishment, and come weal, come woe he would henceforth devote his whole life to promote the well-being of the working classes…..
> The language of O'Connor, to ears accustomed to little else than the Barnsley dialect spoken by pale-faced weavers and swart cobblers, sounded like rich music.[25]

The most remarkable examples of the traditional leaders' linguistic accomplishments are to be found in the courtroom dramas they fought when put on trial by the authorities for allegedly seditious or threatening language. The sense of awe and devotion supporters felt towards their 'gentlemanly' leaders is neatly captured in the observations of one eye-witness, the Stalybridge activist William Aitken. He noted, from a seat in the public gallery, how during his trial in August 1839 at Chester, Dr

McDouall 'spoke with the dignity of a man, and the language of a scholar and a gentleman'.[26] McDouall, not surprisingly, lost his case but both O'Brien at Newcastle in February 1840 and O'Connor at Lancaster in March 1843 respectively managed either an acquittal or escaped sentence. Again, Chartists en masse marvelled at the way in which their leaders used these occasions to display their self-confidence, speak extempore, analyse the evidence, as Gammage recorded, 'in a truly lawyer-like manner,'[27] and turn the tables on their embarrassed accusers on their own linguistic territory.[28]

As Dorothy Thompson has observed, Feargus O'Connor was always the gentleman demagogue, making no attempt to present himself as 'ordinary'.[29] Indeed, he was very much a romantic in an age steeped in popular romanticism.[30] His sincerity was proved by the sacrifice of time and money in the people's cause. For O'Connor, flamboyant even foppish clothes were the order of the day. Just as his adoption of fustian dress outside York Castle on his release in August 1841 sent out an immediate message to the rank and file, so in the early years did his dashing appearance confirm his gentlemanly standing as 'natural' at the head of the movement. The same sartorial kudos - picturesque or unconventional - underlined the romanticism of other leaders in this group and, thus, their right to lead. The redoubtable Dr John Taylor wore striped coloured, open-neck shirts which made him look like 'a cross between Byron's Corsair and a gypsy king';[31] O'Brien's garb registered a distinct scholarly appearance;[32] McDouall wore black clothes and a long cape which gave him, in Adams' words, 'the appearance of a hero of melodrama';[33] and Stephens' self-dramatizations transfixed audiences because of 'the spectacular effect produced by the black robe of a minister of the gospel'.[34] Clearly for these men of letters trying to gather up support, particularly in the early years, personal appearance was very important in the presentation of self to themselves, to their audiences and to one another;[35] it was an important signifier and well-calculated to produce a decidedly favourable impression. Dress codes were therefore virtually as striking as the oratory itself.

The common denominators uniting the second group of Chartist orators were their experience of near or actual poverty, little formal schooling, an attendance to various regimens of autodidactism and involvement in radical political or trade union affairs. Typical among the early apostles from this route were Samuel and George Bartlett, shoemaker brothers in Bath, William Carrier, a hatter in Trowbridge, R.J. Richardson, a master-carpenter in Salford, Ben Rushton, a weaver in Halifax, T.M. Wheeler, a baker in London, and Richard Marsden, a Preston weaver. In their radical debating societies, mutual improvement groups and in the public agitation on behalf of the unstamped press, they learnt how to structure arguments, marshall facts and figures, state a case, argue cogently and confidently, and answer critics. Others learnt the art of public speaking from an additional or passing involvement in school-teaching and organised religion, particularly Methodism. These included John McCrae at Dundee, William Thornton in Halifax, and no less than three in Manchester - James Scholefield (a Swedenborgian), William V. Jackson, and James Cartledge. All of them became very articulate speakers and enjoyed at least a regional political standing for their powers of oratory. Wheeler, for example, was known for the 'clarity and rigour of his style'.[36] Marsden came to display 'a heart-stirring eloquence'.[37] William Carrier possessed 'a fiery rhetoric' and cultivated a romantic image when he appeared at West Country meetings mounted on 'a white charger'.[38] Not surprisingly, Carrier's impact as a local demagogue was such that he was lambasted in a poem composed by one of his leading opponents.[39] In Thornton's case, so impressed was O'Connor with his 'fine speech' at the Whit Monday gathering on Peep Green in 1839 that, notwithstanding the Irish leader's tendency to hyperbolize, he put his hand on the lay preacher's shoulder and said 'Well done, Thornton, when we get the People's Charter I will see that you are made the Archbishop of York'.[40]

The most outstanding of all however in this group were men like the Hull printworker, Henry Vincent, the sailor turned London shop-boy, Julian Harney, and the lame South Shields tailor, Robert Lowery. Henry Vincent quickly gained national popularity. According to Gammage, Vincent's fluency, facility, passion, versatility, and powers of mimicry earned him the title 'the young Demosthenes of English Democracy'.[41] Among the West Country and South Wales Chartists he was a particular favourite, not least with the women in their ranks who, it was reported, took to him because of his good looks and consistent advocacy of their rights.[42]

Vincent was a humourist, too, with a funny little chuckle when he said something intended to cause laughter. The kind of banter he was perennially capable of making was revealed by one eye witness thus:

> Once when people were still trying to squeeze in after the oration had begun, and there were angry cries of 'Shut the door!' from the audience already seated, he held up in his hand and said 'Never mind the door. Keep the door open and the mouth shut'.[43]

Despite a noticeable tendency to be hesitant in his early speeches, Harney, by speaking regularly, emerged as a fluent and effective first rank speaker, who could range from 'such subjects as emigration and Corn Law repeal to proletarian internationalism, and find a ready response'.[44] Like 'gentlemanly' radicals, too, he had a goodly spice of vanity, enough to cultivate a romantic appearance on the platform: he grew his curly brown hair to his shoulders in the fashion of the time, wore a tricolour sash and red cap of liberty; self-consciously, in the early confrontation with the authorities he also liked to be considered the 'Marat of the English Revolution'.[45]

Robert Lowery's autodidactic zeal for acquiring the arts of verbal communication demanded a certain kind of evangelism: it earned him a reputation as a second-rank speaker whose oratory, delivered without notes, was acclaimed to be slow, deliberate, clear and reasoned.[46] Yet in Lowery's fascination with oratory we gain a rare insight into what one working man felt about dialect, the lingua franca of ordinary people. As Dorothy Thompson has reminded us, although Lowery was an outstanding speaker in the early years of the movement, he later became a full-time lecturer for the middle class temperance movement and wrote his autobiography in the first instance for members of that constituency.[47] Thus he was keen to stress his respectability in terms of, among other things, the conscious shedding of his Geordie accent as an encumbrance, and the need to acquire a 'correct' pronunciation as part of his personal, professional development. Dick Leith and other linguistic scholars have shown how, in the Victorian period, 'h' dropping, glottal stops and ellipses were all aspects of dialect, vernacular, or demotic speech.[48] At best, dialect came to be viewed as comic; at worst it was stigmatised as hideous and vulgar, the antithesis of the language those with superior breeding or socio-economic success spoke.[49] Lowery's eschewing of dialect might be viewed in two different ways. In practical terms, going around the country as he did in the summer of 1839 as a Chartist missionary for the Convention, he needed to be understood in order to help move Chartism forward as quickly as possible. In this case a Geordie accent might well have been a hindrance outside his native North East. On the other hand, if he was motivated more by individual ambition than most men of his background, and bearing in mind that language pronunciation in society became slowly allied to power, learning and authority, then it is clear that Lowery, in pursuit of respectability, lived with the corrosive illusion that his own tongue was somehow 'ignorant' or 'wrong'.[50] Other Chartist orators in this group did not appear to have suffered the same kind of tension over what language to use in speech-making. R.J. Richardson retained his 'rude provincialism of speech'[51] when he was extending the Chartist movement around Salford, and Ben Rushton in Ovenden, near Halifax, kept his broad Yorkshire dialect and 'never failed to make an impression upon an audience'.[52]

Slightly more difficult to categorise, or define, is the third group. These were young men from humble backgrounds in their teens or early twenties. They might well have honed their speaking skills in radical clubs in the late 1830s, but, more often than not, were more prominent because they were naturally gifted orators, the products of a rich working class oral culture. Around the fire-side, in the social mixing of the workshop, public house, street-corner, fair or market place, they expressed and developed verbal fluency and facility, cracked jokes and sallied forth, told stories, knew when to be sarcastic, change facial expression and gesticulate just as the mood or tone of their discourse dictated. Moreover, if all of them matured into natural spell-binders and raconteurs, some were also endowed with the artistic powers of singing and reciting their own poems on the platform. Thus, they came into Chartism as versatile performers: they knew how to sway audiences not only by their impassioned oratory, but also by utilizing theatrical devices in the form of songs, recitations or dramatic acts. One distinct cluster of these 'naturals' came from poor, Irish Catholic parentage. Street-wise and oratorically skilled before they left their impoverished homeland, their geographical mobility, dictated by the search for work in England, encouraged still further socialization with new groups of influential workers; it also helped instil independence and radical political awareness. George White was certainly one of the best known of the Irish born Chartist 'voices'.[53] He was a rousing speaker who established himself as a fearless, specialist Anti-Corn Law League-baiter. John West, who settled and worked as a handloom silk-weaver in Macclesfield, was said to electrify Chartist meetings: he was a real 'Leviathan of the Platform,'[54] a speaker who was in fact offered a post as a professional lecturer with middle class organizations.[55] Christopher Doyle, a power-loom weaver, was another who emigrated: an avowed republican, he became noted for his 'fine singing voice' on Chartist platforms.[56] Perhaps the most outstanding of all in this Irish coterie were David Ross and Thomas Clark. Ross settled in Manchester where, untypically of his peers, he actually earned a living as 'a teacher of rhetoric and elocution' – in the pay initially of the Anti-Corn Law League.[57] However, following a debate over the merits of the Corn Laws with the influential Chartist, James Leach, in 1840, he converted to Chartism, becoming an outstanding speaker and well known worker-poet.[58] Thomas Clark of Stockport, who became one of O'Connor's most important lieutenants, was described by him as 'one of the most eloquent men in this or any other country'.[59] 'Paddy Clark,' as he was affectionately known, was well-travelled in the Chartist cause and earned a reputation amongst audiences for reasoned arguments, with humour and occasional sarcasm.[60]

Irish-born Chartists, of course, did not monopolise the ranks of the naturally gifted communicators. Amongst indigenous speakers of a similar standing were the young Liverpool shoe-maker William Jones, who Gammage rated as 'the best of the new orators' of the 1840s;[61] W.H. Chadwick, the Mancunian, who first made his debut in public life as a sixteen year old lecturer on temperance; and John Snowden, the highly articulate Halifax woolcomber, who could neither read nor write, yet by eighteen was a leader of the West Riding Chartists.[62] Two others worth noting for their innate skills and accomplishments were J.B. Leno, the printer-Chartist in Uxbridge, and Samuel Kydd, from Arbroath, who became a bookseller in South Shields following a brief spell as a shoemaker in Glasgow. From an early age Leno was 'conscious of his superior speaking and argumentative powers,' ability to sing, act and give impromptu recitals in taverns or theatres.[63] Kydd's lectures on general economic subjects were very well received in Scotland and the north of England, because they were so carefully prepared, reasoned, vigorous and fluent, and delivered with a thick Scottish accent. Such skills also provide an important clue as to why Kydd became a successful barrister in later life.[64]

It is important to recognise that these three types of orators were not in any way mutually exclusive. Individuals did straddle categories, learnt from one another and worked together at times to get their messages across. In the missionary work, for example, surrounding the activities of the Convention in 1839, Robert Lowery shared the platform with gentlemen radicals such as O'Connor and Stephens and fellow autodidacts like Harney. From them, too, it is clear that he learned a great deal about how to use ambivalent language, rhetorical questions, and the dramatic pause.[65] But he was equally concerned to point out that for all their combined efforts no overall lecturing strategy was employed.[66] As a result, there was little co-ordination: some places or regions were overworked; others were marginalised or left entirely unattended.[67]

The role of the orator in the Chartist movement took on a new and added importance with the formation of the National Charter Association, in the summer of 1840. Under this organizational structure, lecture circuits were set up on a more professional and systematic basis to promote Chartist propaganda on the platform. The national leaders were gradually supplemented by paid or unpaid lecturers, who built up reputations as regional, district, or local speakers. A nationally integrated political culture was gradually established. The local associations, or branches of, the National Charter Association were also extremely important in creating a 'movement culture,' in which both home-grown talent and the naturally gifted orators were encouraged to take up public speaking. Weekly meetings, lectures, communal newspaper readings, and public dinners all provided 'a more systematic basis for men and women to become articulate or consolidate their platform skills as speakers'.[68] What was also highly significant at this time, as James Epstein has stressed, was the fact that the

National Charter Association had been founded in a period in which the great majority of Chartism's 'gentlemanly' radical leaders were either in prison or broken in health.[69] This situation threw a considerable burden on the local rank and file activists and the 'movement culture,' which was taking shape or regrouping after the confrontational politics of 1839. As a result, a sizeable number of either entirely new speakers emerged, or those who were only of minor importance in 1839 now rose to prominence.[70] To explore the oratory of the new personnel of the 1840s is to ensure that some more of the lesser-documented figures in Chartism are accorded their proper place in the movement's history.

In order to equip missionaries for their demanding oratorical work, every encouragement was given to 'improve' the capacity for self-expression and mastery of speech. In the debating societies and discussion clubs of the N.C.A. branches, aspiring lecturers, as well as the more practised, learnt how to develop their powers of analysis on their feet, to arrange in consecutive order all their arguments, and, in a general return to the strategy of persuasion rather than menace, to stress the importance now of facts, figures, and dates.[71] Before delivering their first speech, many had gained in self-confidence and verbal fluency through learning by stages: it involved giving a toast or a vote of thanks; reading aloud a resolution or notice of future events; singing at the end of an experienced speaker's peroration; and taking the chair for the proceedings. The need to prepare and practice skill remained vital as Robert Crowe, the London Chartist and a former temperance lecturer, remarked when he joined in the mid 1840s:

> I was not slow to discover my deficiency as a speaker. I realised there was something needed, so I adopted the following novel expedient: I selected a retired, secluded spot (Soho Square) and every night, after 11pm, and continuing for about three months, I made the railings and trees my imaginary audience, and soon learned to shudder at the echo of my voice.... I acquired a name throughout London as a youthful orator.[72]

To appreciate the nature of how an oratorical apprenticeship like this was undertaken, is to begin to understand why speakers were not overawed when they addressed meetings of a different type or function. Whether it was standing in front of the large set-piece, open-air meeting, or contesting an election, or giving a lecture in a hall, engaging in a debate with rivals, preaching a sermon or delivering a funeral oration, Chartist speakers were remarkably versatile and resourceful; indeed, it was not uncommon for some of them to give a lecture, preach, and take part in a debate all on the same day!

The Chartist press played its part too. The *Northern Star*, for example, provided assistance across an impressively broad front. It ran editorials praising the role of orators, published schedules of their forthcoming tours, complimented up-and-coming speakers on their eloquence, advertised manuals on English Grammar and public speaking written specifically by radicals,[73] encouraged readers to learn by studying reprints of Robert Emmet's memorable speech when on trial for High Treason in 1803,[74] eulogised orators in poetic form[75], and, in prose reports, singled out experienced American public lecturers for their superior oratory and polished stage-craft.[76] One of the latter, for example, was the American traveller, George Catlin, who toured England in 1843. The radical press praised his reputation as a fearless advocate of the rights of Red Indians and marvelled at the way in which he used visual aids and actors in Indian dress on the platform to persuade English audiences out of their racial prejudices.[77]

Out of this 'movement culture' emerged a new generation of Chartist orators in the early 1840s. Overwhelmingly male, they had strong connections, engaging personalities, flair, dedication, and an enormous capacity for hard work. Prison experiences underlined their sincerity and credibility on the platform. Among the group were self-publicists like the shoe-maker Thomas Cooper of Leicester. 'Possessed of a dashing style of oratory,' Cooper became a national celebrity.[78] Alongside John West and Thomas Clark, the two most influential men to emerge at a national level with the gift of oratory were the Leicester handloom weaver, Jonathan Bairstow, and the Manchester factory operative, James Leach. Noted for his 'Herculean lungs,'[79] Bairstow was certainly an orator for all occasions. Whether preaching indoors or lecturing outside, his declamatory style drew on 'figures of speech which set some of his audience gaping with wonder as to what could be his meaning'.[80]

'In James Leach,' wrote O'Connor in the *Northern Star*, 'we discover the philosopher, the philanthropist and the debater, full of that statistical knowledge so highly essential to the advocacy of our cause, with a coolness of manner, a simplicity of eloquence, and grace of delivery which is peculiarly his own'.[81] Among others who had considerable impact on lecturing tours almost immediately were John Campbell, William Dean Taylor, John Mason and Edward Preston Mead. Campbell rapidly rose through the ranks because he combined his power of the pen as General Secretary of the N.C.A. with a reputation for 'forceful oratory' based on cold logic.[82] Taylor enjoyed popularity because of his wordy and ostentatious style; Mason, a Birmingham shoemaker, was known to be a very rousing and rapid speaker; and E.P. Mead, the old sailor, was famed for his 'dry, droll but cutting sarcasm' conveyed 'with irresistible force.'[83] By 1843, their ranks had been further strengthened through the accession of such up and coming crowd-pullers as Samuel Kydd, the East End tailor Philip McGrath, and the Northampton coach-maker, Robert Gammage.[84] All these speakers became, as David Jones and Philip Howell have noted, famous for their different styles, specialized knowledge and pet interests; they also enjoyed close relationships with Chartist audiences in different parts of the country when they resided in a centre which served as a base for proselytizing a county or region.[85]

The abiding impression bequeathed by contemporary observers is that Chartist oratory was an exclusively male domain. Both Dorothy Thompson and Jutta Schwarzkopf in their researches on the role of women in Chartism have found this to be entirely without foundation. Female help in sustaining the movement oratorically was not substantial, but nor was it slight. Whilst Schwarzkopf has identified two women orators (a Mrs Theobald and Helen M'Donald, an eighteen year old from Perth), Thompson has offered interesting profiles of a further eight.[86] Three of these, who were single, hailed from London (Susanna Inge, Mary Ann Walker and Emma Miles); two came from Leeds (Mrs Anna Pepper and Miss Mary Grasby); two from within one family at Nottingham (Mrs Caroline Blatherwick and Miss Eliza Blatherwick); and one married woman from Manchester (Mrs Fields). At least two more married women have been identified here as active speakers in the early 1840s: Mrs Parkinson of

Oldham delivered Sunday lectures at a number of branches of the
N.C.A. at Manchester; and Mrs Martin, a native of Sunderland,
addressed audiences both in her home town and in neighbouring
Newcastle.[87] In limiting themselves to speaking within their home
towns and neighbourhood, and on topics concerning political rights
for the working people as a whole, rather than specifically female
issues, both Mrs Parkinson and Mrs Martin were reiterating
precisely the political and social sentiments enunciated by other
members of this small but courageous band of women orators.[88]

In recommending the use of local lecturers the N.C.A. gave an
important boost to indigenous talent communicating in localised
forms of speech or dialect. For Thomas Cooper in Gainsborough,
however, the pursuit of knowledge and self-improvement with an
almost desperate intensity meant getting rid of his dialect and
conversing in the 'most refined English'. This move took 'some
courage' because in his neighbourhood it 'roused positive anger
and scorn in some, amazement in others'.[89] Elsewhere, Chartist
orators were not quite so desperate as Cooper was to be counted
'among the scholars'. For many in Manchester and Halifax, for
example, dialect carried important and positive connotations, such
as emphasizing credibility, honesty, native shrewdness, suspicion
of strangers, a no-nonsense approach, an ability to deflate
pretension, and a sense of class pride in how one spoke. This was
certainly the case in the life and struggles of the Yorkshire Chartist,
John Snowden. According to one report he acquired in lecturing
around Halifax:

> a rugged eloquence of no copyist type, and a skill of
> speech welcomed by ears of toilers, because it spoke
> through sympathy of touch with horny hand at workshop
> and loom, a sympathy cemented, too, by fellowship in
> poverty.[90]

In addition, dialect speakers would in certain situations have
advantages over outsiders who were distinguished by their standard
or different speech. This would almost certainly have applied in the
debate between local Chartist R.J. Richardson and James Acland of
the Anti-Corn Law League held in Salford. One observer, Lloyd
Jones, an Owenite missionary, found R.J. Richardson 'almost

uncouth by his rude provincialism of speech and awkwardness of manner'. But to an audience drawn from the Salford industrial area, his native accent obviously paid off since he won the debate with acclaim.[91] In Scotland, too, Samuel Kydd spoke with 'a broad Scotch accent'; it was only when he stepped outside his native country on tour that his pronunciation was considered vulgar and comical by his detractors.[92]

Whether in dialect speech or not, many orators had to contend with considerably practical difficulties, such as the sheer size of the audience, extraneous noises, and routine throat weaknesses affecting their voice timbre and pitch. Not surprisingly the new generation became adept at handling non-verbal forms of communication as part of the subtleties of platform rhetoric. Just as the symbolic language of fustian clothes (clothing peculiar to working men) was adopted and worn by Feargus O'Connor after his release from York prison in August 1841 to signal his re-assertion of 'gentleman' leadership of the Chartist movement, so local leaders, too, recognised 'the power of the working class uniform'.[93] John Campbell may have reinforced his language of plain speaking by emphasizing that he was still 'one of yourselves, a hard working man, a fustian jacket'.[94] James Scholefield, too, although a clergyman, represented himself to the Manchester Chartists as 'a working man like themselves and at times wore fustian'.[95]

Body language, tone and gesture were all aspects of delivery with which these Chartist orators could shape their performances to perfection. William Aitken recalled how Chartist audiences in Ashton and Stalybridge were visibly moved by the demeanor of local orator George Johnson who was:

> Terribly in earnest when he spoke publicly, his face used to get swollen red – the veins in his forehead dilate – his voice raised to that peculiar high pitch common to the Primitive Methodists formerly, he was a sight once seen not easily forgotten.[96]

Slightly less dramatic but no less effective was the skilful use of gesture, hand and arm movements. Very large crowds might well find these platform features adequate compensation for unclear and continuous articulation on the part of the speaker, and all kinds of interruptions. In Wales, there was an even greater reliance on non-verbal language, as Gammage discovered when he addressed Welsh-speaking audiences: they came to understand him precisely because of his changes of emphasis, variations in tone and many gestures.[97]

Consummate performers like Feargus O'Connor and Henry Vincent combined a use of non-verbal language with great, if not incomparable, powers of mimicry. Audiences, it is made clear from reports in the *Northern Star*, thrilled to the platform theatricals performed by both as they imitated 'the foible and fashions of the day'.[98] While O'Connor was adept particularly at satirising 'Harry Brougham' and clergymen who were antagonistic to Chartism,[99] Vincent's star turn was to mimic 'the grave stammerings of the Marquis of Londonderry'.[100] Mimicry was delivered, of course, in conjunction with stirring statements denouncing the conduct of the aristocracy and middle classes 'who lived upon the blood and marrow of the labouring classes'.[101]

From time to time orators did face considerable difficulties. Among them were personality clashes, the strategic demands of audiences with varying levels of political awareness or linguistic differences, and confrontations with the authorities, over which they risked arrest and imprisonment. It is interesting to discover from private letters how Chartist orators perceived one another when they were, politically, at loggerheads. Gammage, for example, judged Robert Kemp Philp, the Bath printer and another of the speakers who rose to prominence after 1839, to be a mild man, whose speeches were almost free from declamation, eloquent, instructive and delivered with little force.[102] Writing to Thomas Cooper in July 1842, three months after Philp had defected to the Complete Suffrage Union, Bairstow offered a completely different view of both the man and his oratory. Bairstow declared that Philp:

> was playing a double game. That soft, milky, affable, easy, feminine deportment is all damnable affectation..... He really was a reckless drunken, devil-may-care sort of fellow.[103]

Linguistic difference in Wales was a perennial problem. Morgan Williams, the Merthyr Chartist leader, was not the first of his kinsmen to complain when he addressed delegates assembled for the 1842 N.C.A. Convention thus:

> The great and only want, throughout the district which I represent, is that of lecturers who understood two languages: it was not so material that they should be eloquent men, as they should be able to lay down the principles in language all could understand.[104]

Merthyr had to depend on such locals as Henry Thomas and David Rees; no Chartist orator ever served Wales bilingually; like Gammage they all had to rely on getting their message across by symbolic means alone. In the adjacent West of England region, strategic problems of a more representative nature surfaced, when delegates gathered at Bath in October 1841 to assess the progress of itinerant orators since 1840. Predictably, delegates from the market towns of Mere and Salisbury clamoured for more speeches by John Cluer, the Glasgow weaver, and Henry Vincent. George Bartlett, however, 'with characteristic insight,' called for more propaganda in the villages, and thought 'men of more humble abilities' were better suited than Vincent 'to address the ignorant agricultural labourers'.[105] Clearly, Bartlett was aware of Vincent's oratorical strengths and weaknesses: his passion, sound, and fury was more readily appreciated in 'advanced' market towns; yet in the purely agricultural areas of the West Country what was needed was more reasoning to cultivate the labourers' understanding. Only six months later W.P. Roberts of Bath, now released from prison, requested that lecturing in the region be placed on a more systematic basis. He noted that in some places orators were needed 'who would lay down the first broad principles' whilst in others 'men of more philosophic cast' were appropriate'.[106]

Chartist rhetoric over the use of force calmed considerably after 1839. The dominant strategy adopted by itinerant orators of the N.C.A. was a disciplined, gradualist, robust constitutionalism. Nevertheless, ambivalent or ironic language on the platform brought clashes with zealous authorities, who considered them seditious at a time of economic and political crises, as in the Plug

Plot Strikes of August and September 1842. Hitherto, Chartist orators had become adept at incorporating certain religious modes and forms of rhetoric into their speeches as a powerful source of legitimation for action.[107] The particular theme of redistributive social justice grounded in Biblical language was a favourite one. In the heated political atmosphere of the Plug Plots the religious rhetoric used by orators like William Jones and John West was ambiguous, calculated to insult the authorities, but nevertheless still within the law. However, the authorities went on the offensive and took figurative or metaphorical language quite literally. Thus when William Jones spoke metaphorically at the Pastures in Leicester of 'the boiling of the unboiled blue vampires' and John West, again in Leicester, quoted Isaiah in order to 'break open the locks of the prison doors, and let our incarcerated brethren free,' the authorities prosecuted and successfully incarcerated them.[108] A similar fate befell John Mason, Jonathan Bairstow, George White and Thomas Cooper in 1842.

In the mid and late 1840s, there was no shortage of fresh autodidactic orators. Among the new recruits to figure prominently by 1847 were the ex-Socialist George J. Holyoake, Benjamin Wilson of Halifax and three London workers - Edmund Stallwood, W.J. Vernon, and William Cuffay, a black by birth, and a tailor by trade. The rather depleted ranks of the 'gentleman' radicals also received two very important additions: the one was Ernest Jones, who became an effective orator and leader of national standing; the other was Joseph Cowen Jr from Tyneside. Both Jones and Cowen added fresh zeal but in different ways.

Jones was very much in the tradition of the romantic 'gentleman' leader of popular movements. Family wealth, a classical education and legal training had not only increased his self-assuredness, but also honed the linguistic powers necessary for 'correct' pronunciation in his speech. In the opinion of one Preston Chartist, when Jones spoke to the 30,000 assembled on Blackstone Edge in August 1846, his noble and striking appearance was underlined by a stentorian voice and 'various figures and graces of oratory'.[109] Although a skilful orator, he lacked the charisma of O'Connor and never achieved the status of the gentleman demagogue.[110] Nevertheless, like Thomas Clark, Samuel Kydd, and Philip McGrath, Jones did much both on behalf of proselytising

O'Connor's Land Plan and making a stir on the platform by standing as a Chartist in the 1847 General Election. In Halifax, Jones's oratorical flourishes no doubt helped him receive a respectable 279 votes but he was still bottom of the poll; some time after the election he was presented with a gold watch and chain by the grateful Halifax Chartists.[111]

Cowen, like Jones, was wealthy, educated, oratorically gifted, and no less genuine a Chartist convert. Yet here the similarities virtually finish. Cowen was a man of simple tastes. He dressed like 'a workman, with a black comforter around his neck'; he 'talked the Tyneside tongue'[112] and easily identified with working class causes in Newcastle. The symbolic language of fustian was not his only strength. Cowen also effectively personified the power of dialect in the later Tyneside Chartist movement for when 'he denounced the enemies of liberty from the platform,' he obtained an added force to those listening from his 'deep and mystical burr'.[113] By nature of his political enthusiasm and unique oratorical powers Cowen rekindled from 1847 an aggressive Chartist-Republicanism on the Tyne and was known as the 'Tribune of the North'.[114]

One final issue needs to be addressed: how effective was Chartist oratory? The complex and symbiotic relationship of expectation, performance and response between speakers and audiences, both verbally and symbolically, has been explored by a number of historians.[115] Whether leading or swaying an audience, or expressing what it desired to hear, orators like O'Connor, by virtue of the use of the first person and of rhetorical questions, appeared 'to touch a chord which vibrated from one end of the kingdom to the other'.[116] District lecturers were no less adept at carrying audiences off their feet. Whatever their style and regardless of subject matter, it is abundantly clear from newspaper sources, autobiographies and private papers, that men like McDouall, Ross, Kydd and Jones spoke the language of class with great passion, anger and feeling. They were able to articulate the shared concerns of their audiences about political exclusion, capitalist exploitation in the work place, poverty, and the erosion of civil liberties.

The test of successful oration is also revealed in the respect and authority speakers generated. Just as O'Connor and McDouall were blessed with cognomens, so, too, did others become platform celebrities and heroes in the 1840s. Robert Wilkinson, the veteran Halifax Chartist, was popularly known as 'Radical Bob'; Ruffy Ridley of Chelsea as 'Rough and Ready' Ridley; Thomas Dickinson, as 'the Manchester packer'; E.P. Mead as 'the old Commodore'; William Beesley as the 'lion of North Lancashire'; and James Scholefield was dubbed 'the Chaplain of the Manchester Chartists'.[117]

Another indicator of the effectiveness of Chartist oratory is to be found in the reactions of the authorities themselves. In Gloucestershire, they were certainly fearful of the impact which Henry Vincent might have on his release from prison in January 1841. Vincent recalled how the authorities tried to play on popular superstition in order to warn them off attending his scheduled meetings:

> The Tory *Gloucestershire Chronicle* had called him an ugly, bloodthirsty, villain with high cheek-bones and a terrible squint in the eyes, and that women with large bellies would bring forth monsters if they were unfortunate enough to catch a glimpse of him.[118]

By the end of April 1841, Vincent was again remarking that 'some of the villagers think that the Chartists wish to run away with their grandmothers out of their graves..... The people expected to find me at least eighteen feet high'.[119] The power of the orators was still evident here in April 1848 when a local J.P. complained that 'Chartists have during the last week been busy inveighing against the Government and poisoning the labourers' minds'.[120]

Perhaps the most telling evidence of the power of orators is revealed in the statistical growth in N.C.A. membership. At the end of December 1841, there were 282 localities and 13,000 members; by April 1842, 50,000 members and 401 localities were claimed; and in the full year of 1847 about 600 branches of the Land Company had been formed.[121] As Stephen Roberts has pointed out, 'a movement of tens of thousands of people could not have been held together by only the printed word'.[122] Orators and oratory remained at the centre of the N.C.A. agitation throughout the 1840s and, like the *Northern Star,* were crucial to the unity and vitality of the movement.

The role of Chartist oratory still awaits full historical investigation. A more detailed analysis of the 1850s would surely show that the lingering coherence of the movement in decline still relied heavily on the power of the spoken word. Ernest Jones certainly wished to revive in 1851 the efficacy of the public meeting as one of 'the most potent agents of democratic power and change'.[123] After the formal end of the movement Chartist orators were, it is clear, much in demand. Bronterre O'Brien and J.B. Leno, for example, were firm favourites at the Cogers and other debating halls in London in the early 1860s.[124] Thomas Cooper, Henry Vincent and Robert Lowery became successful professional lecturers.[125] W.H. Chadwick and C.L. Robinson, a young Bradford Chartist in the 1850s, carried on in the best Chartist traditions of public speaking as they served, respectively, the platforms of the Liberal Party and the Independent Labour Party.[126] The Chartist critique, clearly, 'was by no means limited to print. It was vividly associated with the spoken word as well..... [and] the movement's orators became its heroes'.[127] Gammage was certainly correct in his judgement that with the Chartist movement, the age of the working class Cicero had arrived.

NOTES

I wish to thank the following for their help or advice: Darrell Hinchliffe, Lyn Hodgkiss, Paul Pickering, Debbie Roberts, Stephen Roberts, and Miles Taylor.

[1] Alfred Plummer, *Bronterre*, London, G. Allen & Unwin, 1971, p.107
[2] *Ibid.,* p.192.
[3] Edward Royle, *Chartism*, London, Longman, third edition, 1996, p.22
[4] John Belchem, 'Beyond *Chartist Studies*: Class, Community and Party in Early-Victorian Populist Politics,' pp.105-7 in Derek Fraser (ed.), *Cities and Communication: Essays in Honour of Asa Briggs,* London, Harvester Wheatsheaf, 1990
[5] David Jones, *Chartism and the Chartists,* London, Allen Lane, 1975, p.102
[6] Royle, *Chartism*, p.10.
[7] Dorothy Thompson, *The Chartists*, London, Temple Smith, 1984 and James Epstein, 'Feargus O'Connor and the *Northern Star,*' *International Review of Social History*, Vol.XXI, Pt.1, 1976, pp.51-97.

[8] Michael S. Edwards, *Purge this Realm: A Life of Joseph Rayner Stephens,* London, Epworth Press, 1994; James Epstein, *The Lion of Freedom: Feargus O'Connor and the Chartist Movement, 1832-1842,* London, Croom Helm, 1982. It is also clear from Epstein's work that O'Connor revelled in exploiting platform heckling in order to encourage audience participation.

[9] Gareth Stedman Jones, 'Rethinking Chartism,' pp. 90-178 in his *Languages of Class: Studies in English Working Class History 1832-1982,* Cambridge, C.U.P., 1983.

[10] Patrick Joyce, *Visions of the People: Industrial England and the Question of Class 1848-1914,* Cambridge, C.U.P., 1991; James Vernon, *Politics and the People: A Study in English Political Culture c.1815-1867,* Cambridge, C.U.P., 1993.

[11] James Epstein, Chapter 3: 'Understanding the Cap of Liberty: Symbolic Practice and Social Conflict in Early Nineteenth-Century England,' pp.70-99, in his *Radical Expression: Political Language, Ritual and Symbol in England 1790-1850,* Oxford, O.U.P., 1994; Paul Pickering, 'Class Without Words: Symbolic Communication in the Chartist Movement,' *Past and Present,* No.112, August 1986, pp.144-162 and Paul Pickering, *Chartism and the Chartists in Manchester and Salford,* London, Macmillan, 1995, Chapter 9: 'Class without Words: Rank-and-File Communication in the Chartist Movement,' pp.159-172.

[12] Martha Vicinus, 'To Live Free or Die': The Relationship between Strategy and Style in Chartist Speeches, 1838-1839,' *Style,* Vol. X, Fall, 1976, pp.481-503.

[13] John Belchem, '1848: Feargus O'Connor and the Collapse of the Mass Platform,' pp.269-310 in James Epstein and Dorothy Thompson (eds.), *The Chartist Experience: Studies in Working Class Radicalism and Culture, 1830-1860,* London, Macmillan, 1982.

[14] Philip Howell, 'Diffusing the Light of Liberty'. The Geography of Political Lecturing in the Chartist Movement,' *Journal of Historical Geography,* Vol.21, Pt.1, 1995, pp.23-38; Philip Howell, 'A Free-Trade in Politics': A Geography of Chartism's Political Culture c.1838-1848,' Ph.D. thesis, Cambridge, 1993, particularly pp.83-188. See also Humphrey Southall, 'Mobility, the Artisan Community and Popular Politics in Early Nineteenth-Century England,' pp.103-153 in Gerry Kearns and Charles W.J. Withers (eds.) *Urbanising Britain,* Cambridge, C.U.P., 1991. Both Howell and Southall, as historical geographers, have stressed the link between oratory and Chartist mobilization. They emphasize the way in which speeches and lecturers were instrumental in inspiring the formation of local Chartist associations, and their maps reveal a remarkable linkage between the two.

[15] Howell, Ph.D. thesis, Chapter 3, pp.119-187.

[16] Pickering, 'Class Without Words: Symbolic Communication in the Chartist Movement,' p.148.

[17] Thomas Cooper, *The Life of Thomas Cooper,* with an introduction by John Saville, Leicester, Leicester University Press, 1971; R.G. Gammage, *History of the Chartist Movement 1837-1854,* London, Merlin Press, 1969; Brian

Harrison and Patricia Hollis (eds.), *Robert Lowery, Radical and Chartist*, London, Europa Publications, 1979.

[18] Martin Hewitt, *The Emergence of Stability in the Industrial City: Manchester 1832-1867*, Aldershot, Scolar Press, 1996, p.257.

[19] W.E. Adams, *Memoirs of a Social Atom*, with an introduction by John Saville, New York, Augustus M. Kelley, 1968; William Aitken, *Remembrances and Struggles of a Working Man for Bread and Liberty*, in Robert G. Hall and Stephen Roberts (eds.) *William Aitken. The Writings of a Nineteenth Century Working Man*, Tameside, Libraries and Heritage, 1996; Robert Crowe, *The Reminiscences of Robert Crowe, the Octogenarian Tailor*, reptd., New York, Garland, 1986; William Farish, *The Autobiography of William Farish: The Struggles of a Hand-Loom Weaver*, reptd., London, Caliban Books, 1996; and Benjamin Wilson, *The Struggles of an Old Chartist: What he knows, and the Part he has taken in Various Movements*, reptd., in David Vincent (ed.), *Testaments of Radicalism*, London, Europa Publications, 1977.

[20] For McDouall see Raymond Challinor 'Peter Murray McDouall and 'Physical Force Chartism,' *International Socialism*, Series 2, No.12, Spring 1981, pp.53-84 and Paul Pickering and Stephen Roberts, 'Pills, Pamphlets and Politics: The Career of Peter Murray McDouall (1814-54),' *Manchester Region History Review*, Vol. XI, 1997, pp.34-43; for Roberts see Raymond Challinor, *A Radical Lawyer in Victorian England. W.P. Roberts and the Struggle for Workers' Rights*, London, I.B. Tauris, 1990; for Beaumont see W.H. Maehl, jr 'Augustus Hardin Beaumont: Anglo-American Radical (1798-1838),' *International Review of Social History*, Vol. XIV, Pt.2, 1969, pp.237-250. For Binns see Stephen Roberts, *Radical Politicians and Poets in Early Victorian Britain*, New York, Edwin Mellen Press, 1993. For Larkin see Harrison and Hollis (eds.), *Robert Lowery, Radical and Chartist*, pp.64-65; for Gaskell see Owen R. Ashton, 'Radicalism and Chartism in Gloucestershire, 1832-1847,' Ph.D. thesis, University of Birmingham, 1980, pp.33-48. See also John Belchem and James Epstein, 'The Nineteenth Century Gentleman Leader Revisited,' *Social History*, Vol. 22, Pt. 2, May 1997, pp.174-193.

[21] Dick Leith, *A Social History of English*, London, Routledge, 1983, second edition, 1997, pp.56-57.

[22] Plummer, *Bronterre*, p.31.

[23] Challinor, 'Peter Murray McDouall and Physical Force Chartism,' p.55.

[24] Adams, *Memoirs of a Social Atom*, p.211.

[25] Thompson, *The Chartists*, p.99.

[26] Aitken, *Remembrances and Struggles of a Working Man for Bread and Liberty*, p.39.

[27] R.G. Gammage, *History of the Chartist Movement 1837-1854*, with an introduction by John Saville, New York, Augustus M. Kelley, 1969, p.238. In all subsequent references, this edition is cited.

[28] James Epstein, Chapter 2: 'Narrating Liberty's Defense: T.J. Wooler and the Law,' pp.29-69 in his *Radical Expression*, particularly p.32.

[29] Thompson, *The Chartists*, p.99.

[30] Epstein, *The Lion of Freedom*, p.10.

[31] Adams, *Memoirs of a Social Atom*, p.211.

[32] Gammage, *History of the Chartist Movement*, p.76.

[33] Adams, *Memoirs of a Social Atom*, pp.211-212.

[34] Frank F. Rosenblatt, *The Chartist Movement in its Social and Economic Aspects*, New York, Columbia University, 1916, reptd., London, Cass, 1967, p.124.

[35] See Pickering, 'Class Without Words: Symbolic Communication in the Chartist Movement,' p.156 for a discussion of Clifford Geertz's notion of personality.

[36] Howell, Ph.D. thesis, p.185.

[37] *Northern Star*, 27 December 1845, Manchester Convention. It notes Marsden's 'heart-stirring eloquence, which no man in the movement can imitate'.

[38] R.B. Pugh, 'Chartism in Somerset and Wiltshire,' p.79 in Asa Briggs (ed.) *Chartist Studies*, London, Macmillan, 1959.

[39] M.J. Lansdown, *The Trowbridge Chartists 1838-1848,* Trowbridge, Historical Association West Wiltshire Branch and The Friends of Trowbridge Museum, 1996, iii-iv. The poem is as follows:

Then noble Carrier silence broke –
But scratch'd his whiskers ere he spoke –
  (And well their fiery hue became
That spacious mouth, those eyes to flame) –
Then forth that luckless army went,
Like ghosts to Pluto's region sent;
The blasts on which their banners flew
Displayed their tattered raiment, too;
But neither wind nor driving rain
Could those unhappy dupes restrain…
    W.H. Tucker

[40] Thompson, *The Chartists*, p.183.

[41] Gammage, *History of the Chartist Movement 1837-1854*, p.11.

[42] *Ibid.*, p.12

[43] H.J. Jennings, *Chestnuts and Small Beer*, London, Chapman & Hall, 1920, pp.38-39. It is interesting to note that Vincent in a letter dated November 1878, a month before his death, prophesying the triumph of Liberalism and liberty, signed himself, 'Henry Vincent, Chartist Orator'. A copy of this letter is in the Dorothy Thompson Chartist Collection at Staffordshire University Library, Stoke on Trent.

[44] A.R. Schoyen, *The Chartist Challenge. A Portrait of George Julian Harney,* London, Heinemann, 1958, p.103.

[45] Gammage, *History of the Chartist Movement 1837-1854*, p.30.

[46] *Ibid.*, p.30.

[47] Thompson, *The Chartists*, p.190.

[48] Leith, *A Social History of English*, p.44 and James Milroy and Lesley Milroy, *Authority in Language: Investigating Language, Prescription and Standardization*, London, Routledge, p.20.

[49] Patrick Joyce 'The People's English: Language and Class in England c.1840-1920' p.157 in P. Burke and R. Porter (eds.), *Language, Self and Society. A Social History of Language*, Cambridge, Polity Press, 1991.

[50] *Ibid.*, p.158.

[51] Dorothy Thompson, 'Chartism as a Historical Subject,' *Bulletin of the Society for the Study of Labour History,* No.20, 1970, Conference Report, pp.10-12, particularly p.11.

[52] Wilson, *The Struggles of an Old Chartist*, p.22.

[53] Roberts, *Radical Politicians and Poets in Early Victorian Britain*, Chapter 1: George White; Thompson, *The Chartists*, pp. 228-229.

[54] *The Macclesfield Courier and Herald*, 22 January 1887, Obituary of John West, copy in Dorothy Thompson Chartist Collection.

[55] Thompson, *The Chartists*, p.227.

[56] Pickering, *Chartism and the Chartists in Manchester and Salford*, pp.194-195.

[57] *Ibid.*, p.204

[58] *Ibid.*, p.204; Y. Kovalev (ed.) *An Anthology of Chartist Literature*, Moscow, 1956, pp.113-115.

[59] Howell, Ph.D. thesis, p.181.

[60] Roberts, *Radical Politicians and Poets in Early Victorian Britain*,' Chapter 5: Thomas Clark, particularly pp.90-91; Howell Ph.D. thesis, p.181.

[61] Gammage, *History of the Chartist Movement 1837-1854*, p.211.

[62] Thompson, *The Chartists*, p.246.

[63] John Bedford Leno, *The Aftermath*, reptd., New York, Garland, 1986, pp.12-15 and p.53.

[64] Roberts, *Radical Politicians and Poets in Early Victorian Britain*, Chapter 6: Samuel Kydd.

[65] Harrison and Hollis (eds.), *Robert Lowery, Radical and Chartist*, p.16.

[66] *Ibid.*, p.249.

[67] Gammage, *History of the Chartist Movement 1837-1854*, p.107; K. Judge, 'Early Chartist Organization and the Convention of 1839,' *International Review of Social History*, XX, Pt.3, 1975, pp.370-397, see generally.

[68] Epstein, *The Lion of Freedom*, p.236.

[69] J. Epstein, 'Some Reflections on National Chartist Leadership, Strategy and Organization,' *The Consortium of Revolutionary Europe 1750-1850 Proceedings*, University of Georgia, Athens, Georgia, 1989, Vol.11, pp.25-37, particularly p.31. Beaumont died in December 1838; Dr Taylor, ill from 1840, died in December 1842.

[70] Gammage, *History of the Chartist Movement 1837-1854*, p.210.

[71] Robert Gammage, *Reminiscences of a Chartist*, with Introduction pp.7-17, and editorial annotation by W.H. Maehl, reptd., Manchester, Society for the Study of Labour History, 1983, p.15; and Adams, *Memoirs of a Social Atom*, pp.116-117.

[72] Crowe, *The Reminiscences of Robert Crowe, the Octogenarian Tailor,* p.5.

[73] These included: George Mudie, *The Grammar of the English Language Truly Made Easy and Amusing by the Invention of Three Hundred Moveable Parts of Speech,* London, 1841; William Hill, *Fifteen Lessons on the Analogy and Syntax of the English Language, for the Use of Adult Persons who have neglected the Study of Grammar,* London, 1841; and George J. Holyoake, *Rudiments of Public Speaking and Debate,* London, 1849.

[74] The *Northern Star,* almost weekly in 1840 and 1841, carried advertisements for Emmet's speech, which was published in a penny edition. The full title of the speech was, 'The Speech of Robert Emmet who so nobly defended the cause of universal freedom'.

[75] See the poem by F. Goodfellow in the *Northern Star,* 4 February 1843, set out in the Appendix.

[76] For the role and importance of the public lecturer in the U.S.A. see Donald M. Scott, 'The Popular Lecturer and Creation of a Public in mid-Nineteenth Century America,' *Journal of American History,* Vol. 66, No.4, March 1980, pp.791-809.

[77] *Northern Star,* 28 January 1843, Catlin's Lectures.

[78] Gammage, *History of the Chartist Movement 1837-1854,* p.202; and Stephen Roberts 'Thomas Cooper in Leicester, 1840-1843,' *Transactions of the Leicestershire Archaeological and Historical Society, (T.L.A.H.S.),* Vol. 61, 1987, pp. 62-76; and Roberts' 'The Later Radical Career of Thomas Cooper, c.1845-55,' *T.L.A.H.S.* Vol.64, 1990, pp.62-72.

[79] *Northern Star,* 11 June 1842, Lecture in Peterborough by Thomas Bairstow.

[80] Gammage, *History of the Chartist Movement 1837-1854,* p.210.

[81] *Northern Star,* 2 April 1842, Feargus O'Connor on James Leach.

[82] Gammage, *History of the Chartist Movement 1837-1854,* p.211, and *Northern Star,* 23 July 1842, Hull, Lecture by John Campbell.

[83] For Taylor, Mason and Mead, see Gammage, *History of the Chartist Movement 1837-1854,* p.211 and p.213, and *Northern Star,* 2 July 1842, Ilkeston, Lecture by Mead.

[84] See, for example, *Northern Star,* 12, August 1843, Newcastle, Lecture by Samuel Kydd; *Northern Star,* 3 June 1843, Manchester, Lectures by R. Gammage; *Northern Star,* 21 Oct 1843, Greenwich and 25 November 1843, Lectures by P. McGrath.

[85] Jones, *Chartism and the Chartists,* p.104 and Howell, 'Diffusing the Light of Liberty', pp.29-30.

[86] Jutta Schwartzkopf, *Women in the Chartist Movement,* London, Macmillan, 1991, pp.216-217; Thompson, *The Chartists,* pp.120-151.

[87] *Northern Star,* 6 March, 1841, Manchester, Mrs Parkinson lectured at the Tib Street Rooms and in the Brown Street Rooms. In Sunderland Mrs Martin lectured at the Golden Lion Inn on the 'Rights of the People'. See also *Northern Star,* 20 March, 1841, Newcastle, Mrs Martin on 'National Sins and Sorrows'.

[88] Schwarzkopf, *Women in the Chartist Movement,* p.217; Thompson, *The Chartists,* p.149. 'Women speakers might…' Thompson also notes, 'illustrate

the particular sufferings of women as workers and as victims of the Poor Law'.

[89] Cooper, *The Life of Thomas Cooper*, pp.56-57.
[90] Royle, *Chartism*, p.127.
[91] Thompson, 'Chartism as a Historical Subject,' p.11.
[92] Roberts, *Radical Politicians and Poets in Early Victorian Britain*, p.123, note 5.
[93] Pickering, *Chartism and the Chartists in Manchester and Salford*, p.170.
[94] *Ibid.*
[95] *Ibid.*, p.171.
[96] Aitken, *Remembrances and Struggles of a Working Man for Bread and Liberty*, p.42.
[97] Gammage, *Reminscences of a Chartist*, p.29.
[98] Jennings, *Chestnuts and Small Beer*, pp.38-39. Vincent's mimicry was witnessed at first hand by Jennings as a young reporter.
[99] *Northern Star*, 11 November 1843, Carlisle, Public Meeting addressed by O'Connor. See also W.J. O'Neill Daunt, *Ireland and Her Agitators*, Dublin, 1845, p.138. Daunt wrote of O'Connor: 'His talents as a mimic were first-rate'.
[100] Gammage, *History of the Chartist Movement 1837-1854*. p.39.
[101] *Northern Star*, 28 October 1843, Newcastle, Grand Demonstration in honour of T.S. Duncombe, extract from O'Connor's speech.
[102] Gammage, *History of the Chartist Movement 1837-1854*, pp.212-213.
[103] *TS 11/601*, Bairstow to Cooper, Bristol, 1 July 1842.
[104] *Northern Star*, 23 April. 1842.
[105] Pugh, 'Chartism in Somerset and Wiltshire,' p.198.
[106] Howell, Ph.D. thesis, p.132 and *Northern Star*, 23 April 1842, West of England Delegate Meeting.
[107] James Epstein. 'Some Organisational and Cultural Aspects of the Chartist Movement in Nottingham'. pp.221-268, particularly pp.251-253, in James Epstein and Dorothy Thompson (eds.) *The Chartist Experience: Studies in Working Class Radicalism and Culture, 1830-1860*, London, Macmillan, 1982.
[108] See the *Northern Star*, 29 October 1842, 'Incarceration of Mr John West'.
[109] Thompson, *The Chartists*, p.308.
[110] *Ibid.*
[111] Wilson, *The Struggles of an Old Chartist*, pp.9-10.
[112] Nigel Todd, *The Militant Democracy: Joseph Cowen and Victorian Radicalism*, Whitley Bay, Bewick Press, 1991, p.5.
[113] Adams, *Memoirs of a Social Atom*, pp.496-497.
[114] *Ibid.*, p.495, and Todd, *The Militant Democracy*, generally.
[115] Vicinus, 'To Live Free or Die: The Relationship between Strategy and Style in Chartist Speeches, 1838-1839,' pp.487-490; Harrison and Hollis (eds.) *Robert Lowery, Radical and Chartist*, pp.15-17; Pickering, 'Class Without Words: Symbolic Communication in the Chartist Movement,' pp.150-151.
[116] Adams, *Memoirs of a Social Atom*, p.157.

[117] For Wilkinson, see *Northern Star*, 5 September 1840, Huddersfield; for Ridley, see Lansdown, *The Trowbridge Chartists 1838-1848,* p.39; for Dickinson, see *Northern Star*, 27 August 1842, Nottingham; for Beesley, see *Northern Star*, 5 November, 1842; and for Scholefield, see Pickering, *Chartism and the Chartists in Manchester and Salford,* p.114.

[118] *John Miniken/Henry Vincent Papers.* Vincent to Miniken, 19 January 1841, Oakham Gaol.

[119] *The English Chartist Circular and Temperance Record*, 1841-1843, reptd., Augustus Kelley, New York, 1968, see Vol. 1, No.17, May 1841, p.68, Henry Vincent on Tour, letter to the Editor.

[120] *HO 45/2410D, 1848*, Part III, Gloucestershire, letter from G. Milward J.P. to Sir George Grey, Home Secretary.

[121] *Royle,* Chartism, p.29.

[122] Roberts, *Radical Politicians and Poets in Early Victorian Britain,* p.3.

[123] John Saville, *Ernest Jones: Chartist*, London, Lawrence and Wishart, 1952. pp.115-118.

[124] *Newcastle Weekly Chronicle*, 11 April 1896, 'Some Men I have Known' by Robert Applegarth.

[125] Gammage, *Reminiscences of a Chartist*, p.15.

[126] T. Palmer Newbould, *Pages From a Life of Strife, Being Some Recollections of William Henry Chadwick, the Last of the Manchester Chartists,* reptd., New York, Garland, 1986, p.2; E.P. Thompson, 'Homage to Tom Maguire,' pp.276-316, particularly p.288, note 5 on C.L. Robinson, in Asa Briggs and John Saville (eds.) *Essays in Labour History*, London, Macmillan, 1960.

[127] Gammage, *Reminiscences of a Chartist*, p.14.

Appendix

Chartist poem in praise of N.C.A. orators (*Northern Star,* 4 February 1843)

TO CHARTIST LECTURERS

To Chartist orators, who preach long and loud,
Exposing senators' vile tricks to a crowd
Of miners and nailors, shoemakers, and cads,
Old women, and tailors, and bare-footed lads;
Of grim faces gaping, and anxious to know
The means of escaping from hunger and woe;
It still ye persist in the lending poor fools,
They'll shortly be miss'd in our churches and schools;
Think then of the ruin of Sunday-school teachers,
You're even undoing our bishops and preachers.
Tis really appalling to hear a vile throng

Vehemently bawling a democrat's song:
While a speaker "rejoices" and finds that the "truth
Can mingle the voices of age and youth".
So apt, so discerning, so full of rare knowledge,
Ye flourish your learning like "students" from college;
From every occurrence ye can, if ye choose,
Extract some inference to favour your views,
And when other parties a meeting convene,
Ye "impudent Chartists" by dozens are seen
To flock on the rostrum, without a request,
And carry your "nostrum" in spite of the rest.
For a "purpose unholy on Sabbaths ye meet,"
And the meek and the lowly your doctrines greet,
With ardour quite charming to Radical ears,
Though strangely alarming to parsons and peers.
Your tenets, so strange, is to cause men to grumble,
And work a sad change in the "patient" and "bumble"
Mother church they forsake her, call ministers knaves,
And swear by their Maker they'll not remain slaves.

The parish priest passes without e'en a bow
From the "consummate asses of clod-hoppers," now;
No longer enslaved by their "spiritual pleaders,"
They hope to be saved by their Radical leaders,
That cringing submission once seen in a lad,
Is changed to "sedition," or something as bad;
In fact it is flown from the whole of the masses,
And is now only known among spaniels and asses;
The "mitre," the "crown", and the "coronet", too,
Alike meet the frown of the Radical crew,
Who teach their admirers that "profligate drones,"
Were always aspirers to pulpits and thrones;
But away with this jesting, this mocking comment,
My rhymes have been dress'd in the garb of dissent,
Still ardent and zealous, though seeming to chide,
I hail the brave fellows with Radical pride,
May those of the *heroes* destined to survive
The reign of our Neros still prosper and thrive,
And their death-stricken brothers though sunk to their rest,
Still live with the others in memory bless'd.

F. GOODFELLOW,
Sub-secretary to the National Charter Association.
Stourbridge.

THE TRANSPORTED CHARTIST:
THE CASE OF WILLIAM ELLIS

Robert Fyson

Over a hundred men were transported to Tasmania for crimes associated with Chartism: ten in 1839-40, at least eighty-five in 1842-3, sixteen in 1848.[1] Only a small number of these were definitely active Chartists.[2] Most convicted Chartists served prison sentences of up to two years in England. Even though a few of these died in prison, it was the Chartist transportees, or 'political exiles' who were singled out above all by the harshness of their punishment as the movement's pre-eminent 'victims and martyrs'. Some of them attracted intense sympathy, interest, and support for themselves and their families from the Chartist movement as a whole.

Most historians of Chartism have not paid much attention to the fate of the transportees, except for Frost, Williams, and Jones, leaders of the 1839 Newport rising.[3] Although Asa Briggs suggested some lines of approach to the subject nearly forty years ago, the only general study of transported 'social and political protesters' is disappointingly incomplete.[4] The subject of this essay, William Ellis, a leading Potteries Chartist, was undoubtedly the most well-known Chartist exile in the mid-1840s, apart from Frost, Williams, and Jones, with whom his name was often linked in Chartist toasts, petitions and appeals for pardon. He was wrongfully convicted on perjured evidence, transported for twenty-one years, and was the subject of a moving memoir by his fellow-Chartist Thomas Cooper, which included sixteen of his letters.[5] He never returned. It is time that his story was told.[6]

I

William Sherratt Ellis was born in Liverpool on 18 September 1809, one of a family of thirteen children. When he was about five his family moved to Stoke, and when he was nine or ten to Hanley, where he attended first the National, later the British, schools. The latter was more in keeping with the family's allegiance to New Connexion Methodism, and William was for a time a Sunday School pupil, then a teacher, probably at the Bethesda Methodist

Sunday School in Hanley. But his formal education soon ended, he was apprenticed as a china potter, and the family moved again, to Burslem, where his father, John Ellis, a retired sergeant-major and a member of the local volunteer force, found work as a lodgeman and gatekeeper at the factory of Enoch Wood, the town's leading manufacturer and a staunch Tory.[7]

A voracious reader with a questioning mind, Ellis began to think for himself and to question religious and political orthodoxies during the 1820s. According to one account, in 1825, as a boy of sixteen, he associated with Joseph Thomas, a twenty-five year old Burslem potter, who was the president of the first potters' trade union, which flourished briefly in 1825-6.[8] A few years later, in August 1829, Ellis married his childhood sweetheart, Emma, daughter of Jonah Read, a Burslem earthenware manufacturer. Read, who qualified in 1825 as one of the first Burslem Improvement Commissioners, paying £35 annual rent, was part of the town's ruling élite. He did not welcome his daughter's marriage to 'a young man of unsettled opinions and empty pockets' and 'considerable family uneasiness' resulted.[9] But the marriage lasted, and by 1842 William and Emma Ellis had four children.[10]

All who remembered Ellis stressed his intelligence, his liveliness, his ability as a speaker and debater. During the 1830s he became a temperance advocate and a teetotaller, belonging to a group who met in each other's houses for discussion and non-alcoholic drinks.[11] He also became an Owenite socialist and trade unionist, activities not emphasised in the memoir by Cooper, who hoped to procure a pardon for him. One account refers to Ellis meeting Robert Owen in the Potteries in 1833, as a member of a deputation of trades delegates concerning a proposal for an 'equitable labour exchange' in the Potteries. The Potters' Union of the 1830s was at pains to conceal the identity of most of its activists, but a partial list leaked to the local press during the great strike of 1836-7 included Ellis' name as president of the Hanley Lodge of China Potters, i.e., branch chairman for his own section of the trade in Hanley.[12] It must have been after the defeat of this strike and the disintegration of the Potters' Union that Ellis, a marked man, moved with his family to work in Liverpool for a year.[13] He retained his Owenite beliefs into the Chartist years: in 1839 he addressed a socialist meeting in Macclesfield; in 1842 he enthused to Cooper about the utopian book *Paradise Within the Reach of All Men* by J.A. Etzler, which was promoted by the Owenite press; and the local committee appealing for help to Chartist prisoners stressed Ellis' anti-clericalism.[14]

However, Ellis achieved public prominence as a Chartist rather than an Owenite. First mentioned in the press as a Chartist speaker in October 1838, it was he who made the platform speech in November at the great open-air Potteries radical demonstration, proposing John Richards as Potteries delegate to the National Convention, and, to loud applause, declared the meeting to be 'the death-knell of the spirit of despotism in the Potteries'. Throughout 1839 he was a prominent and militant activist, with a taste for dramatic rhetoric: chairing an open-air meeting near Burslem in April, he predicted that the army would be used to attack the people, but that, 'the moment when the first gun was fired among the working men of England, would be succeeded by a short but awful pause, and that the future history of this country would be written in characters red with human gore!' Unlike many who were active in 1839, he persevered when Chartism suffered its first decline, and was still addressing small Chartist meetings in the winter and spring of 1840.[15]

This activity came to an end when Ellis lost his job because of his Chartist allegiance. He was sacked, first from Samuel Alcock's Hill Top pottery in Burslem, then from his father-in-law's factory. He spent many months on the tramp in search of work, going as far as Glasgow, and travelling five hundred miles without finding employment. In one letter to Emma, written from Chesterfield in December 1840, he admitted that he had fallen into 'one of my old bygone drunken weekends,' which he bitterly regretted. At home in Burslem again for the 1841 census, he supported his family for a time by making picture frames out of plaster of Paris. This was the life of a poor workman fallen on hard times and preoccupied with making a living. For nearly two years Ellis' name did not appear in reports of Chartist meetings.[16]

II

William Ellis had already twice been victimised for his beliefs, as a trade unionist in 1837 and as a Chartist in 1840. But, like so many others, as depression deepened during 1842, he was drawn back into Chartist activity, impelled by a mixture of desperation and hope.[17] First reappearing as a Chartist speaker in Hanley in March, he re-entered the fray in earnest in June, when it was announced that 'Mr. W.S. Ellis will lecture at the following places,' with a schedule of five successive meetings throughout the Potteries in one week.[18] Ellis, who was not unduly modest, thought that his intervention at this time was crucial: in December, awaiting transportation, he wrote that

> I am pleased now at the part I have taken - that I never became a partizan, and owing to that I was always unfettered - so, last summer, when party feeling had almost crushed Chartism, I came out, took the market-places of the Potteries towns, and the result he (fellow-Chartist George Mart) well knows.[19]

Certainly Ellis was back in the thick of things as one of the most prominent Potteries Chartist speakers in the summer of 1842. He addressed meetings of striking colliers, as well as Chartists; he spoke at, and chaired, demonstrations by paupers on out-relief; in August he chaired a public meeting of protest about the state of acute and widespread distress in the Potteries.[20]

One among Ellis' many meetings brought him into the limelight especially. On June 13 a public meeting of the nobility, gentry, clergy, freeholders, and electors of Staffordshire was summoned in the Shire Hall, Stafford, to congratulate the Queen on escaping assassination. The hall was invaded by Chartists from Stafford and the Potteries who interrupted, made Chartist speeches, and carried on with their own meeting after the respectables had withdrawn. Ellis spoke at length, the only Potteries Chartist identified by name in the press and clearly a ringleader.[21]

The Chartist upsurge of 1842 culminated in the Potteries on August 15 and 16, when Chartists and striking colliers joined forces in calling a general strike for the Charter which degenerated into an outbreak of rioting, looting, arson, and destruction, checked only by a confrontation with the military, who fired upon the crowd at Burslem. Ellis' movements on August 15 are unknown; and his whereabouts on August 16 became a critical issue at his trial. From newspaper accounts as well as his own admission, it is clear that he was one of the speakers at an open air meeting in Hanley on the afternoon of Tuesday 16th, which was curtailed by the arrival of troops in the town.[22]

In the aftermath of the riots, all the leading Potteries Chartists were likely to be arrested. It was Ellis' misfortune that he was the subject of the first information laid before a magistrate: John Williams of Sandbach, a grocer, claimed on August 17 that he had been in Hanley early in the morning the previous day and had heard Ellis haranguing a crowd which then moved off to attack Burslem. Thomas Powys, the magistrate in question, who had been with the soldiers at the scene of the shooting in Burslem, forwarded the deposition to the Home Office with a note that 'An *immediate* step ... would be desirable against Ellis'. The Home Secretary, Sir James Graham, who was under pressure from Queen Victoria to act decisively against the rioters, noted 'Ellis ought to be immediately apprehended,' suggesting he might be guilty of treason, and a letter to that effect was sent to Powys by return of post. On August 20 a meeting of magistrates decided to arrest Ellis, and issued a warrant.[23]

But Ellis had already fled the previous day. He made his way to Liverpool, took ship for Glasgow, and found work in a pottery under an assumed name. According to Cooper he was planning to escape to America. Information of his whereabouts, however, soon reached the Burslem police, and a Metropolitan Police officer was sent to arrest him and bring him back to the Potteries, where he was initially held at Newcastle-under-Lyme police station. From there he wrote two abject letters to his former employer, Samuel Alcock, saying that he was innocent of using violent language, and asked Alcock to vouch for his character and assist his family. Alcock, then Chief Constable of Burslem, is unlikely to have given Ellis any assistance.[24]

When Ellis attended court at Newcastle on September 13 for committal proceedings before two magistrates, he was faced with not only John Williams, but seven other witnesses: between them they testified that they had heard Ellis make violent, blasphemous and seditious speeches in June and July, heard him speak out inciting the crowds on both days of the riots, seen him at the burning of Hanley parsonage on the night of August 15/16, and running away from the soldiers in Burslem on the 16th. The hearing lasted four or five hours; Ellis vigorously cross-examined the witnesses, though the cross-examination was not recorded; he was committed for high treason, and was removed to join the other prisoners already in Stafford gaol. He was the only prisoner among several hundred who faced this capital charge. The Potteries Chartists' defence fund committee explained this when they described him as 'a person of commanding and respectable talent, marked out by the more wealthy portion of society on account of his fearless and eloquent exposures of their ignorance, tyranny and hypocrisy, and more particularly that of the clerical order'.[25]

Writing to Emma from prison, Ellis described the testimony against him as a 'frightful mass of false swearing and perjury': in particular, he singled out the evidence of Thomas Smith, a special constable who claimed to have heard him speaking after Thomas Cooper on the evening of the 15th, and George Goodwin, a cabinet maker who claimed to have seen him standing outside the burning Hanley parsonage, with his face blackened at 2 a.m. on the 16th.[26] During the weeks leading up to the Special Commission of Assize at Stafford in October, the authorities had still not decided which charges to press: Ellis' name appeared on four different prosecution briefs for demolition of Hanley parsonage with others, riot at Burslem with others, conspiracy and sedition with Thomas Cooper, John Richards and Joseph Capper, and high treason, allegedly committed on his own.[27] John Ward, Tory solicitor of Burslem, was especially keen on the last of these, writing to the Treasury Solicitor that 'we shall spare no pains to maintain the capital charge by evidence ...' According to Cooper, at this time the Tory gentry were betting bottles of port in Hanley that he and Ellis would be hung. It was only the day before the Assizes opened that the Solicitor-General, Sir William Follett, decided that the evidence could not sustain the charge of high treason against Ellis.[28]

On the first of the remaining charges to come to trial, the burning of Hanley parsonage, Ellis was arraigned with seventeen others in the Shire Hall, Stafford, before Sir Nicholas Tindal, Lord Chief Justice of Common Pleas, on Friday October 7th. George Goodwin appeared against Ellis on Saturday, but was an unsatisfactory prosecution witness, vague and shifty, and Ellis' barrister effectively cast doubt on his testimony, before calling defence witnesses, including Ellis' landlady, and fellow-lodgers, or neighbours, who testified that he had been at home in bed all night, and men who admitted being at the burning of Hanley parsonage and insisted Ellis was not there. One said Goodwin was drunk at the time. However, on Sunday the prosecution procured fresh witnesses to discredit the testimony of Ellis' neighbours and contest his alibi: these were heard on Monday and the jury found Ellis guilty. On Friday 14th, sentence was passed, and the judge, claiming that Ellis was 'one of those who might be considered as the most immediate promoters of the crime by the violent and intemperate speeches which you delivered,' sentenced him to be transported for twenty-one years.[29]

In the evening, herded in the cell below the court with about forty other prisoners, William Ellis and Thomas Cooper met and had their only conversation, during which Cooper promised to work for Ellis' release. Ellis 'spoke of the coming age of universal brotherhood, of the world-spread establishment of the great community'; the two men discussed socialism, Christianity, and the state of the Chartist movement, before they were taken back to Stafford gaol and separated.[30]

The events of the succeeding weeks were sadly inexorable. Talk of a petition to the Home Secretary for the right to appeal, at a time when there were many Chartists facing charges arising from the widespread disturbances, came to nothing. After a harrowing family visit in Stafford gaol, Ellis and about fifty other convicts were removed to the York Hulk in Portsmouth Harbour early in November. According to one report, Ellis was taunted by other prisoners as he left Stafford, with such cries as 'we've got the Charter, haven't we, Billy?'[31] Arrived in Portsmouth Harbour, kept in chains and put to work, his departure to Australia was delayed for a further month by contrary winds. He continued to protest his innocence, recapitulate the details of his trial, and pour out his heart, in letters smuggled to shore, especially to J.D. Leggett of Portsea, presumably a local Chartist. Emma Ellis followed her husband to Portsmouth for a last heart-breaking farewell. Ellis, via Leggett, wrote to his wife asking to be supplied with, 'a quart can, a tin plate, a Bendigo cap, Walker's Pronouncing Dictionary, Burns's Poems, and likewise the poetical works of Percy Bysshe Shelley'.[32]

On December 6 the convict ship *John Renwick*, with 160 male

convicts aboard, set sail from Portsmouth, and William Ellis saw
the last of England.

III

A campaign to secure the return of William Ellis, and in the
meantime support his family, soon got under way, boosted by the
powerful advocacy of Thomas Cooper. During the four years after
Ellis' conviction, over a hundred Chartist localities from all parts of
Britain sent money for Mrs Ellis and her children, passed
resolutions, signed petitions, and drank toasts to 'Frost, Williams,
Jones, and Ellis'.[33] Out of many deserving Chartist prisoners, the
draconian punishment of Ellis, and the widespread belief in his
innocence, attracted especially strong support for him and his
family.

Cooper announced his intention to write a memoir of Ellis, with
the help of information from the Potteries Chartists, within a week
or two of Ellis leaving the country. Although he was busy
preparing for his own second trial, he saw Thomas Duncombe, the
radical pro-Chartist M.P., and succeeded in interesting him in Ellis'
case. He also handed his memoir of Ellis over to John Cleave,
leading radical journalist and publisher, before he entered prison.[34]
Cooper's incarceration in Stafford gaol, from May 1843 to May
1845, removed Ellis' most urgent and vociferous champion from
the scene of action. In his absence, his memoir of Ellis did not
begin to appear until November 1843, in the *English Chartist
Circular*, a paper of small circulation published by Cleave, rather
than the movement's main organ, the *Northern Star*. However, a
letter from Ellis to his wife from Tasmania was published in the
Northern Star in August 1844, which helped to maintain interest in
the case: Ellis urged Emma not to follow him to Tasmania while he
was still serving his period of probationary labour in a chain gang.
In December Duncombe wrote to the Home Secretary asking for a
pardon for Ellis, but was bluntly refused.[35]

Serious campaigning for Chartist transportees resumed in 1846,
when the Chartist executive recommended mass petitioning for the
return of Frost, Williams, Jones, and Ellis. George Mart wrote from
the Potteries claiming to have new defence evidence. Cooper
renewed his efforts, and Julian Harney suggested a special
commission to bring to London witnesses who could prove Ellis'

innocence, and make out a case to lay before the government.[36] In
the Potteries a meeting was held on behalf of all the Chartist exiles,
and then another one for Ellis alone.[37] In most cases, though,
petitions for Ellis were kept separate from those for the Welsh
Chartists, in line with Duncombe's parliamentary tactics: when he
opened a debate in the Commons, calling for the release of the
transportees, he judged it best to restrict himself to the cases of
Frost, Williams, and Jones, and Ellis was not mentioned.[38]

At the end of October, John Shaw of Tower Hamlets suggested
that only the *Northern Star* could mount an effective campaign for
Ellis, but Harney, the paper's editor, thought the initiative must
come from the Potteries:'When the friends of Mr Ellis in the
Potteries commence action, they may hope for assistance
elsewhere; but until they move, nothing effectual can be done for
the exile'.[39] This was, perhaps, to overestimate the resources
available to Potteries Chartists. In any case, the campaign petered
out. Feargus O'Connor's Commons motion in April 1848 did
include 'all political prisoners,' without mentioning Ellis
specifically, but had no chance of success.[40] 1848 produced a fresh
cohort of Chartist 'victims and martyrs,' and Ellis' case faded from
the forefront of Chartist attention.

The plight of Emma Ellis and her four children was a matter of
more immediate, practical concern. Ellis was concerned that his
family would be persecuted if they remained in Burslem, but they
had at first no alternative.[41] A friendly Chartist family at
Wednesbury in South Staffordshire offered a home to the only Ellis
daughter, five year old Jane, and this was accepted.[42] Emma and
her three sons lived off the money sent in by Chartists, until
January 1844, at the home of Fletcher Mandley, a Burslem Chartist
shoemaker and friend of William Ellis. Nevertheless, by December
1843 Emma was selling some of their clothes to get money to buy
food for the children.[43]

Early in 1844, new hope dawned when the Tower Hamlets
Chartists invited Emma to come to London and go into business.
They set her up in a newsagent's and general provision shop off
Brick Lane, Spitalfields, in March. A fund-raising committee,
meeting weekly, guaranteed her an income of fifteen shillings a
week for the first three months. But by July the shop was in
difficulties, and by the end of the year Emma Ellis was again

appealing for help, reduced to selling her bedclothes, and devastated by the death of her daughter in Wednesbury.[44] Her business folded in May 1845, and she returned to the Potteries and lived for a time with her father, who was himself now in reduced circumstances. She pleaded with the parish authorities for outdoor relief, eked out an existence on donations and the three shillings a week earned by her eldest son. She heard again from William, who offered hope that when he could get his ticket of leave, his wife and family could join him, and he would establish himself as a potter.[45] But when she applied to the Stoke Poor Law Board for assistance to emigrate to Tasmania, in July 1846, her application did not find favour.[46] The family continued, presumably, to live in desperate circumstances until, having lost touch with William, Emma and her three boys emigrated in 1849, not to Australia but to the U.S.A., in search of a new life.[47]

William Ellis was still sometimes remembered, and his fate was a subject of surmise and speculation, sometimes of definite assertion. In 1851 Harney suggested that, even if Frost and Ellis had not participated in the forming of a democratic association, 'It is, however, morally certain that the expatriated patriots have largely contributed to the birth of Democracy in the land of their exile'.[48] In 1856 John Frost returned to England, but William Ellis' name was not on the list of those offered a free pardon. The state, which had punished him so severely, now appeared to have forgotten his existence, and even Thomas Duncombe M.P. did not raise the matter.[49]

William Owen, a Potteries trade union and labour leader born in 1844, knew the main outlines of the Ellis story and presented them in a dialect serial for the entertainment of readers of his short-lived local monthly, *The Archer*, in 1872. He believed that 'William Elton the Chartist' (a deliberate alteration of the name) was still alive and prospering. 'His family went ait tu him many years ago, an William Elton found in Australia that breadth of popular freedom which, especially in his dey, wonner easy found in owd England'.[50] Lloyd Jones, recalling Ellis in 1879 as one of the 'Poor Chartists Not to Be Forgotten,' was more cautious, admitting he did not know what had become of him.[51] But Henry Allen Wedgwood, writing in the early 1880s, confidently informed Potteries readers that Ellis had become a wealthy businessman. Furthermore, 'From being created a magistrate he rose to be a member of the highest legislative assembly in Australia, equal to being a member of Parliament ...When a candidate he sent a copy of his address to his friends in England'. The reference to Ellis as a magistrate is reminiscent of Dickens' Micawber.[52]

Interest in the subject was revived in 1905 by a personal advertisement in the *Sentinel*. 'William Ellis, son of late Chartist Ellis, would be glad to meet friends if there are any. He has been away 56 years'. William Ellis junior from the U.S.A., born in 1840, was interviewed by a journalist: he believed that his father 'by his industry and integrity, gained the confidence of those who were in charge of the settlement at the Antipodes. He established a pottery business which flourished, and the last that was heard of the Chartist was that he had left a fortune of £20,000'. Ellis enjoyed a warm reception in the Potteries, but left without finding out any more about his father, and died in 1913.[53]

The reality of William Ellis' life in Tasmania was different from these hopeful imaginings.

IV[54]

The *John Renwick* had an uneventful four month voyage to Tasmania, or Van Diemen's Land as it was then known. The ship touched at the Cape of Good Hope, to take on fresh provisions, vegetables and water, and Ellis was able to send a letter to his wife. The surgeon superintendent, T.E. Ring, recorded in his log book that 'the prisoners were allowed to be upon deck, as much as possible, and such amusements as Gymnastics, singing and dancing were encouraged, thus promoting cheerfulness and keeping the mind employed'. He also mentioned, however, the 'marked and almost general despondency' among the transported Staffordshire rioters. There were no serious illnesses or deaths during the voyage, but forty prisoners suffered from minor ailments, Ellis among them with a five-day attack of dyspepsia. He kept out of trouble, worked as an inspector of provisions, and was 'very attentive to his duties' until the ship anchored in the Derwent River, and disembarked its convicts on April 15.[55]

Ellis was now subject to the rigorous discipline of the Australian convict system.[56] After an initial registration in the prisoners' barracks at Hobart, he began the most severe part of his sentence, three and a half years probationary labour, on a chain gang, at Cascades, on the Tasman peninsula near Port Arthur. By 1846 there were 445 convicts at Cascades, 200 of whom were employed in agriculture. The land was heavily wooded, and the main industry was felling timber. Wheat and vegetables were also grown during Ellis' time there.[57] Correspondence in the *Northern Star* affords only very brief glimpses of his experiences. Writing to Emma in January 1844, he referred to 'the moral desolation that now surrounds me' and added 'I find myself in the same situation as those who have committed the blackest crimes that stain the dark calendar of human guilt'. This was a recurring theme; in a letter written on Christmas Day 1844, he again complained that he was compelled to herd with the 'vilest outcasts of society and bloodstained men, the most degraded of human kind'.[58] Unlike many convicts, Ellis was not charged with any criminal offence during his years on the Tasman peninsula, and, according to a letter Emma received from a friend in Hobart, he was exempted from hard labour as a reward for good conduct, and employed as a schoolmaster at Port Arthur, probably early in 1845. But, working in Australia's 'Hell on earth,' he must have witnessed or been aware of appalling brutalities, horrific floggings, and widespread sodomy.[59]

However, Ellis was not devoid of Chartist friendships. In January 1844 he wrote that he had repeatedly seen Frost, Williams, and Jones, and that Frost had been in the same place with him for six months, but all three had now left the Tasman peninsula. He referred again to Frost in his Christmas Day letter.[60] At about the time Ellis wrote, Frost in Hobart heard from him that he was in pretty good health, but sadly tired of his situation. Frost asked his correspondent, James Sweet of Nottingham, to tell Mrs Ellis that it was very difficult and dangerous to make any contact with Port Arthur prisoners.[61] Uncertain as communications were, the links maintained by the Chartists in Tasmania helped to maintain morale. But conditions were such that early in 1844 Ellis was adamant that he could not see his wife, and did not want her to come to Australia, until he had completed his period of probationary labour. By the end of the year, he was beginning to look forward to the future possibility of getting a ticket of leave, setting himself up as a potter, and being joined by his wife and family.[62]

In October 1846 Ellis was released from his period of probationary labour, and was hired as a labourer by James Tibbs of Goulburn Street, Hobart, an ex-convict with a market garden in which Ellis probably worked. He worked for a month at Swansea on the east coast in the spring of 1847, and then for two months as a police constable in Hobart, before going north in July to work for a butcher called Green in Launceston, the second largest Tasmanian town.[63] It was here that Ellis made a determined effort to escape from the island, in company with fellow-Chartist Zephaniah Williams, at the end of October. Allegedly Williams and Ellis tried to row a small boat to the harbour mouth and get on board the *Opossum*, a cutter bound for New Zealand. This was preceded by a long and arduous walk of many miles, but, according to different versions, the *Opossum* sprang a leak and had to return to port and discharge her cargo, and the two convicts had difficulties with navigation and could not get past the police stationed at the river's mouth. The escape attempt had already failed when Williams and Ellis were arrested walking home in Launceston late at night. Ellis, who was very fatigued, had been left in charge of Green's premises while his master was away for the weekend. He had taken £15 of Green's money with him, and another employee, a free man, had informed the police. Ellis tried to bluff it out, and would not admit his guilt. Williams, who had tried to escape before, got a year's sentence; Ellis was sentenced to only six months' imprisonment with hard labour, because it was his first offence and he was thought to have been led astray by Williams.[64] He served his time in the prison barracks at Launceston and Hobart.[65]

After an exemplary record of good behaviour for four years, Ellis had made a determined attempt to escape from Tasmania and regain his freedom. His capture and imprisonment was a major setback. Thereafter, he probably became reconciled to remaining in Tasmania for the foreseeable future, and decided to make the best of it.

In May 1848, having served his sentence, he was re-employed by James Tibbs in Hobart, where he remained until the end of 1851.[66] Now he was able to achieve his ambition to work as a potter. In December 1848 a newspaper advertisement appeared for an ornamental pottery producing flowerpots in Goulburn Street with Charles Tibbs, James' eighteen year old son, as the proprietor: he announced that he intended to start an earthenware factory.[67] This venture must have relied on Ellis' skills as a potter. William Cartledge, another Staffordshire potter transported in 1842, was also working there from November 1848 on. A few years later, Ellis seems to have been managing the pottery. In a controversy about the merits of rival potteries in August 1851, the Goulburn Street works were defended thus: 'Mr Ellis assures us that the articles turned out from the manufactory are not to be surpassed, if equalled, in durability and virtue'.[68]

Ellis, who had been granted his ticket of leave in January 1850, now began not only to work at his old trade, but also to emerge as a public figure in Hobart, playing a prominent role first of all in the temperance movement. He appeared frequently in reports of meetings and social functions of the Hobart Town Total Abstinence Society from March 1850 to January 1851. Inn signs, he told a meeting in August, were 'the frightful monuments of a people's degradation,' and in October he 'hoped to rescue the drunkards of the land from impending ruin'. He spoke at a meeting at Richmond, fifteen miles from Hobart, and chaired the Hobart teetotallers' Christmas teaparty. In January he claimed that 'he had been a pledged teetotaller for fifteen years and during that time had never deviated from the principle': despite temptations and difficulties, he had been enabled to stick to his beliefs by 'a supernatural interposition'.[69]

From the autumn of 1850 Ellis was also actively involved in a new political movement. The Tasmanian Union, founded in October, aimed to ensure equal rights and freedom from discrimination for ex-convicts who comprised about 40% of the island's population.[70] It was a response both to the anti-convict propaganda of the Anti-Transportation League, and to the prospect of elections for a new Legislative Council under the Australian Colonies Government Act of 1850. Early in November Ellis was on the management committee. At a large, overcrowded public launch meeting for the new movement, he was a member of the platform party and declared that 'we are about to enter upon a new era in the history of Tasmania'. A week later he led an unsuccessful attempt to start a branch of the Tasmanian Union in Richmond, claiming that he had 'chosen to leave for a time the privacy of retired life to advocate the cause of the Union'.[71] The meeting, packed by the Union's opponents, declined to start a Richmond branch, and later a hostile paper complained pointedly that

> Chartist rioters, and men of that class, are not only permitted to attend such meetings, but to be actually on committees and on delegations to the inland district, there to move resolutions tending to divide society, and in known connection with the press, to write articles for publication...[72]

But Ellis was not deterred, and contrived to make more than one 'lengthy eulogium' calling for the Union to make its members 'strong, independent and free'; they were, he declared 'capable of legislating for themselves'.[73]

Thus in 1850 and 1851 Ellis was running a pottery business, and becoming a prominent public man in the temperance movement and Tasmanian politics. Possibly at this time he wrote to friends in the Potteries exaggerating his prospects, and giving rise to the legends mentioned earlier. This was a time of hope which did not last long.

The pottery business failed and Ellis joined the police force as a constable for the second time in December 1851, resigning again in February 1852.[74] There were also personal complications in his life: a prominent newspaper advertisement by Samuel Boltz, an ex-convict labourer or storeman, in May 1851 announced that he would no longer be responsible for the debts of his wife, Elizabeth Boltz, who had 'broken up my home and absconded with my property whilst I was at work, and is now cohabiting with that cloven-footed teetotaller, long Ellis, the potter'. A longer impassioned denunciation on similar lines appeared a year later: this time Boltz, who had seven daughters, complained that, 'Government allows that fornicator, Ellis, the Chartist to go at large to ruin other families as he had ruined my wife and children ... this deceiver Ellis acts under the garb of religion and teetotalism. All good people will be aware of the cunning, crafty, smooth-tongued fellow'. Boltz denied that he was living with his wife again. The implication is that her liaison with Ellis may have ended.[75]

This sort of publicity would not have helped Ellis to establish himself in public life, but other factors also checked his political activity in 1851. New regulations introduced in March ordered that, 'Ticket-of-leave holders are not to enter any theatre or billiard-room, nor attend any public meeting. They are likewise prohibited from becoming members of any society, religious and temperance societies excepted'.[76] By the end of 1852 Ellis had ceased to be a ticket of leave man, and had been granted a conditional pardon: he was free as long as he remained in Tasmania.[77] Meanwhile, however, by the summer of 1851 the Tasmanian Union had collapsed due to internal disputes, and the Legislative Council elections, held in October on a restricted property-based franchise, saw the election of two conservative anti-convict members for Hobart.[78]

For the rest of William Ellis' lifetime Tasmania, unlike the other Australian states, was a stagnant backwater, economically, socially, and politically. Transportation to the colony ended in 1853, but because of economic depression there was little new immigration, while thousands of the most active Tasmanians joined in the gold rush to the Australian mainland, especially in the 1850s. A rigid social division persisted between free settlers and emancipists, most of whom were poor. Manhood suffrage was not introduced until 1900, but by 1870 Hobart had 80% of adult males on the voting register.[79] 'William Ellis, householder, Forest Street,' off Goulburn Road, appeared on a list of electors in 1851, although as a ticket of leave holder he should have been disqualified. His name does not appear on any subsequent Hobart electoral register, though he could have qualified from 1856 had he earned £100 p.a. or occupied a house worth £10 p.a.[80]

It remains to outline Ellis' sad decline after 1851. In June 1852 a police register of ticket of leave holders shows that he was living in the house of N. Ferguson, baker, Goulburn Street, and he joined the police for the third time in the same month, though he may, again, not have remained a policeman for long.[81] In April and again in June 1853 he was fined for being drunk and disturbing the peace in Hobart.[82] In October 1853 he married for the second time, probably bigamously, at St. George's Anglican Church, Battery Point, Hobart; his bride was Catherine McGovern or Farrelly, an illiterate Irish Catholic housemaid aged 28 or 29, transported from Edinburgh in 1847 for killing her husband's mistress.[83] She had a daughter, Mary Ann, aged two.

The marriage did not bring Ellis peace and stability. In January 1854 he was fined for indecent exposure. Despite this, he once more found employment with the police in February, but after being found drunk in Richmond, he was dismissed from the post of police clerk, and was marked down as totally unfit ever to enter the police service again. In November he again became a father: his son, another William Ellis, was baptised a Catholic by his mother in Richmond.[84]

Between 1853 and 1870 William Ellis appeared in court in Hobart and Richmond 31 times, and there may have been other appearances elsewhere. In July 1857 the Ellises were living apart. A city missionary applied for Ellis' son and stepdaughter to be admitted to an orphanage, since 'being of dissipated and irregular habits' Ellis was doing nothing to support his wife and her children, but the Chief Constable maintained that Ellis could support them if he wished and that Mrs Ellis was surviving by taking in washing and doing needlework.[85] From 1857 to 1861 Ellis disappears from the police and court records of Hobart and Richmond. In June 1861 he was discharged with a caution for assaulting his wife; with his usual grandiloquence, marred by inaccuracy, 'Defendant desired to observe that he had been 15 years a total abstainer out of 17 in the colony'.[86] In 1863 Ellis completed his 21 year sentence, but by this time he was past redemption.

In June 1864, facing a charge of vagrancy after being found sleeping rough, Ellis was said by a detective to get his living 'by writing petitions and letters for publicans and others; he also wrote for the newspapers and he knew he had got articles inserted'.[87] In 1865 he was imprisoned for three months with hard labour, having failed to pay maintenance to his family under a court order.[88] There were also various disputes and assault cases involving the Ellises and their landlords. In 1867 Mary Ann, his stepdaughter, was sent to prison for a month for soliciting, and in 1870 she got three months for stealing money from a sailor.[89]

In 1869 Ellis was found in an outhouse, drunk and suffering from the cold, and taken to hospital. His last known court appearance was in July 1870.[90] He made one more public appearance in October 1870, outside the Parliament House 'followed by about fifty persons, principally boys,' whom he haran.gued on

> 'the advantages of Parliamentary government, the merits
> of the Main Line Railway, and on various other
> interesting subjects ... The time will come when the sun
> that looks down on this fair isle of the sea will witness a
> thriving people here. The prosperity of the country will
> be far beyond what we at present have any conception
> of, when the steam engine runs through the length and
> breadth of the country'.

Ellis broke off to cheer Sir Robert Officer, the Speaker of the
House of Assembly, and after speaking for twenty minutes,
'adjourned to a neighbouring public house to refresh his wasted
energies'.[91]

William Ellis died in Hobart General Hospital from heart
disease on November 17, 1871, aged 62, and was buried in a
pauper's grave. He had started life with considerable talents, highly
literate and articulate, an autodidactic intellectual of the younger
generation of early Chartist leaders, with a background in New
Connexion Methodism, the temperance movement, Owenite
socialism and trade unionism. Always a highflown and impulsive
orator, and given to militant rhetoric, it is very likely that in 1842
he laid himself open to a charge of using seditious language; but it
is virtually certain that he had not committed the crime of arson for
which he was sentenced. The hardships endured by his family
throughout the 1840s were typical of many other Chartists'
families, but more protracted. The remarkable, tragic, story of his
life in Australia resembles a classic Victorian morality tale. He was
a stalwart of the temperance movement who became a drunkard.
For how many others was the Victorian temperance movement the
nineteenth-century equivalent of Alcoholics Anonymous? Yet,
even in his old age as a drink-sodden vagrant, he was still able to
use his superior literary skills to eke out a living; and his stump
oratory in 1870 still, perhaps, bore traces of the utopian hopes of
his youth. William Ellis the potter, a forgotten and neglected figure,
may be seen, not as typical but as archetypal, in the sufferings
which he endured as a result of his Chartist beliefs. He deserves to
be remembered, despite his human failings, as one of the most

notable Chartist 'victims and martyrs'.

NOTES

[1] Figures calculated from George Rudé, *Protest and Punishment*, Oxford, Clarendon Press, 1978, pp.131-144, with the addition of five more transportees involved in the 1842 riots, omitted by Rudé: see *North Staffordshire Mercury* (N.S.M.), 25 March, 12 August 1843, 6 January 1844.

[2] Among the largest group, the fifty-six men transported for involvement in the 1842 Potteries riots, only two, Richard Croxton and William Ellis, are known to have been Chartist activists.

[3] David Williams, *John Frost: A Study in Chartism*, Cardiff, University of Wales Press Board, 1939, reprinted New York, Augustus M. Kelley, 1969. For a brief account of the most famous Chartist exile of 1848, see John Saville's entry on William Cuffay, in J.M. Bellamy and J. Saville (eds.), *Dictionary of Labour Biography, Vol. VI*, London, Macmillan, 1982, pp.77-80.

[4] Asa Briggs, 'Chartists in Tasmania: A Note,' *Bulletin of the Society for the Study of Labour History*, 3, Autumn 1961, pp.4-8; Rudé, op.cit. See also the critical review of Rudé's book by E.P. Thompson, 'Sold Like A Sheep for £1', *New Society*, 14 December 1978, reprinted idem, *Persons and Polemics*, London, Merlin Press, 1994, pp.193-201.

[5] Thomas Cooper, 'A Brief Memoir of W. Sherratt Ellis, The Chartist Exile', *English Chartist Circular*, (E.C.C.), 145-150, 152, n.d. c. Nov.-Dec. 1843, Jan. 1844.

[6] Brief discussions of Ellis are in Rudé, *Protest and Punishment*, pp.134, 216; Thompson, *Persons and Polemics*, p.197; Dorothy Thompson, *The Chartists*, London, Maurice Temple Smith, 1984, p.300. Frank Burchill and Richard Ross, *A History of the Potters' Union*, Stoke-on-Trent, Ceramic and Allied Trades Union, 1977, is dedicated 'to William Ellis, potter, transported and forgotten'.

[7] *E.C.C.* 145, 148; *Weekly Sentinel*, 4 June 1881.

[8] *Ibid.*

[9] *Staffordshire Mercury*, 22 August 1829; Stoke-on-Trent City Archives, Burslem Commissioners' Minutes, 3 August 1825, 26 July 1826, 4 January 1827, 19 December 1828, 20 March 1829; *E.C.C.*, 145.

[10] 1841 Census, Burslem, Upper Pitt Street.

[11] *E.C.C.*145; *Staffordshire Sentinel*, 25 May 1905.

[12] *Weekly Sentinel*, 4 June 1881; *N.S.M.*, 31 December 1836.

[13] *E.C.C.*, 145.

[14] *New Moral World*, 21 Dec. 1839; *E.C.C.*, 147; *Northern Star* (N.S.), 24 September 1842. For Etzler see Gregory Claeys, 'John Adolphus Etzler, technological utopianism, and British socialism ...', *English Historical Review*, 1986, pp.351-375.

[15] *N.S.M.*, 20 October, 17 November 1838, 6 April 1839, 25 April 1840; *N.S.*, 15 February, 25 April 1840; *Staffordshire Gazette*, 16 May 1840.

[16] *N.S.M.*, 17 Sept. 1842; *E.C.C.*145.

[17] For the general context of events, see my 'The Crisis of 1842: Chartism, the Colliers' Strike and the Outbreak in the Potteries', in James Epstein and Dorothy Thompson, (eds.), *The Chartist Experience*, London, Macmillan, 1982, pp.194-220.

[18] *N.S.M.*, 19 March 1842; *N.S.*, 4 June 1842.

[19] *E.C.C.*, 150, Ellis to J.D. Leggett, 3 December 1842.

[20] *N.S.M.*, 18 June, 9 July, 6, 13 August 1842; *N.S.*, 11, 25 June, 20 August 1842; *Staffordshire Advertiser* (S.A.), 9 July, 13 August 1842.

[21] *N.S.M.*, *N.S.*, *S.A.*, 18 June 1842. *E.C.C.* 145, says Ellis took the chair at the meeting, an error by Thomas Cooper which I carelessly repeated in 'The Crisis of 1842', p.205.

[22] *N.S.M.*, *N.S.*, *S.A.*, 20 August 1842.

[23] Public Record Office (P.R.O.), Home Office papers (H.O.) 45/260, Disturbances, Staffordshire 1842, ff.285-8, 308-9; H.O. 41/17, Sutton to Powys, 18 August 1842; British Library (B.L.), Peel Papers, Additional Manuscripts (Add. Mss.) 40, 434, ff.317-319, Queen Victoria to Sir Robert Peel, 17 August 1842.

[24] *N.S.M.*, 17 September 1842; *E.C.C.*, 146; Staffordshire Record Office, Stafford, Microfilm 49, Samuel Alcock Letter Book, Ellis to Alcock, 11, 13 September 1842.

[25] P.R.O. Assizes 6:6, Depositions in Case 213; *S.A.*, 17 September 1842; *N.S.*, 24 September 1842.

[26] *E.C.C.*, 148, Ellis to Mrs Ellis, 15 September 1842.

[27] P.R.O., Treasury Solicitor (T.S.) 11/597-8, 601-2.

[28] P.R.O., T.S.11/600, Ward to Treasury Solicitor, 27 September 1842; *E.C.C.*, 146; *N.S.* 26 November 1842; B.L., Peel Papers, Add. Mss. 40, 447, Graham to Peel, 26, 30 September, 3 October 1842.

[29] *E.C.C.* 146, 147.

[30] *E.C.C.* 147.

[31] *N.S.M.*, 5 November 1842.

[32] *E.C.C.* 149, 150, 152.

[33] Calculated from *N.S.*, 1842-6.

[34] *N.S.* 17 December 1842, 18 February, 4 March, 29 April 1843.

[35] *N.S.*, 3 August, 14 December 1844.

[36] *N.S.*, 17, 31 January, 14 February 1846.

[37] *N.S.*, 28 February, 21 March 1846.

[38] *Hansard*, Commons Debates, 10 March 1846.

[39] *N.S.*, 31 October 1846.

[40] *Hansard*, Commons Debates, 6 April 1848.

[41] *E.C.C.*, 150, Ellis to Leggett, 3 December 1842.

[42] *N.S.*, 26 November 1842, 28 January 1843.

[43] *N.S.*, 22 April, 16 December 1843, 20 January, 3 February 1844.

[44] *N.S.*, 17 February, 2, 23 March, 13 April, 3 August, 28 December 1844; 4, 11 January 1845.

[45] *N.S.*, 17, 31 May, 28 June, 6, 20 September, 22 November 1845.

[46] P.R.O., M.H. (Ministry of Health) 12/11461, Stoke Poor Law Union

Correspondence, Thomas Griffin to Poor Law Commissioners, 9 July 1846.

[47] *Staffordshire Sentinel*, 23 May 1905.

[48] *Friend of the People*, 3 May 1851.

[49] Details of Chartist prisoners and transportees serving sentences in 1848-56 are in P.R.O., H.O. 12/2/81, but Ellis is not mentioned. Perhaps his conviction for arson disqualified him from consideration as a political prisoner.

[50] *The Archer*, June, 1872, p.134. Compare E.P. Thompson's similar conjecture, *Persons and Polemics*, p.200: 'many ... experienced their new life as in part a liberation from the tight class structure and obligatory deference ... of the old country ... perhaps William Ellis's dreams of universal brotherhood ... blended naturally into a more humdrum and practical egalitarianism'.

[51] *Newcastle (on Tyne) Weekly Chronicle*, 11 October 1879.

[52] *Staffordshire Sentinel*, Summer Number, June 1905, pp.34-5. This was a reprint: Wedgwood died in 1885. For Micawber as a magistrate in Australia, see Charles Dickens, *David Copperfield*, London, 1850, Chapter LXIII.

[53] *Staffordshire Sentinel*, 19, 23, 25, 27 May 1905; 4 December 1913.

[54] I am deeply indebted for research assistance to my friend John Taylor, who, when travelling in Australia, spent several weeks in the Tasmania Archives Office on my behalf. Without his help, this part of Ellis' story could not have been written.

[55] P.R.O., Admiralty 101 39/4, Surgeon-Superintendent's Log Book, John Renwick 1842-3; *N.S.*, 3 August 1844; Archives Office of Tasmania, Hobart (A.O.T.), Convict Conduct Registers, CON. 33/38, 9122.

[56] See, generally, A.G.L. Shaw, *Convicts and the Colonies*, London, Faber, 1966; Robert Hughes, *The Fatal Shore*, London, Collins Harvill, 1987; John Hirst, 'The Australian Experience: the Convict Colony' in Norval Morris and David J. Rothman (eds.), *The Oxford History of the Prison*, New York and Oxford, Oxford University Press, 1995, pp.235-265. I have also been helped by Julia Macneill-Ferguson, 'The Wages of Sin: a study of transportation as a punishment of North Staffordshire convicts 1818-1853,' unpublished B.A. dissertation, Keele University, 1983.

[57] Anne McMahon, 'The Convict Stations of Norfolk Bay,' *Proceedings of the Tasmanian Historical Research Association*, Vol.13 No.3, May 1966, p.65.

[58] *N.S.*, 3 August 1844, 20 September 1845.

[59] *N.S.*, 31 May 1845. For the régime at Port Arthur and on the Tasman peninsula, see John Frost, *The Horrors of Convict Life*, Preston, 1856, reprinted Hobart, Sullivan's Cove, 1973; Hughes, *The Fatal Shore*, pp.398-414.

[60] *N.S.*, 3 August 1844, 20 September 1845.

[61] *N.S.*, 3 January 1846, letter from John Frost, 24 January 1845, quoted by Feargus O'Connor.

[62] *N.S.*, 3 August 1844, 20 September 1845.

[63] Convict Conduct Register, CON 33/38, 9122. For Tibbs' garden, A.O.T., L.S.D. 1/80 p.52.

[64] *Launceston Examiner*, 3, 6, 10, 20 November 1847; *Cornwall Chronicle* 6, 20 November 1847. David Williams, *John Frost*, p.310, mentions this incident without naming Ellis or noticing that he was a Chartist, and claims that William Jones informed on Zephaniah Williams.

[65] CON 33/38, 9122.

[66] *Ibid.*

[67] *Hobart Town Courier* (H.T.C.), 13 December 1848.

[68] CON 33/38, 9105; *Hobart Town Guardian (H.T.G.)*, 30 August 1851.

[69] *Temperance Banner*, 22 August, 10 October, 22 November, 20 December 1850, 31 January 1851.

[70] Henry Reynolds, 'The Island Colony, Tasmania: society and politics 1880-1900,' unpublished M.A. thesis, University of Tasmania, 1963, pp.1-2.

[71] *H.T.G.* 9, 27 November, 4, 7 December 1850.

[72] *Britannia and Trades Advocate*, 26 December 1850. Newspaper articles by Ellis have not been found, but may have appeared anonymously.

[73] *H.T.C.*, 7 December 1850; *H.T.G.*, 25 December 1850, 19 February 1851.

[74] CON 33/38, 9122; *Hobart Town Gazette*, 9 March 1852.

[75] *Colonial Times* (C.T.), 13 May 1851, 25 May 1852. 'Long' Ellis was six feet tall: CON 33/38, 9122.

[76] *Hobart Town Gazette*, 4 March 1851.

[77] CON 33/38, 9122.

[78] Lloyd Robson, *A History of Tasmania, Vol. I*, Melbourne, Oxford University Press, 1983, p.511; *H.T.G.*, 29 October 1851.

[79] Reynolds, 'Island Colony,' pp.1-25, 119.

[80] *C.T.*, 2 September 1851; information from John Taylor on 1856 Electoral Act.

[81] A.O.T., POL 29/22; *Hobart Town Gazette*, 29 June 1852.

[82] A.O.T., LC 247/23.

[83] Marriage certificate No.1956, 25 October 1853, St. George's Church, Battery Point, Hobart; CON 41/11, Convict Conduct Register of Catherine McGovern.

[84] LC 247/22; *Hobart Town Gazette*, 21 February, 30 May 1854; LC 445/2; University of Tasmania Archives, R.C. Church records, baptism certificate of William Ellis, 26 November 1854.

[85] A.O.T., Colonial Secretary's Department, CSD 1/116/3959.

[86] *Hobart Town Advertiser* (H.T.A.), *Hobart Town Mercury* (H.T.M.), 25 June 1861.

[87] *H.T.A.*, 18 June 1864; *H.T.M.*, 16 June 1864; LC 247/31.

[88] *H.T.M.*, 3 May 1865; A.O.T., GD 67/2/312, 14 June 1865.

[89] LC 247/32, 23 November 1867; LC 247/33, 16 December 1870; *Tasmanian Times*, 22 December 1870.

[90] *H.T.M.*, 19 May 1869; LC 247/33, SC 243/2, July 5 1870.

[91] *H.T.M.*, 19 October 1870. For Sir Robert Officer, see *Australian Dictionary of Biography, Vol.2*, Melbourne University Press, 1967, pp.297-8.

[92] Hobart Death Certificates 1871, No.660; Hobart General Hospital Death Book, HSD/145-6; *H.T.M.*, 18 November 1871.

FEARGUS O'CONNOR IN THE HOUSE OF COMMONS, 1847-1852

Stephen Roberts

Amongst labour historians, there is now general agreement on the subject of Feargus O'Connor. The last book to subscribe to the readings of Chartism offered by R.G. Gammage and William Lovett appeared in 1973[1]. A 1989 biography of Lovett put in a persuasive plea on behalf of its subject, but made no attempt to re-establish the old anti-O'Connor orthodoxy.[2] The way O'Connor is seen has changed for good. It changed because of the appearance in 1982 of James Epstein's revisionist account of O'Connor and early Chartism and the reinforcing of this interpretation two years later by Dorothy Thompson.[3] Epstein's portrayal of his subject as an immensely talented agitator stands as one of the most important contributions to the historiography of Chartism, but his study considers O'Connor's leadership only up to the strikes of 1842. Of course, the later Chartist agitations have been expertly explored in other books and articles, but O'Connor's story certainly remains incomplete. In particular there has been no attempt to examine his exertions in the House of Commons. O'Connor was returned for Nottingham in July 1847, the only Chartist ever to be elected an MP - yet all that is noted in the standard histories is the fact of his election and the way his parliamentary career ended in 1852. O'Connor's unexpected victory was undoubtedly a highly significant moment in the long years of the Chartist struggle. Here was the voice of Chartism in the chamber of the House of Commons itself - in a way that Thomas Attwood or even the radical MP for Finsbury, Thomas Slingsby Duncombe, never could be. This chapter seeks to explore this neglected aspect of O'Connor's career, and will suggest that, like Henry Hunt and William Cobbett before him, his contribution as a parliamentary radical was not without some signal successes.

On 9 June 1852 Feargus O'Connor was arrested in Westminster Hall by the Deputy Sergeant-at-Arms of the House of Commons.[4] He spent the next seven days in custody in the House until his sister, Harriet O'Connor, with whom he lived in Finsbury, arranged for his transfer to the Chiswick asylum of Dr. Harrington Tuke.[5] It was clear, by spring 1851, that O'Connor's health was breaking down. He was often absent from the House and, in an attempt to recruit his health, had spent the summer months in travel on the continent. There was to be no recovery: O'Connor was suffering from general paralysis of the insane, induced by syphilis. 'I was very ill last night,' he wrote, in November 1851, after addressing a meeting, 'and I am still very poorly'.[6] It was the final letter he wrote for the *Northern Star*, and a fortnight later the newspaper he had founded in 1837 was sold for £100. The incidents which marked O'Connor's mental breakdown were reported with amusement and little sympathy in the middle class press.[7] When, in February 1852, the Speaker read from a magistrate's letter in the Commons concerning O'Connor's arrest and imprisonment for striking a police constable at the Lyceum Theatre, there was laughter from many MPs.[8] Amongst these men, he was a hated figure.

In the House itself O'Connor's appearances had become excruciating. He would walk around the chamber offering his hand to other MPs, push and pull colleagues and sit in the seat of the Speaker.[9] Then, on 8 June 1852, as the MP for Marylebone, Sir Benjamin Hall, was calling on the House to divide, O'Connor turned round and struck him in the side. Hall, it should be noted, had taken a special interest in O'Connor. He had read Feargus' letters in the *Star* aloud in the House, and had become one of his principal parliamentary tormentors over the Land Company. A very vocal member of the Select Committee on the Company in summer 1848, he had continued to harry O'Connor on the subject. On one occasion, in March 1850, O'Connor had angrily defended himself when Hall presented petitions from allottees at Snigs End and Minster Lovell and asked repeated questions about his conduct and the winding up of the Company.[10] O'Connor's arrest took place the day after he had struck Hall. During a debate on the County Polls Bill, he gave T.S. Duncombe a blow in the side and then pushed his hand into the face of E.B. Denison, MP for the West Riding. If O'Connor's parliamentary career ended tragically, it had begun triumphantly - with his election campaign and return in Nottingham and, in his first session, with his firm and confident resistance to the passing of the Whig Irish Coercion Bill.

Invited by local Chartists, Feargus O'Connor arrived by train in Nottingham at dusk on Monday 26 July 1847 to contest the parliamentary election. Only a few years earlier the framework knitters and lace hands of Nottingham had made their town a Chartist stronghold. The largest meetings had drawn tens of thousands of working people, and, in 1842, Nottinghamshire had contributed 40,000 signatures to the National Petition.[11] The local leaders, George Harrison and James Sweet, unlike those in nearby Leicester, had been united in their support for O'Connor. 'Jimmy' Sweet was a barber, a bookseller and, in 1847, O'Connor's 'little general'.[12] He was to become O'Connor's main line of communication with Nottingham during his years in the House of Commons and he never afterwards abandoned either his leader or his Chartist principles: he visited Feargus at Tuke's asylum and, on Reform League platforms in the mid-1860s, declared himself 'a Chartist still'.[13] He died in 1879 and half a century later was still remembered in Nottingham as 'brave ... kindly and courteous'.[14]

Nottingham was represented by two Whigs. Thomas Gisborne had been elected in a by-election in 1843 as a supporter of the repeal of the Corn Laws. Though he declared himself in favour of the ballot and some extension of the franchise, his name was known mainly for opposition to the ten hours bill. Sir John Cam Hobhouse, MP since 1834, was one of the biggest beasts in the forest. He had achieved fame early in life as a travelling companion in Spain, Greece, and Italy of Byron and had begun his parliamentary career in 1820. He had joined Grey's administration in 1832 and, at the time of the 1847 election, was, as President of the Board of Control, responsible for India. Whatever radical views Hobhouse may once have espoused, he was now regarded 'by his colleagues ... (as) one of the most conservative members of the Cabinet'.[15] In Nottingham he was seen as a puffed-up politician; Feargus informed him, as the two stood on the hustings, that he was 'a scoundrel'.[16]

There was one other candidate in the Nottingham election of 1847. This was John Walter (1818-1894), who did not actually appear in the town. His father, John Walter (1776-1847), had been elected MP for Nottingham in a by-election in April 1841. The Tory proprietor of *The Times*, his opposition to the 1834 Poor Law had won him the support of the Chartists. Walter was defeated in the 1841 general election, but returned in another by-election in August 1842, when O'Connor and the Chartists intervened on the side of the middle class reformer, Joseph Sturge, and then was unseated again in 1843. In July 1847 he was on his deathbed, and his son allowed his name to go forward in the Tory interest.

Across the country in July 1847 there were Chartist candidates, including Julian Harney in Palmerston's seat, Tiverton, Thomas Clark in Sheffield, and Samuel Kydd in Greenwich. Mostly they withdrew after meeting their opponents 'teeth to teeth' on the hustings.[17] Only Feargus and Ernest Jones in Halifax proceeded to the poll. O'Connor had issued his election address in June. In the House of Commons, he declared, he would be the advocate of the six points and repeal of the Act of Union - and also of the appointment of a Minister of Agriculture. In his manifesto O'Connor also made clear that, at the end of each session, he would return to Nottingham and seek the support, in a public meeting, of both electors and non-electors. He had done this when he was MP for County Cork in 1833-5. It was, in his own constituency, an endorsement of the Chartist principles of universal male suffrage and annual elections. Each September after his election, O'Connor submitted himself for re-election in the market place at Nottingham - although another plan for him to be paid an annual salary of £600 came to nothing.[18]

O'Connor's victory in Nottingham was entirely unexpected; for the Tory *Nottingham Journal* the outcome appeared 'altogether like a dream'.[19] The Chartist had been expected to withdraw after the show of hands - and Hobhouse had expected Walter and Gisborne to be elected. 'O'Connor's people were astonished at his success,' Hobhouse noted in his diary, '& the shabby dissenters affected to be equally surprised and vexed. The bells of the Churches rang and bands of music paraded the town & stopt under my windows to shout and play "Johnny so long at the fair", "Oh dear what can the matter be ..."' (sic).[20] Soirees, suppers, tea parties and camp meetings were immediately organised in the Chartist localities; there was even a 'most crowded' meeting in Philadelphia in the United States to celebrate O'Connor's election.[21] Feargus' close friend, the wealthy stockbroker, Thomas Allsop, meanwhile provided him with the property qualification required to take up his seat.

At nomination day, Wednesday 28 July, in the Exchange Hall, O'Connor had demonstrated his considerable skills as a popular orator. In the highest of spirits, in front of his own people, his was a brilliant performance, 'the speech of the day ...,' 'a slasher ...'.[22] He had chastised the two Whig MPs and their 'soup kitchen government,'[23] and had caused considerable hilarity by reading 'Grateful Paddy,' a tough satirical poem of his own composition, in a pronounced Irish accent. 'I am,' Feargus had told his working class followers, 'no leveller ... I am your elevator'.[24] Hobhouse and Gisborne, for their part, had tried to emphasize their support for O'Connor's principles. 'I am ... for the Charter,'[25] Hobhouse had desperately declared; but he lost the show of hands and the next day came bottom of the poll:

> ' ... I'm out
> By Nottingham rudely rejected;
> My ears tingle still
> With the rabble's loud shout
> Proclaiming my rival elected ...
>
> I cannot sit still, for my seat I have lost;
> My foes meet my smiles with their mockings
> When I last put my foot (to my very great cost)
> In that borough so famous for stockings ... [26]

Hobhouse must have been glad to get out of Nottingham. In March 1848 he was returned for Harwich in a by-election; Gisborne put himself forward again in Nottingham in 1852, but died a few weeks before the contest.

There were several reasons for O'Connor's victory. He certainly benefited from Hobhouse's unpopularity; the former Whig MP, Lord Rancliffe, was amongst those who voted for him while other Whig electors did not use their votes.[27] Catholic electors also united in endorsing O'Connor.[28] The main feature of the election, however, was the support given to him by much of Walter's Tory vote - including John Bowley and T.R. Redgate, the two men who had proposed and seconded Walter. 'I am very pleased you returned Mr Walter,' Bowley told a Tory meeting, 'and I am no less pleased that you also returned Feargus O'Connor'.[29] Amongst the Chartist leaders who stood for election in 1847, Feargus was the only one who was successful. His national reputation and his own talents on the hustings undoubtedly contributed to his victory; had another member of the Chartist leadership stood in Nottingham, he probably would have been defeated.

Amongst the Nottingham Whigs shock soon turned to bitterness. 'Nottingham is disgraced by the choice she has made,' declared the writer of an open letter to O'Connor. 'But, sir, the day of retribution with you is at hand ...'[30] A petition was launched against O'Connor's return, but eventually abandoned.[31] The attack on O'Connor was led by Thomas Bailey, editor and owner of the *Nottingham Mercury* and author of some poems dedicated to Lord John Russell.[32] In his newspaper he denounced the Land Plan as a 'vulgar combination of autocratism, helotism and Irishism,'[33] but refused to accept O'Connor's challenge to meet him in public debate unless it was a ticketed meeting.[34] The local press was to remain unremittingly hostile to O'Connor and his Land Plan. He instigated and lost a libel action against Job Bradshaw, proprietor of the *Nottingham Journal*, in February 1850; when the local Chartists encountered Bradshaw they 'hissed him, hooted him and pelted him until he was obliged to take refuge in a shop'.[35]

During his first year in the House of Commons, O'Connor returned on several occasions to Nottingham. He was back in October 1847 to address a public meeting in reply to Bailey and, in November 1847 and April 1848, to attend celebrations to mark his election victory and the withdrawal of the petition against him.[36] He invited electors and non-electors to visit him in his hotel on these occasions, receiving, in October 1847, deputations from, amongst others, the lace trade, the National Association of United Trades, and the Manchester Unity of Oddfellows. But O'Connor did not look only to the people of Nottingham for approval of his efforts in the Commons. He declared that 'when I speak in the House of Commons I do not speak, as Feargus O'Connor only, I do not speak as the representative of Nottingham solely, but I speak as the mouthpiece of every industrious man in England, Ireland,

Scotland, and Wales'.[37] He emphasised that his support for, and from, the unenfranchised made him a different kind of MP, and he offered himself to them as their 'faithful friend and unpurchasable representative,' their 'independent and uncompromising representative'.[38]

In the Reform Parliament of 1833-5 O'Connor had sat as one of two MPs for County Cork, the largest county in Ireland. Though a member of the Irish party, he had several times found himself in opposition to Daniel O'Connell. In June 1833 he had led a revolt against O'Connell's refusal to move the repeal of the Act of Union. O'Connell had resented the actions of 'this interloper'; but there were to be other disagreements.[39] The inevitable breach between the two men had occurred in 1836 after O'Connor had left the Commons, but, in 1847-52, it meant that there was some bitterness between the Chartist leader and other members of the deceased O'Connell's family. In February 1848 the *Star* denounced Morgan John O'Connell, MP for Kerry, as 'the deadly enemy of Mr O'Connor' - for which Feargus had to apologize in the Commons.[40]

During his first period in the Commons O'Connor had been a relentless critic of the Whigs. He had censured them for their broken promises on reform, and had supported a reduction in taxation and Cobbett's determined resistance to the Poor Law Bill. When re-elected in 1847, the *Nation* warned that O'Connor would 'assuredly be a sharp thorn in the side of the Whigs'.[41] He began as he had begun in 1833 - with strenuous opposition to the Bill for the coercion of Ireland. Whilst one MP wailed about 'a war against property in Ireland' and the ultra-Tory, Colonel Sibthorp, called for a measure 'ten times more coercive,'[42] O'Connor declared that the Crime and Outrage (Ireland) Bill would give the authorities excessive and unconstitutional powers. During the second reading of the Bill, he read aloud from his legal texts, condemning the Whigs with the words of Beccaria, Blackstone, and, mischievously, Lord John Russell. When such reasoning was ignored, there was also the passion of the platform. Feargus spoke of 'English persecution,' of the 'piteous poverty' of the Irish peasantry and of 'the vicious principle on which was based the relationship between landlord and tenant in Ireland'.[43] He called for an end to 'the vicious principle': 'Give the tenantry perpetual tenures and corn rents ... until they did that, the Irish people would eternally be coming to the Government for assistance and the landlords for Coercion Bills'.[44] Days before the Bill went into its committee stage in December 1847, O'Connor introduced a Repeal motion. It was massively defeated - but O'Connor's vigorous opposition to the Whig Bill contrasted starkly with the votes of support of some members of the Irish party. In Dublin the Confederates were impressed. 'There is one Irishman in this House indeed who seems determined to give this Bill staunch resistance,' John Mitchel observed, 'and I honour him for it - I mean the hon. member for Nottingham, Mr Feargus O'Connor'.[45] O'Connor's efforts in the House in late 1847 were undoubtedly significant in creating an alliance between the Confederates and the Chartists.

Soon after the passing of the Coercion Bill, Russell and his cabinet decided that it was also necessary for Habeas Corpus to be suspended in Ireland. In July 1848 the Bill was rushed through the House. Russell was there to hear O'Connor's protests, and Peel's dismissal of 'this mock king of Munster'.[46] When, in February 1849, an extension of the suspension was put to the House, O'Connor was again on his feet. He maintained that the Whigs were relying 'entirely upon the subserviency of the House to destroy the last remnant of Irish liberty'.[47] Amidst loud cries of 'time,' he spoke for an hour-and-a-half when the measure received a third reading; Joseph Hume supported an extension of the suspension, John Bright abstained and only eleven MPs, including O'Connor, voted against.

Whenever Irish issues were raised in the Commons, there were usually interventions from O'Connor. The Whigs were committed to spending as little money as possible in Ireland; for O'Connor, Russell led 'an exterminating government'.[48] As for emigration, which was strongly encouraged by such Irish MPs as William Monsell, it reminded O'Connor 'of the practice adopted by some persons to get rid of an old dog - that of sending him out to get lost'.[49] Though he welcomed such measures as the Encumbered Estates Act (1849), which allowed bankrupt landlords to sell up, O'Connor never ceased to remind the Whigs that what was really needed was to give tenants fixity of tenure. 'What the people wanted,' he informed the Chief Secretary for Ireland, Sir William Somerville, 'was ... to work for themselves not other men ...'[50] Three decades later O'Connor's demand was to be incorporated in Gladstone's Irish land legislation.

On Ireland O'Connor followed his own course. He had intended, in other matters, to follow the lead of Duncombe, but the MP for Finsbury was not a particularly active parliamentarian. When he moved the second reading of a Mines and Collieries Bill in July 1849, it was the first time Duncombe had addressed the Commons in two years. After 1847, Miles Taylor has stated, the reform party in the Commons consisted of about 60 MPs. These were the MPs, including Hume, Lord Dudley Stuart, J.A. Roebuck and Thomas Wakley, who regularly voted against the Whigs on such issues as electoral and financial reform. Taylor has suggested that O'Connor 'hitched his fortunes to those of the reform party'.[51] Certainly there were numerous occasions when O'Connor spoke and voted in the same way as the radical reformers. He expressed support for retrenchment.[52] He voted for William Ewart's Bill in March 1848 for the abolition of capital punishment - though he did have some doubts. Believing that it was important not to 'render the lives of persons who are not murderers less secure,' he declared that he did not think the punishment should be totally done away with.[53] Similarly O'Connor voted for Hume's annual motions for a partial extension of the franchise, but, in 1848, this was anything but an amicable alliance. Feargus condemned those who 'upon his soul and conscience he believed only intended to use the people for their own purposes' - which provoked a sharp reply from Cobden.[54] Hume's motions secured the support of 80-90 MPs, far more than O'Connor's own motions for the whole Charter, in 1849 and 1850, ever managed. On the first occasion O'Connor introduced such a motion, there were barely enough MPs present to enable the debate to take place; Feargus 'without going so far as to say he would die on the floor of the House' promised his continued advocacy of the Charter, Russell responded with 'a direct negative' and 13 MPs registered their support.[55] O'Connor believed his was a solitary voice in the Commons which drew authority from the unenfranchised, and it is perhaps as well not to align him too closely with the reform party. Certainly most of these MPs voted in favour of the repressive measures taken in Ireland in 1848-9 and it was O'Connor, not Hume or Wakley, who offered the fiercest parliamentary resistance to the Crown and Government Security Bill which the Whigs rushed through both Houses of Parliament in April 1848. Russell and his cabinet sought to create the offence of treason-felony; it was under the provisions of this measure that those involved in the Orange Tree conspiracy in London were transported later in the year. Condemning the Bill as 'a disgrace to the Statute Book' and 'in reality a suspension of the Habeas Corpus Act,'[56] O'Connor refused to allow it an unopposed first reading and, at the beginning of the second reading, proposed that it should be put off for six months; when this was rejected, he argued that the measure should lapse as soon as Russell ceased to be Prime Minister. 'Let it become law,' O'Connor declared in one of several ardent speeches, 'and he would traverse the country, morning, noon and night, and his constant cry would be "Down with the base, bloody, and brutal Whigs"'.[57] O'Connor was to prove to be as good as his word.

The Whigs introduced their Bill only a few days before the presentation of the third Chartist petition. Feargus, in the first half of April 1848, was under immense pressure. In the Commons he faced unremitting hostility and subsequently ridicule. The cabinet, on Thursday, 6 April, decided to prohibit the planned procession from Kennington Common to the House of Commons. They derived their authority for this step from a seventeenth century statute which stated that only ten persons could accompany a petition to Parliament. Russell declared that the Chartist procession was intended to 'overawe' MPs.[58] This O'Connor denied. It would, he informed MPs, be peaceable and, in addition, was 'a constitutional right ... he had precedents for it both before and after the era of the Reform Bill'.[59] The same day Feargus introduced a motion for the pardon of all Chartist prisoners, including Frost, Williams and Jones. 'Since this trial we have had a royal marriage, we have had many royal births,' he commented, 'but, instead of taking the opportunity of pardoning political offenders, the hulks and the gaols were searched and pickpockets and thieves were let loose, and to them the royal clemency was extended'.[60] When the motion was rejected, O'Connor recognized immediately that there would be no concessions or negotiations from Russell and the Whigs. Despite this he did not immediately climb down. The next day, Friday, 7 April, O'Connor again argued in the Commons that the demonstrators should be allowed to cross the river. 'My intention is to attend this meeting,' he stated. 'My intention is to come, in the procession, not to the House of Commons but over Westminster Bridge with that petition ...'.[61] It did not happen; by the morning of Monday, 10 April, O'Connor had decided on the abandonment of the proposed procession.

The petition delivered to the House of Commons on four rolls in the afternoon of 10 April became the responsibility of the Select Committee on Public Petitions. The Committee ordered the petition to be examined and, at midday on Wednesday, 12 April, O'Connor was informed by a member of the cabinet that thirteen clerks, working over a period of seventeen hours in one of the committee rooms, had calculated that the number of genuine signatures amounted to 1.9 million. When this information was revealed to the Commons the next day, O'Connor, amidst 'a brutal howl,' maintained that the figure was considerably greater and expressed his scepticism that such a small body of clerks in such a limited period of time could have examined the petition with such precision.[62] At this point one of the members of the Committee, the Peelite MP for Cirencester, William Cripps, launched a vitriolic personal attack on O'Connor; he would, he declared, 'never believe the hon. member again'.[63] O'Connor managed to reply calmly, but then, in great anger, left the chamber. Amongst MPs it was soon rumoured that Feargus intended fighting a duel with Cripps, but nothing so dramatic actually happened. O'Connor was briefly arrested for failing to obey an order from the Speaker to return to the chamber, and Cripps apologized. One month later Cripps was dead, struck down by 'an attack of brain fever'.[64]

April 1848 was the most testing period of O'Connor's Chartist leadership. He came through it, both in the House of Commons and outside, more creditably than has been allowed. The Kennington Common demonstration was not a 'fiasco,' and equally O'Connor was not a frightened blusterer. When he shook hands with the Police Commissioner, Richard Mayne, on 10 April or, in the lobby of the Commons that evening, expressed his relief that there had been no bloodshed, these were the actions and words of a concerned, not a frightened, man. O'Connor was concerned to avoid a violent confrontation between the soldiers and the Chartists. He knew that, in such an event, it would be the demonstrators and not the soldiers who would be killed or wounded. In the Commons, in the days after the demonstration, O'Connor, in the face of much derision and animosity, remained resolute in his support for the Charter and the petition. He withdrew his motion for the petition to be discussed - but persisted in his dubitations about the speed of the work of the clerks and the number of signatures they claimed to have counted. His scepticism was surely shared by the thousands of working people across the country who had collected signatures for the great petition of 1848.

In the *Northern Star* Feargus O'Connor's speeches at public meetings were very fully reported. The official reports of his parliamentary speeches, however, are not so comprehensive. Moreover, it is not always apparent in *Hansard* how many MPs were listening to a debate, or what their reactions were. It has nevertheless been possible to construct a narrative of O'Connor's parliamentary career, and to suggest that he established himself as a conspicuous figure of dissent.[65] O'Connor sat on the opposition benches, unlike John O'Connell and a number of other Irish MPs who sat with the Whigs. In 1849 he sometimes sat on the opposition front bench close to Peel and Disraeli;[66] later on he seems to have sat next to Duncombe, who, after 1850, was more frequently in the House. In the Commons O'Connor mostly operated alone. Roebuck made plain his animosity, and William Ewart referred to O'Connor 'as one of the most notorious fabulists that ever existed. So says everyone who knows him in the House of Commons'.[67] In his last years as an MP, O'Connor was mostly concerned with introducing a Bill to wind up the Land Company - but, in 1847-8, he had demonstrated his defiance and courage. MPs heard exactly what the Chartists hoped they would hear - passionate advocacy of the cause of Ireland and unflagging denunciations of the restringent legislation of the Whigs. 'Was it not something,' he declared in March 1848, 'for him to be able to defend John Mitchel in the House of Commons?'[68] O'Connor did not succumb to the attractions and allurements of House of Commons life. He did not move away from championing the People's Charter, and he did not make himself a 'respectable' radical. 'Mr Feargus O'Connor, baited on all sides,' the *Nation* noted after one debate, 'exclaimed "the People's Charter and no surrender" - just as Barnaby Rudge's raven, perched on a tombstone, croaked "never say die"'.[69]

Nottingham did not elect another Chartist MP. The people's candidate in 1852, the barrister, Charles Sturgeon, was overwhelmingly rejected, and Ernest Jones' two election campaigns at the end of the 1850s also ended in defeat.[70] Nottingham was soon again a Whig town. But, in 1859, a proposal for a statue of O'Connor was discussed by the town council. The Chartist's old opponents of 1847 were enraged:

> 'Has Sherwood's new member nought better to say,
> That because poor O'Connor in Kensal Green lay,
> That Nottingham workmen, altho' he did cheat 'em,
> Should erect a stone in their own Arboretum? ...
> So retrace your false step and let commonsense reign,
> And wipe from your records this damnable stain;
> Or perhaps the next time you wiseacres meet,
> You'll vote for a statue to one Jimmy Sweet.'[71]

The statue was erected. O'Connor's supporters declared that it 'would be appreciated by the respectable and intelligent portion of the inhabitants of this town and neighbourhood and add to the embellishment of the Arboretum as well as the encouragement of the fine arts ...' .[72] With his left hand across his chest and the People's Charter held firmly in his right, Feargus still gazes across a park in the centre of Nottingham.

NOTES

I would like to thank Paul Pickering, Miles Taylor and Dorothy Thompson for their help and encouragement during the writing of this chapter.

[1] J.T. Ward, *Chartism,* London, B.T Batsford, 1973; R.G. Gammage, *History of the Chartist Movement,* London, 1855; William Lovett, *Life and Struggles,* London, 1876.
[2] Joel Wiener, *William Lovett,* Manchester, Manchester University Press, 1989.

[3] James Epstein, *The Lion of Freedom, Feargus O'Connor and the Chartist Movement 1832-1842*, London, Croom Helm, 1982; Dorothy Thompson, *The Chartists*, London, Temple Smith, 1984.

[4] *The Times*, 10 June 1852; *Leader*, 12 June 1852; *Hansard*, CXXII (9 June 1852), 367-74, (10 June 1852), 417, (14 June 1852), 611, (16 June 1852), 816.

[5] For a detailed description of O'Connor's mental collapse see Laurence M. Geary, 'O'Connorite Bedlam: Feargus and his Grand-Nephew, Arthur,' *Medical History*, Vol. 34, No.2, April 1990, pp. 125-143; for O'Connor's funeral, attended by 40,000 people, see *The Times*, 11 September 1855.

[6] *Northern Star* (NS), 29 November 1851. Also see *Ibid.*, 4 October, 18 October, 1 November, 15 November 1851; attempts were made by middle class reformers to prevent O'Connor attending or speaking at meetings organised to welcome Lajos Kossuth to England.

[7] *The Times*, 27 April, 28 April, 26 May 1852, for reports concerning O'Connor's short visit to America.

[8] *Hansard*, CXIX (9 February 1852), 252; *NS*, 14 February 1852.

[9] *The Times*, 4 June 1852; *Nottingham Journal* (NJ), 11 June 1852.

[10] *Hansard*, CIX (1 March 1850), 234-9. Also see *Ibid.*, XCVIII (10 April 1848), 89-91, (12 May 1848), 927-8, CX (18 April 1850), 495-6, CXXII (8 June 1852), 273-4. Hall was a very active parliamentarian; Big Ben was named after him.

[11] See James Epstein, 'Some Organisational and Cultural Aspects of the Chartist Movement in Nottingham,' in James Epstein and Dorothy Thompson (eds) *The Chartist Experience. Studies in Working Class Radicalism and Culture, 1830-1860* , London, Macmillan, 1982, pp. 221-268.

[12] *NS*, 7 August 1847.

[13] John Rowley, 'James Sweet' in Joyce M. Bellamy and John Saville (eds), *Dictionary of Labour Biography, Vol.4*, London, Macmillan, 1977, p. 172. Another prominent supporter of O'Connor in 1847 was William Linwood, Unitarian minister in Mansfield and editor of the *Nottingham Review*.

[14] *NJ*, 24 January 1934; *Ibid.*, 5 March 1934, for a reference to 'Mopstail' Jack Sylvester, a baker and radical colleague of Sweet's.

[15] *Edinburgh Review*, CXXXIII, p. 337, review of Hobhouse's *Recollections of a Long Life* (1865). Hobhouse's radical credentials were made clear by the 1831 Act he initiated which lowered the municipal franchise.

[16] *Nottingham Mercury* (NM), 13 August 1847.

[17] A.R. Schoyen, *The Chartist Challenge. A Portrait of George Julian Harney*, London, Heinemann, 1958, p. 150.

[18] See *NS*, 23 September 1848, 1 September 1849, 7 September 1850. These meetings were well attended; on each occasion O'Connor answered questions e.g. on his admiration for Palmerston and was overwhelmingly supported in shows of hands. Also see *Ibid.*, 7 August 1847: the annual salary was to be paid by constituencies across the country in return for reports of proceedings in the House

of Commons produced by staff employed by O'Connor; *Ibid*, 5 June 1847, for
O'Connor's election address.
[19]
Quoted in A.C. Wood 'Nottingham Electoral History 1832-1861,' *Transactions
of the Thoroton Society of Nottingham*, Vol. LIX, 1955, pp. 65-83. Also see J.V.
Beckett, 'Parliament and the Localities: The Borough of Nottingham,'
Parliamentary History, 1998, pp. 58-67.
[20]
Hobhouse, Diary entry, 27 July 1847, Broughton Papers, British Library Add.
MS 43, 751, p.3
[21]
NS, 21 October 1847. The meeting was chaired by a native-born American,
Robert Taylor.
[22]
Nottingham Review (NR), 30 July 1847; *NS*, 31 July 1847.
[23]
Ibid.
[24]
Ibid.
[25]
NM, 30 July 1847.
[26]
From the Satirist, reptd. *NS*, 21 August 1847.
[27]
Thrice-elected MP for Nottingham (in 1812,1818 and 1826), Lord Rancliffe
(1785-1850) of Bunny Hall did not agree with Whig support for repeal of the Corn
Laws; see J.B. Firth, *Highways and Byways in Nottinghamshire*, 1916, pp. 72-5.
[28]
NS, 14 August 1847.
[29]
NJ, 13 August 1847.
[30]
NM, 5 November 1847.
[31]
See *Ibid.*, 3 March, 28 April 1848; *NS*, 29 January, 19 February, 4 March 1848.
[32]
Thomas Bailey (1785-1856) became wealthy as a wine and hop merchant. He
dedicated *Ireton* (1827) to Lord John Russell and, though elected to the town
council (1836-43), his main ambition seems to have been to become MP for
Nottingham; see William Wylie, *Old and New Nottingham*, London, Brown,
Green & Longmans, 1853, pp. 187-91.
[33]
NM, 17 September 1847. The paper launched a sustained attack on O'Connor
and the Land Plan throughout September, October and November 1847.
[34]
See *Ibid.*, 29 October 1847; *NR*, 12 November 1847.
[35]
NS, 7 September 1850; also see *Ibid.*, 23 February, 30 November 1850.
[36]
NR, 29 October, 12 November 1847; *NS*, 6 November, 20 November 1847, 29
April 1848, 17 February 1849.
[37]
Ibid., 20 November 1847.
[38]
Ibid., 19 February 1848, 7 September 1850.
[39]
Oliver MacDonagh, *O'Connell. The Life of Daniel O'Connell 1775-1847*,
London, Weidenfield and Nicolson, 1991 edn., p. 378; Epstein, *The Lion of
Freedom*, pp. 14-15. Also see Anon., *Random Recollections of the House of
Commons from the year 1830 to the close of 1835*, London, Smith, Elder & Co,
1836, pp.322-4

[40] *NS*, 26 February, 4 March 1848; *Hansard*, XCVI (28 February 1848), 1389-92. The offending words had been written by O'Connor himself.

[41] Quoted in *NS*, 14 August 1847.

[42] *Hansard*, XCV (23 November 1847), 138, (11 December 1847), 962.

[43] *Ibid.*, XCV (6 December 1847), 733, 731.

[44] *Ibid.*, XCV (23 November 1847), 142.

[45] Quoted in Takashi Koseki, *Patrick O'Higgins and Irish Chartism*, Tokyo, Hosei University Ireland-Japan Papers, No. 2, 1990, p. 19.

[46] *Hansard*, C (22 July 1848), 718.

[47] *Ibid.*, CII (6 February 1849), 333.

[48] *Ibid.*, XCVII (24 March 1848), 1011.

[49] *Ibid.*, CV (15 May 1849), 528.

[50] *Ibid.*, XCVI (15 February 1848), 697.

[51] Miles Taylor, *The Decline of British Radicalism 1847-1860*, Oxford, Clarendon Press, 1995, p. 110. Also see David Nicholls 'Friends of the People: Parliamentary Supporters of Popular Radicalism,' *Labour History Review*, Vol. 62, No 2, 1997, pp. 127-146. For a series of motions O'Connor planned to introduce into the House of Commons see *NS*, 9 September 1848.

[52] *Hansard*, XCVI (25 February 1848), 1365.

[53] *Ibid.*, XCVII (14 March 1848), 584.

[54] *Ibid.*, XCVIII (23 May 1848), 1309-11. Also see *Ibid.*, CIV (5 June 1849), 1181-4; CIX (28 February 1850), 171-3.

[55] *Ibid.*, CVI (3 July 1849), 1276-7, 1302; also see *Ibid.*, CXII (11 July 1850), 1282-4; *NS*, 4 January 1851.

[56] *Hansard*, XCVIII (7 April 1848), 229, (12 April 1848), 375.

[57] *Ibid.*, XCVIII (14 April 1848), 377.

[58] *Ibid.*, XCVIII (7 April 1848), 19.

[59] *Ibid.*, XCVII (6 April 1848), 1355.

[60] *Ibid.*, XCVII (6 April 1848), 1371. Also see *Ibid.*, CIII (22 March 1849), 1121 and CVI (12 June 1849), 50 for O'Connor's questions about the prison conditions of the Chartists, John Shaw and Ernest Jones.

[61] *Ibid.*, XCVIII (7 April 1848), 12.

[62] *NS*, 15 April 1848.

[63] *Hansard*, XCVIII (13 April 1848), 291. Disraeli expressed his dismay at Cripps' words: *Ibid.*, (13 April 1848), 295-6.

[64] *The Times*, 12 May 1848. For Cripps see *Wiltshire and Gloucestershire Standard*, 22 May 1848, 15 June 1889.

[65] For views of O'Connor's parliamentary career see Samuel Kydd, *History of the Factory Movement*, London, Simpkin, Marshall & Co., 1857, p. 131; Henry

Weisser, *April 10: Challenge and Response in England*, Lanham, University Press of America, 1983, pp. 285-6; Roland Quinault, '1848 and Parliamentary Reform,' *The Historical Journal*, Vol. 31, No. 4, 1988, p. 837.

[66] See John Vincent (ed.) *Disraeli, Derby and the Conservative Party. Journals and Memoirs of Edward Henry, Lord Stanley, 1849-1869*, Hassocks, The Harvester Press, 1978, p. 2.

[67] *Hansard* CXVII (30 May 1851), 261; Ewart Papers, Jedburgh, Scotland, William Ewart to Charlotte Rutson, 26 April 1848: I have not been able to obtain the address of the copyright holder of this letter, and would be grateful for any information.

[68] *Manchester Examiner*, 18 March 1848.

[69] *Nation*, 9 March 1850.

[70] Sturgeon (512 votes) was bottom of the poll, as was Jones in 1857 (614 votes) and in 1859 (151 votes).

[71] University of Nottingham, Department of Manuscripts and Special Collections, *The O'Connor Monument*, Nottingham, 1859, pp. 2-4.

[72] *Records of the Borough of Nottingham*, IX, pp. 135-6. Also see fascinating note in *Yorkshire Gazette*, 26 April 1851: 'A man named Haigh, living at Illingworth, near Halifax, was found dead in bed on Wednesday last. By his will he has left £2000, all the savings of a long and laborious life, to the hon. Member for Nottingham'.

'REPEAL AND THE SUFFRAGE': FEARGUS O'CONNOR'S IRISH 'MISSION,' 1849-50.[1]

Paul A. Pickering

During his seven years in prison for his part in the 1867 rising, Michael Davitt, the secretary of the Irish Republican Brotherhood and later a leading figure in the Irish land war, recorded great surprise in his prison journal that a fellow prisoner, an old English worker, held 'extremely liberal views on England's rule of Ireland'. Davitt went on to suggest to the old prisoner 'that very few more advocates of separation would be found among his countrymen'.[2] For his trouble Davitt got a history lecture. The old worker had been a Chartist. He told Davitt of a 'democratic Yorkshire' where the walls of many hundreds of houses displayed a portrait of Robert Emmet - probably the one given away with the *Regenerator and Chartist Circular* in 1839. To prove his sympathy for the Irish cause he offered to recite the whole of Emmet's oration from the dock at his trial for treason in 1803. Despite Davitt's incredulity, the old prisoner's performance would not have been unusual. Chartists in cities and towns all over England had staged the 'Trial of Robert Emmet' as an inspirational play, and well before Davitt's incarceration the transcript of Emmet's trial had gone through at least a dozen popular editions in England.[3] Davitt was later to name his youngest child after the hero of the United Irishmen, but he was not alone. During the 1840s birth notices in the *Northern Star* regularly told of new generations of eponymous Robert Emmets running around the Pennine moors.[4]

The old Chartist prisoner might also have told Davitt that in November 1838 one hundred and ten Radical Associations in England and Scotland had put their names to an Address to the Irish People which identified '*exclusive legislation*' as the 'same curse which plunders, oppresses, and blights the happiness of both countries...*whether Parliament meet in London or Dublin,*' and offered them a union in the struggle against it.[5] He might have pointed out that the 1842 National Petition, which had been signed by millions of working people in England, called for the repeal of the Union as well as the implementation of the Charter.[6] If he was old enough the Chartist prisoner might even have explained that 'Orator' Henry Hunt's post-war campaigns had been for '*universal* political and religious liberty,' and had, at their basis, a belief in the unity of the cause of the 'radical reformers, male and female,' of 'England, Scotland and Ireland'.[7] Instead the old Chartist concluded his lecture by 'boasting' of his conversations with Feargus O'Connor, the most popular leader of the Chartists, who was himself an Irishman. Davitt can be forgiven for his ignorance. He had grown up in Lancashire at a time when, as Marx wrote in 1870, 'all the large industrial centres of England' were 'divided...into two hostile camps' as a result of the 'profound antagonism between the English proletarian and the Irish proletarian'. Although the tenor of community relations differed from place to place, tension was undoubtedly higher following the corrosive effects of large scale post-Famine immigration and the emergence of Fenianism on the one hand and popular Toryism on the other.[8]

The question of the relationship between Ireland and the Chartists remains controversial. There is an ongoing debate among historians about the role of the immigrant Irish in the Chartist movement - a question which one commentator has described as one of the most important to confront historians of nineteenth century English radical politics.[9] Some aspects of the debate have received more attention than others. While there has been important work addressing the situation in England, comparatively little has been written about the Chartists' attempts to establish their movement in Ireland. The chapter which follows is offered as a contribution to the broad debate, and as an attempt to go some way towards supplying this gap. Focusing on the period regarded by historians as late Chartism, it will explore Feargus O'Connor's Irish 'mission' - as it was later called[10] - which involved separate trips to Dublin in 1849 and 1850.

During the first of these visits, in November 1849, O'Connor sought to regain the place among the leaders of Irish nationalism that he had foregone fifteen years before. In 1835, having quarrelled with Daniel O'Connell, then at the height of his domination of the Irish political landscape, and lost his Irish seat in the House of Commons on the grounds that he lacked sufficient property qualification, O'Connor moved to London where he subsequently established himself as the most popular leader of the Chartists' campaign for democratic reform of the British political system. On his return to Dublin O'Connor sought to convince an aggregate meeting of nationalists that their best prospect for success lay in joining this campaign. By this time, however, the Chartism that he offered as the basis of an alliance was a pale imitation of the movement that he had led in the early 1840s. Gone were the halcyon days when he had convinced a generation of British working people, through his countless public speeches and the columns of his newspaper, the *Northern Star*, that he could lead them to a better world. The mass movement of the early 1840s had dwindled into a rump of committed activists, the sales of the once great *Northern Star* were in free fall, and a new generation of leaders with new ideas were causing division and acrimony in the diminishing ranks. After 1845 O'Connor had devoted his energy to the promotion of the Chartist Land Plan, but by the time of his Irish 'mission' this scheme to resettle urban workers on small farms was facing serious legal and financial difficulties. O'Connor had finally regained a seat in the House of Commons, winning Nottingham in 1847, but his broader audience were increasingly no longer listening.

Returning to Ireland represented going back to his roots and the chance for a new beginning. The thunderous applause O'Connor received from the audience in Dublin's Music Hall must have reminded him of better days, but his appeal to the conference failed. Subsequently O'Connor threw his weight behind a rival organisation, the Irish Democratic Association, attending its inaugural conference during a second trip to Dublin four months later in March 1850. By doing so he joined an organisation that had more significance than has been allowed by historians. The IDA is not mentioned in any of the general histories of Chartism, nor in the only study devoted to the movement's decline. According to Rachel O'Higgins, the historian who has written most extensively about Chartism in Ireland, the 'comparatively ineffectual' agitation for the Charter there was brought to a close in 1848. Despite a passionate plea for a reappraisal of Irish Chartism, Takashi Koseki also concludes that 'after 1848 Irish Chartism was never revived any more'.[11] Where it has been noticed, the IDA has been dismissed. For O'Connor's biographers, Donald Read and Eric Glasgow, the influence of the IDA was 'slight'; and John Boyle, the most recent historian of the Irish Labour movement, declares that the IDA is 'difficult to take seriously'.[12] Admittedly, the IDA too ended in failure, but the terms of its collapse provide important signposts to later developments in Irish politics and warn against what L.M. Cullen has called a 'simple episodic view of

Irish political history'.[13] It deserves to be taken seriously. Rescuing O'Connor's Irish 'mission' enhances our understanding of his contribution to Anglo-Irish politics, adds a new page to the neglected history of Irish Chartism, and sheds new light on Irish nationalism at a time of transition.

Late in 1849 a requisition was widely circulated in Ireland convening an 'aggregate meeting of nationalists' to be held in the Music Hall, Dublin on 21 November. The requisition was supported by a large number of prominent individuals including, so the *Nation* boasted to its readers, '[f]orty landed proprietors, Baronets, Magistrates or substantial county gentlemen, upwards of 100 Catholic Clergymen, including several ecclesiastical dignitaries; ninety Merchants, shop-owners, Aldermen, Town Councillors, Poor Law Guardians... fifty professional gentlemen, barristers, solicitors, doctors and engineers; and a mass of...substantial shopkeepers'. The conclusion to the editorial - 'And behind, the PEOPLE' - made them appear to be an afterthought, a point that was not lost when it reached the Chartist *Northern Star* which described support for the Conference as emanating from the 'great bulk of the middle class'.[14] The principal promoter of the meeting was Charles Gavan Duffy. As a co-founder of the *Nation*, the journal of the Young Ireland movement, Duffy had helped to cause the split with O'Connell during the mid-1840s that culminated in the formation of an Irish Confederation to rival his Repeal Association in 1847. Duffy's initiative came at a time when the ranks of the Irish nationalists were in a parlous state. By 1849 he was the only leading Young Irelander still active in politics. The others were either dead, in self-imposed exile, or undergoing imprisonment or transportation for their part in the desperate uprising of July 1848 which had taken place in the aftermath of the unprecedented national tragedy of the Famine. Early in 1848 the Council of the Confederation had itself been badly divided, culminating in the secession of John Mitchel on 7 February. 'Old Ireland,' in the form of O'Connell's Repeal Association, had fared no better than the Young Irelanders. Following O'Connell's death in 1847, the Association, under the leadership of his uninspiring son, John, had declined sharply in terms of numbers and influence. After the revival of the Association in October 1849, the word most often used to describe attendance at its meetings in Conciliation Hall was 'miserable'.[15] Efforts were made to reunite the fissiparous factions of repealers and nationalists in a new organisation, the Irish League, but these were close to breaking down over the vexed questions of constitutionalism and the right to bear arms when the shots that were fired in Ballingarry brought them to a precipitate close.[16]

Duffy's objective in calling the conference was twofold. First, he sought to launch a new organisation, called the Irish Alliance, that would effect the reconciliation that had eluded the Irish League. As a moderate among the Confederates, however, Duffy left no doubt that his initiative was not a revolutionary enterprise by reverting to strategy that had characterised Daniel O'Connell's repeal campaign: the 'concentration of public opinion' and the 'exercise of...moral, social and political influence'. Duffy's second objective in calling the conference was to provide a national platform for an agitation on the issue of 'the land'. Foreshadowing the now famous Tenant Rights Conference in August 1850, Duffy called for the formation of 'tenant right associations from sea to sea'.[17] Recognising that high rents and evictions were the most immediate and burning grievances of the rural peasantry, Duffy's proposal, which would, in various forms, help to shape the relations between Irish nationalists and British governments until the Wyndham Act of 1903, was a legislative solution - the codification of the rights of Irish tenants in a law passed by the British Parliament.[18]

By calling an aggregate meeting of Irish nationalists, however, Duffy got more than he bargained for; he got Feargus O'Connor. O'Connor's visit to Dublin in 1849 was by no means the first attempt to establish a Chartist movement across the Irish Sea. As early as 1839 the Chartist Convention had sent Robert Lowery to Dublin, but his attempts to explain the benefits of Chartism to Ireland had ended in riot. O'Connor himself visited Ireland in October 1839, ostensibly for business reasons, but his efforts at setting up a radical association in Cork while he was there proved fruitless.[19] Nonetheless, by 1842 there were Chartist cells operating in several Irish towns and a coordinating body, the Irish Universal Suffrage Association, had been established in Dublin. At a time when O'Connell was boasting at Conciliation Hall that finding an Irish Chartist was like looking 'for a needle in a bundle of straw,' membership of the Dublin group had climbed to approximately one thousand - no insignificant number - and Chartist petitions were collected in various places: Dublin (3000),

Belfast (2200), County Limerick (927), Waterford (3730), and County Clare (504).[20] The Irish Universal Suffrage Association, however, could never lay claim to being the vanguard of a mass movement; they distributed pamphlets and held weekly discussions, but they did not hold the large public meetings or parades that characterised Chartism on the other side of St. George's Channel.[21]

Following a hiatus between 1844 and 1846, Irish Chartism was spectacularly revived in 1847-8, culminating in an alliance with the radical wing of the Confederates.[22] O'Connor had laid the foundation for the alliance (and his later 'mission') by his opposition to an Irish Coercion Bill in the House of Commons during 1847. While the remnants of O'Connell's 'tail' of Irish MPs sat mute (or voted for the Bill), O'Connor condemned it as 'disgracefully tyrannical' and opposed it at every stage, earning him praise from John Mitchel as Ireland's only determined representative.[23] Subsequently, Mitchel used the columns of his newspaper, the *United Irishman*, to broadcast the message that O'Connor, in the face of O'Connell's denunciations, had struggled for years to convey to the Irish people. 'Every Chartist is a *Repealer*,' Mitchel told his readers, 'In all there is nothing for which we should hate the Chartists. Hate them! why they are our brethren and allies: we are bound to help them to their ends, as they offer to help us to ours.'[24]

From the outset efforts to establish Chartism in Ireland had been strongly supported by the British Chartists. In Lancashire during the early 1840s, for example, the Chartists had a standing committee devoted to the extension of Chartism in Ireland. Many local branches collected back issues of the *Northern Star* to send to Ireland for distribution and by July 1842 the Glasgow Chartists had collected 1600 *Chartist Circulars* and 1000 *Northern Stars* 'besides a number of other democratic journals to send to Dublin'. Despite being technically one of the authors of the Charter and endorsing Joseph Sturge's Complete Suffrage Union in 1842, O'Connell's hostility to O'Connor kept many Irish immigrants out of the ranks of Chartism. In the Manchester district, for example, the feud between O'Connor and O'Connell precipitated a deep division within the immigrant community. Paradoxically, the growing splits in the ranks of the nationalists in Ireland during the 1840s had a unifying effect on the immigrant community. The Chartists' critique of O'Connellism as a system of 'get-what-you-can,' 'bit-by-bit' reform anticipated many of the complaints of the Young Irelanders. After the formation of the Irish Confederation a network of Confederate Clubs was set up in England that provided a meeting place for Chartists and former O'Connellites. In Manchester the leading Confederates included a seventy year old Chartist named John Murray, a 'hero of 1798' who had fled Ireland after Emmet's rising of 1803, and George Archdeacon, an immigrant labourer who had been expelled from the Repeal Association for refusing to renounce violence before going on to edit a Chartist newspaper, the *English Patriot and Irish Repealer*, and regard O'Connor as his leader.[25] By July 1848 reports in the press indicated that there were numerous Clubs in the Manchester region involving anything up to 20,000 members, who were unanimously offering to support the proposal for an Irish League intended to unify nationalists in Ireland.[26]

The basis of the alliance between the Chartists and the Confederates was the ultra-democratic tradition of the United Irishmen and United Englishmen. As the title of his newspaper, the *United Irishman*, indicated, Mitchel's appeal was to the spirit of 1798. Despite his later pretensions to Irish royal ancestry, O'Connor also appealed to the struggles of the 1790s. This is not to suggest that O'Connor was a Paineite or a Jacobin, but he was well placed to claim a place in the ranks of Irish nationalists on the basis of that tradition. As rebellion spread through many of the capital cities of Europe following the abdication of Louis Philippe in February, O'Connor shared a Manchester platform with leading Confederates, Thomas Meagher and Michael Doheny, to celebrate the formal inauguration of the alliance on St. Patrick's Day in March 1848. Speaking in both the English and Irish languages, O'Connor invoked the memory of Emmet, Fitzgerald, and his own uncle, Arthur O'Connor.[27] Although part of the Protestant ascendancy, his father, Roger, and his uncle, Arthur, dabbled with rationalism and republicanism and, during the late 1790s, both were prominent members of the United Irishmen, suffering imprisonment for their commitment to the cause of Irish national independence. Arthur O'Connor spent the last fifty years of his life in exile in France, where he married the daughter of the revolutionary *philosophe*, Condorcet, and became a general in Bonaparte's army.[28] Feargus O'Connor revelled in his heritage; he borrowed the title of his Chartist newspaper, the *Northern Star*, from a journal of the United Irishmen, and before English audiences he referred to himself as: 'one of a persecuted family and an outlawed race'.[29] In the year of revolutions, he was also keen to establish his revolutionary credentials. Although his early career is shrouded in mystery and tinged with the unreliability of memoirs, in 1848 O'Connor claimed to have been deeply involved in the violent rural opposition to tithes undertaken by the notorious 'Whiteboys' a quarter of a century earlier in 1822. Later he boasted that he led a section of the Cork peasantry in two pitched battles with the military, where he was allegedly shot in the leg and subsequently spent 13 months in hiding.[30]

Unfortunately for O'Connor, by 1849 many of his new Irish allies were in hiding, prison, or Van Diemen's Land. He was back to square one. Free of Mitchel's violent counsel and attempting to forge a new direction, the last thing Gavan Duffy wanted to do was embrace Arthur O'Connor's nephew. In response to O'Connor's announcement that he intended to attend the conference, Duffy's *Nation* condemned the 'threatened interruption': 'alliances and friendships must be spontaneous and voluntary; the affection or confidence of a people can not be carried by rape'.[31] Undeterred, O'Connor explained that the principal object of his mission was 'to announce the fact that at length it has been discovered that the cause of the working Celt and the working Saxon must be fought by the workers of both countries'.[32] During the conference O'Connor needed little encouragement from supporters among the crowd to hijack the proceedings and address the meeting. His speech was a classic statement of the Chartist belief that political action provided the means to achieve social objectives. '[T]he question is not simply the land,' he told the delegates, 'the question is, how you are to get your land'. He had 'devoted much...time to social reform,' he continued, including the Chartists' own Land Plan, 'but I tell you...you may look upon everything else that is proposed to you as mere moonshine, until your order is fully and fairly represented in the House of Commons'.[33] Throughout the 1840s O'Connor had made it clear that 'Repeal and the Suffrage must go hand in hand'. By itself, Repeal of the Union would merely give Ireland a 'House of Landlords sitting in College Green'; only the Charter could ensure that Repeal was followed by 'every measure of justice'.[34] O'Connor's appeal was not to the town councillors, professionals and merchants who made up the bulk of those who signed the requisition, but to the ordinary delegates and the spectators in the hall. He pleaded for an understanding that the working people of England were 'as much oppressed and trampled on by the aristocracy as you are...' Despite a promise to say nothing divisive, O'Connor could not resist an attack on John O'Connell and the other 'lick-spittles' that represented Ireland in the House of Commons, explaining that they must be replaced by the 'labouring man with the fustian jacket, the tanned trousers and the brawny hands'. In a country where nationalist - and religious - aspirations often cut across class lines, this was an explicit call for a class based alliance with the English working class.[35]

O'Connor concluded his speech by stating that it was the strategy of their 'enemies' to excite division between 'working Saxon and Celt' and he emphasised the support of the Chartist population with the fanciful boast that he could get 3,000,000 English signatures on a petition for repeal. The press in both England and Ireland reported that the speech had been greeted with 'tremendous cheering' from the audience, and O'Connor claimed that he had taken part in bringing about a 'union of the working class of England and Ireland'.[36] Within weeks, however, it was clear that the conference had failed to produce a structure for cooperation and the promise of the Irish Alliance remained unfulfilled. The first reason for the failure of the Alliance had nothing to do with O'Connor; it was because Duffy had not secured the support of the O'Connellites before launching his initiative. Under intense pressure from the nationalist press outside Dublin,[37] he and other former Confederates, such as his lieutenant, Maurice Leyne,[38] continued to negotiate with the remnants of the Conciliation Hall Repeal party after the Conference, but without success. For others the problem was Duffy. Their objection was not so much to Duffy's polices, but to his friends. Prior to O'Connor's speech at the conference, Duffy had indicated that one of the objectives of the Alliance would be an extension of the suffrage. In this respect, he told the delegates 'the hopes of the Irish people' lay with a 'powerful association formed by Bright, Cobden and the men who beat the aristocracy of England in their fiercest contest'. Readers of Duffy's newspaper, the *Nation*, which had been revived in September, would have known that he was referring to the Parliamentary and Financial Reform Association which he had admired from afar.[39] As a vehicle for an alliance between middle- and working class reformers, the Parliamentary and Financial Reform

Association turned out to be a dismal failure, but Duffy's public identification with Cobden and Bright saw him condemned in some nationalist eyes as a Whig. The *Irishman*, for example, anticipated the formation of the Independent Irish Party by urging nationalists to regard all Tories, Whigs, liberals, and radicals as enemies until they gave an unequivocal commitment to support Irish national independence.[40]

Initially O'Connor did not join the attacks on Duffy; he had also flirted with the PFRA. Once it became clear that his appeal to Duffy's Alliance had fallen on deaf ears, however, he began lending his support to a rival organisation, the Irish Democratic Association. This followed on from his burgeoning relationship with the *Irishman*, a Dublin Chartist newspaper, that he described as a 'sterling representation of the Irish democratic mind'.[41] After an ephemeral appearance in mid-1848, the *Irishman* commenced publication under the control of Bernard Fullam in January 1849. The circumstances under which the paper reappeared were controversial. Fullam had worked as office manager-cum-book keeper for the *Nation* before its suspension. With Duffy in prison, Fullam issued a prospectus for a paper to be called the *National*. No doubt he intended to attract Duffy's supporters, but he also succeeded in attracting the attention of Dublin Castle and sought refuge in flight. After some months underground, Fullam emerged as the owner of the *Irishman*. Later Fullam's opponents, in particular Maurice Leyne, alleged that he had avoided prosecution by agreeing to the Castle's condition that he use the pages of his new paper to attack Duffy, but the evidence was only circumstantial and hotly denied.[42]

It is true that, despite Fullam's former close association with Duffy, the *Irishman* became increasingly critical of the latter's new direction, condemning the 'Duffy clique' for abandoning 'all that it is great, virtuous and sacred in our past' and accusing Duffy himself of coveting O'Connell's mantle.[43] In response to the *Irishman's* barbs, Duffy complained of everything from fraud and treachery to plagiarism. Both in the *Nation* and his voluminous later writings, Duffy portrayed his dispute with Fullam as personal: Fullam, we are encouraged to believe, was the ungrateful former servant who kicked his 'dearly beloved friend and master' while he was on the ground.[44] But there were larger issues at stake. Fullam was not alone in attacking the Irish Alliance for its constitutional objectives. The *Cork*

Reporter, for example, lamented that the 'sword drawn by the Confederates...is returned to its scabbard by the Alliance'.[45] When it was published in 1854, Mitchel's jail journal revealed that the celebrated exile regarded Duffy as a 'pitiable' 'traitor' and believed the *Irishman* to be the true 'representative of the old *Nation*' and the preacher of the 'doctrines of me, J.M'. Although often consumed with recrimination and mutual mistrust, the new generation of Chartist leaders could at least agree about the value of the *Irishman*. According to G.W.M. Reynolds it was the 'only true organ of the democratic party of the Emerald Isle' and Julian Harney, 'England's Marat,' used the columns of his *Red Republican* to 'heartily recommend' it to 'British and Irish Republicans' as 'a master-piece of democratic eloquence'. With his characteristic knack of getting to the heart of the matter, Feargus O'Connor commented that while Duffy's revived *Nation* sought to represent 'the pockets of the shopocracy,' the *Irishman* championed 'the interests of the toiling millions'.[46]

Duffy's concern was hardly inspired by the *Irishman*'s effect on his newspaper's circulation. Having enjoyed an initial readership of 15,000, by January 1850 the *Irishman* was struggling to survive with a circulation of between three and six thousand.[47] Nevertheless the paper had played a crucial role in launching a rival organisation to Duffy's Alliance in the week of the aggregate conference. The impetus for a new organisation came from a group of 'thorough-going Nationalists and resolute Democrats,' including Fullam, who had been excluded from the preparations for the aggregate meeting. Unlike O'Connor, they chose not to gate-crash, but to call on the 'Dublin Democrats and Nationalists...to withhold their adhesion from any WHIGGISH or EXPEDIENCY SOCIETY,' pending the formation of a 'National Democratic Association'. Based in the premises formerly occupied by the Mechanics Institute in Dublin's Lower Abbey Street, the Irish Democratic Association was Ireland's last chance for Chartism. By December the provisional committee had set an ambitious target of 1,000,000 members 'before Spring passes,' with a branch association 'in every town and village'. This optimism was infectious. Following a meeting with Fullam in London, O'Connor reported his delight to readers of the *Northern Star* at the 'strength that the Democratic Party [in Ireland] was likely to possess,' although he concluded his epistle on a cautious note:

'Now, Irishmen, let me implore you not to be disheartened if your beginning is weak...'[48]

Within weeks, however, there was evidence that the organisation was indeed flourishing. In February 1850 the committee issued a public invitation to O'Connor to attend a national aggregate meeting 'on an early day'. Accompanied by two of his closest Chartist allies, the Irishmen, Thomas Clark and Philip McGrath, O'Connor undertook his second visit to Ireland in four months to attend this conference at the Music Hall in Lower Abbey Street, Dublin, early in March 1850. In addition to a Dublin contingent, there were deputations from Kilkenny, Carlow, Cork and Glasgow. It was clear, even at this early stage, that 'branches' of the IDA had been formed in Cork, Limerick, Kilkenny, Drogheda, Dundalk, Carlow, Belfast, Leeds and Glasgow.[49] After just four months operation, boasted the editor of the *Irishman*, the IDA had recruited an 'army of Democrats,' that had assured it 'a broad and recognised existence in the hearts and history of this country'.[50] The degree of success varied from place to place. In Kilkenny, for example, the IDA branch claimed a membership of 16,000 and even the hostile *Kilkenny Journal* conceded that support for the movement was 'not, by any means, insignificant'. In Cork, on the other hand, the antipathetic *Cork Examiner* estimated that IDA membership was 'confined to a very few,' a point conceded by the local democrats.[51] Even allowing for exaggeration (and underestimation), the movement clearly deserves to be taken seriously.

What did the IDA stand for, and who was attracted to its banner? To answer both these questions the aggregate meeting is a good place to start. The chairman, Thomas Graham, opened proceedings with a blunt declaration that set the tone: 'they would not make a compromise for the miserable end of endeavouring to get men of property to join them,' a phrase that evoked Wolfe Tone's well known description of the United Irishmen as 'men of no property'.[52] O'Connor also evoked the struggles of the 1790s by reminding the audience with characteristic self-aggrandisement that 'his family had suffered more in supporting them than any other family that ever was born'.[53] Significantly, O'Connor went on to declare that 'he was not only for a Repeal of the Union, but for a separation,' going beyond his usual prescription, and earning him 'loud cheering, which lasted for several minutes'. The response to O'Connor's statement underscores the fact that these were nationalists first: 'separation' from England was the defining object of the IDA. 'Ourselves alone,' declared the *Irishman*, using a phrase that would grow to have enormous significance in Irish nationalist politics, 'must be the key-stone on which the proud edifice of our National Democracy must be erected'.[54]

Beyond this a seven point programme was agreed to, and it is worth lingering over its details. Firstly, the IDA was committed to the 'elevation of the character and condition of the working classes,' defined to include 'artisans' and the 'tiller of the soil'. Second, they would: 'inculcate the necessity of every Irishman encouraging native manufacture, and...lay a plan for the revival of Irish trade'. Third, they would educate the people as to the 'position they occupy, and the position they are entitled to occupy' and lead an agitation for a 'complete and entire restoration of the social and political privileges they have been unjustly deprived of'. Fourth, the association was committed to 'the development of Irish talent, and diffusion of a national literature'. Fifth, they undertook to co-operate with all existing democratic organisations that shared the aim of recognising the 'rights of labour, and the overthrow of a heartless and useless oligarchy'. Sixth, they would seek to 'break down the barriers of religious prejudice' between Catholic and Protestant by showing 'respect... [for]...every man for his conscientious opinions, and the free expression of the faith that is within him'. And, finally, they were committed to holding 'our Irish martyrs' in 'grateful remembrance so long as they are expatriated under British law'.[55]

In some respects this is an unexceptional statement of late Chartism; this is 'Chartism and something more' that could just as easily have been proclaimed in Soho, the Gorbals or Salford. In particular, students of later Chartism will recognise the sentiment expressed by one of the executive, Thomas Cullen; their objective, he later wrote, was 'Socialism', the formation of a body to 'watch over, to protect, and to advocate, the sacred rights of labour.' 'We must become Socially Democratic as well as politically so,' observed the *Irishman*, as 'no great benefit can be derived from struggling for half a victory'.[56] Just as in Britain, this became a source of dissension. At a time when the Manchester Chartists were condemning their London counterparts for mixing Chartism 'pure and simple' with a 'kind of mongrel Socialism...borrowed from the Parisian school of philosophers,' the direction of the IDA was of grave concern to veterans of the Irish Universal Suffrage Association, such as Patrick O'Higgins. By the end of 1850 he had issued his own call for Chartism 'pure and simple' and informed the readers of the *Northern Star* that he was no longer connected with any political organisation.[57]

In a country prone to sectarian violence, the United Irishmen had been committed to religious toleration, non-sectarianism and to co-operation with other democratic bodies. Students of Chartism will also recognise these objectives as part of the universalist political tradition, encompassing 'the illustrious dead of every nation who, by their actions or their writings, have contributed to the cause of freedom,' which many Chartists saw themselves as part of.[58] Other features of the IDA programme are more distinctively Irish. By committing themselves to promote native manufacture, the IDA was picking up the threads of an economic nationalist campaign that had dominated the Irish political agenda for a short period during the early 1840s, and the commitment to cultural nationalism both carried on the literary mission of the Young Irelanders and anticipated the cultural objectives of Fenianism and the later work of Eoin MacNeill and Douglas Hyde in the Gaelic League and the Irish Literary Society.[59] For some opponents it was the IDA's cultural and educational objectives that posed a greater threat than their plots. The *Clonmel Chronicle*, for example, warned:

> We do not require such a tainted body for the education of our mechanics, artisans, and people. Nothing but a noxious weed can spring from the dunghill of an ignorant and rebellious democracy.[60]

With scarcely more sympathy the editor of the *Cork Examiner* pointed out that it was necessary to read the language of the IDA programme in the light of 'other circumstances'. 'Considered with the illustration thus thrown upon them,' he continued, 'we have no hesitation in pronouncing the objects of the Democratic Association as dangerous in the highest degree'. What was being hinted at here was the fact that, at one level, the IDA was the quasi-constitutional face of a secret organisation that had a shadowy pre-history during 1849. A number of those involved in the public IDA and the *Irishman*, including its editor, Joseph Brenan, had been among the leaders of a network of secret Democratic Associations extending from Dublin to Cork during 1849. Under the watchful eye of the police, the members of these clandestine cells, many of them veterans of 1848, collected arms, hatched plans to kidnap Queen Victoria on her visit to Dublin in August 1849 and undertook a little known assault on the police barracks at Cappoquin, County Waterford in September.[61]

The matter of how to implement the programme was in many ways a more important consideration than the programme itself. As the cheering subsided following his declaration in favour of 'separation,' O'Connor eschewed the use of 'violence, riot, or revolution' to achieve that objective. For many among his audience, however, the IDA was not an alternative to armed rebellion. As one IDA member later recalled, the *Irishman* reflected the mental attitude of the 'hotter heads of the party': 'It was not avowedly revolutionary, but neither could it be considered exactly legal and constitutional, and controversial it certainly was...'[62] For Joseph O'Grady, an IDA member from Tipperary, 'every Irishman of spirit must feel himself pressed into the earth beneath a burden of shame...Our people are the withering and prostrate victims of a subtle and depraved barbarism'. He had 'no patience with parliamentary agitation as a weapon with which to settle our gigantic quarrel with England'.[63] This attitude was not unknown among Chartists in Britain. For example the members of the Glasgow IDA were opposed to 'another fifty years agitation, or any agitation at all, which holds out any hope in the present Constitution or Parliament'. In Ireland, however, the development of a separatist nationalism went further, undermining the very premise of O'Connor's Irish mission. O'Grady, for example, went on to conclude that the only tolerable position that an Irishman can at present occupy is that of an armed antagonist, or a chained and stubborn foe of English oligarchy. After O'Connor's speech, the secretary of the IDA, Andrew English, called on his 'brother democrats' to 'cast aside forever...the debasing system of parliamentary agitation,' 'even at the expense of losing the aid of their English friends'.[64]

The message could not have been clearer. Mitchel had welcomed the support of the Chartists on the basis that '[t]hey are as eager to get rid of us as we are to be free of them' and he abjured any attempts to articulate his cause within the British polity: 'we deny the right or power of the Imperial Parliament to legislate for us in any shape,' he told readers of the *United Irishman*, 'even to give us the franchise'. In October 1850, Michael Doheny, a leading Confederate who had shared the platform with O'Connor at the formalisation of the alliance in 1848 (calling himself an 'Irish Chartist') before fleeing into self-imposed exile in the United States, argued that the objects of the English and Irish Democrats are not identical. 'They are not even analogous, save to a limited extent,' he wrote to the *Northern Star*, '[n]or would they be identical, in my estimate, if the "Repeal of the Union" were made the first point of the Charter.' The Charter could not deliver what was needed: 'total extinction of the English interest in Ireland'.[65] Many of those who cheered O'Connor at Dublin's Music Hall, both in November 1849 and in March 1850, believed, or would come to believe, that Ireland's salvation could only be achieved through force of arms. In this sense the IDA was defeated by its own ideology.

For other commentators it was not so much the IDA programme that was notable, but the personnel. For George Fleming, editor of the *Northern Star*:

> The formation of an independent Democratic Association in the sister country...may be taken as the commencement of a new era in the history of Irish public movements. Heretofore, lawyers and priests have been the moving powers, and the masses have been made subservient to the advancement of their selfish class-schemes and individual aggrandisement.

These views were shared by the press in the United States. 'It is truly refreshing to notice,' wrote the *Irish American*, for example, 'for the very first time in Ireland, the people throwing off the yoke of slavish subserviency'.[66] John Boyle dismisses the IDA because '[n]o prominent artisan ever had any connection with it,' but this is to miss the point. As one correspondent to the *Irishman* put it, the fact that the IDA had been formed 'unassisted by wealth, known talent or influence' was a source of pride. A fortnight later the editor took up the theme: 'For the first time in Irish history, a National movement has been organised by the people'.[67] Duffy would later describe these people as 'honest Hotspurs,' whose 'unselfishness, sincerity and genuine passion' was 'mixed with folly and gasconade,' but can we say more?[68] What sort of people participated in the IDA? As always with 'history from below,' this is a challenging and sometimes unsatisfactory enterprise. All that can be offered is a few glimpses. Apart from Fullam, about whom little is known, the Dublin contingent at the National Conference included Patrick O'Higgins,[69] a wool merchant and stalwart of the Irish Universal Suffrage Association, and Thomas Mooney, a baker and provision dealer from the Liberties, who was a veteran of the Operative Association for the Promotion of Native Manufacture.[70] One of the editors of the *Irishman*, Joseph Brenan, was born in Cork in 1829 into a 'comfortable family'. As an eighteen year old firebrand he had been involved with the Young Irelanders in Cork while working as a journalist. In 1848 he moved to Dublin where he joined the staff of Mitchel's *United Irishman*, and later the *Irish Felon* and *Irish Tribune*. After taking part in a violent uprising in Waterford during August, he was arrested and spent eight months in prison. A month after his release in March 1849 Brenan became the editor of *Irishman* while continuing to pursue revolutionary objectives in secret.[71] Thomas Clarke Luby was born in Dublin in 1822, the son of an episcopal clergyman. Educated at Trinity College, Luby was regarded as a 'man of scholarly attainments'. He was in his twenties when he joined the Young Ireland movement and contributed to the *Nation*. In 1848 Luby joined the Confederates and was subsequently arrested with Smith O'Brien. Upon his release he became Brenan's co-conspirator and co-contributor to the columns of the *Irishman*.[72]

These relatively privileged backgrounds, however, were atypical of the IDA membership. On the day Luby joined the Dublin Branch of the IDA, Michael Doheny was also nominated in his absence. What Doheny thought about this is not known, but his background among the poor was far more typical of the IDA membership.[73] Thomas Graham, chairman of the March conference was a coffin-maker by trade which caused the hostile *Clonmel Chronicle* to speculate that he would 'no doubt, be glad to deposit Queen, Lords and Commons in one of his own shells'; the leader at Carrick-on-Suir was John Power, a 'dealer in cast cloths'.[74] Graham had opened the National Conference by rejecting compromise with 'men of property,' implying that the IDA could be identified with Tone's constituency: men of no property. From a range of newspaper reports

- hostile and supportive - general descriptions indicate that the IDA ranks were filled by artisans, mechanics, 'respectable tradesmen,' 'labouring men,' 'working men,' the 'lowest class of workmen,' such as 'small shopkeepers assistants,' and specifically, 'men of no property (or business)'.[75] O'Connor called them the 'toiling millions,' 'working Celts,' or simply the 'fustian jackets'.

Other characterisations suggest that the typical IDA member was young. In a range of different newspaper accounts they were described as 'ill-conducted young lads,' 'youthful,' 'young artisans' and 'youngsters and scamps'.[76] If the neo-Young Irelander was young, like Luby and Brenan, this was not a barrier to previous political experience, especially among the Confederates. Andrew English, Secretary of the provisional Dublin Committee, was a former treasurer of the Dr Doyle Confederate Club who had been tried and convicted of drilling a 'troop of rebels,' but escaped a sentence of twelve months imprisonment on 'a point of law'.[77] Edward O'Sullivan, a leading member of the Cork branch, had been vice-president of the Bantry Donald Combh Confederate Club in '48 and was, 'a personal friend of many of the martyrs and exiles'. Meetings of this branch were chaired by a Scot named Peacock, who had been a Fraternal Democrat, and had represented Greenock at the Chartist National Assembly in 1848.[78] Two members of a branch that was centred on a reading room in Francis Street in Dublin were the Farrell brothers, Thomas and Edward, who had been stalwarts of the Felon Confederate Club. Another member of this branch, Dennis Byrne, staked his revolutionary credentials on his bloodline, being a relative of 'William Byrne of '98'.[79]

In the months following the March conference there is evidence of IDA branches operating in Dublin, Cork, Carrick-on-Suir, Kilkenny, Tipperary, Callan, Clonmel, Waterford and Sligo as well as in Liverpool, Manchester, Glasgow, Sheffield, Wigan, Barnsley, Bradford, London, and Leeds (where the Chairman was a native of Cork, the irascible Chartist veteran George White).[80] At one meeting of the IDA at Carrick-on-Suir in Tipperary in May there were reports of a crowd of 10,000. At about this time, a veteran Irish democrat, L.T. Clancy, who had been chased out of Dublin by O'Connell's henchmen early in 1840, estimated that there were as many as 100 branches of the IDA in the three kingdoms, although it is unclear on what basis he offered this calculation.[81]

Notably absent from the Carrick-on-Suir meeting was a deputation from Dublin. The reasons for this were significant. On the one hand, the organisation had moved to new premises and a new Secretary had taken office. On the other hand secret negotiations - involving the central Dublin branch - had commenced in June 1850 with a view to a union with the remnants of Duffy's Irish Alliance.[82] According to the new IDA Secretary, Tom Cullen, the pretext for the discussions was that 'some of the best Confederates of '48, who stand on neutral ground outside both the Alliance and the Democratic Association,' had 'been dinging "Union" in our ears every day since the Association was formed'.[83] Initially the negotiations threatened to stall over whether to make disestablishment of the Church of Ireland part of the objectives of a unified organisation, and the vexed issue of whether to participate in parliamentary elections. The IDA had adopted a position of non-interference in parliamentary elections and scorned the Alliance's commitment to parliamentary and constitutional activity, as well as its association with English liberals.[84]

Compromise on these points - dropping any reference to religion and leaving involvement in elections as an 'open question' - paved the way for the central Dublin branch to seek endorsement of a joint programme that would seal a union. This prospect, however, drew fire from within the organisation that underscores the contradictions at its heart. From Glasgow came a stern warning to the Dublin comrades not to be 'made the unconscious tools of the wily Duffy' and, in Dublin itself, the proposed union was rejected out of hand by the branch in Francis Street. As residents of a part of south Dublin renowned for its poverty and its propensity to riot, the Francis Street members had a reputation for militancy having, for example, previously threatened to 'slay' Maurice Leyne 'like a dog'.[85] The upshot was a formal split that saw the accession of many members of the IDA to the new Irish Democratic Alliance. Socialism was an issue in determining which way members went. The compromise involved an explicit repudiation of 'continental socialism,' which brought the new organisation into line with the stance of the Alliance and the editorial policy of the *Nation*, while those who resisted Duffy's embrace were regarded as the 'Red party' for their commitment to *la republique democratique et sociale*.[86]

In the aftermath of the schism and the collapse of the *Irishman* in mid-1850, the momentum that had been established quickly dissipated. In January 1851 Harney's *Friend of the People* reported that a number of 'earnest patriots' had formed a Joint Stock Association to finance a successor to the *Irishman*, to be known as the *People*, but, like so many of the schemes of the later Chartists, it came to nothing.[87] The democratic agitation was also overtaken by events, specifically the new direction being forged by Duffy. While the negotiations continued over reunion, Duffy's Tenant Rights Conference was successfully convened in Dublin in August 1850. As early as May the *Irishman* had foreseen the Tenant Right movement 'rising with a giant's growth,' and, by September, even the *Northern Star* was predicting that the Tenant Rights League 'promises to become powerful'. At the same time, the unified Democratic Alliance was promising to 'act behind the Tenant League' and ensuring its own rapid irrelevance by embracing a strategy of 'propagandism, rather than agitation'.[88] It is difficult to assess the involvement of IDA members in the Tenant Rights campaign as the platforms of this agitation heralded the return of the 'lawyers and priests'.

Despite its relatively brief efflorescence the Irish Democratic Association is worthy of more attention than it has received. On the one hand it brought together a number of disparate strands of popular politics: the ultra-democratic, or Paineite, tradition of the United Irishmen and radical Confederates, O'Connor's brand of democratic populism, the cultural nationalism of the Young Irelanders, and the pragmatic economic nationalism of the campaign to revive and promote native manufacture. On the other hand, the IDA served as a time capsule. L.M.Cullen has pointed out that one of the consequences of an episodic view of history is that the 'underlying strength of political movements can be underestimated': 'the next phase of politics is seen as almost entirely new'. Taking up the point in *Outsiders*, Dorothy Thompson speculates that 'the Jacobin/Chartist element in Irish artisan politics was to some extent kept alive and later fed back into Irish politics from Britain and America'.[89] George Archdeacon is a case in point. As the police were simultaneously arresting a clutch of leading Confederates and Chartists on the night of 15 August 1848, Archdeacon slipped out of Manchester in disguise. Dressed as a weaver he went from safe house to safe house, being helped by 'many hundreds' of common folk along the way, until he got to the river Clyde where he boarded a ship for New York. From there he wrote to the *Irishman* to offer his services as a correspondent. Archdeacon reappeared in Liverpool in 1861 when he became chairman of the National Brotherhood of St Patrick, a direct forerunner of the Irish Republican Brotherhood. By the mid-1860s, when the Fenians were exploring a possible alliance with British radicals, Archdeacon was the intermediary.[90] Was he the exception that proves the rule? More research is called for on this point, but there is evidence that the IDA provided a stepping stone in the careers of later Fenians.[91] These included John O'Leary, Thomas Clarke Luby, and Joseph Brenan, who were all members of the IDA and its shadowy forerunner, and who all subsequently contributed to the *Irishman*.

After leaving the *Irishman,* Brenan emigrated to the United States where he became active in émigré politics, and continued to pursue journalism as a vocation, writing for Mitchel's *Citizen* and *Delta* in New Orleans.[92] John O'Leary went on to a prominent career in Fenianism as well as a role as W.B. Yeats' literary mentor.[93] After his stint at the *Irishman*, Luby went to Paris with the intention of joining the Foreign Legion, and then to Australia and the United States in the company of the man who would lead the 1867 uprising, James Stephens. After he returned to Ireland, Luby co-edited the *Tribune* and later the *Irish People*, and he is credited with formulating the Fenian Oath for the IRB. Arrested in 1865, Luby was released in 1871 and went into exile in America. After settling in New York he continued to write, chronicling Irish history from Brian Boromha (Boru) to the Wild Geese, becoming one of Daniel O'Connell's legion of biographers during the 1870s, and contributing articles on Fenianism to the newspaper the *Irish Nation* as late as 1882.[94] The Fenian Davitt might have owed more to Chartism than even his fellow prisoner could have told him.

In his *Labour in Ireland*, published after he had been executed for his part in the Easter Rising of 1916, James Connolly also recognised that the IDA had 'spread amongst the Irish workers in Great Britain'. Here too it acted to preserve values and solidarity among the immigrant communities where it took root. As late as November 1851 the Bradford Branch of the IDA was still holding regular meetings at the Neptune Inn in Bridge Street, agreeing to renew their subscription to both the *Nation* and the *Northern Star*, and hatching plans to add to the three Irish representatives they had already secured on the local council.[95] O'Connor might have pointed to Bradford as evidence of the success of his 'mission,' but his broader objective to create a common programme between radicals in England and Ireland, that was reflected in his visits to Dublin in 1849 and 1850, failed. Some of those whom he hoped to attract to the Chartist banner followed Gavan Duffy into the campaign for Tenants' Rights and the disappointment of the Independent Irish Party; others came to, or continued to, believe that Ireland's salvation could only be achieved through armed rebellion; whereas others simply accepted Doheny's argument that, in the end, the interests of the Irish and the English were not the same. O'Connor's appeal to the 'fustian jackets' of Ireland excited insufficient response in a country where the loyalties to nation and religion were often more powerful - but it is important to rescue Ireland's last chance for Chartism precisely because it represented a call for an alliance between English and Irish workers that had few proposers in subsequent generations.

NOTES

[1] *Northern Star, (NS)*, 1 February 1840, p. 4. A version of this chapter was presented to the Fourth Annual Chartist Conference, University of Birmingham, September 1998. I am grateful to Alex Tyrrell, Dorothy Thompson and Suzanne Pickering for their comments on the paper and a subsequent draft.

[2] M. Davitt, *Leaves from a Prison Diary; Or Lectures to a Solitary Audience*, London, Chapman and Hall, 1885, p. 142.

[3] *Ibid*, pp. 141-3; *Regenerator and Chartist Circular*, 7 December 1839, p. 56; HO 40/54, fol. 887; *NS*, 23 February 1850, p. 8; *Red Republican*, 23 November 1850, p. 180. Editions of Emmet's trial were published in 1803, 1832, 1835, 1836, 1847, 1850, 1852, two in 1840, and three in 1845. Accounts of his life and trial were serialised in the *Regenerator and Chartist Circular* (1839-40); *English Chartist Circular*, (1841); Scottish *Chartist Circular* (1841); and *NS* (1850).

[4] For young Emmets named during 1842 alone see *inter alia NS*, 15 January 1842, p. 5; 30 April 1842, p. 5; 23 July 1842, p. 5; 30 July 1842, p. 5; 8 October 1842, p. 5; 3 December 1842, p. 5.

[5] *NS*, 3 November 1838, p. 6.

[6] *NS*, 16 October 1841, p. 4.

[7] See I. McCalman, '"Erin go Bragh": the Irish in British Popular Radicalism,' in O. MacDonagh and W.F. Mandle (eds), *Irish-Australian Studies*, Canberra, Australian National University, p. 176; J. Belchem, 'English Working-Class

Radicalism and the Irish, 1815-50,' in R. Swift and S. Gilley (eds), *The Irish in the Victorian City*, London, Croom Helm, 1985, pp. 87-9.

[8] Davitt, *Prison Diary*, pp. 141-3; K. Marx, 'To the Federal Council of French Switzerland' (1870), in K. Marx and F. Engels, *Articles on Britain*, Moscow, Progress Publishers, 1978, p. 353. See also N. Kirk, *The Growth of Working Class Reformism in Mid-Victorian England*, London, Croom Helm, 1985, pp. 310-348.

[9] J. Belchem, 'English Working Class Radicalism and the Irish, 1815-1850,' *North West Labour History Society Bulletin*, No. 8, 1982-3, p. 7. For other contributions to the debate see R. O'Higgins, 'The Irish Influence in the Chartist Movement,' *Past and Present*, No. 20, 1961, pp. 83-96; J.H. Treble, 'O'Connor, O'Connell and the Attitudes of Irish Immigrants Towards Chartism in the North of England 1838-48,' in J. Butt and I.F. Clarke (eds), *The Victorians and Social Protest*, Newton Abbot, David and Charles, 1973, pp. 33-70; D. Thompson, 'Ireland and the Irish in English Radicalism before 1850,' in J. Epstein and D. Thompson (eds), *The Chartist Experience: Studies in Working-Class Radicalism and Culture, 1830-60*, London, Macmillan, 1982, pp. 120-151; W.J. Lowe, 'The Chartists and the Irish Confederates: Lancashire, 1848,' *Irish Historical Studies*, Vol. XXIV, No. 94, 1984, pp. 172-196; G. Davis, *The Irish in Britain 1815-1914*, Dublin, Gill and Macmillan, 1991, pp. 159-190; D. Thompson, 'Seceding from the Seceders: The Decline of the Jacobin Tradition in Ireland, 1790-1850,' in *Outsiders: Class, Gender and Nation*, London, Verso, 1993, pp. 134-163.

[10] *NS*, 16 March 1850, p. 1.

[11] P.W. Slosson, *The Decline of the Chartist Movement*, New York, Colombia, 1916, pp. 78-114; O'Higgins, 'The Irish Influence,' p. 89. T. Koseki, 'Patrick O'Higgins and Irish Chartism,' Tokyo, Hosei University Ireland-Japan Papers, No. 2, 1990, p. 20. I am grateful to Stephen Roberts for providing me with a copy of this paper.

[12] D. Read and E. Glasgow, *Feargus O'Connor: Irishman and Chartist*, London, Edward Arnold, 1961, p. 138; J. Boyle, *The Irish Labour Movement in the Nineteenth Century*, Washington, Catholic University of America Press, 1988, p. 53.

[13] L. M. Cullen, 'Comment on T. Koseki,' Hosei University Ireland-Japan Papers, No. 2, p. 31.

[14] *Nation*, 3 November 1849, p. 152; *NS*, 20 October 1849, p. 7; 3 November 1849, p. 6.

[15] *Nation*, 16 March 1850, p. 457; *NS*, 25 May 1850, p. 6; 15 June 1850, p. 6

[16] *NS*, 8 January 1848, p. 2; 17 June 1848, p. 3; 24 June 1848, p. 3; 12 August 1848, p. 5; 19 August 1848, p. 8; *Irish Felon*, 1 July 1848, p. 24; 15 July 1848, pp. 60-1. For the divisions between Young and Old Ireland see R. Clarke, 'The Relations between O'Connell and the Young Irelanders,' *Irish Historical Studies*, Vol. 3, No. 9, 1942, pp. 18-30.

[17] *Cork Examiner*, 23 November 1849, p. 6; *Freeman's Journal*, 21 November 1849, pp. 3-4.

[18] *Cork Examiner*, 23 November 1849, p. 6. See also P.J. Bull, *Land, Nationalism, and Politics: A Study of the Irish Land Question*, Dublin, Gill and Macmillan, 1996.

[19] *Charter*, 1 September 1839, p. 510; 8 September 1839, p. 526; *Pilot*, 19 August 1839, p. 1; *NS*, 19 October 1839, p. 1; 26 October 1839, p. 1; B. Harrison and P. Hollis (eds), *Robert Lowery: Radical and Chartist*, London, Europa Publications, 1979, pp. 144-8.

[20] *Weekly Freeman's Journal*, 11 September 1841, p. 1; 14 May 1842, p. 4; *NS*, 9 April 1842, p. 7; 21 May 1842, p. 1; 25 June 1842, p. 1; 20 August 1842, p. 7; *Reports of the Select Committee of the House of Commons on Public Petitions*, Session 1842, Vol. 130, pp. 377, 399.

[21] *NS*, 27 July 1839, p. 7; 7 November 1840, p. 3; 30 January 1840, p. 5; 8 May 1841, p. 6; 16 July 1842, p. 5; 17 September 1842, p. 1; 29 December 1849, p. 1.

[22] See Koseki, pp. 15-20.

[23] *Hansard*, XCV (6 December 1847) 729; *NS*, 18 December 1847, p. 1. On the Second Reading half a dozen repealers, including M.J. O'Connell, voted for the Bill, while John O'Connell and William Smith O'Brien, a leader of the moderate wing of the Confederate Council, voted with O'Connor in the minority.

[24] *United Irishman*, 24 February 1848, p. 41. See also Koseki, p. 19; R. Davis, *The Young Ireland Movement*, Dublin, Gill and Macmillan, 1987, p. 191.

[25] See P.A. Pickering, *Chartism and the Chartists in Manchester and Salford*, Basingstoke, Macmillan, 1995, p. 96, 201.

[26] *Irish Felon*, 15 July 1848, p. 61; *English Patriot and Irish Repealer*, 22 July 1848, pp. 6-7.

[27] *NS*, 25 March 1848, p. 1.

[28] See Epstein, *Lion of Freedom: Feargus O'Connor and the Chartist Movement, 1832-42*, London, Croom Helm, 1982, pp. 8-9. For a hostile portrait of Roger and Arthur O'Connor see M. Elliot, *Partners in Revolution: the United Irishmen and France*, New Haven, Yale University Press, 1982, pp. 99-103.

[29] *NS*, 13 May 1848, p. 1

[30] *NS*, 13 May 1848, p. 1; *National Instructor*, 29 June 1850, pp. 89-90.

[31] *Nation*, 17 November 1849, p. 185; *Cork Examiner*, 19 November 1849, p. 3.

[32] *NS*, 24 November 1849, p. 1.

[33] *Cork Examiner*, 23 November 1849, p. 3.

[34] *NS*, 1 February 1840, p. 4; 21 August 1841, p. 1; 1 January 1848, p. 1

[35] *Cork Examiner*, 23 November 1849, p. 3. For the significance of fustian see P.A. Pickering, 'Class Without Words: Symbolic Communication in the Chartist Movement,' *Past and Present*, No. 112, August 1986, pp. 144-162.

[36] See *Cork Examiner*, 23 November 1849, p. 3; *Freeman's Journal*, 21 November 1849, p. 4; *Irishman*, 24 November 1849, p. 739; *Clonmel Chronicle*, 24 November 1849, p. 1; *Kilkenny Journal*, 24 November 1849, p. 1; *NS*, 24 November 1849, p. 1.

[37] See *Dundalk Democrat*, 17 November 1849, p. 2; 24 November 1849, p. 2; *Cork Examiner*, 23 November 1849, p. 2; *Kilkenny Journal*, 24 November 1849, p. 2; *NS*, 22 December 1849, p. 7.

[38] For Leyne see *Irish Felon*, 15 July 1848, pp. 60-1; *NS*, 19 August 1848, p. 6; 3 March 1849, p. 6; 10 March 1849, p. 6; *Nation*, 27 April 1850, p. 555-6; C. Gavan Duffy, *My Life in Two Hemispheres*, London, T. Fisher and Unwin, 1898, Vol. 2, p. 9;

M. Doheny, *The Felon's Track: Or History of the Attempted Outbreak in Ireland*, Dublin, Gill and Son, 1914, p. 308.

[39] *Cork Examiner*, 23 November 1849, p. 3; *Nation*, 8 September 1849, p. 3; 12 January 1850, p. 312; 27 April 1850, p. 553.

[40] *Irishman*, 20 October 1849, p. 664. A similar policy was to prove crucial to the subsequent establishment of the Independent Irish Party (whose historian credits Duffy with its formulation). See J.H. Whyte, *The Independent Irish Party 1850-9*, Oxford, Oxford University Press, 1958, pp. 10-11.

[41] *NS*, 1 December 1849, p. 1. Koseki claims, incorrectly, that the *Irish National Guard*, published in 1848, was the 'first and last Irish Chartist newspaper,' 'O'Higgins,' p. 24.

[42] *NS*, 23 February 1850, p. 4. See *Nation*, 1 December 1849, p. 217; 27 April 1850, pp. 555-6; 4 May 1850, p. 568; *NS*, 15 December 1849, p. 7; 18 May 1850, p. 1

[43] *Irishman*, 1 September 1849, p. 552; 13 October 1849, p. 648

[44] *Nation*, 1 December 1849, p. 217; C. Gavan Duffy, *My Life in Two Hemispheres*, Vol. 1, pp. 310-11. This was also how T.D. Sullivan remembered it. See *Recollections of Troubled Times in Irish Politics*, Dublin, Sealy, Bryers and Walker, 1905, pp. 9-10. Duffy even alleged that Richard Pigott, the author of the infamous Parnell letters, got his start in journalism on the staff of the *Irishman*.

[45] *Cork Reporter* cited in *The Times*, 27 November 1849, p. 5.

[46] John Mitchel, *Jail Journal*, (1854), Dublin, Gill and Son, [1913], pp. 207-8; *Reynolds Political Instructor*, 3 April 1850, p. 178; *Red Republican*, 27 July 1850, p. 44; 17 August 1850, p. 69; *NS*, 18 May 1850, p. 1. See also Harney's *Democratic Review*, May 1850, p. 465. The other prominent leader of the later Chartists, Ernest Jones, was in prison during 1849-50.

[47] *Irishman*, 1 July 1848, p. 16; *NS*, 23 February 1850, p. 4; 1 June 1850, p. 1.

[48] *Irishman*, 29 December 1849, p. 824; *NS*, 26 January 1850, p. 1.

[49] *Irishman*, 31 November [sic]1849, p. 755; 29 December, 1849, p. 824; 19 January 1850, p. 34; 16 February 1850, p. 105; 23 February 1850, p. 121; 9 March 1850, p. 146-8; *NS*, 1850, p. 1.

[50] *Irishman*, 9 March 1850, p. 152.

[51] *Kilkenny Journal*, 23 February 1850, p. 2; *Cork Examiner*, 8 March 1850, p. 2; *Irishman*, 16 March 1850, p. 162. See also M. Cronin, *Country, Class or Craft? The Politicisation of the Skilled Artisan in Nineteenth-Century Cork*, Cork, University Press, 1994, p. 156.

[52] See F.S.L Lyons, *Ireland Since the Famine*, London, Fontana, 1973, p. 54. The same phrase was used by William O'Brien in the United Irish League and in framing the Democratic Programme of the first Dáil in 1919.

[53] *NS*, 9 March 1850, p. 1.

[54] *Irishman*, 12 January 1850, p. 25. Arthur Griffith's biographer, Calton Younger, attributes the phrase *Sinn Féin amháin* (ourselves alone) to a poem by Douglas Hyde: C. Younger, *Arthur Griffith*, Dublin, Gill and Macmillan, 1981, p. 26. As Richard Davis has noted, however, the English version of the phrase preceded the Irish version and was widely used by Young and Old Ireland in the 1840s. See R. Davis, *The Young Ireland Movement*, Dublin, Gill and Macmillan, 1987, p. 239.

[55] *NS*, 9 March 1850, p. 1.

番

[56] *NS*, 27 July 1850, p. 7; *Irishman*, 29 December 1849, p. 824.

[57] *NS*, 23 November 1850, p. 1; 7 December 1850, p. 5; 8 March 1851, p. 1; 19 April 1851, p. 1; 13 December 1851, p. 1. Koseki, 'O'Higgins,' pp. 9-10, points out that the Irish Universal Suffrage Association had explicitly rejected socialism.

[58] *Manchester and Salford Advertiser*, 9 June 1838, p. 4. See also H. Weisser, *British Working Class Movements and Europe 1815-1848*, Manchester, Manchester University Press, 1975.

[59] See J. Hutchinson, *The Dynamics of Cultural Nationalism: the Gaelic Revival and the Creation of the Irish Nation State*, London, Allen and Unwin, 1987; M.J. Brown, *The Politics of Irish Literature from Thomas Davis to W.B. Yeats*, London, Allen and Unwin, 1972; P.A. Pickering, '"Irish First": the Native Manufacture Campaign and Economic Nationalism, 1840-44,' (forthcoming).

[60] *Clonmel Chronicle*, 9 March 1850, p. 2.

[61] See R.V. Comerford, *The Fenians in Context: Irish Politics and Society 1848-82*, Dublin, Wolfhound Press, 1985, p. 18; D. Lynch, *The Fenian Chief: A Biography of James Stephens*, Dublin, Gill and Son, 1967, pp. 51-2; J. Newsinger, *Fenianism in Mid-Victorian Britain*, London, Pluto Press, 1994, p. 18; D.N. Buckley, *James Fintan Lalor: Radical*, Cork, Cork University Press, 1994, pp. 23-4. If only in passing references, both Comerford and Newsinger recognise the link between the 1849 movement and the Chartist IDA.

[62] J. O'Leary, *Recollections of Fenians and Fenianism*, (1896), Vol. 1, Shannon, Irish University Press, 1969, p. 34.

[63] *Nation*, 22 June 1850, p. 686

[64] *NS*, 3 August 1850, p. 7; *Nation*, 9 March 1850, p. 446; 22 June 1850, p. 686.

[65] *United Irishman*, 26 February 1848, p. 41; 4 March 1848, p. 60-1; *NS*, 12 October 1850, p. 1. See also D.G. Boyce, *Nationalism in Ireland*, London, Routledge, 1995, pp. 154-191.

[66] *NS*, 16 March 1850, p.1; *Irish American* extract in *Irishman*, 20 April 1850, p. 242. See also the extract from the New York *Truth Teller* in *Irishman*, 27 April 1850, p. 259.

[67] Boyle, *Irish Labour Movement*, p. 53; *Irishman*, 2 March 1850, p. 137; 16 March 1850, p. 168.

[68] Duffy, *League*, p. 28.

[69] For O'Higgins see Koseki, 'O'Higgins,' *passim.*

[70] For Mooney see *Pilot*, 19 October 1840, p. 3; 23 October 1840, p. 1; *Irishman*, 16 March 1850, p. 160; *Nation*, 9 February 1850, p. 384; 9 March 1850, p. 442; D. O'Connell to J. O'Connell, 4 December 1840, in M.R. O'Connell (ed.), *The Correspondence of Daniel O'Connell*, Vol. IV, Dublin, Blackwater, 1972, p. 387; W. O'Brien and D. Ryan (eds), *Devoy's Post Bag 1871-1928*, Dublin, C.J. Fallon, 1948, pp. 193-4; Pickering, 'Irish First,' *passim*. He is not the same Thomas Mooney, a Fenian known as 'Trans-Atlantic,' who contributed to the *Irish World* and was later editor of *Mooney's Express* in San Francisco, although, coincidentally, both had a bad reputation in financial matters.

[71] *Irishman*, 21 April 1849, p. 248; *Irish Felon*, 15 July 1848, p. 50; J. Savage (ed), *Fenian Heroes and Martyrs*, Boston, Patrick O'Donohoe, 1868, pp. 52-3; M. Bourke, *John O'Leary: A Study in Irish Fenianism*, Tralee, Anvil books, 1967, p.

21; Comerford, *Fenianism*, p. 35; Mitchel, *Jail Journal*, p. 435; M. Doheny, *The Felon's Track*, p. 302.
[72] *Irishman*, 23 February 1850, p. 121; 2 March 1850, p. 137; M.F. Ryan, *Fenian Memories*, Dublin, Gill and Son, 1945, pp. 82-4; R.F. Foster, *Modern Ireland 1600-1972*, London, Penguin, 1989, p. 392n.
[73] *NS*, 25 March 1848, p. 1; 12 October 1850, p. 1; *Irish Tribune*, 10 June 1848, p. 12; Mitchel, *Jail Journal*, pp. 437-8.
[74] *Clonmel Chronicle*, 9 March 1850, p. 2; *Nation*, 18 May 1850, p. 598.
[75] *Nation*, 26 January 1850, p. 341; 9 March 1850, p. 2; 13 April 1850, p. 524; 18 May 1850, p. 598.
[76] *Nation*, 26 January 1850, p. 341; 1 June 1850, p. 632; 8 June 1850, p. 643; *Cork Examiner*, 8 March 1850, p. 2.
[77] *Nation*, 4 May 1850, p. 572; *Clonmel Chronicle*, 9 March 1850, p. 2.
[78] *NS*, 13 April 1850, p. 8.
[79] *Nation*, 28 December 1850, p. 1.
[80] *Irishman*, 31 November 1849, p. 770; 23 March 1850, p. 178-9; 6 April 1850, p. 211; 27 April 1850, p. 259; 4 May 1850, p. 275-6; 11 May 1850, p. 293; 25 May 1850, p. 323; *NS*, 1 June 1850, p. 1; 1 November 1851, p. 1. For White see S. Roberts, *Radical Politicians and Poets in Early Victorian Britain*, Lampeter, Edwin Mellen Press, 1993, pp. 11-38.
[81] *NS*, 6 June 1840, p. 2; 25 May 1850, p. 1; 8 June 1850, p. 1. The hostile press such as the *Kilkenny Moderator* and the *Tipperary Free Press* described this meeting as a great failure. See *Nation*, 18 May 1850, p. 598.
[82] *NS*, 27 July 1850, p. 7; *Nation*, 29 June 1850, p. 693; 27 July 1850, p. 756.
[83] *NS*, 27 July 1850, p. 7. See also *Nation*, 8 June 1850, p. 652; 29 June 1850, p. 699.
[84] *Nation*, 26 January 1850, p. 341; 17 August 1850, p. 805; *NS*, 27 July 1850, p. 7.
[85] *NS*, 3 August 1850, p. 7; *Nation*, 11 May 1850, p. 584.
[86] *Nation*, 18 May 1850, p. 600; 1 June 1850, p. 628; 29 June 1850, p. 699; 17 August 1850, p. 805; 16 November 1850, p. 179; 28 December 1850, p. 276.
[87] *Friend of the People*, 18 January 1851, p. 45. See also *Red Republican*, 17 August 1850, p. 69.
[88] *Irishman*, 11 May 1850, p. 295; *NS*, 28 September, 1850, p. 4; *Nation*, 17 August 1850, p. 805; 26 October 1850, p. 134.
[89] L.M. Cullen, 'Comment on Koseki,' p. 30; Thompson, 'Seceding from the Seceders,' p. 148.
[90] *Irishman*, 22 September 1849, p. 594; J. Denvir, *The Life Story of an Old Rebel* (1910), Irish University Press, Dublin, 1972, pp. 52-3; T. Frost, *The Secret Societies of the European Revolution, 1776-1876*, London, Tinsley Brothers, 1876, Vol. 2, pp. 284-5; W.J. Lowe, *The Irish in Mid-Victorian Lancashire*, New York, Peter Lang, 1989, p. 192. Lowe suggests that he was the only link between the revolutionary movements of 1848 and the 1860s in Lancashire.
[91] J. Connolly, *Labour in Ireland: Labour in Irish history*, Dublin, Maunsel, 1917, pp. 191-2. According to M. Bourke, *John O'Leary*, p. 29: 'the members of the 1849 secret society must have provided the nucleus of Stephens' newly-founded

society in 1858'. See also Maura Cronin, *Country, Class or Craft?*, pp. 156-7, for the links between the IDA and the Fenians in Cork.
[92] See Mitchel, *Jail Journal*, pp. 405, 435.
[93] See M. Bourke, *John O'Leary*; Foster, *Modern Ireland*, p. 392n.
[94] See: T.C. Luby, *Life of Daniel O'Connell*, Glasgow, R and T Washbourne, 1872; *The Lives and Times of Illustrious and Representative Irishmen*, New York, Thomas Kelly, 1878; Connolly, *Labour in Ireland*, p. 192; H. Boylan, *A Dictionary of Irish Biography*, Dublin, Gill and Macmillan, second edition, 1988, p. 202.
[95] *NS*, 1 November 1851, p. 1; 8 November 1851, p. 1; Connolly, *Labour in Ireland*, pp. 191-2.

FROM THE LAND OF LIBERTY TO LAND MONOPOLY: THE UNITED STATES IN A CHARTIST CONTEXT

Jamie L. Bronstein

Although British labour history has often focused on the 'peculiarities of the English,' the Chartists have been shown to have been fervent internationalists, interested in the fates of workers in other countries and in movements for national freedom.[1] The United States, with which Britain shared so many cultural values, had since Jacobin times been a refuge for British radicals.[2] It is not surprising, therefore, that many British workers saw the United States as a symbol of successful democracy in the English tradition which they could wield as a rhetorical weapon in their own quest for political inclusion. Nor is it surprising that those who came under direct pressure from the government, or from material scarcity, used the United States as a refuge. More notable is the effect which the United States, as a political symbol, had on the Chartist movement. The United States which the Chartists constructed through their discourse in newspapers and memoirs changed over time, reflecting the realities of transatlantic contacts and visits. Generally speaking, as British leaders learned about life in the United States, they became less willing to promote the United States as an example of the way in which political inclusion could help to abolish class legislation. In turn, this new construction of the United States as a land of social and economic inequality fed back into radical policy proposals, helping to shift Chartists' preoccupations from the political to the economic realm.

Two points of pressure helped to re-mould radical thinking about the United States during the Chartist period. First, the persistence of slavery in a land of liberty led workers to criticize the nation they had once upheld as an example. This became a particular problem in the 1830s and 1840s as American labour gained its own voice and press, but refused to condemn slavery. Second, under the influence of emigration proponents and individual immigrants alike, hopes of individual betterment in the United States had come to be associated with land. By the mid-1840s, however, close association with American reformers had convinced British workers that even in America, land was far from being a free commodity. Close ties between American and British workers, and particularly between the Chartists and the Americans struggling to achieve land reform, cast doubt on universal suffrage as a panacea.[3] After all, if land monopoly could flourish in a system in which working men could vote, perhaps economics had to underpin politics and not the other way around. These American experiences helped to intensify the Chartists' already evident shift from political to social solutions like the Chartist Land Company, land nationalization, and 'The Charter and something more.'

I

From the inception of their movement, Chartists and other political radicals had no choice but to deal with the American question, since the United States was a political football for those opposed to universal suffrage as well as those who supported it. This was particularly the case in the wake of the election of President Andrew Jackson - an election which had been made possible by the transformation of the American electorate. No longer was property ownership the standard by which citizenship was measured; and the election of an outwardly populist president produced a violent rhetorical backlash from those who saw democracy as the antithesis of good government. In one anti-Jacksonian tract, 'An Anglo-American of Several Years' Residence' categorized the negative impact which democracy, in the form of universal white male suffrage, had produced in the United States. In his estimation, under the pressure of popular government, a once wisely-governed nation, led by representatives who followed their own best judgments rather than the fickle will of the populace, had become sadly perverted. And if the political excesses and demagogueries of Jacksonianism could occur in a country like the United States, where the population was relatively well-educated and spread out, how much more likely would they be in a country like Great Britain, full of the poor and uneducated? 'The calamities we have suffered here . . . may be considered light compared with those which would be likely to overwhelm yourselves, should you be rash enough to force upon the country the so-called Charter,' the correspondent warned.[4]

Another traveller to the United States, A. Thomason, who called himself a 'passive radical,' was equally pessimistic about the prospects for democracy as illustrated there. Thomason had a difficult time finding work as a teacher in America, and was disgusted by American trade unionism, American slavery, and by the ease with which the American press distracted workers from their real interests.[5] Rather than producing a materialist utopia, democracy in America had led to homelessness on one hand and to worship of the dollar on the other. 'I have seen such abject submission in American workmen, to the searching tyranny of domineering capitalists and their underlings, as involved the dereliction of all manhood, and would not have been borne by Englishmen or Frenchmen for an hour,' Thomason sneered.[6]

These manifestoes about the United States were double-edged. Like Tocqueville's musings on his own visit to America, they were as much answers to political movements at home as dispassionate analyses of affairs abroad.[7] It is thus not surprising that, as proponents of universal suffrage, the political radicals of the London Working Men's Association felt proprietorial about the reputation which the United States enjoyed in the press. William Lovett noted that newspapers constantly mocked the partisan wrangling which so characterized Jacksonian politics, drawing the conclusion that democracy was an unfit system. To counteract that tendency, the Association tried to co-opt the American story for their own purposes, producing an address to the Americans, which praised the republican institutions which had been purchased at the price of so much blood and valour.[8] Of course, the L.W.M.A. admitted, the United States had fallen victim to some maldistributions of power, in the form of crony capitalism and land monopoly, but these were blamed on the process of voter education rather than on the viciousness of the electorate.

Republican and Chartist Peter Murray McDouall also described the United States as a successful test case for democracy. McDouall noted that universal suffrage in America 'gives value to labour in payment for its work - because the suffrage protects the rights and the interests of the workingman, and elevates him above the degrading drudgery of a slave, who is hired for his master's work.' He argued that this was a characteristic of universal suffrage in all countries. Although the Americans were lucky to enjoy a material bounty, a richness of resources, that Britain lacked, the Americans' political institutions protected and invigorated that material growth:

> 'The cotton, the leather, the wood and the iron are all
> brought cheap and abundant to the workshop; but the
> moment the hand of the labourer touches the least of
> these supplies, it instantly assumes a fresh value in the
> eyes of the buyer . . . The hand of labour being thus
> encouraged socially, is protected politically, and thus it
> is that America acquires that vigour which we are so
> much addicted to ascribe to her youth.'[9]

Radicals' portrayal of the United States was never uniformly
rosy. While they felt a need to defend the results of universal
suffrage when arguing in the larger public sphere, within their own
public sphere of labour periodicals, they sometimes highlighted the
shortcomings of the Americans in order to goad their own
constituents to further action. Thus John Francis Bray, who would
be influential in Leeds Chartism before he emigrated to the United
States, noted in 1839 that universal suffrage was not a sufficient
condition for equality.[10] He argued that, in fact, Americans were
worse off than the English. Their ability to vote, he claimed, made
American workers sanguine about their ability to change their
oppression, when, in reality, they were just as helpless as their
English counterparts:[11]

> 'The possession of political power by a people, although
> in accordance with the principle of that equality which
> all good men wish to see established and enjoyed, does
> not of itself constitute the equality of rights; for although
> no equality of rights can be enjoyed by a nation without
> the accompaniment of universal suffrage, yet universal
> suffrage is neither accompanied with, nor productive of,
> equal rights.'[12]

Bray had been born in the United States and continued to
correspond with his brothers there; his opinions were therefore
based on first-hand information. His recommendation, for a linkage
between political rights and a better system of labour and
distribution, reverberated not only in England but also in America,

where artisans in Northern cities had spent much of the 1830s calling for a similar species of 'Equal Rights.'[13]

The persistence of slavery - and the willingness of American workers to condone that institution - was another issue which prevented British political radicals from completely idealizing the United States.[14] British and American workers generally stood quite far from each other on the question of race. American workers - particularly Irish immigrants - might reap what David Roediger has called 'the wages of whiteness,' or certain psychological satisfactions from the mere fact of being white. These satisfactions served both to compensate in part for low wages, long hours, and social disapprobation, and to prevent the white workers from imagining any kind of solidarity with black workers, free or slave. Leaders of American working men used the phrase 'white slavery' to describe their own plight and that of working-class women and children, and to redirect middle-class sympathy and energy from black bondsmen to themselves.[15] While some of this rhetoric did resonate in Britain, British workers did not have the same particular experiences of race - working in a country alongside slaves - which made the 'wages of whiteness' possible.

Many British workers and radicals who have left a record of their feelings found slavery abhorrent. The London Working Men demanded of the Americans an explanation for the persistence of slavery.[16] British socialist John Finch was disgusted about American attitudes toward blacks, noting that 'there is something in the construction of American character, customs and habits, that destroys all correct notions of universal liberty.' In a utopian narrative which was not published during his lifetime, John Francis Bray mounted a scathing attack on white workers for condoning slavery in the south and perpetuating racism against free blacks in the north.[17]

The memoirs of William Aitken, an Ashton-under-Lyne Chartist who went to the United States on an extended visit in 1843-4, capture his own personal loss of faith in America as an example for his own country to follow. While Aitken had many criticisms, his most trenchant ones were reserved for the institution of slavery. With horror and revulsion, Aitken recounted his visit to a slave auction and to a sugar plantation, where white men purporting to be Christians upheld the local work regime at the point of a lash.

Aitken even recalled a conversation he had had with a female slave - a conversation, about the possibilities for freedom, which had brought a tear of sentiment to the bondswoman's eye. Aitken was furious; 'Here was a female, sensitively alive to her degraded condition, and speaking in language as gentle and refined as any lady I have ever met with; but God and nature made her black, and the cupidity of man stamped inferiority upon her race.'[18] When he came to summarize his experiences in the United States at the end of his memoir, Aitken wondered whether the slavery issue would finally bring about serious trouble in the republic, and warned Americans to pay attention to their own rhetoric about all men being free and equal.[19]

Helping to emphasize the connections between American democracy and support of slavery were the writings of two Chartists who did emigrate to the United States. Upon relocating to the United States and taking his place among the workingmen land reformers of the urban North, former Chartist John Campbell wrote *Negro-Mania*, a compilation of pseudoscientific information which supported his view that blacks were racially inferior. Campbell's conclusion - that blacks must therefore remain enslaved lest they serve as debased competitors for wages with free white workers - was one he shared with many American working people: 'Will any one dare to say that were the whole slave population thrown into the free white labour market at once that the results would not be most disastrous to our mechanics and working men?'[20] Similarly, former Newcastle Chartist Thomas Devyr became a virulent racist and - not coincidentally - a supporter of the Democratic party, when he emigrated to New York.[21] The fact that these ordinarily enlightened individuals publicly expressed distaste for the prospect of freeing the slaves supported the idea that slavery was a systemic problem in American democracy, and not an institution which could be defeated by better voter education.

II

The United States was more than just an object of political discourse. The country had, since the seventeenth century, been the 'marchlands' of the British Empire, the rough edges to which indentured servants were sent and in which new labour systems and political systems were re-negotiated.[22] Even though by the Chartist period the United States had made its decisive political and cultural break with Great Britain, the tides of emigration continued. It was commonly understood on both sides of the Atlantic that the growing populations of the United States and Britain faced different futures; the United States supposedly enjoyed an embarrassment of riches in land, whereas the British workforce found itself penned up in cities. Competition between British firms in the same industry, combined with surplus workers, allowed - or compelled - low wages. This competition for wages led working-class radicals, and middle-class reformers alike, to promote migration within, or from, Britain as a safety valve for unemployment. W. Cooke Taylor noted with hope that 'the 'Far West' will for years to come afford refuge to all who cannot find employment in the older states. New factories must be the 'Far West' of England, whether they be extensions of the system in the branches already established, or an application of it to untried fields of industry.'[23] Other middle class reformers promoted the emigration of the British workforce to Australia - and, as Robin Haines has shown, attracted an audience committed to taking advantage of all possible public and private sector assistance in order to get there.[24]

Although emigration to Britain's colonies and former colonies helped lift former farm labourers and urban workers from poverty, English radicals felt ambivalent. They worried that the mass migration of English workers contributed nothing to improving their collective political lot, and in fact symbolized their marginalization. For many, emigration echoed transportation, the government's policy for punishment of criminal offenders and political radicals alike. Thus, the *Northern Star*'s editors opposed emigration as early as 1838, on the grounds that the unjust establishment which oppressed workers at home was being replicated in all the colonies. Furthermore, there was abundance at home, if only it were properly distributed.[25] Joseph Rayner Stephens, the political preacher with a devoted personal following in Lancashire and Cheshire, was an early proponent of home colonization, which came to be seen as the radical alternative to emigration.[26] The editors of the *English Patriot and Irish Repealer* were firm in the belief that there is no country in the world more suited to the health and prosperity of Englishmen than their own country, nor is there one that can offer a richer reward for industry than England, if justice were done the labourer . . . we shall henceforth oppose and expose, with all our might, these deluding schemers of emigration...[27]

To emigrate was to bear great transportation expense, to run the risk of illness, and to compromise the national defence - all while exculpating the ruling classes of their responsibilities to the poor.[28]

Even as working-class leaders felt understandable conflict about losing the constituency for their reform programme to other countries, in the early Chartist period they portrayed the United States as the least bad of all the possible emigration options. As the *Northern Star*'s editors noted:

We . . . recommend those who have money and who wish to emigrate, go to America, and those who have not money we recommend also to go to America. If they go to Canada, or Australia, they meet with branches from the basting, blighting, destroying Upas tree, which has driven them from house and home, and if they go to America they at once become their own masters.[29]

Those wishing to go to America might find encouragement about the prospect there in emigrant guides and colonization tracts. Books like Charles Knight's *British Mechanic's and Labourer's Handbook and Guide to the United States* portrayed the United States as a material utopia, with plentiful and various foods, pubs which carried English newspapers, authentically free public schools, and plenty of jobs available for boys, girls and women as well as tradesmen.[30] Publicity pamphlets intended for European audiences touted the United States as a new garden of Eden. In Texas, for example,

the nights are cool and refreshing; while the south winds prevail, the transparent clearness of the skies, the balmy softness of the atmosphere, realize all that poets have sung of the Aegean era . . . Peaches of delicious flavor, figs, oranges, pomegranates, quinces, grapes; and in the forests, the pecan, hickory-nut, persimmon, wild grape, wild plum, various species of the blackberry, flourish in high perfection.[31]

Middle-class observers contributed to this utopian view of the United States by favourably contrasting the American factory system with its British counterpart. Henry Scoresby visited Lowell, Massachusetts in 1844, and came back to lecture about it to the Church Institution in Bradford:

Here, with us, everything, externally, is discoloured with smoke; buildings, streets and causeways, alike bearing a sooty covering; the mud of the streets in colour and consistency, like blackish-grey paint, and the air of heaven darkened as by a dense cloud; there, nothing is discoloured, neither houses nor mills nor trees.[32]

The factory operatives who worked in Lowell were uniformly described as neatly dressed, clean and happy, in contrast with British operatives who had become slaves to the machine.[33] The American worker was described as having few cares; the strike era of the mid 1830s had quickly evaporated under the hostility of public opinion, and workmen had little time for political activism.[34] Thus, Owenite socialist John Finch was reflecting the general optimism of the time when he described America as an 'untaxed land, flowing with milk and honey.'[35]

Responding to these appeals, British workers sought solace on land in the United States, sometimes through elaborate schemes of mutual aid.[36] The Potters' Joint Stock Emigration Society, which in the Staffordshire Potteries competed with the Chartist Land Company, proposed to buy land in Wisconsin, and by ballot to choose emigrants who would be eligible for plots of farmland there.[37] The Bradford Co-Operative Emigration Society was established in June 1849

to secure the emigration of all the members as soon as possible. We think by cooperating together for a certain period - say five years- a sufficiency of land and stock will be had, to enable each individual member to commence farming on his own account.[38]

Smaller, less formally organized emigration schemes were also suggested. Members of the Manchester iron trades considered sending their 'surplus labour' to the Western United States, also through a process of balloting.[39]

The message flowing back from individual emigrants to the United States was somewhat qualified. Many emphasized that the urban economy was uncertain in America and held up the land as by far the best option to provide permanent security.[40] Sometimes these appeals were printed in the *Northern Star*. Samuel Davies, a Birmingham Chartist, conjured up a picture of an endless line of English and Irish mechanics begging their way westward, unable to find work. 'At New York I saw many who had not the means to purchase a meal, some of whom I had known in this country.' In Davies' estimation, only the land was the guarantor of pure happiness.[41] Wortley Chartist Joseph Barker, whose brothers had already moved to the United States, agreed, noting,

> There is room in the United States for all the people of the British Islands. There is land enough to make everyone rich, and every one, by temperance and persevering industry, may obtain a fair portion of that land. And the land is infinitely productive. And the climate is not at all unfriendly.[42]

The multiplicity of working-class and radical voices attempting to claim and make sense of the United States illustrates that there was no single prevailing view of that experiment in democracy. This would change by the end of the 1840s, as the voices of optimism gave way to a more pervasive disillusionment based on the failure of the United States to measure up in the one area that had been relatively uncontested - its position as a materialist utopia. Both the discourse about emigration and the material experiences of English emigrants had helped to classify the United States as a region which provided the answer to poverty through an abundance of land. Rather perversely, this optimism about the abundance of

American land opened the way for British disillusionment with the United States. Once American workers began to agitate for land reform within their own country, their activism showed the British that the promise of free land was rapidly becoming an empty one.

III

Disillusionment with the United States was facilitated by increased Chartist travel to the United States, and by the maintenance of close connections of communication between British labour newspapers, like the *Northern Star*, Bronterre O'Brien's revived *National Reformer*, and the *Potter's Examiner and Workman's Advocate*, and American newspapers which reported on workers' issues - particularly the New York *Working Man's Advocate* (later *Young America*).[43] Readers of the British newspapers learned that even Chartists who emigrated to the United States remained involved in reformist politics, demonstrating with their lives the notion that universal suffrage was not a total panacea. John Cluer crusaded for the ten-hour day in the textile factories of Massachusetts and New Hampshire; Thomas Devyr was more famous as a proponent of American land reform and the anti-rent movement in upstate New York than he had been as an outspoken member of Newcastle's Northern Political Union.[44] As Devyr wrote in a passage which reached across the Atlantic,

> our descendants wish to raise themselves from the condition of hirelings, but they wish it in vain. They cannot approach a field on which the capitalist has not made his mark, and each succeeding age their condition becomes more and more hopeless . . . When our posterity look back to the opportunity that we are now losing, they will not bless our memory if we leave them nothing but a heritage of toil and dependence.[45]

British emigrants warned their friends at home that the economic picture of the United States was not as rosy as it had originally been painted. A former Leeds Chartist, who had emigrated just in time for the recession which followed the Panic of

1837, reported that thousands in New York were out of work, and relying on alms houses for food:

> Scores are compelled to lie in the open air, under trees, in the public walks in the city, for the want of money to pay for beds. . . I have had, several times since my arrival, to give money out of my pocket to starving families, that I was keeping to buy food for myself and family.[46]

John Smyles, who was in contact with Chartist Lawrence Pitkeithley, wrote from Rochester, New York, to complain about the way the wealthy had gained an upper hand in the United States. 'Special, class legislation, has [been] obtained to a great extent, and unless the evil be remedied, our institutions will become a mockery and a byeword.'[47] Similarly, Pitkeithley, who visited the United States as the *Northern Star's* correspondent in 1843, warned that 'no one should depart their native land, unless under complete arrangements for entering upon THE LAND at the place of their intended destination.' He states that from the immense numbers that flocked to the United States during the last and two previous years, there is a great 'redundancy of hands' in every department of labour.'[48] Pitkeithley was relentless in his exposure of poor conditions in the United States, painting New York as a land of crooked, stinking streets steeped in mire and flanked by bizarre and unmatched architecture, and obstructed by merchandise.[49] Agents for the *Northern Star* helped to mould the Chartist view of America by selling American manifestoes of discontent along with other cheap tracts.[50]

After a long journey by steamship to the American West, William Aitken had found not a land of plenty but rather a rough, poor region, devoid of the markers of civilization to which he was accustomed, and surprisingly lacking in economic opportunity.[51] Like other observers of American politics, he quickly noticed the extent to which the general good of the country had been subsumed in party politics.[52] On the social side, Aitken found Americans vulgar and rough. He reserved especial revulsion for the Mormon prophet Joseph Smith, who Aitken judged had lured thousands of innocent Lancashire folk to the no-man's land of Nauvoo, Illinois, forcing them, for starvation wages, to work building his temple, while they lived in the meanest hovels.[53] Aitken found himself imploring the Americans to mend their ways and become the example of freedom for their oppressed British brethren to follow:

> I would fain hope that the people of America will justify that high opinion which the democratic party in England form of their country, because it is to you that the oppressed of every country look for carrying to the acme the blessings of political equality to every human being . . .[54]

These criticisms continued throughout the 1840s. A British emigrant to Paterson, New Jersey in 1849 noted that

> the first thing that struck me was the dirty, ill-paved streets. The morning had been wet before I landed, and the streets were literally canals of filth and mud of every description . . . the houses are in some parts densely crowded as the worst of Glasgow.[55]

Other emigrants complained about the low wages or the demanding pace of work at American manufacturing jobs.[56] Former Chartist Peter Bussey was more philosophical. As he wrote from Lowell, Massachusetts,

> I like the country, and shall spend the remainder of my days in it. Many who come, feel disappointed in consequence of forming too high an estimate of the political and social arrangements of the Republic . . . Others do well, and send exaggerated accounts to their friends, whom they induce to come, perhaps to experience disappointment.

Bussey reiterated the fears about urban blight and competition, which many emigrants to America were now sharing, but continued to be confident in the redemptive powers of the land.[57]

Although the news from the cities was bad, the United States had at least always offered the prospect of free land. Now,

however, through the working-class press and these personal
connections forged across the Atlantic, British working people
would learn the lesson that despite the so-called 'American
frontier,' American working men had little chance of becoming
independent peasant proprietors. Although his influence as a
Chartist leader was limited by the mid-1840s because Feargus
O'Connor did not like him and kept his ideas out of the *Northern
Star*, Bronterre O'Brien was one of the main forces behind
publicity of the land question. As he pointed out in 1840, no
country could have real freedom unless its people had absolute
dominion over the land. Besides being represented and educated,
every man should be a part proprietor in the soil.[58] O'Brien was one
of the first on either side of the Atlantic to point out that, no matter
what temporary legislative expedients were tried in order to
distribute free public lands in the United States, land monopoly
might return as soon as crowding occurred again through
immigration.

Through his *National Reformer* O'Brien focused attention on
the American National Reform movement, a political and cultural
expression by northern working people who sought free
homesteads on the public lands, a limitation on the amount of land
that any one man might own, and an exemption so that the family
homestead could not be confiscated in case of debt. Between 1844
and 1862, the National Reformers would inundate Congress and
their state legislatures with petitions calling for these reforms; but
they also created an extrapolitical culture of meetings, songs and
literature which echoed that of the Chartists in its richness.[59]
O'Brien also brought to the attention of British workers the
Americans' other grievances. Their demands included provisions
for the equitable adjustment of debt, the elimination of chartered
privileges, a reformation of the legal system, and direct taxes on
property. They sought free public schools, mechanics' liens to
ensure that they got paid, and the abolition of a system of prison
labour which flooded the market with cheap, competitive goods.[60]
British readers of the working-class press were exposed to the
details of the Americans' annual Industrial Congresses, at which
labour radicals promoted such reforms as the ten-hour day, free
homesteads, homestead exemption, and cooperative workshops and
stores.[61] The Americans' decision to lobby for these changes

outside as well as inside the political system would have shown observant Chartists that, even in the midst of universal suffrage, working people lacked the power to repeal 'class legislation.'

As the proprietor of the Chartist Land Company, Feargus O'Connor also enjoyed a close relationship with the American land reform movement. Open letters and the exchange of personnel dedicated to returning man to a more 'natural' life on the land exposed British workers to the European-sounding arguments for social equality made by American land reformers - their complaints about monopolies, aristocracies, and land-related despotisms.[62] At the National Reform Convention held at Cleveland, Ohio, in May 1848, American workers passed resolutions that

> The right to live involves and includes the right to the means of sustaining life. There is no known means of raising supplies for sustaining life but from the soil. Thence the monopoly of the soil - of the means of sustaining life - is equal to the monopoly of life itself; therefore, 'resolved, that the monopoly of the soil includes within the enthrallment of the tiller of that soil; or in other words, that land monopoly was the foundation of chattel slavery, and now involves consequences worse than it . . . though the Revolution of '76 gave to the Americans the liberty to vote, *they have not yet voted for liberty.*

These stirring sentiments were filtered back to British workers through extensive reportage in their own press.[63] That the land reform movement was a transatlantic cause favoured even by the Americans helped O'Connor build his list of Land Company subscribers.[64]

When Chartists and American workers joined together to condemn land monopoly as the underpinning of political oppression, it was logical to conclude that political representation was a sham without economic power to back it up.[65] Ebenezer Jones noted that the social power of the propertied classes conferred political power, maintaining that 'the investigator of the moral condition of the upper and middle classes must ask not what laws they break, but what laws they make; not what social institutions they attack, but what social institutions they establish.'[66] The *Northern Star*'s editors reported that just such a power imbalance, based on the monopoly of land, was beginning to show itself in the United States. They called the American Far West a 'mockery to the masses,' and claimed that speculators had pre-empted most of the land there, taking it out of the reach of actual settlers.[67] The *Northern Star*'s readers learned of railroad speculators who threatened to foreclose all of the American land beyond the existing states, depriving Americans of their birthright in the soil - and by extension, of the meaningfulness of their votes.[68] Joseph Barker likened land monopoly in Britain to American slavery; 'If our aristocrats have a right to the land of the country, they have, in effect, a right to the bodies and souls of the inhabitants.'[69]

Former Chartist John Campbell entered this discourse in 1848, with his *Theory of Equality*.[70] Although Campbell had begun his new life in America as a Jacksonian democrat - and therefore a convinced proponent of universal suffrage - he was disappointed with the way in which the Jacksonians had provided for the economic and social needs of the working men.

> Has the party been consistent advocates and defenders of the rights of man? has it, when it has had the power, destroyed paper money in each state? has it made the land of the United States free to actual settlers? has it established free trade? has it abrogated usury? has it abolished slavery? has it prevented monopoly? I ask for proofs.[71]

Campbell would admit no difference between the way in which factory workers and other urban labourers were treated in America and the way that they were treated in Britain. 'Are the populations of Lowell, or of Manayunk, less at the mercy of the capitalists than those of Lyons, or of Manchester? Is a factory master kinder to his wage slaves in America than in Europe?'[72] Campbell's solution to this problem - a solution just as dear to the hearts of members of the Chartist Land Company as to the American land reformers - was to return the working man to an independent farming life.[73]

British radicals with socialist leanings rejoiced that the United States was such a fertile ground for Owenite and Fourierite experiments.[74] Even the American advocates for free land for the workers were susceptible to these communitarian enthusiasms, as the British reading public would discover.[75] The rage for Owenite and Fourierite communities in the United States reinforced the call for social change, since it could be interpreted as an admission that the suffrage alone was insufficient to produce a reordering of society.[76] As early as 1842 John Smyles had made the connection between the failures of universal suffrage as a panacea in the United States, and the need to use the Charter to gain social reforms. The system of Republican government outstripped the present intelligence of the English people, he contended. 'The Charter, as a mere instrument to confer rights, such as voting for representative, etc., would do little good to the people of England in itself.' Smyles looked forward instead to

> the revolution that it would necessarily bring about - the destruction of a splendid but frivolous and useless government, which all their earnings are taxed to support - the annihilation in some way of the national debt - the abrogation of the laws of primogeniture - and the permission of the more equal division of the soil among the many.[77]

By the late 1840s and early 1850s, the socially-based Chartist critique of the United States - a critique which had largely grown out of the land issue - was complete. Despite the fact that the Chartist Land Company was floundering under negative attention from a Parliamentary Select Committee, many Chartist leaders had accepted home colonization, or some similar social reform, as a necessary concomitant of political representation, if for divergent reasons. 'Why are we poor?' asked the Kirkdale Chartist prisoners, proceeding to blame the misappropriation of land as the primary cause of poverty in all countries:

> We go still further and fearlessly denounce the monopoly of the soil as the fruitful source of human misery and degradation in all civilized countries . . . for

even in Republican America, the evil is found to operate.[78]

Ernest Jones considered and rejected the solution of emigration to the United States in 1851 for the same reason; 'In almost every large town of the United States, mass meetings are being held, far greater than this, of the unemployed, starving hopeless and workless, who are rolling in the glut of their surplus labour.'[79] Once a test case for democracy, the United States now demonstrated the limitations of a purely political reform.

Although the United States had run its race as a political symbol by the early 1850s, eclipsed somewhat by newer and more vital republics, it did not disappear completely as a point of reference for British reformers. At the end of the Chartist period, as some Chartists themselves began to rethink their early folly and recast themselves as Liberals, the United States served as a symbol of failed hopes and youthful enthusiasm gone awry. James Dawson Burn, author of *Autobiography of a Beggar Boy,* spent three years among the American working classes and published his thoughts on their plight in the last year of the American Civil War.[80] Many of his criticisms of the United States were predictable. He found Americans too individualistic, turned by the spirit of competition into automatons working at the speed of their machines.[81] He felt that democracy reigned to a ridiculous extent, to the point that domestic servants even claimed to have no masters.[82] He reported that the Americans were corrupt and that they allowed their newspapers to run roughshod over men's public reputations instead of promoting useful political knowledge.[83]

Burn concluded his visit to the United States with a sense of disillusionment, not only about that country, but about some of the radical demands, including the ballot and universal suffrage, for which he had campaigned in his own past. Political corruption was one major factor in his disillusionment; the Civil War, which illustrated the limits of democracy, was another. As had many writers before him, Burn drew conclusions for England from the failed experiment in America:

In England, the question of the extension of the franchise, is one of serious importance, and to none more than to the working classes themselves. I can form some small idea of the anarchy and confusion which would have existed in Great Britain in 1837, if the people had had the power of returning the men of their choice to the House of Commons. The interests of the working men, so far as their representatives were concerned, would have been in the hands of such men as Fergus O'Connor, Bronterre O'Brien, Julian Harncy, Dr. McDugall, Dr. Taylor, the un-Rev. Mr. Stevens, and a number of others of the same class whose names have slipped from my memory [sic]. Had all or any of these men been elected, the Government then in being would have immediately closed their patriotic jaws by trifling bribes, unless we make an exception in favour of the disinterested folly of Mr. O'Connor.[84]

A reader would hardly have known that Burn had identified himself with Chartism while living in Greenock in the 1830s and that he had once even expressed approval of the theory behind O'Connor's land plan.[85] By dismissing democracy in the United States, Burns found a way to close the book on an embarrassing chapter of his own political life.

For decades, the United States of America in its material and its cultural expressions not only had been constructed by Chartists in different ways, but also had helped to construct their movement. At the beginning of the Chartist period many looked upon America with fond hopes, and even fled there under the pressure of economic or political repression. While the People's Charter was home grown, summarizing as it did British radical demands that had been mooted about since the eighteenth century, the existence of that other, culturally English democratic republic across the Atlantic helped to make the Chartists' cause seem practicable. By the mid-1840s, much of the bloom was off the rose, as Chartists learned more about the failure of the United States to meet their material expectations, and also considered the persistence of slavery in a country in which liberty and virtue were the national slogans. Their disillusionment added to the energies which the Chartists collectively were investing in social reform, and impelled their attempts to acquire the land. Still, the meaning of 'the United

States' which any individual Chartist chose to appropriate - by joining the Land Company, by emigrating to the United States, by railing against slavery, or by continuing to seek universal suffrage - was not determined by this larger movement within Chartism. As Burn's repudiation ironically shows, after Chartism, the war-riven United States might once again become a symbol of the folly of democracy, helping former radicals to link the radicalism of their youthful pasts with the more measured politics of their later lives.

NOTES

[1] Edward Thompson originated this phrase in a rather different context in his essay, 'The Peculiarities of the English,' which is reprinted in Edward Thompson, *The Poverty of Theory and Other Essays*, New York, Monthly Review Press, 1978, pp. 245-301. On internationalism, see Margot Finn, *After Chartism*, Cambridge, Cambridge University Press, 1993.

[2] Michael Durey, *Transatlantic Radicals and the Early American Republic*, Lawrence, University of Kansas, 1997, p. 8.

[3] Gregory Claeys identified this as one of four competing strains of radical thought from 1820 to 1850. See "The Example of America a Warning to England?' The Transformation of America in British Radicalism and Socialism, 1790-1850,' in Malcolm Chase and Ian Dyck, eds., *Living and Learning: Essays in Honour of J.F.C. Harrison*, Aldershot, Scolar Press, 1996, pp. 66-80. While I do not deny that for some radicals the United States continued to be thought of as a beacon of freedom, this essay explores what I consider to be the most influential Chartist evaluation of the United States.

[4] An Anglo-American of Several Years' Residence, *Letters from the United States of America, Exhibiting the Workings of Democracy in that Country for the Last Twenty Years*, London, James Gilbert, 1844, p. 5.

[5] Thomason's particular critique was the work-scales which American craftsmen had arrived at, creating a situation whereby 'the veriest bungler, both in amount of work dealt out to him, and in its price, could insist on an equality with the accomplished workman. Thus did the round balls of dung, floating cheek-by-jowl with the fruit in the inundated farmyard of the fable, say 'How we apples swim!'' A. Thomason, *Men and Things in America: Being the Experience of a Year's Residence in the United States*, London, William Smith, 1838, p. 119.

[6] *Ibid.*, p. 193.

[7] George Wilson Pierson, *Tocqueville in America*, Baltimore, Johns Hopkins University Press, 1996, pp. 31-33.

[8] William Lovett, *The Life and Struggles of William Lovett*, London, MacGibbon & Kee, 1967, p. 107.

[9] *McDouall's Chartist Journal*, 14 August 1841.

[10] A good, short biography of Bray is M.A. Lloyd-Pritchard's introduction to John Francis Bray, *A Voyage from Utopia*, London, Lawrence and Wishart, 1957, pp. 7-34.

[11] Bray, *Voyage from Utopia*, p. 141.

[12] John Francis Bray, *Labour's Wrongs and Labour's Remedy*, Leeds, David Green, 1839, p. 18.

[13] Sean Wilentz, *Chants Democratic*, New York, Oxford University Press, 1986, pp. 191-216.

[14] Gregory Claeys, *Citizens and Saints*, Cambridge, Cambridge University Press, 1989, p. 296.

[15] On the racism of white workers in the American north, see David Roediger, *The Wages of Whiteness*, London, Verso, 1991; Marcus Cunliffe, *Chattel Slavery and Wage Slavery*, Athens, University of Georgia Press, 1979; and Noel Ignatiev, *How the Irish Became White*, New York, Routledge, 1995.

[16] Lovett, *The Life and Struggles of William Lovett*, p. 110.

[17] Bray, *Voyage from Utopia*, p. 147.

[18] William Aitken, *Journey up the Mississippi River, From its Mouth to Nauvoo, the City of the Latter Day Saints*, Ashton-under-Lyne, John Williamson, 1845, p. 18.

[19] *Ibid.*, p. 52.

[20] John Campbell, *Negro-Mania!*, Philadelphia, Campbell and Power, 1851, p. 459.

[21] See, for example, Devyr's letter to Andrew Johnson, December 9, 1859, in Andrew Johnson papers, Library of Congress.

[22] Bernard Bailyn, *Voyagers to the West*, New York, Vintage Books, 1986, pp. 4-5.

[23] W. Cooke Taylor, *Factories and the Factory System*, London, Jeremiah How, 1844, p. 115.

[24] Robin F. Haines, *Emigration and the Labouring Poor*, New York, St. Martin's Press, 1997.

[25] *Northern Star*, 1 December 1838; 11 December 1841; *Spirit of the Age*, 19 August 1848.

[26] *People's Magazine*, August 1841.

[27] *English Patriot and Irish Repealer*, 7 October 1848.

[28] *English Patriot and Irish Repealer*, 14 October 1848; see also *New Moral World*, 3 December 1842.

[29] *Northern Star*, 10 April 1841.

[30] Charles Knight, *The British Mechanic's and Labourer's Handbook and Guide to the United States*, London, Charles Knight & Co., 1843, passim.

[31] *Texan Emigration and Land Company, Texas: Being a Prospectus of the Advantages Offered to Emigrants*, London, Richardson, 1843, pp. 16-17.

[32] Henry Scoresby, *American Factories and their Female Operatives*, London, Longman, 1845, p. 11.

[33] *Ibid.*, p. 12; cf. A. B. Reach, *Manchester and the Textile Districts in 1849*, Helmshore Local History Society, 1972, p. 2; and for an American view of the

same subject, see John Aiken, *Labor and Wages, at Home and Abroad*, Lowell, D. Bixby, 1849.

[34] Charles Knight, *The British Mechanic's and Labourer's Handbook and Guide to the United States*, London, Charles Knight & Co., 1843.

[35] *New Moral World*, 6 July 1844.

[36] See Charlotte Erickson, 'Emigration from the British isles to the USA in 1841: Part II: Who were the English immigrants?' *Population Studies*, vol. 44, 1990, p. 40.

[37] On the Potters' Joint Stock Emigration Society, see Jamie Bronstein, *Land Reform and Working Class Experience in Britain and the United States, 1800-1862*, Stanford, Stanford University Press, 1999; Grant Foreman, 'Settlement of English Potters in Wisconsin,' *Wisconsin Magazine of History*, vol. 21, June 1938, pp. 375-396; and Horst Rössler, 'The Dream of Independence: The 'America' of England's North Staffordshire Potters,' in Dirk Hoerder and Horst Rössler, eds., *Distant Magnets: Expectations and Realities in the Immigrant Experience, 1840-1930*,' New York, Holmes and Meier, 1993, pp. 128-159.

[38] *The People: Their Rights and Liberties, their Duties and their Interests*, vol. 2 no. 62, p. 79. Hereafter cited as *The People*.

[39] *English Patriot and Irish Repealer*, 14 October 1848.

[40] See Charlotte Erickson, *Invisible Immigrants*, Ithaca, Cornell University Press, 1972, pp. 164, 166, 168, 303, 312. This point is also well-made in Rössler, 'Dream of Independence,' pp. 142-144.

[41] *Northern Star*, 20 May 1843.

[42] *The People*, vol. 1, no. 15, p. 119. Barker would be a steady proponent of emigration to the United States, but with the caveat that only those who could afford land should go; see also vol. 1 no. 28, p. 221; vol. 1 no. 38, pp. 300, 303; vol. 1 no. 39, p. 307; vol. 2 no. 70, p. 139; vol. 2 no. 75, p. 179. On Barker, see Michael Brook, 'Joseph Barker and the People, the True Emigrants' Guide,' *Publications of the Thoresby Society*, vol. 13, 1963, pp. 331-378.

[43] For details on these interactions, see Bronstein, *Land Reform and Working-Class Experience in Britain and the United States*, chapter 5.

[44] On the general problem of Chartist emigration to the United States, see Ray Boston, *British Chartists in America*, Manchester, Manchester University Press, 1971; and Cynthia Anne Paul Swajkowski, 'Chartist Contributions to the American Workers,' Ph.D. thesis, George Washington University, 1996. On Cluer's activities, see Theresa Murphy, *Ten Hours' Labor: Religion, Reform, and Gender in Early New England*, Ithaca, Cornell University Press, 1992.

[45] *Evening Star*, 6 January 1843.

[46] *Northern Star*, 1 October 1842.

[47] John Smyles, *A Letter Addressed to Mr. Pitkeithly*, London, J. Watson, 1842, p. 3.

[48] *Northern Star*, 1 April 1843.

[49] *Northern Star*, 29 April 1843. On Pitkeithley's journey to the United States, which helped to cement the ties between British and American reformers, see Michael Brook, 'Lawrence Pitkeithley, Dr. Smyles, and Canadian Revolutionaries in the United States, 1842,' *Ontario History*, vol. 57, 1965, pp. 79-84.

[50] *Northern Star*, 10 October 1840.

[51] Aitken, *Journey up the Mississippi River*, p. 7.

[52] *Ibid.*, p. 30.

[53] *Ibid.*, p. 37.

[54] *Ibid.*, p. 31.

[55] *Spirit of the Age*, 18 August 1849.

[56] *The People*, vol. 2 no,. 67, p. 117; vol. 2 no. 69, p. 133.

[57] His letter, addressed to 'Friend Sutcliff' and dated July 14, 1849, can be found in *The People*, vol. 2 no. 65, p. 99.

[58] *Chartist Circular*, 19 December 1840.

[59] The National Reformers are discussed in detail in Bronstein, *Land Reform and Working-Class Experience in Britain and the United States*; Helene Zahler, *Eastern Workingmen and National Land Policy*, New York, Columbia, 1941; Sean Wilentz, *Chants Democratic*; and John Reeve Huston, 'Land and Freedom: The Anti-Rent Wars, Jacksonian Politics and the Contest over Free Labor in New York, 1765-1865.' Ph.D. thesis, Yale University, 1994.

[60] *National Reformer*, 10 October 1846.

[61] *National Instructor*, 20 July 1850; 31 August 1850; *Red Republican*, 27 July, 1850.

[62] See Bronstein, *Land Reform and Working-Class Experience in Britain and the United States*, pp. 150-159.

[63] *Spirit of the Age*, 11 November, 1848.

[64] Bronstein, *Land Reform and Working-Class Experience in Britain and the United States*, chapters 5 and 6.

[65] Ernest Jones, *Notes to the People* vol. 1, London, J. Pavey, 1851, p. 339; see also 'The Charter and the Land,' in *The Labourer*, vol. 1, 1847, p. 81. On the American side, see the comments of former London Owenite, turned Wisconsin reformer, Thomas Hunt in *Spirit of the Age*, 11 November 1848.

[66] Ebenezer Jones, *The Land Monopoly: The Suffering and Demoralization Caused by It, and The Justice and Expediency of its Abolition*, London, Charles Fox, 1849. See also W.J. Linton, *The People's Land: And an Easy Way to Recover It*, London, J Watson, 1850.

[67] *Northern Star*, 12 October 1850.

[68] *Northern Star*, 13 March 1847.

[69] See 'Property in Man, and Property in the Land,' *The People*, vol. 3, no. 117.

[70] John Campbell, *A Theory of Equality: or, the Way of Making Every Man Act Honestly*, Philadelphia, John Perry, 1848.

[71] *Ibid.*, p. 16.

[72] *Ibid.*, p. 25.

[73] *Ibid.*, pp. 94, 103.

[74] *People's Journal*, vol. 3, 1847, p. 196. On communitarianism in the United States during this period, see Carl Guarneri, *The Utopian Alternative: Fourierism in Nineteenth-Century America*, Ithaca, Cornell University Press, 1991; Christopher Clark, *The Communitarian Moment: The Radical Challenge of the Northampton Association*, Ithaca, Cornell University Press, 1995; and J.F.C.

Harrison, *Robert Owen and the Owenites in Britain and America: The Quest for the New Moral World*, London, Routlege and Kegan Paul, 1969.

[75] See the report on the National Reform village in Ceresco, Wisconsin, reprinted in *Spirit of the Age*, 16 Feb. 1850.

[76] *New Moral World*, 23 December 1843, 21 January 1843; 6 April 1844.

[77] Smyles, *A Letter Addressed to Mr. Pitkeithly*, p. 5.

[78] Kirkdale Chartist Prisoners, *Chartist Tracts for the Times, no. 2*, Wortley, Joseph Barker, 1849, p. 4.

[79] Ernest Jones, *Evenings with the People, An Address Delivered at St Martin's Hall, no. 7*, London, Ernest Jones, 1856, p. 4.

[80] James Dawson Burn, *Three Years Among the Working Classes*, London, Smith, Elder and Co., 1865.

[81] *Ibid.*, p. 12, 186.

[82] *Ibid.*, p. 21.

[83] *Ibid.*, p. 47.

[84] *Ibid*. p. 272.

[85] James Burn, *Autobiography of a Beggar Boy*, David Vincent, ed., London, Europa Publications, 1978, pp. 151-2.

CHARTIST POETRY AND SONG

Timothy Randall

Frank Peel, writing in the late nineteenth century, noted the 'immense masses of people' who attended the Chartist meeting at Peep Green, Yorkshire, on Whit Monday 1839. This was 'the largest political meeting ever held in England... it was calculated that a quarter of a million people were present'. The meeting opened with a Methodist hymn, '[T]he singing of which from such a vast multitude had an indescribable effect, accompanied as it was by thousands of musical instruments'.[1] Such mass singing, whether of hymns or anthems or other forms of verse, was common during Chartist meetings. Most verses were written by the Chartists themselves and published in the Chartist press. John Storey has recently observed that analysis of Chartism should provide the context from which 'the *political* study of popular culture first emerges'.[2] Yet comparatively little study has been undertaken of the popular political culture which Chartists created. Chartist verse has been largely ignored alike by cultural critics, fixated as they have been upon the twentieth century, by historians, wary as they still are of literary textuality, and by literary critics, shy as they always will be of archival research.[3]

Some historians however have found various reasons to attend to Chartist verse: for Paul Pickering, H.R. Nicholls' poems are 'pedestrian,' but are useful because they 'provide a window' on the past; while James Epstein values Chartist verse for providing 'an impressive challenge to the force of emergent industrial capitalism'. Scholars are beginning to draw upon Chartist verse (and fiction) as historical sources.[4]

Literary critics have occasionally edited and analysed Chartist verse. Two anthologies have been published, one in the former Soviet Union and the other in the U.S.A.[5] Two books exclusively on Chartist verse have been published, in France and in Germany. Hugues Journès examines the careers of several Chartist poets and discusses the most important themes of Chartist poetry. Ulrike Schwab combines close analysis of a few poems within a very theoretical categorisation of Chartist verse.[6] A few other literary critics have chapters or sections on Chartist verse.[7] Most recently

Anne Janowitz has devoted several chapters to demonstrate that 'Chartism as a social and political movement made itself culturally intelligible to its constituencies *through* its use of poetry'.[8]

Janowitz succeeds in making Chartist verse culturally intelligible to today's readers, partly through the prism of formal categories such as the 'communitarian lyric'. This chapter might have debated with such critical interpretations of Chartist texts as currently exist. However the primary need is to continue to make visible what remains obscured cultural history.[9] The aim of this chapter is to reconstruct in close detail a popular cultural formation within its historical context.[10]

By 'Chartist verse' I refer to poems and songs written by people who were actively involved in the Chartist movement, and which express a distinctly Chartist political perspective. Many of the verses which appeared in Chartist newspapers were not concerned with political or social issues (such as paeans to nature), and they are not the subject of this chapter. The Chartist press also carried many poems or extracts from the literary canon, especially from those who expressed 'democratic' sentiments: for instance, Burns, Byron, and particularly Shelley. Again, these are not the subject of this essay, although it should be noted that literary classics bore considerable cultural, moral and political authority for Chartists who often enlisted them for their own movement; verse extracts from the canon were frequently cited in Chartist speeches and displayed on public banners.

For reasons of space this chapter will not assess the careers of the numerous Chartist poets, nor will it comprehensively discuss the various themes which informed Chartist verse. Instead I shall focus on the collective functions of Chartist verse within the movement. Various issues will emerge, including: the significances of communal singing; the use of verse to celebrate individual Chartists; the difficulties of poetically representing political agency; the authorship of poetry in prison; the use of poetry to explore utopian visions; and the evolving character of a distinctively Chartist stock of poetic imagery.

Chartist verse possessed a context which historians find difficult to fully recover, and which literary critics are largely oblivious of: the mass open-air gatherings, the anniversary celebrations, the reading groups, the feasts, the evening teas, the workplace lunches, the public house meetings, the extempore singing in prison. This is a literature which existed not only on the page as a literary text, but also as a social event and public demonstration.

The frequent inclusion of melody titles within the printed texts of Chartist verse is our first indication of this. The *Northern Star* advertised a series of 'Songs for the People, or the Poetry of Chartism,' 'for use in the convivial meetings of the people, and on occasions of popular rejoicing'. A Chartist tea party in Manchester in 1843, attended by 'upwards of five hundred persons,' included six Chartist songs, which the assembly sang accompanied by a brass band, and to which they danced from midnight until five in the morning. Clearly, pleasure and ideological purity are not always incompatible.[11]

In 'A Song of Freedom' Benjamin Stott, a Manchester bookbinder, defined the purpose of his verse:

> It shall waken the slave to a sense of his wrongs,
>   And his soul shall delight in the strain;
> It shall tell the poor bondsman what to him belongs,
>   And teach him to burst from his chain.[12]

The act of singing evidently stiffened Chartist defiance. Robert Gammage, when in prison, 'sang the song of my friend, John Leatherland:- 'Base oppressors, leave your slumbers'. And I sang it at intervals through the whole night'.[13] This song contains stanzas such as:

> Tyrants quail- the dawn is breaking,
>   Dawn of Freedom's glorious day;
> Despots on their thrones are quaking,
>   Iron bonds are giving way.[14]

Here both poetic text and social context indicate that Chartist verse was a means of strengthening resolve in adversity and of proclaiming the group's shared defiance of the established order.

Singing was also the opportunity for converting national 'patriotic' tunes and anthems over to the radical political cause. Edwin Gill's 'Spread the Charter' was to be sung to the tune of 'Rule Britannia,' and Thomas Cooper recalled how Leicester stockingers regularly did so. M. Clements' version of 'God Save the Queen,' expressly entitled 'National Chartist Anthem,' overturned its original by wishing the people 'From Queen and Priestcraft free'. Feargus O'Connor usurped the monarch's place at a Chartist dinner, where 'O'Connor's the Man of our Choice' was sung to the melody, 'Victoria's the Queen of the Rose'.[15]

An important function of Chartist verse was to pay public tribute to individual figures of the movement, especially during their imprisonment, release from prison, or their death. The hymn, 'Great God! is this the patriot's doom!,' was composed by John Henry Bramwich, for the funeral of Samuel Holberry, the leader of the Sheffield Chartist rising who had died in jail in 1842. The inscription on Holberry's gravestone included lines of verse by Edwin Gill, which offered the consolatory message that death had 'set the captive free'.[16] A torrent of poems appeared during the months in which John Frost, Zephaniah Williams and William Jones were in prison awaiting their sentence for leading the 1839 Newport rising. These poems alternately condemned tyranny and petitioned for the prisoners' release.[17] The youngest of the twenty-two fatalities at Newport was lamented by John Watkins in 'Lines on Shell, killed at Newport'. On Palm Sunday 1841 lines of commemorative verse were placed on the graves of those who had died.[18] The poet's own experience of personal witness was sometimes included within poetic commemoration. James Elmzlie Duncan's 'The Murdered Chartist' laments Henry Hanshard, a silk weaver who was fatally attacked by police during a Chartist meeting at Bethnal Green on 4 June 1848 at which Duncan had been present.[19]

Although Chartism was often riven by factious disputes between individual leaders, the verse consistently celebrated individuals for their contribution to the whole movement, thereby promoting Chartism's sense of coherence and self-confidence. Poems about individuals were often integrated into symbolically charged occasions, helping to articulate at a communal level feelings of grief, outrage and consolation which may otherwise have had little outlet for expression.

This is perhaps most apparent in two consecutive reports of funerals which appeared in the *Northern Star*. On 22 September 1849 the paper described the funeral of Joseph Williams, who had died in jail. There were no fewer 'than twenty thousand persons in the cemetery,' and near the end, 'a hymn composed as a tribute of respect to the memory of the deceased Joseph Williams, by Mr Bentley...was sung at the grave to the tune of "Base Oppressors," the whole audience joining in chorus'. The very next week the *Northern Star* reported the funeral of yet another Chartist to have died in jail, Alexander Sharpe. Here too lines of verse 'composed for the occasion by Mr John Arnott...were sung over the grave, the whole audience harmoniously joining in chorus'. Both elegies seek various consolations for the deaths; in Arnott's hymn, death is depicted as the captive's liberator, and in Bentley's hymn, Williams and Sharpe are 'from pain set free'.[20]

We have seen that singing reinforced defiance, but frequently also the verbal expression of militancy was mitigated by the ritualisation of a public occasion such as a funeral. Indeed, outbursts of violent feeling may have been openly vented in verse, at exactly the same time as they were being discouraged in public behaviour. Bentley's elegy includes a clear threat that the freedom for which Williams died will be achieved 'Whether gain'd by peace or war,' but immediately after the hymn was sung, the London Chartist, Edmund Stallwood, delivered a closing speech specifically 'exhorting all friends to depart in peace'.[21] Individual Chartists were sharing with each other the ardent expression of their desire for change, while containing this desire within a disciplined moderation as a movement. The tensions between verbal militancy and (usually) moderate behaviour is indeed a recurring feature of Chartist verse.

A singing crowd seems more often to have been the victim of violence than its agent. Frank Peel described a protest in Halifax, during the summer strikes of 1842, in which the Riot Act was read to the crowd, but a group of women remained and sang together 'The Union Hymn':

> Our little ones shall learn to bless
> Their fathers of the union,
> And every mother shall caress
> Her hero of the union.

Peel continued: 'Singing this stirring hymn they defiantly stood in their ranks as the special constables marched up, but their music did not save them, for the constables did not hesitate to strike them with their staves'.[22] Here, in an unintentional pun, we perceive the true difference between moral force and physical force, where the moral force of Chartism confronts the manifest physical force of the state: the wooden staves wielded by the constables silencing the musical staves sung by the women.

There are several contemporary references to groups of Chartist women singing in public. Regrettably, however, I have found few Chartist literary works known to have been written by women. I am certain that Chartist women composed stories and songs, but I have also become certain that they were seldom written down, that those which were written down have seldom been preserved, and those which have been preserved form a large part of the Chartist writings which are pseudonymous and anonymous. For example, Thomas Cooper popularised a song, 'The Lion of Freedom,' which glorified O'Connor, and was used as an anthem wherever O'Connor went.[23] Gammage identified Cooper as the song's author, but Cooper corrected him, saying it 'was understood to be the composition of a Welsh female Chartist. [A] Leicester working man (Valentine Wooley) first set it to an air'.[24] It appears that men, through their greater public prominence in Chartist activity, appropriated women's writing in a careless, casual, unthinking manner. Even Cooper, in the act of correcting Gammage's historical record, identifies the man who composed the music, but not the woman who composed the poem. She is simply a 'Welsh female Chartist': a triply marginalised figure.

Where Chartist women writers are identifiable, their verse is usually contained within a male discourse. In 'Self-Deceit' by the Bristol Chartist, Caroline Maria Williams, the female narrator refuses to purchase exciseable articles (one sphere of action identified with Chartist women), but disavows separate female agency or speech:

> Woman's influence is powerful, says man
> Their zeal effects wonders; if true,
> I'll vow I'll do all that I can,
> And provoke men to act as I do.[25]

Women have influence, but only through men's actions; and even in a poem written by a woman, the man's voice ('says man') intrudes his viewpoint.

Chartist verse was aware of itself as the expression of the working class, but this was a consciousness which stressed 'working' as much as 'class'. Chartists frequently expressed pride in being able to combine poetic creativity with productive labour: according to the *Labourer*, the Scots poet 'Tannahill contrived to weave, at the same time, threads of cloth and lines of song'.[26] Marxist commentators in particular have made large claims for Chartist poetry's valorisation of class;[27] but where class is specifically mentioned in Chartist verse it is always in a pejorative sense, as something which embodies inequality and oppression and which needs to be eradicated. Joseph Radford, from Birmingham, envisages the glorious time when the Charter is attained: 'When class-distinctions shall wither and die'. Benjamin Stott asserts: 'And class legislation, of freedom the curse, / Doth the natural rights of the people reverse'. William Jones attributed the cause of his wretchedness to '*class legislation's vile law!*'; and John Athol Wood refers also to 'vile class-made laws'; while E. P. Mead anticipated the time when 'Class legislative tyrants are confounded'.[28] In Chartist verse the concept of class is insistently associated with oppressive law-making. Chartist poets were less concerned to articulate a working class consciousness than they were to assert the rights of the working class in the face of social oppression and constitutional discrimination.

Indeed, whenever revolution was envisaged, its heroic protagonist was invariably referred to as 'the people,' rather than 'the working class'. The language and imagery used to express social conflict commonly rested upon a number of antithetical abstractions, such as poverty and wealth, light and darkness, the people and the rulers. The most important binary to Chartist poetry was variously characterised as liberty or freedom, against tyranny or oppression or slavery. Patrick Joyce claims these binaries were primarily inherited from romanticism which supplied, not only an ideology, but 'a kind of language of feeling'.[29]

Chartists followed the Romantics in using images of nature as an analogy or symbol for revolutionary change. M. H. Abrams has listed some of these images, as used by the Romantics: 'the earthquake and the volcano, the purging fire, the emerging sun, the dawn of glad day, the awakening earth in springtime'.[30] The Chartists deployed these analogies even more repeatedly. From a plenitude of examples I cite one for each of Abrams's images: the people's voice 'like the earthquake shall fill with dismay, / The hearts of the tyrants and sweep them away'; tyrants will 'Dread the burst of an Etna'; the day will come when 'the whole broad land is tongued with fire on Freedom's harvest day!'; a day when 'the sun of old freedom is born'; for 'Who bids us backward- laggards, stay! / As soon wave back the light of day!'; finally, let the spring of continental revolution 'Breathe on our northern ice till England move'.[31]

Chartist poetry teems with other images including fountains overflowing, cataracts dashing, winds clearing the clouds, and especially storms gathering.[32] Ernest Jones's 'We are Silent' is compounded of several such analogies of nature with revolutionary liberation. Jones stresses the gradual, unnoticed preparation which will climax into nature's liberating violence:

> All in silence glides the larva
> Thro' its veins of red-hot ore;
> All in silence lightnings gather
> Round the mountain's glacier hoar;
> Weight on weight, and all in silence,
> Swells the avalanche's snow,
> Till a scarce-heard whisper hurls it
> Crushing on the world below,
> ...
> Silent as the snowflake sinking
> Truth on truth keeps gathering strong,
> [33]
> ...

In addition a river bursts its banks, flame is kindling, the sea rises against a continent, and, of course, 'the tide is turning'.

Brian Maidment has pointed out that this Chartist reappropriation of Romantic images of nature serves to 'stress the "naturalness" of the revolutionary process,' thereby legitimating revolution. Ashraf also notes that the working man will in nature, 'see revealed a power greater than that of his oppressors'.[34] However, in 'We are Silent' the two images of the sea's rise and the tide's turn are used in contradictory directions (where the sea is both the people's strength and the adversary), and the cumulative use of such imagery leads to mixed metaphors and a mixed political message. For nature is incorrigibly cyclical; if freedom arrives with spring, tyranny will return with winter. The metaphorical images enact a temporary victory in the time of reading or singing of the verse, but no guidance as to how this victory will be achieved. On the contrary, in stressing the natural inevitability of liberty's conquest of tyranny, such images appear to foreclose on the need for human action.

Representations of the revolution were also prone to various tautologies. The revolution will be achieved when the people sufficiently desire it; as Thomas Willey tells them: 'If you but resolve to be free, / Your freedom you'll certainly gain'.[35] Similarly, the revolution will spontaneously happen in a single instant of time, usually conceived as 'the day' or 'the hour'; as in David Ross's poem 'A Call to the People':

> Brighter than the dawn when breaking
> O'er the wild unfettered sea,
> Will be the hour when all awaking
> Shall determine to be free.[36]

Nature's antithesis, scientific progress, was also frequently depicted by Chartist poets as a means of revolutionary change. Even where poets identified the evils of industrialism these evils were usually ascribed, not to the technological processes of industrial change, but to individual humans, tyrants who had temporarily perverted science. In the hymn, 'What mighty mind?,' science is deified as the agent of political, as well as technological, progress:

> Great Science' self the world illumes;-
> Directs the lightning- quells the wave,
> And rends the fetters from the slave![37]

Science inspired many with exuberantly imaginative prophecy, as in William Jones' poem, *The Spirit*:

A World of light, there sovereign Knowledge reigned,
Science the lightning checked, the tempest chained;
Dissolved, at will, the storm in rich'ning dew;
... [38]

But some Chartists were critical of science, depicting it as inherently oppressive; in E.P. Mead's 'The Steam King,' steam is a false idol worshipped by those who should instead be ministering to the people's welfare.[39]

The contemplation of science was a prominent theme for the many Chartist poets who wrote while in prison, and I shall return to this; but I shall turn now to examine the distinctive genre of Chartist prison poetry. After he had inspected Ernest Jones' conditions of imprisonment at Tothill Fields prison, Thomas Carlyle concluded that prison was the ideal place for a person to devote themselves to writing, and he envied Jones, a 'literary Chartist...the world and its cares quite excluded...the master of his own time and spiritual resources'.[40] Carlyle was partially accurate in his assessment of how the imprisoned writer could use the generous amount of leisure available, a commodity so rarely enjoyed by working class poets. In addition, prison granted authority within the movement for the writer's words. In the view of George Jacob Holyoake: 'To have spent, without shrinking, some portion of life in prison in defence of public liberty, gives the same authority among the people as having graduated at a university does among scholars'.[41] Such authority was particularly important when the poet addressed his readers on topics such as self-sacrifice for the cause, and the oppressive tyranny of the ruling classes.

Even the obstacles which imprisonment presented to the physical composition of writing (since the prisoner was often denied pens, paper and books) proved a psychological stimulus to writing. Prisoners used various means to acquire writing materials and to smuggle manuscripts out of prison for publication, and their successful strategies for getting into print came to form an exciting and triumphant narrative in itself. According to one biography of

Ernest Jones, '[P]ens he got by finding occasionally a feather from a rook's wing that had dropped in the prison yard. ...an ink bottle he contrived to make from a piece of soap he got from the washing-shed'. Feargus O'Connor placed his poetic production, 'The Mirror of York Castle,' within the looking glass of his servant, who, when released, took this to publication. The most sensational means of composition was Jones' claim to have written some of his prison poems with his own blood.[42]

Prison was itself an important subject matter for poets. Robert Peddie, a Scottish master staymaker, who led the Bradford insurrection of January 1840, was imprisoned for two years, during which time he produced the poetic anthology, *The Dungeon Harp*; and the dungeon is, indeed, the generative metaphor for Peddie's poetry. In 'The Weaver's Address to his Fellows' Peddie uses his own imprisonment as a metaphor for the condition of the working man, who is imprisoned by the tyranny of industrial work:

> While fifteen hours a day, in this damp unwholesome room,
> We are chain'd to the shuttle, we are fetter'd to the loom,
> By irons more galling- more enduring and strong
> Than any that e'er bound the slave to his much-pitied wrong;[43]

Peddie's poetry exemplifies a recurrent feature of Chartist prison poetry, whereby the individual mind, through memory and imagination, is the key which releases the prisoner. In 'Verses' he remembers roaming the Scottish mountain sides:

> My mind's creative power
> Anticipates future scenes,
> Whose shadows now live in my fancy's eye,
> In bright prophetic dreams. [44]

And in 'A Voice from Beverley: no.1' his imagination seemingly returns him to his wife Jane: 'Soon as I close my waukrif' e'e, / On fancy's wings I'm borne to thee'.[45] However, in 'The Imprisoned Chartist to his Wife' Peddie acknowledges the inability of 'fancy' to actually bear him to his wife, and expresses

the gulf between the reality of his situation and the intense
hallucinatory powers of the imprisoned imagination:

> Sweet music I hear from the lips of my fond one,
> Enraptured as on thy fair bosom I lean.
> But, alas! there's no voice wakes the still of my dungeon,
> Save the groans of some suff'rer in anguish and pain,
> Which fancy converts to the voice of affection,
> While the music I hear's but the loud rolling chain!
>
> But still there's a pleasure in that fond delusion,-
> Joy with the shadow, though substance be gone;
> 'Tis thus the poor maniac is cheer'd in his dungeon,
> And empire enjoys on his straw-fabric'd throne.[46]

Peddie often oscillates between celebrating the power of his
mind to elevate the poor dungeoned maniac into an enthroned
imperial sovereign, and lamenting the impotence of his solitary
imprisoned mind to effect actual social change.

George Binns, a Sunderland Chartist 'missionary,' was
imprisoned for sedition between July 1840 and January 1841. In his
narrative poem *The Doom of Toil* the material confinement of the
body again generates its antithesis, the boundless vision of the
mind. Binns gazes at the stars:

> At night, beyond my window's iron bar,
>   Upon a bed of straw, within my cell,
> I've watched some pale and bonny twinkling star,
>   Till gentle sleep has bound me in her spell.
> In chainless thought, by fetters unsubdued,
>   I've wandered to that distant world alone,
> To ask, in midnight's breathless solitude,
>   If slaves and palace despots there are known?[47]

Here Binns depicts sleep as his gaoler ('bound me'), but one
which actually releases his mind ('chainless thought'), and allows
him to roam around the stars to find a world free of tyranny.
Clearly Binns believed that Britain was far away from utopia, for in
1842 he emigrated to New Zealand.[48]

In Chartist prison poetry affirmation was both a personal need for the suffering poet and a political need also, since his suffering was representative of the Chartist cause. Peddie sent some poems to the *Northern Star* 'as a proof that my spirit is not yet broken down'.[49] The poet's spiritual triumph in imprisonment could be identified as the actual political triumph of the oppressed. On one level this again evaded identifying the social and political mechanisms which would cause this victory. However, many Chartist writers believed that the individual mind was not only the source for the poet's resistance, it was also symptomatic of the wider social progress, and would ultimately prove the source for the people's eventual victory. Peddie's 'Spirit of Freedom' concludes:

> Yes, vain all arts will tyrants find,
> To cramp or bind the human mind;
> For onward with resistless force,
> The stream of mind shall hold her course.[50]

Similarly Binns asserts to tyrants 'Ye cannot chain the world's awakening mind'.[51] The fact of writing poetry in prison symbolised the freedom of the mind; and in contrast to the confinement of the poet's body, the poet's mind freely explored in verse the far-flung territories of imaginative fantasy, allegorical interpretations of history, and utopian prophecies for the future.

The Purgatory of Suicides by Thomas Cooper is the most ambitious journey undertaken by the Chartist poetic mind. This is an epic poem, three hundred pages long, written in Spenserian stanzas, crammed with Biblical and classical erudition, poetic archaisms and Hebraic and Latinate words. Its very composition was in itself an engagingly dramatic narrative: here was a full-scale epic poem authored by a self-educated working class man, moreover, a Chartist writing the poem while imprisoned for seditious conspiracy.

The narrator receives dream-visions which prophesy moral, spiritual, and political revolution in Purgatory and on earth; 'kingship' and 'Mystery' will in the course of 'mind's progression' be usurped by 'fair Equality'. The epic progresses towards nothing less than the march of mind and the 'endless afterlife of jubilee'.[52]

This chapter is primarily concerned with the role of Chartist verse within the movement, and is not the place for a full textual analysis of *The Purgatory*, this 'extremely complicated text'.[53] What I will briefly outline is the significance of 'mind' in the poem: both Cooper's mind and the mental progress of the working class.

Cooper wished to use his time in prison to write, but initally he was denied access to any reading or writing materials. However Cooper responded: 'I thought I could defeat their purpose by composing the poem and retaining it in my mind,' and he duly authored the first thirty stanzas of his own epic text within his head and memorised them.[54] Despite Cooper's body being imprisoned, the existence of the epic asserts the inviolability of his mind, his memory, and his imagination, which are enthralled to no one. Cooper recurrently characterises these visionary characteristics of the mind in terms of properties which an imprisoned working class man might not be supposed to possess: freedom ('the unbound mind'), wealth ('this opulence / Of intellective might'), and sovereignty ('The regal mind').[55]

Cooper redefines what imprisonment truly is: not the spatial incarceration of the body, physically enforced; rather, a mental confinement, ideologically conditioned. The concept of Purgatory has been part of that mental conditioning; the progress however of 'Knowledge,- the new-born world's great heroine' will unravel false thought and prove 'the great Enfranchiser'.[56] The very fact that a working man can now write epic poetry is symptomatic of the transformation of an earthly purgatory into the Chartist utopia. There are a number of passages in the epic which attempt to depict the future utopia and which affiliate educational and cultural advance with the emergence of political democracy.[57]

Cooper's epic manifests problems of political agency we have seen already in Chartist verse; for instance, in the conclusion he characterises the transition from Error to Truth as 'The day,' a miraculous instant of time, rather than as a carefully specified process of change. However, the direction of Cooper's own activism was clear and consistent; for instance, he set up an adult school in Leicester in 1841/2, and proposed that members compose hymns for the Sunday meetings which he collected and published as *The Shakspearean Chartist Hymnbook*.[58] Cooper's fervent educational evangelism contributed to the process of mental progress which he envisions and celebrates in the epic.

Like Cooper, Ernest Jones wrote much verse in prison, including a complex, prophetic narrative poem entitled 'The New World'.[59] Here Jones describes how scientific progress will be the instrument for social and moral progress, ushering in the future utopian society: 'But Science gathers, with gigantic arms... / Throughout the world expands her hallowing reign'.[60] Jones continues with a remarkable series of prophecies of the specific benefits science will bring:

> Then, bold aspiring as immortal thought,
> Launched in the boundless, mounts the aeronaut;
> ...
> Or, mocking distance, send, on rays of light,
> Love's homeborn smiles to cheer the wanderer's sight.
> Mechanic power then minister to health,
> And lengthening leisure gladdens greatening wealth:
> ...
> No fevered lands with burning plagues expire,
> But draw the rain as Franklin drew the fire;
> ....
> With steely fingers on twin dials placed,
> The thoughts of farthest friends are instant traced;
> ....
> Then each disease shall quit the lightened breast,
> By pain tormented while by vice oppressed;
> ....
> Those halcyon days shall witness discord cease,
> And one great family abide in peace;
> ...
> One language then endearingly extends;
> Shall tongues be strangers still, when hearts are friends?[61]

Air flight, television (or video), leisured affluence, mastery of the climate, the telephone, a cure for all diseases, world peace, and one shared language: some of this has now been achieved, but much remains to be done before we attain the Chartists' millennium.

As with Cooper, Jones was not content to only imagine and depict this ideal world; he was actively seeking to achieve it. Under his influence the programme of the Chartist Convention of 1851 emphasised, more than at any other time, a comprehensive vision of socal welfare for all members of society. Its manifesto was a description of a model socialist society and was the corollary in practical terms to the imaginative writing of Jones's poem.

Such audacious prophesying into the future may appear incongruously juxtaposed with Jones's use of the traditional heroic couplet. Yet the confident symmetrical balance of these heroic couplets perfectly harmonises with Jones's rational conception of science. However, and once again, Chartist verse shows little sense of human agency. Science assumes a semi-religious aura ('hallowing'), and functions in the narrative like a *deus ex machina*, omniscient and paternal, ('gathers, with gigantic arms'); its reassuring, self-sufficient power obviates any need to analyse how individuals can work to bring about these changes. Jones's depiction of political revolution is an event occurring in a single instant of time lacking any prior causation:

> At last, when least expected friends and foes,
> Grandly and silently the People rose!
> None gave the word! - they came, together brought
> By full maturity of ripened thought.[62]

The words 'At last' convey the felt need for a revolution and, 'when least expected,' express the retrieval of a seemingly lost position characteristic of much Chartist poetry: the willing suspension of doubt which constitutes Chartist poetic faith. Jones' science stands in this context too, as an agent which can be invoked in the poetry without need for explanation itself. This ungrounded affirmation constitutes the poem's major flaw, but it also provides the flights of technological and political imaginativeness which are the poem's strengths.

The existence of a large corpus of Chartist verse provided a repository of images which Chartists could draw upon in varying contexts. W.J. Linton wrote a large number of wittily ironic poems against monarchy, such as 'A Song of Rejoicing on the Birth of the Prince of Wales' which ends with Linton's bitter recommendation to a starving artisan: 'Yet gild thy starved lip with a smile, bend low on servile knee, / And pray that God preserve *thy* Prince - to prey on thine and thee!'.[63] Linton gets neglected by literary critics, or miscategorised as a 'High Victorian' poet.[64] His brand of 'Victorianism' was shared by numerous Chartist poets. The 'pray'/ 'prey' pun was repeated a year later in 'A Starvation Anthem for the Royal Christening': 'For ought we not to *pray for him* / Who'll *prey on us* enough some day?'; and exactly those lines are repeated after another royal birth in 1850, in 'On Birth of Arthur Baby Royal'.[65] Chartist poets frequently repeated images, phrases, puns and specific ideas from other Chartist poets. Such borrowing may be regarded, in Ashraf's words, as 'a form of common property,' rather than as plagiarism; for example, such borrowings occurred when yet another royal child was produced to be a parasite upon the state, or when yet another Chartist was imprisoned.[66] They should then be seen as a collectively established means of countering repeated instances of privilege and oppression.

In other ways also, verse could be borrowed and modified in the course of time. Cooper's popularisation of 'The Lion of Freedom' was followed by several variations which illustrate the range of contexts for Chartist (and anti-Chartist) verse. One autobiographer recalled how, following Cooper's 'harangues' during the Pottery Riots of 1842:

> The mob, thousands strong, marched along singing the Chartists' hymn of the day- 'The lion of freedom's let loose from his den, / And we'll rally round him again and again.' The rough rhyme suited the rough singers in their desperate march.[67]

In contrast William Jefferson, a Primitive Methodist preacher, was alarmed at the mass following for Chartism and composed a hymn entitled 'The Lion of Judah' to the tune of 'The Lion of Freedom,' which substituted heavenly for political salvation and preached political quietism.[68] Chartists reclaimed the tune with at least two further versions which deepened the song's significance within Chartist history. Shortly after O'Connor was committed to an asylum in 1852, an elegiac version was written anonymously (by 'S.R.'), commencing 'The Lion of Freedom has gone to his den'.

After O'Connor died, at the end of the funeral service, a hymn was sung over his grave by John Arnott (' 'Tis not at the grave.'), to the tune of 'The Lion of Freedom'.[69] The recurrence across time of specific melodies, rhetorical tropes, or metaphorical images enabled Chartists to respond to changed circumstances while simultaneously reaffirming communal identity.

However, by the late 1840s Chartist poetry began to register the frustrations of a movement which had existed for ten years without achieving its goals. As the movement was diminishing and fragmenting, the optimistic defiance of the early poetry became increasingly problematic. In 1847 John Peacock uses the familiar image of the morning dawn, but now it is with uncertainty: 'When-when, oh, God! will Freedom's morning dawn'. The refrain of 'Labour's Anthem,' by Sheldon Chadwick, a Chartist poet of the 1850s, is 'How long, O God! how long?,' and this became the refrain of his poetic career.[70]

Chartism continued, although diminished, throughout the 1850s, and much poetry continued to be written in this decade. There tended to be fewer songs for communal singing and more printed narrative poems, reflecting an attenuated connection between verse and political agitation. Thinly masking a mood of pessimism and doubt, much of the Chartist poetry written in the three or four years after 1848, was of a largely metaphoric militancy. This is best seen in the career of Gerald Massey.

Much of Massey's earlier verse was published in the papers of Julian Harney, one of Marx's Chartist correspondents. In 'The Red Banner' Massey's poetic rhetoric displays militant class warfare:

> Fling out the Red Banner! the patriots perish!
> But where their bones moulder the seed taketh root-
> Their heart's-life ran red the great harvest to cherish,
> Then gather ye Reapers, and garner the fruit.[71]

However, by 1855 Massey had published a volume on the Crimean war, *War Waits*, whose political sentiments have transformed. The first lines of the first poem, 'War Rumours,' reveal Britain to be the haven of liberty:

> There sits in her Island-home,

Peerless among her Peers!
And Liberty oft to her arms doth come,
To ease its poor heart of tears.[72]

In 'England goes to Battle' the 'tyrant's rage' is abroad, and
'our red-cross banner' is now heralded by England's soldiers, not
her workers.[73]

What is most significant here is not that Massey changed his
opinions, but that alongside his political shift is the unchanging
character of his poetry. Images which had previously been used in
the fiery Chartist verse were retained in his later jingoistic verse,
but used in an antithetical direction; and in this he was typical of
later Chartist verse. Throughout his career Massey frequently drew
upon the figure of the martyred patriot, which appealed also to
many other Chartist poets and writers. This rhetorical figure
became more resonant in later Chartist writing, perhaps because it
confronted the sense of defeat which was seeping into Chartism.
Around the martyred patriot clustered a series of interlocking
images: the martyr's earthly blood providing the seed which
posterity will harvest for a heavenly future.[74] Linton draws upon
this imagery in his poems, 'English Reapers' and in 'Harvest
Home':

What of the harvest? patriot, say!-
Seed is sown for the harvest day:
Freedom's seed for the Future's food,
Sown in many a martyr's blood,
[75]
…

We have already seen how Massey deploys this imagery in 'The
Red Banner'. From the mid 1850s Massey continued to deploy the
image of the martyr's blood, but this time in the context of the
Crimean war. In the earlier poetry the struggle between the
martyred patriot and tyranny had been conceived as a political
struggle within the nation. However, by 1854, tyranny is
exclusively located as a foreign entity and the martyr's sacrifice is
on behalf of his nation. Massey replaces a perspective of class
antagonism with that of national antagonism. Consequently ultra-
militant verse had become intensely, and conservatively,

nationalistic. Massey ennobles the slaughter of British soldiers, in such verses as 'Before Sebastopol':

> Thick are the groves on Alma, see
> What costly seed lies sleeping!
> God! but thy Sun shall stand, while we
> That Harvest-field are reaping![76]

Massey went on to deploy identical imagery for later imperial wars, as in the poem 'Cawnpore'. 'The Old Flag' reads like an antithetical rewriting of 'The Red Banner'; Massey is unproblematically patriotic (with lines such as 'We love our native land and laws'), and celebrates those who have died in foreign wars: 'Will God the Martyrs' seed forget? / No. Keep the Old Flag flying yet'.[77]

Massey's shift was not exceptional. Earlier Chartist poetry had been critical of both war and imperialism. In 'War! - War!' Linton had condemned those who 'Who taketh up arms in the tyrants' wars'.[78] Yet in 1854 Linton published a series of *War Cries*, in support of the British struggle to free the Poles from Russian oppression. The cry 'God Save our England,' was to be sung to the tune of the national anthem, and contains lines such as: 'Till all the nations be, / Even as England, free'.[79] Similarly Cooper turned his energy to 'rousing performances of "Rule Britannia" during the Crimean War'.[80] Such activity was consistent with radical support for Poland, but it bore stark contrast to Linton's previous poetic utterances against imperialist warfare, and contrasted with earlier Chartist practice, in which Cooper was involved, of inverting the national anthems against themselves.

This possibly demonstrates the vulnerability of abstract binary oppositions, such as 'freedom' and 'oppression,' which had featured so much in Chartist poetry; both binaries were capable of shifting their point of reference, even to the extent of exchanging positions, as here. The confrontation depicted in verse between working class radicalism and ruling class tyranny had been starkly polarised but abstractly non-referential. Such a depiction slid readily into an equally stark confrontation between British freedom and foreign (especially Russian) despotism. The role of the Crimean war in reorienting the object of these images, and thereby articulating a much moderated political radicalism in Britain, appears to have been immense, and so far under-estimated. The connotative history of political vocabulary has yet to be written.

For two broad reasons, Chartist literature existed on the edge of creative possibility. Firstly, most Chartists did not enjoy the material comforts which facilitate, or make possible, the writing of literature: education, leisure, light and warmth. As Gerald Massey wrote: 'Poverty is a cold place to write Poetry in'. The biographical memoirs attached to so many working class poetic anthologies recurrently lamented poverty's frosty climate. Roger Quinn recounted his situation as 'the father of twelve children, for whose maintenance I had often, while composing some of the following pieces, to work sixteen hours a day in a very cheerless, enervating, and unpoetic atmosphere'.[81]

Secondly, as I have recurrently pointed out, Chartist writers were confronted with the problem of how to represent in artistic form the processes of revolutionary change in society. Perhaps it was an unresolvable problem and Chartist writers were attempting to represent the unrepresentable; as Cooper writes at one point in *The Purgatory*:

> But unimagined, unconceived, unknown,
> Unspeakable, by man, seemed all revealed
> To those awed travellers...[82]

And yet it is worth recalling that despite the defeat of Chartism, most of the Chartist political programme was gradually achieved, and that it was achieved as part of a wider social process rather than as a consequence of political victories by individuals. In an analogous manner individual Chartist poets did not achieve lasting influential careers, but the poems and songs which Chartists composed and printed and which Chartists read and sang around the nation proclaimed the cultural potential of the working class, and announced a cultural, as well as political, democracy. To understand the emergence of political democracy in Britain we have to observe the presence of those 'immense masses' who sang at Chartist demonstrations. To understand the emergence of mass culture we should listen to what they sang.

NOTES

[1] Frank Peel, *The Risings of the Luddites, Chartists and Plugdrawers*, (1880) 4th ed., London, Frank Cass, 1968, pp.317-8.
[2] John Storey, *An Introductory Guide to Cultural Theory and Popular Culture*, Hemel Hempstead, Harvester, 1993, p.21.
[3] Throughout this chapter there is a distinction between: 'poetry,' which refers primarily to a printed text; 'song,' to words intended for singing; and 'verse,' which encompasses both.
[4] Paul Pickering, ' "Glimpses of Eternal Truth": Chartism, Poetry and the Young H.R. Nicholls,' *Labour History*, vol.70, May 1996, p.59; James Epstein, *The Lion of Freedom: Feargus O'Connor and the Chartist Movement*, London, Croom Helm, 1982, p.315; e.g. Margot Finn, *After Chartism: Class and Nation in English Radical Politics, 1848-1874*, Cambridge, C.U.P., 1993.
[5] Yuri Kovalev (ed.), *An Anthology of Chartist Literature*, Moscow, Foreign Languages Publishing House, 1956; Peter Scheckner (ed.), *An Anthology of Chartist Poetry; Poetry of the British Working Class, 1830s-1850s*, New Jersey, Fairleigh Dickinson University Press, 1989. See Timothy Randall, 'Review of *An Anthology of Chartist Poetry*, by Peter Scheckner,' *Clio*, vol.20, Spring 1991, pp.307-9.
[6] Hugues Journès, *Une Littérature Revolutionnaire en Grande-Bretagne: la Poesie Chartiste*, Paris, Publisud, 1991; Ulrike Schwab, *The Poetry of the Chartist Movement: a Literary and Historical Study*, (1987), Dordrecht, Kulwer Academic Publishers, 1993.
[7] Brian Maidment, *The Poorhouse Fugitives: Self-Taught Poets and Poetry in Victorian Britain*, Manchester, Carcanet, 1987, pp.23-94; Martha Vicinus, *The Industrial Muse; a Study of Nineteenth Century British Working-Class Literature*, London, Croom Helm, 1974, ch. 3; Mary Ashraf, *Introduction to Working Class Literature in Great Britain*, 2 vols., East Berlin, 1978, 1979; Isobel Armstrong, *Victorian Poetry: Poetry, Poetics and Politics*, London, Routledge, 1993.
[8] Anne Janowitz, *Lyric and Labour in the Romantic Tradition*, Cambridge, C.U.P., 1998, chs. 4-7; pp.137-8.
[9] This can be treacherous terrain for critics, and interpretative analysis has not always been grounded on factual accuracy. For instance, when Armstrong claims that the 1840s 'may have been the only time in the century when middle-class and working-class poetry ran almost *pari passus*,' her example of working class poetry, 'The Pauper's Drive,' anonymously printed in the *Northern Star* (*NS*), was actually written by Thomas Noel, a middle class priest: Armstrong, *Victorian Poetry*, p.158.
[10] This chapter emerges out of my continuing research in Chartist verse and fiction: see Timothy Randall, 'Towards a Cultural Democracy: Chartist Literature, 1837-1860,' D.Phil thesis, University of Sussex, 1994, and a forthcoming book on Chartist literature.
[11] *NS*, 29 Oct. 1842; 12 April 1843.
[12] Benjamin Stott, *Songs for the Millions*, Middleton, Horsman, 1843, p.83.

[13] Robert Gammage, *Reminiscences of a Chartist*, (1883-5), (ed.) W.H. Maehl, Manchester, Society for the Study of Labour History, 1983, p.23.

[14] *Western Vindicator*, 24 Aug. 1839.

[15] *Evening Star*, 20 Jan. 1843; Thomas Cooper, *The Life of Thomas Cooper*, (1872) Leicester, Leicester University Press, 1971, p.175; *Western Vindicator*, 30 Nov. 1839; *Evening Star*, 8 Dec 1842.

[16] *English Chartist Circular*, vol.2, pp.275-6; *NS*, 25 May 1844.

[17] e.g. ['Iota,' pseud.], 'The Mountain Minstrel's Appeal,' *NS*, 6 June 1840.

[18] *NS*, 26 Sep. 1840; *Midland Counties Illuminator*, 1 May 1841.

[19] James Elmzlie Duncan, *Pe-ans for the People*, n.p., 1848, no.3.

[20] *NS*, 22 & 29 Sept. 1849. This is Leatherland's song, mentioned earlier.

[21] *NS*, 22 Sept. 1849.

[22] Peel, *Risings of the Luddites*, 334. Samuel Bamford (not a Chartist) wrote this song in the 1830s.

[23] *NS*, 11 Sept. 1841.

[24] Robert Gammage, *History of the Chartist Movement, 1837-1854*, (1854-5), London, Merlin Press, 1969, p.203, p.207. Stephen Roberts has shared with me his suspicion that Cooper did compose the poem but was later too embarrassed by his idolisation of O'Connor to admit to it. I clutch at my faith in Cooper's absolute honesty.

[25] *NS*, 4 June 1842.

[26] 'Robert Tannahill,' *Labourer*, vol.II (1848), p.114.

[27] e.g. Ashraf, *Introduction*, vol.1, p.63.

[28] 'The Charter,' *NS*, 2 Jan. 1841; 'King Death,' Stott, *Songs*, p.25; 'The Unemployed Weaver's Appeal,' *English Chartist Circular*, vol.2, p.208; 'Thou art a Self-Degraded Slave,' *Friend of the People*, 29 March 1851; 'Address to the Starving Millions,' *NS*, 16 July 1842.

[29] Patrick Joyce, *Visions of the People; Industrial England and the Question of Class, 1848-1914*, Cambridge, C.U.P., 1991, p.34.

[30] M.H. Abrams, 'English Romanticism: the Spirit of the Age,' in Northrop Frye (ed.), *Romanticism Reconsidered*, New York, Columbia University Press, 1963, pp.53-4.

[31] [W.H.C.], 'The Voice of the People,' *NS*, 4 Dec. 1841; Charles Darlin [various spellings of his surname are printed], 'Questions from the Loom,' *Chartist Circular*, 29 Aug. 1840; W.J. Linton 'The Coming Day,' *Prose and Verse; Written and Published in the Course of Fifty Years, 1836-1886*, 20 Vols., held in British Library, vol.6, p. 51; Peter McDouall, 'The Old Handloom Weaver,' *NS*, 27 Oct. 1849; Ernest Jones, 'Onward,' *Labourer*, vol.2 (1848), p.1; W.J. Linton, 'To the Future (April 1848),' *Prose and Verse*, vol.7 p.187.

[32] A fine example of the latter is Sheldon Chadwick, 'Now Cometh the Storm,' *Red Republican*, 19 Oct. 1850.

[33] *Notes to the People*, vol.1 (1851), p.92.

[34] Maidment, *Poorhouse Fugitives*, p.38; Ashraf, *Introduction*, vol.1, p.75; Abrams, 'English Romanticism,' p.53.

[35] Thomas Willey, *A Song for the Times; Illustrative of Passing Events*, Cheltenham: Willey, 1848, p.5.

[36] *NS*, 30 Sept. 1843.

[37] *English Chartist Circular*, vol.2, p.204.

[38] William Jones, *The Spirit; or, A Dream in the Woodlands*, London: John Chapman, 1849, p.22.

[39] *NS*, 11 Feb. 1843.

[40] Thomas Carlyle, *Latter Day Pamphlets*, 'Model Prisons,' (1850) London, Chapman & Hall, 1898, p.53.

[41] George Jacob Holyoake, *The Last Trial for Atheism in England; a Fragment of Autobiography*, (1850) 4th ed., London, Trubner, 1871, p.118.

[42] [James Crossley?], *Ernest Jones. Who is He? What has He Done?*, Manchester, Heywood, 1867; Feargus O'Connor, 'Life and Adventures of Feargus O'Connor, Esquire M.P.,' *National Instructor*, 7 Sept. 1850 ('The Mirror' appeared in the *NS* on 4 July 1840: the leader of Chartism wrote the worst of Chartist poems); Jones, 'New World,' *Notes*, vol.1 (1851), p.4.

[43] Robert Peddie, *The Dungeon Harp; being a Number of Poetical Pieces Written During a Cruel Imprisonment of Three Years*, (ed.) David Ross, Edinburgh: n.p., 1844, 41. See Stephen Roberts, *Radical Politicians and Poets in Early Victorian Britain: the Voices of Six Chartist Leaders*, Lampeter, Edwin Mellen Press, 1993, ch.3, where Roberts cites generously from Peddie's poetry.

[44] *The Dungeon Harp*, p.135.

[45] *Ibid*, p.59.

[46] *Ibid*, p.80.

[47] [George Binns], *The Doom of Toil; a Poem, by an Ambassador in Bonds*, 2nd ed. Sunderland, 1841, p.14. For Binns' authorship see his obituary in the *NS*, 5 Feb. 1848.

[48] See Stephen Roberts, *Radical Politicians*, ch. 2. Roberts has also helped make available some prison poems and other literary writings, by William Aitken, in *William Aitken: the Writings of a Nineteenth Century Working Man*, (eds.) Robert Hall & Stephen Roberts, Tameside, Tameside Leisure Services, 1996.

[49] Peddie, *Dungeon Harp*, p.67. Also *NS*, 6 March 1841.

[50] Peddie, *Dungeon Harp*, p.69.

[51] [Binns], *Doom of Toil*, 14.

[52] Thomas Cooper, *The Purgatory of Suicides; a Prison-Rhyme in Ten Books*, (1845) 3rd ed., London, Watson, 1851, p.45; p.47; p.296.

[53] Stephen Roberts, 'Thomas Cooper: a Victorian Working Class Writer,' *Our History Journal*, vol.16 (1990), 17.

[54] Cooper, *Life of Thomas Cooper*, p.251.

[55] Cooper, *Purgatory*, p.20, p.122; p.20.

[56] *Ibid*, p.72; p.73.

[57] e.g. *Ibid*, p.268-9.

[58] Cooper, *Life*, pp.162-9. This anthology seems to be lost.

[59] Ernest Jones, 'The New World, a Democratic Poem Dedicated to the People of the United Queendom, and of the United States,' *Notes to the People*, vol.1 (1851), pp.1-15.

[60] *Ibid*, p.14.

[61] *Ibid*, p.14.

[62] *Ibid*, p.12.

[63] Linton, *Oddfellow*, 27 Nov. 1841. For a biographical study, see F.B. Smith, *Radical Artisan: William James Linton, 1812-97*, Manchester, M.U.P., 1973.

[64] J.R. Watson (ed.), *Everyman's Book of Victorian Verse*, London, Dent, 1982, pp.619-25.

[65] [Anon.], *National Vindicator*, 29 Jan. 1842; [J.C.]. *Democratic Review*, vol.2 (1850), p.50.

[66] Ashraf, *Introduction*, vol.1, p.38.

[67] ['An Old Potter,' pseud. Charles Shaw], *When I Was A Child*, (1903) Llanbydder, Caliban Books, 1993, p.158; pp.160-1.

[68] B. Aquila Barber, *A Methodist Pageant: a Souvenir of the Primitive Methodist Church*, London, Holborn Publishing House, 1932, p.74.

[69] *People's Paper*, 23 April 1853; 15 Sept. 1855.

[70] John Peacock, 'The Voice of a Slave,' *NS*, 24 April 1847; Chadwick, *Red Republican*, 28 Sep. 1850.

[71] *Red Republican*, 22 June 1848. For a biography see David Shaw, *Gerald Massey: Chartist, Poet, Radical and Freethinker*, London, Buckland, 1995.

[72] Gerald Massey, *War Waits*, 2nd ed., London, David Bogue, 1855, p.1.

[73] Alfred Miles (ed.), *The Poets and the Poetry of the Century*, (1892) 12 vols., London, Hutchinson, 1905-7, vol 5, p.330; p.331.

[74] This metaphor originates from Tertullian, a second century Carthaginian theologian: 'The blood of the martyr is the seed of the Church'.

[75] W.J. Linton, *Ireland for the Irish; Rhymes and Reasons against Landlordism*, (1850-3) New York, The American News Company, 1867, pp.84-5.

[76] Massey, *War Waits*, p.19.

[77] Gerald Massey, *Havelock's March, and Other Poems*, London, Trubner, 1861, pp.25-9; Gerald Massey, *Robert Burns, a Centenary Song, and other Lyrics*, London, Kent, 1859, p.8; p.11. The image was reclaimed by the socialists: Jim Connell's 'The Red Flag' (1889) starts, 'The people's flag is deepest red; / It shrouded oft our martyred dead'.

[78] *The Oddfellow*, 31 Oct. 1840.

[79] W.J. Linton, *War Cries*, London: n.p., 1854, p.8.

[80] Stephen Roberts, 'Thomas Cooper,' in Joyce Bellamy & John Saville (eds.), *Dictionary of Labour Biography*, vol.9, London, Macmillan, 1993, p.54.

[81] Gerald Massey, *The Ballad of Babe Christabel*, 5th ed., London, Bogue, 1855, 'Preface,' p.viii; Roger Quinn, *The Heather Lintie; Being Poetical Pieces, Spiritual and Temporal, Chiefly in the Scottish Dialect*, 2nd ed., Dumfries, Maxwell, 1863, 'Preface,' p.iv.

[82] Cooper, *Purgatory*, p.19.

SUBJECTIVITY, COMMUNITY, AND THE NATURE OF TRUTH-TELLING IN TWO CHARTIST AUTOBIOGRAPHIES

Kelly J. Mays

The first volume of John Burnett, David Mayall, and David Vincent's invaluable reference work *The Autobiography of the Working Class: An Annotated Critical Bibliography* (1984) identifies 36 extant autobiographies by authors who claimed to have once been Chartists. Not surprisingly all 36 autobiographers are men, but they are otherwise a quite diverse group - differing in terms of the nature and extent of their involvement in Chartism and their attitudes toward it and in terms of occupation, region of origin, and family background. Expressing and compounding the diversity apparent among their authors is the diversity among the texts themselves, which range from the 17 'Reminiscences' that Robert Gammage contributed to the *Newcastle Weekly Chronicle* between 1883 and 1885, to the six-page autobiographical preface that opens Chartist poet John Teer's *Silent Musings* (Manchester, 1869), to W. E. Adams' 650-page *Memoirs of a Social Atom* (2 vols.; London, 1903).

Any scholar hoping to make a study of 'Chartist autobiography' is thus immediately faced with a range of questions about the slipperiness of that very category and of the two terms that comprise it. Does, or should, the category include the autobiographies of those who recounted their involvement in Chartism only to repudiate it? Texts, such as Gammage's, that self-consciously present themselves less as autobiographical narratives proper than as a hodgepodge of 'Reminiscences'? Autobiographies by writers, such as G. J. Holyoake and Henry Solly, who were active Chartists, but whose middle-class status means their exclusion from the *Bibliography?* Is the category 'Chartist autobiography' itself a viable or valuable one at all?

Obviously the answers to such questions lie not in the texts themselves, but in the goals and methods of scholars; the scholarly producers of the three most recent and extensive studies of these texts - David Vincent's anthology, *Testaments of Radicalism* (1977), Bernard Sharratt's *Reading Relations* (1982), and Regenia Gagnier's *Subjectivities* (1991) - have essentially answered 'no' to

all of these questions insofar as they have chosen to define
autobiographies by Chartists not as 'Chartist autobiographies' *per
se* but as what Bernard Sharratt labels 'working-class political
autobiographies.'[1] As a result, Vincent's anthology includes the
autobiographies of the Chartists Benjamin Wilson, John James
Bezer, and Thomas Dunning, alongside that of the London
Corresponding Society founder, Thomas Hardy; Sharratt looks not
only at the autobiographies of the Chartists Thomas Frost and
James Dawson Burn, but also at those of Samuel Bamford and
Alexander Somerville; and Regenia Gagnier considers the
autobiographies of the Chartists William Lovett and Benjamin
Wilson as part of a group of 'political narratives' by Hardy,
Bamford, the tailors' union leader Lewis Lyons, and the socialist
Robert Blatchford.

What such studies make clear is the extent to which explicit, or
implicit, answers to ostensibly 'literary' questions about genre
inevitably lead one into the very heart of contested socio-historical
terrain. For in explicitly, or implicitly, arguing for a generic kinship
between these autobiographies based on their concern with politics,
on the one hand, and their writers' working-class status, on the
other, Vincent, Gagnier, and Sharratt implicitly seem to offer
versions of a familiar, but increasingly contested, vision of
nineteenth-century history - a vision that posits Chartism as an
integral facet, or phase, of a continuous and distinctively 'working-
class' political struggle that begins with the reform movements of
the late-eighteenth century, and culminates in the socialist and
trade-union movements of the late-nineteenth and early-twentieth.

Though implicit in all three studies, this vision is expressed in
an unusually forthright manner in Gagnier's *Subjectivities*, where
the assertion that the 'general form of these political
autobiographies was established with Thomas Hardy's *Memoirs*'
leads to the assertion that this form is both an expression of, and
medium for, class-based political struggle. Thus Gagnier describes
'the political narrative' both as one in which the 'hero is the
working class, the odyssey is the quest for political power, and the
battle is class warfare' and as 'the self-conscious working-class
answer to the bourgeois novel.'[2] In Gagnier's argument, then, the
'political narrative' becomes in a sense doubly 'working-class' - a
distinctly 'working-class' experience here finding both the

(political) ideology and the form most appropriate to it. Testifying further to that vision of class, ideology, and narrative form is the fact that Gagnier treats the autobiography of former Chartist James Dawson Burn separately from these 'political narratives,' arguing that Burn's repudiation of his former political activity is one among many symptoms of the fact that he has 'adopted' a 'middle-class ideology' and 'upper-class' narrative 'models' that nonetheless do not accord with his experience.[3]

Obviously, such an argument both intersects with, and departs in significant ways from, the accounts of Chartism and of class advanced by such social historians as Gareth Stedman Jones and Patrick Joyce.[4] For while Stedman Jones's *Languages of Class* is very much concerned with establishing the continuity between Hardyean radicalism and Chartism that Gagnier implicitly evokes, he does so precisely in order to argue that Chartism was never the product, or expression, of a class-based ideology in the way Gagnier takes it to be.[5] As a result, Jones obviously challenges the assumed equation between 'Chartism' and/or 'radicalism,' on the one hand, and 'working-class' experience and ideology, on the other. That particular challenge is, moreover, inseparably linked to a much broader critique of a traditional, 'essentialist' socio-historical approach that involves treating particular linguistic utterances as the more or less adequate 'expression' of the 'material situation of a precisely specified social group' or, in other words, of a class.[6]

As Patrick Joyce's remarks about *Subjectivities* make clear, both he and Jones would arguably see precisely this sort of 'essentialism' at the very heart of Gagnier, Sharratt, and Vincent's treatment of Chartist autobiography. And Joyce, in fact, directly critiques Gagnier in particular for employing in *Subjectivities* what he calls 'an obsolete view of class in which "individual" is the sign of "middle class," a "collective self" that of "working class."'[7]

Among the many potential counter-critiques that might be lodged against Joyce and Jones, one of the more powerful takes shape in Anne Janowitz's argument that 'analytical confusion' results from applying the same 'anti-essentialist, structuralist-derived' logic to class that is typically applied to gender and race.[8] For while racism and sexism may be accurately '[u]nderstood as a set of subjectively experienced *attitudes* ' 'contestable through struggles of representation' aimed at 'demystifying the social construction of apparently 'natural' or ineluctable [or 'essential'] features,' 'classism' is by no means a parallel phenomenon, given that the problem, in this case, is not essentialism, but its very opposite - that is, the tendency to 'deny [or mystify] the category of class altogether.'[9]

Thus, from this point of view, a linguistic approach that aims to 'demystify' class essentially risks (in a way that the putatively 'essentialist' approach of Gagnier certainly does not) itself contributing to the 'mistake' it is meant to both reveal and correct.

While adjudicating this disagreement is well beyond the scope of this chapter, it does aim - through a reading of two autobiographies - to consider some of the issues this debate raises about the relation between class, language and narrative form, ideology, selfhood, and Chartism. Specifically, the chapter looks at the autobiographies of two self-identified Chartists - John James Bezer, who used the pages of his autobiography to celebrate and advocate the Chartist cause, and J. A. Leatherland, who devoted his 'Autobiographical Memoir' to repudiating his earlier involvement in the movement. For all the differences between these autobiographies, what they share, and what to some extent differentiates them from many other autobiographies by Chartists, is the extent to which they foreground Chartism and Chartism's role in the formation and/or expression of the author's 'selfhood' or subjectivity, however differently that subjectivity is conceived in the two texts. As a result, they potentially provide interesting case studies of the ways in which Chartism, the self, and the relation between them could be envisioned by differently situated nineteenth-century writers and of the ways in which different visions both took shape in, and shaped, the form and the content of particular autobiographical texts. In exploring such issues, the chapter thus treats what Stedman Jones calls 'the language of Chartism' not by conceiving that language as a unified, consistent whole, but by instead exploring the ways in which languages of the self, and of Chartism, are 'transformed and appropriated by [a] variety of speakers' in part by virtue of the way in which those speakers appropriate the 'available' 'rhetorical for[m]' of autobiography.[10]

A characteristic and crucial element of the rhetoric of that form as it is appropriated by Bezer and Leatherland and one that says much about their vision of the nature, function, and value of that form is an emphasis on the truthfulness of the autobiography. John James Bezer, for example, more than once interrupts his autobiography to remind readers that though particular remarks will 'doubtless displease some,' such remarks are a necessary enactment and demonstration of the writerly commitment to truth. '[W]hen I commenced this history, I determined that it should be a *genuine* one, and that I would put down my thoughts without reserve,' Bezer avows at one point, while insisting at another that 'the truth shall be told - the whole truth.'[11] More typical than Bezer's confrontational interjections, but making much the same point, are introductions and conclusions that insist that the autobiographical narrative is a 'plain, simple, and authentic' one 'faithfully narrated' by a writer devoted to the 'endeavour to give you just what is strictly true.'[12] As these remarks suggest, however, such rhetorical claims of, or to, truthfulness can, to borrow Gagnier's words, 'in fact signify any point within an affective range extending from defensive self-effacement [Davenport's 'plain, simple, and authentic'] through defiant irony' of the kind displayed in Bezer's avowals.[13] Thus, attention to the ways in which the authors explicitly, and implicitly, both define and deploy such claims - and the way they thereby implicitly figure the nature and ends of autobiographical 'truth-telling' - will be a key element of this chapter's exploration of the ways in which these particular Chartist autobiographers appropriate the autobiographical form.

Because the focus here is on the differences, rather than similarities, among Chartist autobiographies, the chapter explores texts that differ from each other thematically and stylistically, that appeared before nineteenth-century readers in different formats and venues, and that have had quite different fates in the twentieth century. Thus, Bezer's unfinished autobiography was originally published serially in *The Christian Socialist,* instalments appearing weekly between 6 September 1851 and the journal's demise in December 1851; apparently never printed in volume form in the nineteenth century, it has been made available in recent years through its inclusion in David Vincent's *Testaments of Radicalism.* Never reprinted in the twentieth century, Leatherland's

'Autobiographical Memoir' functioned as a preface to the volume of *Essays and Poems* published by William Tweedie in 1862.

As the different fates of their autobiographies suggest, these autobiographers came from somewhat different backgrounds. Born in 1812 to a carpenter father who died five years later and to the daughter of a Baptist minister, Leatherland seems to have spent his entire life in his birthplace, Kettering. Taking to the loom under his silkweaver stepfather, Leatherland subsequently became a ribbon- and then velvet-weaver until trade depression forced him to turn instead to manufacturing and hawking men's vests. When, in 1850, an accident led to an illness that made him incapable of manual work, Leatherland became a journalist. Thus at the time he came to write his autobiography, Leatherland was essentially a professional writer, living on salaries from several papers and prize money won in essay contests together with pecuniary assistance from patrons whom he had apparently met through his work as a writer.

However precarious Leatherland's struggle to maintain himself and his small family may at times have been, John James Bezer's was by all accounts more so. Four years younger than Leatherland, this self-styled 'Chartist Rebel' was born in Spitalfields in 1816 to a barber father (whom Bezer labelled a 'drunkard') and a mother who worked as a cotton-winder.[14] When the family's slim finances finally collapsed when Bezer was six or seven, Bezer's father was sent to a workhouse, while he and his mother were granted a minimal stipend by a London parish. After miserably failing at his one attempt to supplement the family's income by hawking buns in the streets, Bezer went to work as a warehouseman and errand-boy for his mother's employer, working over the next several years as an assistant in various shops, as a shoemaker, and as porter at a Bible Society book-bindery before taking to the streets 'To sing, to beg, to cadge.'[15] Though the unfinished state of his autobiography leaves it unclear what exactly Bezer did for a living between this time (c. 1838) and his two-year imprisonment in Newgate (1848-1850), David Vincent indicates that he afterwards opened a radical bookshop in Fleet Street before emigrating to Australia in 1852 at the age of 36.[16]

However different their experiences of work and family life, both the Kettering weaver-poet and the Spitalfields shop assistant turned street-performer were Chartists, even though that shared label potentially disguises the differences between the two autobiographers' experiences of, and attitudes toward, the movement. Secretary of the Kettering Chartist Association from 1838 to about 1842 and a member for longer, Leatherland-the-autobiographer was so embarrassed by his own Chartist past that he provided little detail about the nature and extent of his activities. Given his long-time residence in Kettering and his position with the association, however, it is likely that Leatherland was an important local leader, and it is certain that he was one of the many proselytising-poets so central to the movement (at least one of his poems, by his own admission, becoming 'very popular' after insertion in the 'Chartist Hymn-book').[17]

Not at all embarrassed about his Chartist past, John James Bezer nonetheless never got the chance to tell his readers about the events that occurred between the time of his first Chartist meeting in 1839 (the event with which the autobiography concludes) and the 1848 imprisonment in Newgate (to which he alludes throughout the text) - the *Christian Socialist* failed before the last instalments of the autobiography could appear. After his release and during the months his autobiography appeared, according to David Vincent, Bezer 'gained a seat on the nine-man executive of the National Charter Association,' resigning that position in April 1852 when G. J. Holyoake 'seemed to be gaining the upper hand' over Bezer's hero, Ernest Jones.[18]

Though the actual narrative of John James Bezer's autobiography begins with a more than usually vivid account of its subject's birth (this first instalment in fact being titled 'The Birth'), that account and the narrative it initiates are at once forestalled and framed by two epigraphs - one a verse from the Bible, the other an unattributed poem entitled 'The Past' - and an imaginary conversation between the author and his readers that is enclosed in brackets and that itself includes a quotation from Robert Burns's 'For A' That.' This highly unusual opening - with its multiplicity of real and imagined 'voices' and its almost dizzying movement across a wide affective and stylistic range - does much to set the tone for a text that Alf Louvre aptly describes as 'a politicised, poor man's *Tristram Shandy*.' Full of 'asides, digressions, musing and mimickry,' this text does indeed, as Louvre argues, engage in 'a kind of deconstructive guerrilla warfare - by pun, parody, pastiche and an interventionary persona consciously destabilising the fixities of association that are the cement of ideological power, of orthodoxy.'[19] Central to this 'warfare,' as Louvre suggests, is Bezer's tendency to emphasize 'the narrator ['I'] as against the protagonist' and to render the former a distinctly and self-consciously *'protean'* character/voice who 'adopts the personae of moralists and preachers ... with telling accuracy' in order to 'revea[l] the gap between their rhetoric and their political practice' and who, through such parody and a host of puns, exposes the instability and 'conventionality' of 'language and meaning' themselves.[20]

While Louvre's account is an, at once, apt and illuminating one, it threatens to ignore the extent to which Bezer's emphasis on the instability of language and of the narrative-self in fact serves to assert the fixity and stability of the protagonist-self - a fixity and stability that is, as we shall see, signified in the 'Chartist rebel' label, secured by multivalent appeals to 'nature,' and seen to be realised in Chartism. This notion of a fixed and stable 'rebel' self and the notion of personal and human nature on which it is based, moreover, at once ensure, and are themselves ensured by, a narrative in which the events of the protagonist's life take on a highly stable logic, pattern, and meaning.

Indeed, the fixity of the self and the narrating of life's events as enactments of it is secured, in part, through Bezer's habit of, in Louvre's words, 'anachronistically' deploying 'terms drawn from radical political thinking of the 1850s' to 'depic[t] scenes from his earlier life.'[21] Chief among those terms are those drawn from, and relating to, Chartism, particularly versions of the titular phrase 'Chartist rebel,' which Bezer applies to himself in describing his own birth and his later confrontations with an employer and a policeman. In the former confrontation, as he puts it, 'I was, to all intents and purposes, a "physical force rebel,"' while in the latter he depicts himself 'looking at the gentleman as impudently as an embryo Chartist well could.'[22] Such self-descriptions serve to create a highly fixed notion of the self, as well as a highly stable interpretive framework: Bezer's references to his child-self as a 'physical force rebel' and 'an embryo Chartist' suggest both the way Bezer wholeheartedly embraces the 'Chartist rebel' label as *the* marker of a highly stable, fixed identity, and the way this label thereby serves to give a sense of meaning and coherence both to the self and, as we shall see, to the particular events that make up that self's pathway through life.

At the same time, the phrase 'embryo Chartist' also begins to suggest the extent to which Bezer does vacillate in the autobiography between portraying that identity as essential, or given, and thus as being merely enacted in the events the narrative records, on the one hand, and, on the other, portraying it as the *result* of the events and conditions he describes, and thus figuring such events as formative rather than performative. That vacillating is aptly captured in the stanza of verse with which the autobiography concludes:

> As a boy I *dreamt* of liberty;
> A youth - I said, but I am free;
> A man - I felt that slavery
> Had bound me in her chain.
> But yet the *dream,* which, when a boy,
> Was wont my musings to employ,
> Fast rolling years *shall not* destroy. . . .[23]

Referring to the development of 'boy' into 'youth' and 'man,' the verse seems to imply the kind of developmental scenario that might also be suggested in Bezer's earlier comments about the formative influence of education and in his reference to finally and fully 'becom[ing] a Rebel' on the day he was first led to attend a Chartist meeting.[24] But the verse - like the autobiography it concludes - also undermines the developmental scenario it invokes by making the '*dream*' 'of liberty' the constituent element - or, in Bezer's own words, 'fixed principle' - of a continuous, unchanging self. That 'principle,' in other words, unites, rather than differentiates, 'boy' and 'man'; guarantees the sameness of former, present, and future versions of the self; and thereby serves to make that self seem invulnerable to the 'destroy[ing]' powers of the 'rolling years' and the 'grief and pain' they bring.[25] And, as previously suggested, it is precisely this latter notion of the self that is emphasised and affirmed through Bezer's use of the 'Chartist rebel' label, as well as through the appeals to 'nature' often encoded in that usage.

In Bezer's autobiography, the phrase 'Chartist rebel' thus operates as a kind of master sign that organizes his notions of self and lends pattern and meaning to the events of his life. For Bezer's narrative renders his life history a series of moments of 'rebellion' against a series of individuals, including more than one employer, a policeman, a Rector who enforces an order requiring Bezer to attend church in order to receive his pauper allowance, and several officials of a Mendicity Society who refuse to give Bezer anything other than bread and cheese. Individually and collectively portrayed as enacting what Bezer calls 'Man's inhumanity to man,'[26] these figures become metonymic representatives of the various external forces - economic, social, religious, and legal - that Bezer sees arrayed against him. The behaviour of such men, Bezer suggests, makes utterly hollow traditional representations of Britain as a 'free country' devoted to 'free trade': 'Certainly I could have left my place,' Bezer says in describing his first employment, 'for this is a free country. What then, should I have got another? And if I had, that's not all - my master was my *mother's* master; and if I had discharged myself, he would have discharged her; he has told me so often - which of course is free trade - so I toiled on. . . .'[27] Moving inexorably from references to a labour-market that is anything but free to the inhumane behaviour of this particular individual employer, Bezer insistently humanizes general social forces. In the process, this employer and the various other characters against whom Bezer rebels become living embodiments of the more general, systemic oppression disguised by conventional appeals to 'free trade' and a 'free country.' Through such characters, Bezer's narrative thus renders 'an alien and disembodied idea of social oppression' quite literally human by embodying it within characters who function very like 'the archetypal and highly visible villain[s] of melodrama.'[28]

Such villains are represented as threatening various kinds of external coercion that Bezer conceptually collapses together under the sign of 'tyranny' and 'slavery'; 'rebellion' thus becomes the enactment of Bezer's own fixed 'rebel' selfhood through the repudiation of the 'slave' position. This recurring dramatic structure and the conceptual framework tyrant/slave that underlies it are established in the fourth and fifth instalments, entitled 'My First Employment' and 'Signs of Rebellion.' Here describing his first job as a warehouseman, Bezer constructs a (melo)drama of enslavement and rebellion in which he is cast as a victim of 'white,' 'errand-boy slavery' and his 'Master' as both a 'craven' and a 'tyrant' whose utter control of Bezer's existence can only be (temporarily) escaped through illness.[29]

Here and in the remainder of the episode, 'slave' thus comes to signify not only the subject-position assigned to Bezer in what he figures as an utterly dichotomous social structure - or, that is, by external social, economic, and legal forces - but also the internal, subjective condition of self-abasement and deference that this social structure both demands of, and inculcates in, the slave. Thus Bezer describes the episode's denouement - a quite physical confrontation with the 'master' - not only as the triumph of 'slave' over 'tyrant,' but also as a matter of 'nature predominat[ing] over my fear of offending.'[30] In this way, the external conflict between tyrant and slave gives way to, and becomes inseparable from, an internal conflict between 'nature' and the 'fear of offending' - the ability to physically confront the external 'tyrant' depends upon first overcoming the 'fear of offending', that is the internal mark of the slave. Thus, while the 'fear of offending' comes to signify the deference of the 'slave,' the opposed term, 'nature,' enables and legitimates rebellion both against the tyrannical master and against a slave mentality precisely because it is so conceptually multivalent. For 'nature' here must be seen simultaneously to refer to Bezer's own particular 'rebel' nature and to all men's (and, more particularly, all Englishmen's) 'natural' desire for liberty; to testify to the idea that this desire constitutes fidelity to a 'natural' - rather than social or cultural - order;[31] and, as shall be clarified below, to signify 'nature' in the sense of truth, sincerity, and/or authenticity rather than artifice or hypocrisy. In the denouement of the incident - in which Bezer avows 'The "*signs* of rebellion" were just then rather clear. I was, to all intents and purposes, a "physical force rebel"' - the former sense of individual 'nature' predominates, yet this sense of 'nature' is here and throughout the autobiography anchored in, and inseparable from, 'nature' in these several other senses.[32]

In envisioning this struggle as one both between 'tyrant' and 'slave' and between 'nature' and his own 'fear of offending', and in thereby figuring 'rebellion' as the heroic effort to stand up not only to the tyrants without, but also to the 'unnatural' inner compulsion to obey, and defer to, such tyrants, Bezer interprets the events of his life in terms of a conceptual framework very like that which Ulrike Schwab argues to be central to Chartist poetry. [33] For there, too, Schwab insists, 'The division of society' into two opposed and hostile camps designated by the terms 'tyrant' and 'slave' 'is recorded as the most important social phenomenon,' the word 'slave' designating simultaneously both the external 'forms of compulsion, discrimination and restriction that affect the workers' and the internal, subjective condition of the 'humiliated' worker - 'will-less endurance, apathetic suffering, anxious submissiveness, ... self-abnegation and self-contempt' - that is outwardly enacted through deference and 'passive obedience.'[34]

In rejecting that submissive, 'artificial' subject-position, moreover, Bezer the 'rebel' comes to characterize himself in much the same terms that Schwab describes Chartist poetry as characterising its central, heroic figure - the 'freedom fighter':

> such a fighter is "manly," "gallant" or "brave,"
> "staunch," "stout," "free from fear" ... "honest,"
> "resolute" or "determined" . . . . Armed *inside* like this
> the worker has acquired a high degree of forcefulness.
> Once a freedom fighter he has made the idea of liberty
> his own. ... He is capable of open declaration and ready
> for physical action. . . . [35]

As already suggested, Bezer thus represents himself as a 'natural' freedom fighter, as well as a fighter in nature's cause; he is, in other words, the morally courageous, liberty-loving child of 'nature' in several ways and senses. Yet the valour of rebellion and the heroism of the rebel self depend upon the perpetual threat of becoming, or being made into, the 'slave' who silently suffers and tacitly promotes 'tyranny.'

Throughout Bezer's autobiography, this sense of personal and human 'nature' heroically asserting themselves via acts of rebellion gains legitimacy by being associated with, and anchored in, a family feeling that is also portrayed as 'natural' and, therefore, universal. Thus the ultimate confrontation with his employer occurs because he chooses to visit his sick mother rather than follow orders, while a confrontation with another authority figure - the head of a soup kitchen - is also staged in terms of the conflict between bureaucratic 'rules' and 'natural' family feeling: for when the head insists that Bezer must eat his bread and cheese rather than take it home to his wife and child because 'it's the rule, and you must obey it,' Bezer responds, 'I don't care about your *rules,* I want to share it with those I love, who are as hungry as I am, and if you are a Devil with no natural feelings, I am not.'[36] Moreover, by casting this event as the precursor and trigger to his first introduction to Chartism, Bezer represents his entry into 'Politics' as the 'natural' outcome of such 'natural' family feeling, as well as the ultimate confirmation and enactment of his own rebel nature.[37]

If Bezer's narrative therefore ultimately scouts the Wordsworthian paradigm of the child being father of the man as thoroughly as the verse epigraph 'The Past' scouts the nostalgia for the past inseparable from that paradigm, however, it is implicitly much more certain and emphatic when it comes to the notion of 'manhood' and/or 'manliness.' For while, as Bezer's verse suggests, boys (and women?) may dream of liberty, it is men - often, as we have seen, in the role of true sons and fathers - who stand up for it. Moreover, the danger of not standing up for it is, as he makes clear in reference to his father, 'unmanning':

> Father had been an old "man-o'-wars man," and the many floggings he had received while serving his country, had left their marks on his back thirty years afterwards; they had done more, - they had left their marks on his soul. They had unmanned him; can you wonder at that? Brutally used, he became a brute - an almost natural consequence. . . .[38]

While the unmanned 'brute' thus becomes a figure parallel to the 'slave,' 'man' and 'rebel' thereby become synonymous;[39] as a result, the rebel label becomes rooted in a gender dichotomy that is both like, and obviously intimately related to, the opposition and/or conflict between tyrant and slave.

A key character trait of the tyrant and a major concern of Bezer's autobiography is hypocrisy - a concern stylistically expressed through the frequent deployment of the verbal and dramatic irony and semantic play so aptly analyzed by Louvre. But it is also - again - a crucial structuring element within Bezer's narrative. Thus, while Bezer-the-narrator represents 'craven men,' such as his master and the Mendicity Society workers, as rule-bound hypocrites and points to the gap between mere words and actual things, mere rules and natural feeling, that at once guides and legitimates their actions, he also presents Bezer-the-protagonist's confrontations with such 'tyrants' as confrontations between manly honesty or authenticity, on the one hand, and hypocrisy or artifice, on the other. For Bezer-the-protagonist's 'rebellions' typically involve not only one-on-one confrontations between 'slave-turned-rebel' and 'tyrant,' but also the public revelation of tyranny. Thus the fight with his master culminates with Bezer 'creat[ing] a crowd by telling every one as they passed all about it,'[40] while his encounter with the 'six gentlemen' who interview him at the Mendicity Society ends with a similarly public confrontation between self-serving lies and self-sacrificing honesty:

> ...I retaliated, as every honest man ought to do when he's insulted and belied by a thing that feeds on him according to law. I retaliated, I say, with equal warmth, calling him a liar ... point-blank, and all the *gentlemen* too; - "you advertise lies, said I, wholesale, now lock me up, and I'll show the magistrate and the world that *you* are the impostors, and obtain money under false pretences from the benevolent."[41]

If Bezer the protagonist thus comes to embody 'honesty,' nature, and authenticity - and thus becomes an heroic, masculine martyr to the cause of nature and truth - the same is equally, if not more, true of Bezer the narrator. Thus the autobiographical act itself comes to be figured as an act of morally courageous rebellion similar to, and coextensive with, the confrontations with hypocrisy and tyranny it describes. Defining the very function and value of his autobiography as residing in the effort to tell the 'whole truth,' Bezer in turn suggests that such an effort *is* a simultaneously heroic and rebellious one precisely because it demands both overcoming the feelings of shame he nonetheless testifies to having, and refusing slavish, unnatural concerns about the potential outrage or disapproval of his readers. When, in other words, Bezer fairly invites the displeasure and outrage of his readers - 'I shall doubtless displease some ...'[42] - he sets up exactly the same dynamic between narrator and reader that operates between rebellious 'slave' and tyrannical 'master' within the narrative; in both cases, or at both levels, in other words, 'nature predominate[s] over [the] fear of offending.'[43]

Moreover, by frequently and directly confronting readers in this way, Bezer utilizes another common strategy of the melodrama, in which - as Elaine Hadley argues - 'Actors not only spoke directly to the audience, but encouraged its response and thus broke down the fourth wall that was becoming crucial to the design of Victorian "high" drama and, arguably, to the Victorian novel.'[44] In this way, while the plot of Bezer's narrative again and again turns upon the unveiling of lies to public view and/or the honest man's effort to break down the wall between the semblance - of religiosity or benevolence - and the reality it conceals, the narrative itself also works to break down the wall between, in Hadley's words, 'mere spectators' and 'busy actors,' making readers themselves into participants in, rather than isolated, 'critical[ly] distanced' spectators to, the autobiographical text.[45] In the process, readers are thus encouraged to bring to bear the 'natural feelings' that the villains of Bezer's narrative are seen to lack - or, more accurately, they are faced with the choice of proving themselves to be the unsympathetically villainous readers imagined in the autobiography's opening, or of aligning themselves with the honest man who defies them. Either way, however, Bezer's narrative doesn't really allow readers to opt out altogether - for by the logic of this text, to maintain 'critical distance' would essentially mean adopting the stance of the craven, unfeeling villains portrayed within the text.[46] Ironically or not, given the oppositional logic of Bezer's text and of its protagonist/narrator's persona, such a 'villainous' reading would in fact merely add fuel to the honest man's fire.

As this reading suggests, the manly 'Chartist rebel' subject position is one rooted in a complex logic of sameness and difference, individuality and community belonging. For that label at once differentiates Bezer from others, as the very word 'rebel' implies, and at the same time grounds itself upon likeness - a likeness indicated by the mere hooking of the 'rebel' label to the necessarily collective adjective 'Chartist.' That dual function is indicated through Bezer's oscillation between references to himself as 'a' and as 'the' 'Chartist rebel,'[47] and the same play of sameness and difference (and of relatively 'individualist' and 'collectivist' conceptualizations of subjectivity) is also present in recurring allusions to his imprisonment in Newgate. For Bezer represents that 'Newgate affair' as at once the single 'remarkable' experience that might differentiate his life and his autobiography from that 'of millions in this "happy land"' and as an experience that marks his unity with, and likeness to, other imprisoned rebels past and present.[48] That sense of unity becomes at once literal and figurative in Bezer's references to Bunyan, the literal connection being forged in the insistence that I read you [Bunyan] in Newgate, the figurative in the assertion that his love for 'Glorious Bunyan' is founded on imagined similarity - 'you too were a "Rebel," and I love you *doubly* for *that*.'[49] This play of difference and similarity is equally and not surprisingly fundamental to Bezer's notion of the nature and meaning of his own Chartist activities, which centre on the recognition both of the conditions that he shares with his 'brother slaves' and a difference from them (and likeness to other Chartists) that is founded in his manly willingness to 'rebel' and to fight for freedom, chiefly and ironically by suffering imprisonment.

Despite his paean to liberty and the play between existential and literal imprisonment encoded in his references to 'the Newgate affair,'[50] however, Bezer himself admits that his interest and involvement in 'Politics' via Chartism was first and foremost a 'bread-and-cheese-question' - a point emphasised by the fact that he insists that it was quite literally a fight over bread and cheese that preceded his first Chartist meeting.[51] And it is undoubtedly poverty and socio-economic oppression that are the primary antagonists throughout much of his narrative, dramatic scenes of rebellion literally and figuratively overwhelmed by pages devoted to his and his family's efforts to stave off starvation.

At the same time, however, Bezer's recurrent references to 'slavery,' particularly in his description of his first Chartist meeting, tend to render poverty itself a form of enslavement legitimated, in great part, through the mental slavery that keeps most 'poor men' from questioning their situation and thereby penetrating to the truth beneath the semblance in the way Bezer himself does as both narrator and protagonist throughout the autobiography:

> ...as one after another got up, oh, how I sucked in all they said! "Why should one man be a slave to another? Why should the many starve, while the few roll in luxuries? Who'll join us, and be free?" "I will," cried I, jumping up in the midst. ... And *so,* Lord John, I became a Rebel; - that is to say: - Hungry in a land of plenty, I began seriously for the first time in my life to enquire WHY, WHY - a dangerous question, Lord John, isn't it, for a poor man to ask?[52]

Thus while Bezer's narrative might be seen to, as Gagnier argues of Lovett's, 'replicat[e] the West's three master narratives: the quest for material well-being, or freedom from Nature; the quest for Truth, or freedom from ignorance; and the quest for justice, or freedom from political tyranny and economic exploitation,'[53] it also may be said to collapse the three together and to thereby render Chartism the key and culmination to all three 'quests,' even as, and because, Chartism is the enactment of the honest, manly rebel self - both narrator and protagonist.[54]

In so doing, Bezer's autobiography may be seen to stage a particular version of the equation between the social and the political (or, in Gagnier's words, between 'political tyranny and economic exploitation'[55]) that Gareth Stedman Jones argues was essential to the growth of the Chartist movement, predicated as such a 'political movement' was on 'a shared conviction articulating a political solution to [socio-economic] distress and a political diagnosis of its causes.'[56] For if, as Stedman Jones argues, that 'shared conviction' ultimately rested on a vision of 'the political system itself' as 'totally evil' because it represented a 'monopoly situation in which all other forms of property were afforded political and legal support, while that of labour was left at the mercy of those who monopolised the state and the law,'[57] Bezer's text might be said to forward precisely that vision by presenting characters such as his first employer not only as themselves 'totally evil,' but also, and crucially, as figures whose evil is legally sanctioned - as he puts it in confronting the 'gentlemen' of the Mendicity Society, tyrants 'feed on' the poor slave 'according to law.'[58] Here, in other words, the opposition between bureaucratic 'rules,' or laws, and 'natural' feeling is bolstered by the implication that such rules and laws are both the creatures and creators of 'tyrants.' Bezer's text thus performs the equation between poverty and politics in part through what Elaine Hadley describes as the 'melodramatic mode;' particularly the melodramatic strategy of both humanising in order to vilify general social forces and confronting the reader in ways that ensure that he or she must in the very act of reading choose whether they will embody or defy those forces.

In the process, however, Bezer's narrative supports Stedman Jones' contention that Chartism was not necessarily understood or experienced by its adherents in terms of Marxist notions of class and, perhaps, disproves Hadley's assumption that the melodramatic mode was necessarily antagonistic to, or outmoded by, a Chartist discourse predicated on 'the language of class.'[59] For in large part through its employment of certain elements of the 'melodramatic mode,' Bezer's narrative in both form and content advocates a sense of 'natural' feelings that are seen to at least potentially transcend and heal class divisions - including those presumed to divide Bezer from his readers - and figures such feelings as the antidote to the bureaucratic mentality that threatens to turn all 'men' into 'craven' 'tyrants' and 'slaves', and thus to pit class against class 'where there ought to be no classes.'[60] If Chartism therefore constitutes for Bezer, as it does for many a Chartist poet, a kind of slave's rebellion, it is a rebellion that, in Ulrike Schwab's words, 'first serves dissociation to hopefully serve affiliation in the end'[61] - 'affiliation' being a particularly apt word for an ideal that, in Bezer, hinges so much upon 'family feeling.'

However different, J. A. Leatherland's autobiography is very much like John James Bezer's to the extent that here, too, the writer's involvement with Chartism is cast as *the* definitive event in his life. A major difference, however, is the previously noted fact that Leatherland spends much energy in his autobiography repudiating his former allegiance to Chartism. Thus, Leatherland describes the movement as 'the bane of [his] youth,' depicts the 'period of [his] life' in which he acted as secretary to the local

Chartist Association and wrote 'revolutionary' poetry as one that he 'look[s] back upon with regret and remorse,' and avows - nonetheless - that he was 'never a thorough-going Chartist.'[62] Despite or precisely because of that emphatic 'regret and remorse,' however, Chartism in fact looms as large in Leatherland's autobiography as it does in Bezer's; the story of Leatherland's involvement with Chartism and Chartists taking up fourteen and a half pages of a narrative that is only 39 pages long.

Not surprisingly, in light of this attitude, Leatherland presents himself as distinctly and unusually passive in the pages devoted to Chartism; not only figuring himself as being 'made' the 'tool' of local Chartists,[63] but also quite literally adopting the passive voice both when describing how 'The Charter, and the Charter alone, *was held* to be the great panacea for the cure of every evil' and when listing the dire effects of his adoption of this view: 'the time, money, and energies mis-spent - the excitement produced - the discontent engendered - the reputation damaged - the Utopian hopes raised and frustrated - the maddening disappointment experienced - the restless days and feverish nights constantly passed.'[64] Figuring such effects and Chartism itself in terms of an emotional excess unattributed to any agent or subject - 'excitement,' 'discontent,' 'hopes raised and frustrated,' 'maddening disappointment,' 'restless[ness],' and 'feverish[ness]' - the list, like the section as a whole, is simultaneously self-indicting and exculpatory - the autobiographer quite literally casting himself here as the object, rather than the subject, of his own narrative. Here and throughout the autobiography, Leatherland thus equates Chartism not with thought or conviction, but with unrestrained emotion, asserting in a footnote, for example, that 'those who have studied human nature, know very well that in a time of popular excitement, the passions and feelings often act in advance of, and sometimes contrary to, the judgment of both individuals and nations.'[65] Imagining both himself and 'the people' more generally as quite literally powerless over those 'passions and feelings,' Leatherland suggests that the ultimate agents here - if any - are the movement's leaders ('[t]he madman, O'Connor, and the fire-brand Stevens'[66]) and anonymous *agents provocateurs*. Yet even in assigning blame to the latter, as he does in the following (also passive) sentence, Leatherland consistently de-emphasizes agency:

'This flame was fanned by itinerant demagogues, who went about seeking whom they might devour, ... making a market of the passions and feelings of the people.'[67]

In the terms established by Leatherland's own text, however, the seemingly self-exculpatory casting of the self as object rather than as subject of Chartism is, in fact, ultimately more self-indicting than exculpatory - in this text, in other words, it is precisely the putative lack of self-control and agency that does and should lead to 'regret and remorse' (rather than to rebellion). For Leatherland opens his autobiography by arguing that one of the primary 'service[s]' performed by such texts is

> showing the varying force of circumstances upon different orders of mind - how, while one individual succumbs to them and sinks beneath their pressure, another with heroic vigour rises above them, and bends them to his will, or snaps asunder the bands, as Sampson the green withes that bound his sinewy limbs.[68]

Here, in other words, Leatherland figures heroism as the 'vigorous' assertion and triumph of individual will over external 'circumstances,' insisting that individuals can and should be judged by the extent to which they do or do not succeed in disentangling themselves from the circumstantial 'bands' that threaten to ensnare and enslave them. Thus, it is precisely by insisting on the way he was passively swept up into the Chartist movement and, in the process, essentially lost his individuality and became one of 'the people' that Leatherland figures himself as the erring victim or slave of circumstance.

Ironically or not, however, it is only through this self-indicting drama of enslavement that Leatherland can emerge as a Samson-like hero. Like Samson, in other words, Leatherland must first succumb to the temptation of 'circumstances' in order heroically to defy them, which is precisely what he figures himself as doing when he ultimately resigns the secretaryship of the Chartist Association. Vividly dramatising the heroic individualism of that act, Leatherland describes the 'storm of hisses, mock cheers, and loud exclamations' with which the local members greeted his resignation; this figurative 'storm' then becomes the literal 'pelting rain' in which he has to stand when he returns home only to find himself locked out by a step-father, 'who regarded Radicalism with extreme dislike.' '[K]icked out of the Radical Association Room for not being a Chartist, and locked out of doors for being one,'[69] Leatherland appropriately depicts himself as both literally and figuratively standing alone, heroically defying not only the sentiments of all who surround and threaten to coerce him, but also the very elements. Ironically or not, Leatherland's narrative thus implicitly hinges upon a conflict between enslavement and rebellion that is very like that in Bezer's, the crucial difference being that where Bezer equates Chartism with manly rebellion, Leatherland understands Chartism as the result and marker of his enslavement.

But where Bezer's narrative thus triumphantly and fittingly ends with his first Chartist meeting - an event depicted as the ultimate fulfilment of his life-long desire for 'liberty' and the achievement of individual distinction within community - Leatherland's story of his victory over his enslavement to Chartism ends with a whimper rather than a bang. For, as if testifying to the burdens entailed in figuratively standing alone, the story of the eventful night of his resignation is followed both by the admission that he 'continued to be a member of the [Chartist] society for some time afterwards' even though he 'scarcely know[s] why' and by the story of 'a circumstance that grew out of this connection' to Chartism that Leatherland spends the next nine-and-a-half pages detailing, thus giving it by far the most attention of any incident in the narrative.[70]

That story, told as if Leatherland were giving evidence before a court, begins with Leatherland's late-night encounter ('On the night of Saturday, the 23rd of February, 1839') with a former work-mate who hints that a barley rick burned in the town that morning will only be the first of many, the man 'whom I shall call Harry' avowing that 'There's a plan devised among the Chartists, to rise all over England ... and to burn the ricks down throughout the nation.'[71] Later woken from his bed by cries of 'Fire' and 'believ[ing] the day of ["the most violent Chartists"] vengeance has arrived,' Leatherland helps to put out the fire that is consuming 'two large wheat ricks,' 'work[ing] as hard as I could to restrain the fury of the conflagration.'[72] After discovering 'Harry' himself among those fighting the fire and 'entreat[ing] him to tell me all he knew,' Leatherland goes home with 'Harry' only to find himself locked in, 'alone, in the hands of a desperate incendiary.' After Leatherland makes 'a dreadful vow that I would preserve an inviolable secrecy,' Harry confesses, avowing that though he acted alone and only made up the story of the 'general rising,' 'he had been induced to commit the deed through reading the addresses of Stevens [sic], in the "Northern Star,"' and also been 'greatly excited' by 'O'Connor's harangues.'[73] Over the next several pages, days, and years, Leatherland is again and again tempted to reveal Harry's secret, but only does so when Harry himself decides to confess. Later recanting that confession, Harry is tried anyway, found guilty, and sentenced 'to a term of imprisonment for twelve months only,' Leatherland himself receiving the approbation of the judge for 'act[ing] the part of a faithful friend' by not testifying.[74]

As if justifying the time and energy devoted to the story in the autobiography, as well as his own complicity in these events, Leatherland again and again emphasizes the 'mental anguish,'[75] 'tumultuous anxieties,'[76] 'perplexity, sorrow, and anxiety' he 'suffered' because of Harry.[77] As a result, Harry's activities and their 'most serious consequences' come to be figured in terms of emotional excess in much the same way as Chartism in general is throughout Leatherland's narrative: the 'lurid blaze' that Harry starts in the rickyard comes to seem both the (inevitable) outcome and the literal embodiment of the figurative, emotional 'flame' 'fanned' by Chartist 'demagogues' - that furious 'conflagration' that Leatherland must literally and figuratively 'restrain.'[78]

What is in some ways most interesting, however, is that the horror Leatherland emphasizes is not the fire itself, but the 'secret in [his] own breast' and the 'dreadful dilemma' it entails.[79] Employing conceptual terms very similar to those central to Bezer's narrative, Leatherland figures that dilemma as a conflict between feeling and family, on the one hand, and the 'imperative duty … owed to society' and its rules or laws, on the other.[80] For while Leatherland emphasizes that he fully recognised both that it was his responsibility 'to give up the culprit to justice, and risk all consequences' and that 'by concealing his guilt, I was … becoming myself an accessory, and an accomplice of the criminal,' he justifies his decision not to divulge Harry's secret by calling up the spectre of the emotional impact Harry's inevitable execution would have on his unsuspecting family:

> ...I thought of his poor children being made orphans in this sad way, and of his aged parents' grey hairs being brought down with sorrow to the grave - for he was an only and well-beloved child. His father worked in the very next loom to me, and extremely bitter was he toward the unknown incendiary. ... "Ah," thought I, "poor old man, how little do you suppose it is your own son!"[81]

Fittingly, however, it is Leatherland's own family that he insists is ultimately and irreparably injured by Harry's behaviour when Leatherland's wife, spying him with the police officer who ultimately hears Harry's confession, is 'taken ill' and miscarries.[82]

Obviously, Leatherland's story of 'Harry' is a dramatic and highly specific staging of the conflicts so key to his general depiction of Chartism - here, as in the story of his resignation, Leatherland emerges as a Samson-like hero ensnared by, yet ultimately breaking through, the 'bands' of 'circumstances.' This becomes all the more obviously so given the way Leatherland emphasizes - via a reference to Samuel Johnson - that it was pure chance or 'circumstance' that initiated everything:

> Dr. Johnson - I think it is - says the events of a person's history often turn on very delicate pivots, and that his taking one street or another in a chance walk, which appears at the time of no importance whatever, may be of the greatest consequence through life. So it fell out with me on this eventful night [in which he originally encountered Harry].[83]

By emphasising the extent to which his own actions were motivated by what Bezer calls 'natural family feeling,' moreover, Leatherland demonstrates his fidelity to the 'emotions,' 'griefs and cares' of what his introduction labels 'common humanity,'[84] ironically confirming his membership in a transcendent human community by the very act of violating his 'imperative duty' to 'society' (a point underscored in multiple ways by Leatherland's emphasis on how the judge in Harry's case praised him for his acting the part of a 'friend' by virtue of not acting as the friend of the court). By extension, it is possible to read Leatherland's condemnatory view of Chartism as being based, in part, on the idea that Chartism itself violates this sense of 'common humanity,' if only by leading men like Harry to violate (rather than, as in Bezer, to enact) their duties as fathers and husbands: as Leatherland says to Harry when Harry invokes his 'wife and seven children' in an effort to bind Leatherland to his oath, '... you should have thought of them yourself, and not have done so wicked a deed, for their sakes, if not for your own.'[85] In a sense, in other words, Chartism is represented here as the misguided redirection of 'natural' feelings into political channels that violate, rather than affirm, the community of 'common humanity' in part by emphasising loyalty to 'party' over that to family.

As this suggests, the Harry story, like Leatherland's account of Chartism more generally, hinges upon the opposition between Harry and the Chartists, on the one hand, and Leatherland, on the other. The representation of the former as the passive victims of their 'pseudo-leaders' and of the excessive, misdirected 'passions' those leaders exploit thus dramatizes the distinctiveness of Leatherland's own position as an individualised, reflecting, ethical subject. In this sense, in other words, the isolation entailed in Leatherland's secret merely enacts the more general isolation entailed in the subject position he has defined for himself.

Ironically or not, however, that secret also binds Leatherland to Harry and to the Chartists whom Harry metonymically represents - it is, in other words, the mark of his 'complicity' with, as well as his difference from, them. As a result, it is tempting to see this sense of complicity as the driving force behind Leatherland's fascination with this 'dreadful' story and as an explanation for why Harry's story becomes so large and so integral a part of Leatherland's own. For however fantastic this 'return of the repressed' reading of Leatherland's narrative might be, it is to some extent one to which Leatherland himself gives credence by invoking the classic nineteenth-century story of the repressed, alternative self: 'for years,' Leatherland writes, '[Harry] dogged my footsteps up and down, like the monster in "Frankenstein."'[86]

As a result, 'truth-telling' in Leatherland takes on at once confessional and legalistic overtones and/or functions that differ dramatically from the rebellious ones it takes on and performs in Bezer's text, even as the 'self' becomes at once individualised and divided in a way that much more closely resembles our modern, psychologised notions of the self than it does the fixed, unified 'rebel' self of Bezer's narrative. That these conceptions of self and of truth are conjoined here, is suggested in Leatherland's opening remarks about the way in which autobiography 'reveals, as no other record can, the secret springs of action - the hidden, latent motives which spring up in the heart, and lead to conduct often enigmatical to the keenest and most diligent observer.'[87] Revealing to the reader the 'hidden, latent motives' that might make sense of, and excuse, his own 'enigmatical' 'conduct' - especially his ill-fated involvement with the Chartist Harry - while ultimately attributing the power of judgement to the 'diligent observer,' Leatherland casts himself as a man confessing to the reader rather than as a confrontational rebel, even as he - like Bezer - thereby envisions truthfulness as a process of revealing to view what would otherwise remain hidden. Though here, as in Bezer's autobiography, the author thus renders the reader a necessary participant in an ethical drama in which standards are seen to be those of 'common humanity' and judgement entails the revelation of secrets, Leatherland casts the reader as the ultimate judge and himself as the potentially guilty possessor of secrets, thus effectively reversing the ethical scenario established in Bezer's autobiography - a text in which it is clearly the 'honest' Bezer who, both as narrator and as protagonist, reveals and judges the hypocritical behaviour of others, from Lord John Russell to the reader.

Leatherland thus takes up a deferential stance toward the reader that differs dramatically from that which Bezer adopts, even as Leatherland, like Bezer, thereby manages to render the relationship between author and reader a kind of model for the ideal socio-political situation imagined in the text. For while Bezer much more often and consistently deploys the stylistic devices associated with what Hadley labels the 'melodramatic mode,' it is Leatherland's narrative rather than Bezer's that at least verges on adopting the nostalgic social vision Hadley associates with that mode. As Hadley describes it, that vision centres on the ideal of 'a reciprocal

... relationship ... among the ranks' in which 'traditional sources of authority ... were seen as ... father figures within what was ... considered to be a preordained and patriarchal hierarchy.' Reciprocity and, therefore, order are thus 'maintained through the enactment of ritualized social exchanges,' 'during which deferential roles and their appropriate attitudes were both produced and dramatically represented.' Particularly important forms of such exchange were, in Hadley's words, '[t]he bestowal of benevolence and the expression of gratitude.'[88] Arguably, this is precisely the vision embodied in the author-audience relation constructed in Leatherland's autobiography. For here Leatherland-the-narrator both implicitly and explicitly works to demonstrate his 'deep humility' and his 'respectability,'[89] both by expressing his 'grateful feelings' toward the various benevolent 'gentlemen' who 'kindly interested themselves in [his] welfare' and 'greatly assisted' him and by implicitly asking the reader to occupy the position of such gentlemen.[90] Such fatherly patronage, as Leatherland seems aware, demands not only deference or 'humility,' but also precisely the kind of knowledge of the potential client's character that Leatherland here offers to his anonymous reader. Leatherland thereby offers up his own 'courteous' 'candour' in exchange for the 'pity, candour, and sympathy' that he repeatedly 'beg[s]' of his 'courteous reader,'[91] even as his begging reveals the extent to which both the narrator and his text are haunted not merely by Harry but also and as a result by the spectre of being judged undeserving by the reader - shut out from the deference community he here longs to create as effectively as he was shut out from 'the Radical Association Room' and his own home on the night he ceased to be a Chartist.

As this reading of Leatherland's narrative makes clear, it is certainly possible to interpret his text in very much the same terms that Gagnier reads that of autobiographer James Dawson Burn. For in Leatherland's text, no less than in Burn's, 'Assuming a liberal and masculine ethic of autonomy and progress' certainly leads to a sense of isolation, of individual failure, and of guilt that the autobiography is in many ways devoted both to communicating and over-coming, [92] if not expunging, through deferential appeals to readers and to the community of 'common humanity' in which Leatherland hopes to - but never fully can - affirm his belonging. In the process, autobiography becomes here 'a form, more or less successful, of therapy,'[93] perhaps even to an extent that Burn's text does not in that Leatherland's text arguably presents its protagonist/author more as the divided self assumed in the modern therapeutic model than the utterly fragmented self portrayed in Burn's.

In Leatherland, moreover, that sense of failure and guilt is even more explicitly and inextricably linked with Chartism than it is in Burn's text, even as the similarities between these two autobiographies suggest that it is at least possible to connect their repudiation of Chartism with visions of the self that do, indeed, tend much more toward the 'individualist' than toward the 'collective.' After all, Burn and Leatherland's only visions of an affective and effective collective beyond the family is an exceedingly abstract 'common humanity,' figured in Leatherland's case as a 'deference community,' which they can only hope to realize or claim membership in via the autobiographical act itself. As a result, these two texts do indeed differ dramatically from the autobiography of the affirmed Chartist John James Bezer - for whom Chartism comes to represent a model for, as well as a concrete experience of, affective and effective community of the kind he also tries to create through his autobiography, as well as a potent source of a coherent sense of both selfhood and agency.

Interestingly enough, however, neither of these autobiographies define community in terms of anything like Marxist notions of class. For, as we have seen, Bezer presents a world in which 'men' are divided into 'tyrants' and 'slaves' and in which Chartism constitutes a kind of slave's rebellion that promises to heal such divisions and turn 'tyrants' and 'slaves' back into men. And Leatherland envisions a rank-based 'deference community' in which he can secure membership only by 'Assuming a liberal and masculine ethic of autonomy and progress' that is not only threatened by his political activities, but also itself implicitly at odds with his vision of community.

Equally interesting, however, is the fact that despite the real and dramatic differences between Bezer's and Leatherland's autobiographies and the notions of selfhood and Chartism they each embody, both texts and political visions hinge upon a very similar conceptual vocabulary or 'language,' the profound differences between them resulting from very different interpretations and appropriations of common terms, including enslavement versus freedom or autonomy, passivity versus activity, and 'natural' family feeling versus 'society' and its rules and laws. And however different Bezer's oppositional self and Leatherland's self-divided one, both may well be seen as alike to the extent that they are portrayed as equally fixed and stable. Leatherland's portrait of a self struggling to shake off the 'bands of circumstance,' in these terms, ultimately looks a great deal like Bezer's consistently rebellious self.

To some extent, the effort to account for, and to understand the meaning of, such differences and similarities inevitably entails a return to the theoretical issues raised in the opening of this chapter about the relation between 'the real' and/or 'experience,' on the one hand, and 'representation,' 'discourse,' and/or 'the imaginary,' on the other. For while this investigation of the rhetoric of these texts is based on the conviction that such discursive nuances are worthy of attention precisely because they shape the real, it also seems possible to argue, with Gagnier, that a particular autobiographer's choice of certain rhetorical or conceptual vocabularies and strategies over others was determined by a particular experience that they nonetheless also and inevitably helped to shape. By extension, in other words, it seems possible that *we* might find some version of the concept of class helpful to our understanding of the languages these writers employ even if and when that concept is not one that these writers themselves employ. Thus it seems possible, for example, to imagine that the notion of a unified and consistent self - whether realised in Chartism, as in Bezer, or threatened by it, as in Leatherland - would conceivably be greatly - if not uniquely - appealing to writers who, in Gagnier's words, 'often felt themselves passive victims of economic determinism.'[94] For such experiences, as Joseph Barker insisted, could at least potentially lead to a particularly and quite literally unsettling vision of both world and self: 'One of the greatest, or at least one of the most painful calamities resulting from our long continued poverty,' Barker writes, 'was this: We got the idea that all things on earth were utterly uncertain - ... that chance or a dark and malignant fatality, ruled over all, - that the best days of the world had all gone by, and that risks and ruin were now to be our common and unchanging lot.'[95] For Barker, in other words, the experience of 'long continued poverty' and the perpetual threat of starvation almost inevitably lead to a vision of the world as a kind of chaos in which there is little or no sense of agency or hope of change and in which the world outside the self seems to threaten its disintegration - as it does in Bezer's reference to the threat that 'Fast rolling years' and 'their grief and pain' might 'destroy'[96] - rather than contribute to its growth as is the case in the *bildungsroman* form of both the 'classic realist autobiography' and the classic realist novel.[97] Thus it is not difficult to imagine that, or why, such men might be drawn to the notion of a continuous, unassailable selfhood, whether of the kind so palpably presented in Bezer's autobiography or of the kind that Leatherland's autobiography struggles to affirm.

Such an interpretation might, but does not necessarily, entail the naive 'essentialism' or 'foundationalism' critiqued by Joyce. Thus we might, for example, recognize Barker's assumption that this vision of world and self as a 'great calamity' is itself a discursive, ideological, or 'imaginary' construction of experience rather than the necessary logic of experience itself, while still insisting, as Barker and Bezer in different ways seem to do, that certain such constructions appeal to particular people in particular times and places not only because they somehow accord, or are at least seen to accord, with something for which 'the real' or 'experience' seem apt, or at least sufficient, labels, but also because, leaving 'experience' aside, they are more affectively and rhetorically effective, leading - as Gagnier argues - to 'emotional health and flourishing self-images,' as well as effective political coalition and action, in a way that others quite simply do not.[98] Such a stance would involve, in other words, interpreting and even evaluating such constructions not as more or less adequate 'expressions' of a 'putative experiential reality,' but rather as rhetorical-cum-political acts that are more or less adequate as rhetorical-cum-political acts.[99]

NOTES

1. Sharratt is most explicit on this point, 'broadly' defining 'working-class political autobiographies' 'as autobiographies by people more immediately associated with a working-class background than with any other social position, and connected at some stage with some form of political event or movement.' Bernard Sharratt, *Reading Relations: Structures of Literary Production, a Dialectical Text/Book,* Brighton, Harvester, 1982, p. 237. In concentrating solely on the work of Sharratt, Vincent, and Gagnier, I am obviously (and perhaps problematically) excluding those studies, such as David Vincent's *Bread, Knowledge, and Freedom,* London, Methuen, 1981, and Alan Richardson's *Literature, Education, and Romanticism: Reading as Social Practice, 1780-1832,* Cambridge Studies in Romanticism Series, No. 8, Cambridge, Cambridge University Press, 1994, which treat Chartist autobiographies not as 'working-class political narratives,' but as instances of what Richardson calls the 'autobiography of self-improvement' and/or 'autobiographies of self-educated British writers.' Richardson, *Literature, Education, and Romanticism,* p. 233.

2. Regenia Gagnier, *Subjectivities: A History of Self-Representation in Britain, 1832-1920,* New York, Oxford University Press, 1991, pp. 159-160.

3. *Ibid.,* p. 48.

4. Both Joyce and Stedman Jones are the most prominent proponents and theorists of what has come to be called the 'linguistic turn' within social history. For a discussion of the history of, and theory behind, this 'turn,' see Patrick Joyce, *Democratic Subjects: The Self and the Social in Nineteenth-Century England,* Cambridge, Cambridge University Press, 1994, esp. pp. 1-14.

5. Instead Stedman Jones' analysis of the 'language of Chartism' posits a radicalism whose continuity (and ultimate failure) is ensured by the fact that it was not and 'could never be the ideology of a specific class.' Gareth Stedman Jones, *Languages of Class: Studies in English Working Class History 1832-1982,* Cambridge, Cambridge University Press, 1983, p. 104.

6. *Ibid.,* pp. 18, 21. The term 'essentialist' appears in Joyce, *Democratic Subjects,* p. 6.

7. Joyce, *Democratic Subjects,* p. 86. Arguably, this view is embedded in Gagnier's previously discussed contention that the 'middle-class ideology' at work in Burn's autobiography is symptomatised by his assumption of an individualist, 'masculine ethic of autonomy and progress' and a 'de-identifi[cation] with other workers,' while properly 'political narratives' - like those of Chartist William Lovett - portray 'a self whose desires must be expressed' through a sense of identity with an 'oppositional' community. Gagnier, *Subjectivities,* pp. 47-48, 163. As the word 'arguably' and comments about Gagnier's work later in this chapter are meant to suggest, however, Joyce's criticism of *Subjectivities* seriously underestimates the subtlety of Gagnier's arguments.

8. Though not explicitly linking gender, race, and class, Joyce does imply the equation Janowitz critiques here when he draws upon a series of feminist critics and critiques of the 'naturalised, 'essentialised' categories of 'man' and 'woman'

in order to make his case for the linguistic approach to class. Joyce, *Democratic Subjects,* p. 6.

[9]. Anne Janowitz, 'Class and Literature: The Case of Romantic Chartism,' in *Rethinking Class: Literary Studies and Social Formations,* Wai Chee Dimock and Michael T. Gilmore (eds.), New York, Columbia University Press, 1994, p. 240.

[10]. *Ibid.,* p. 242.

[11]. John James Bezer, 'Autobiography of One of the Chartist Rebels of 1848,' in *Testaments of Radicalism: Memoirs of Working-Class Politicians 1790-1885,* David Vincent (ed.), London, Europa, 1977, pp. 157.

[12]. Allen Davenport, *The Life, and Literary Pursuits of Allen Davenport, Author of the "Muses' Wreath," "Life of Spence," &c. Written by Himself,* Malcolm Chase (ed.), Aldershot, Scolar, p. 3; J. A. Leatherland, *Essays and Poems with a brief Autobiographical Memoir,* London, W. Tweedie, 1862, p. 1; Joseph Barker, *The History and Confessions of a Man, as put forth by himself...,* London, Chapman Brothers, 1846, p. xiv.

[13]. Gagnier, *Subjectivities,* p. 42. Gagnier's words in fact describe what she calls the 'rhetorical modesty' of working-class autobiographies rather than what one might call the 'rhetorical truthfulness' referred to here.

[14]. Bezer, 'Autobiography of One of the Chartist Rebels of 1848,' p. 159.

[15]. *Ibid.,* p. 179.

[16]. *Ibid.,* p. 150.

[17]. Leatherland, *Essays and Poems,* p. 17, n. The 'Chartist Hymn-book' to which Leatherland refers was Thomas Cooper's *Shakespearean Chartist Hymn Book,* a volume that twentieth-century historians have been unable to locate.

[18]. Bezer, 'Autobiography of One of the Chartist Rebels of 1848,' p. 150. Though the choice to focus on the autobiographies of Bezer and Leatherland derives from a desire to select texts by autobiographers whose backgrounds and attitudes toward Chartism differ, this selection is inevitably somewhat arbitrary, and a different selection of texts would undoubtedly reveal a very different picture of representations of self-making and of Chartism in Chartist autobiography. To some extent, however, demonstrating that potential variety is precisely the point of this chapter.

[19]. Alf Louvre, 'Reading Bezer: Pun, Parody and Radical Intervention in 19th Century Working Class Autobiography,' *Literature and History,* Vol. 14, No. 1, Spring 1988, pp. 30, 34.

[20]. *Ibid.,* p. 32.

[21]. *Ibid.,* p. 24.

[22]. Bezer, 'Autobiography of One of the Chartist Rebels of 1848,' p. 165.

[23]. *Ibid.,* p. 187. In Peter Scheckner (ed.), *An Anthology of Chartist Poetry: Poetry of the British Working Class, 1832-1852,* Rutherford, Madison, and Teaneck, Fairleigh Dickinson University Press; London and Toronto, Associated University Presses, 1989, these lines appear as the first stanza of a poem, entitled 'The Poet's Love of Liberty,' attributed to Charles Cole and originally printed in *The Friend of the People* 12 April 1851. (It is worth noting, however, that Scheckner's anthology is harshly criticised by Ulrike Schwab for multiple errors, including those regarding attribution, and for a rather loose definition of 'Chartist'

that leads Scheckner to include poems such as Thomas Hood's 'Song of the Shirt' and Ebenezer Elliott's *Corn-Law Rhymes*. Such criticisms should perhaps be kept in mind both here and in later references to Scheckner's anthology. The chapter nonetheless refers to Scheckner's anthology rather than to Yuri Kovalev's arguably more authoritative *Anthology of Chartist Literature,* Moscow, Foreign Languages Publishing House, 1956, because the former is infinitely more accessible to Anglo-American readers. Readers interested in Kovalev's anthology may, however, find an English translation of its Russian-language introduction in *Victorian Studies* Vol. 2, 1958.)

[24]. Bezer, 'Autobiography of One of the Chartist Rebels of 1848,' pp. 158, 184.

[25]. *Ibid.,* p. 187.

[26]. *Ibid.,* p. 158.

[27]. *Ibid.,* p. 163. Compare the concluding lines of Chartist poet William James Linton's 'Free Trade':

Free to sell, and free to buy, -
    Free to toil for famine wage;
Free to reap, - and free to die, -
    Famish'd youth and foodless age.
'Export' should not mean *despoil*;
    'Free Trade,' - let the words be true:
Free and fair trade on the soil;
    And export grain and landlords too! (*The English Republic* 1851; rept. in Scheckner [ed.], *An Anthology of Chartist Poetry,* p. 243)

[28]. Elaine Hadley, *Melodramatic Tactics: Theatricalized Dissent in the English Marketplace, 1800-1885,* Stanford, Stanford University Press, 1995, p. 125.

[29]. Bezer, 'Autobiography of One of the Chartist Rebels of 1848,' pp. 162, 165.

[30]. *Ibid.,* p. 164.

[31]. Compare the first and last stanza of John Henry Bramwich's 'A Hymn,' which - like Bezer's text - insists upon the unnaturalness of the subjectivity designated by the word 'slave':

Britannia's sons, though slaves ye be,
God your Creator made you free;
He, life to all, and being, gave -
But never, never made a slave!

All men are equal in His sight, -
The bond, the free, the black, the white; -
He made them all, - them freedom gave -
He made the man, - *Man made the Slave!* (*The Northern Star and National Trades Journal* 4 April 1846; rept. in Scheckner [ed.], *An Anthology of Chartist Poetry,* p. 124)

[32]. *Ibid.,* p. 165.

[33]. References to tyranny and to slavery (of both blacks and whites) figure frequently and often in combination in Chartist poetry - perhaps more frequently than any other single phrase or image. Scheckner's anthology of approximately 213 Chartist poems, for example, includes at least 56 poems that include versions

of the words 'tyrant' and 'slave,' 38 more that employ some version of 'slave' (but not 'tyrant'), and a further 30 that include versions of 'tyrant' (but not 'slave'). This number excludes many poems that refer to slavery metaphorically, by referring - for example, to 'chains' and/or 'fetters.'

[34]. Ulrike Schwab, *The Poetry of the Chartist Movement: A Literary and Historical Study,* 'Studies in Social History,' No. 13, Dordrecht, Kluwer Academic Publishers; Amsterdam, International Institute of Social History, 1987, pp. 75. The passively obedient 'slave' is treated with everything from melting pity to harsh contempt in Chartist poetry, the latter attitude being particularly evident in the following lines from 'One and All,' a poem that appeared in the 25 June 1842 edition of *The Northern Star*:

One and all, let us proclaim
He who bears a bondman's name,
And seeketh not to cleanse its shame
Deserves to live in scorn, and die
With the vilest things that lie
Grovelling on their mother earth
'Midst the spawn which gave them birth.
Earth will curse the dastard grave
Of the mean and cringing slave.   (Scheckner [ed.], *An Anthology of Chartist Poetry,* p. 95)

[35]. *Ibid.,* p. 120. The quotations here are taken from poet John Henry Bramwich's 'Some Men That I Like' (Scheckner [ed.], *An Anthology of Chartist Poetry,* p. 125), which Scheckner indicates was first published in *The Northern Star* 18 April 1846. Schwab herself cites the version of the poem contained in Kovalev (ed.), *Anthology of Chartist Literature,* p. 119.

[36]. Bezer, 'Autobiography of One of the Chartist Rebels of 1848,' p. 186; spelling original.

[37]. *Ibid.,* p. 187. Interestingly enough, Bezer apparently confuses (or intentionally fudges?) historical fact in order to bring these events into such a close temporal and thematic relation to each other. For, according to David Vincent, Bezer's narrative has him joining 'the Chartist "Locality" meeting at "Lunt's Coffee House on the Green"' at a time when there was 'no Chartist activity in the capital' and before the Charter itself was even published. While Vincent argues that '"1838" is misprinted or misremembered and should read either 1841 or 1842,' it is possible to see this temporal confusion as an important and revealing instance of the way in which conceptual framework (and/or rhetorical purpose) intervenes to shape Bezer's construction of the facts. Bezer, 'Autobiography of One of the Chartist Rebels of 1848,' p. 179, n. 13.

[38]. Bezer, 'Autobiography of One of the Chartist Rebels of 1848,' p. 159.

[39]. Again, the same equation between 'man,' husband/father, and rebel recurs frequently in Chartist poetry, an example being the following lines from Ernest Jones's 'The Slave-Song':

Will you let your children perish,
    At the rich man's 'scutcheoned gate,
And the wife, you fondly cherish,

Serve his lust and swell his state?

Tell the tyrant - tell the traitor,
    Who grows rich on your distress,
You are a Man - and *who* is *greater*? (*The Labourer* 2 [1847]; rept. in Scheckner [ed.], *An Anthology of Chartist Poetry*, pp. 215-217)

[40]. *Ibid.*, p. 165.

[41]. *Ibid.*, p. 186.

[42]. *Ibid.*, p. 157.

[43]. *Ibid.*, p. 164.

[44]. Hadley, *Melodramatic Tactics*, p. 122.

[45]. *Ibid.*

[46]. In the poem 'Monsters,' William James Linton attributes a similarly cold, unfeeling 'reptile heart' to all those - from 'crowned and purpled Thing' to 'creep[ing]' 'serf' - 'Who ac[t] a loathly part.' Scheckner (ed.), *An Anthology of Chartist Poetry*, pp. 253-254.

[47]. Bezer, 'Autobiography of One of the Chartist Rebels of 1848,' pp. 154, 155.

[48]. *Ibid.*, p. 154.

[49]. *Ibid.*, p. 167.

[50]. Again, this play between existential and literal imprisonment is a recurring theme within Chartist poetry and one eloquently expressed in the following lines from Ernest Jones's 'The Prisoner to the Slaves':
From my cell, I look back on the world - from my cell,
    And think I am not the less free
Than the serf and the slave who in misery dwell
    In the street and the lane and the lea. (*Notes to the People* 1 (1851): 339; rept. in Scheckner [ed.], *An Anthology of Chartist Poetry*, p. 206)

[51]. Bezer, 'Autobiography of One of the Chartist Rebels of 1848,' p. 187.

[52]. *Ibid.*, pp. 186-187; spelling original.

[53]. Gagnier, *Subjectivities*, p. 162.

[54]. Bezer not only deploys a conceptual vocabulary very close to that employed by Chartist poets, but also thereby defines both his own character and the character and goal of Chartism via a quite similar conception of 'liberty' and/or 'freedom.' Defined in opposition to 'slavery,' freedom for Chartist poets designates, in Schwab's words, not only the external, socio-political situation in which all men enjoy 'comprehensive and claimable rights as well as equality before the law,' but also the internal condition of 'intellectual and cultural emancipation' embodied in the very act of 'protest.' Schwab, *The Poetry of the Chartist Movement*, p. 69

[55]. Gagnier, *Subjectivities*, p. 162.

[56]. Stedman Jones, *Languages of Class*, p. 96.

[57]. *Ibid.*, pp. 107, 109.

[58]. Bezer, 'Autobiography of One of the Chartist Rebels of 1848,' p. 186.

[59]. Hadley, *Melodramatic Tactics*, p. 131.

[60]. Bezer, 'Autobiography of One of the Chartist Rebels of 1848,' p. 155. That Bezer's adoption of the 'melodramatic mode' does not entail the nostalgia for a patriarchal 'deference community' that Hadley associates with that mode is made

clear not only by his general emphasis on the dangers entailed in deference, but also by his assertion that his first master's position as both his mother's employer and his own is a negative example of 'tyranny' rather than, as the 'deference community' model would suggest, a positive example of patriarchal care. In this and other ways, then, Bezer's narrative may be said to demonstrate Hadley's (unevenly deployed) contention that the 'practitioners' of the melodramatic mode, 'living in and through the passage of time, subjects of and to uneven development, were often drawn to its expressiveness without wholly adhering to all of its implications.' Hadley, *Melodramatic Tactics,* p. 119.

[61]. Schwab, *The Poetry of the Chartist Movement,* p. 122.
[62]. Leatherland, *Essays and Poems,* p. 17.
[63]. *Ibid.,* p. 18.
[64]. *Ibid.,* pp. 19, 18; emphasis added.
[65]. *Ibid.,* p. 17, n.
[66]. Here and throughout the autobiography, Leatherland clearly intends the radical preacher J. R. Stephens when he refers to 'Stevens.'
[67]. *Ibid.,* p. 19. In the process, of course, Leatherland's representation of Chartism not only comes to resemble that of James Dawson Burn, *The Autobiography of a Beggar Boy,* London: Tweedie, 1855, in David Vincent (ed.), London, Europa, 1978, esp. pp. 150-151, but also comes quite close to that of middle-class writers. For, like Leatherland, middle-class writers from Carlyle to Gaskell to Disraeli persistently depicted Chartism 'as a movement of the subliterate, almost subhuman.' Janowitz, 'Class and Literature,' p. 245.
[68]. Leatherland, *Essays and Poems,* pp. 1-2; spelling original.
[69]. *Ibid.,* p. 21.
[70]. *Ibid.,* pp. 21, 18.
[71]. *Ibid.,* pp. 22, 23. Stephen Roberts (private communication) reports that Harry's real name was Thomas Katterns and that the rick-burning, reported in the local press, occurred in February 1839.
[72]. Leatherland, *Essays and Poems,* p. 24.
[73]. *Ibid.,* pp. 24-25.
[74]. *Ibid.,* pp. 31, 30.
[75]. *Ibid.,* p. 21.
[76]. *Ibid.,* p. 26.
[77]. *Ibid.,* p. 30.
[78]. *Ibid.,* p. 24.
[79]. *Ibid.,* pp. 28, 26.
[80]. *Ibid.,* p. 27.
[81]. *Ibid.*
[82]. *Ibid.,* p. 29.
[83]. *Ibid.,* p. 22.
[84]. *Ibid.,* p. 1.
[85]. *Ibid.,* p. 25.
[86]. *Ibid.,* p. 27.
[87]. *Ibid.,* p. 2.
[88]. Hadley, *Melodramatic Tactics,* p. 15.

[89]. Leatherland, *Essays and Poems*, pp. 1, 2.

[90]. *Ibid.*, p. 14.

[91]. *Ibid.*, pp. 2, 18, 39.

[92]. Gagnier, *Subjectivities*, p. 46.

[93]. *Ibid.*, p. 45.

[94]. *Ibid.*, p. 43.

[95]. Barker, *The History and Confessions of a Man*, p. 79.

[96]. Bezer, 'Autobiography of One of the Chartist Rebels of 1848,' p. 187.

[97]. Gagnier describes the 'classic realist autobiography' as including 'remembered details of childhood, parent-child relationships, the subject's formal education, and [most importantly] a progressive developmental narrative of self,' which both hinges upon 'crises and recoveries' (and, therefore, on a 'climax-and-resolution/action-and-interaction' model) and 'culminat[es] in material well-being and "fame" within greater or lesser circles.' *Subjectivities*, p. 43.

[98]. *Ibid.*, p. 54.

[99]. Stedman Jones, *Languages of Class*, p. 21. The attitude and method here suggested are in some sense merely a logical extension of Joyce's own position, however far they might be from the one Joyce himself employs and advocates. For, as he puts it, 'there is no problem about discriminating ... tenable from untenable arguments' or what are here labelled effective and ineffective constructions of experience: 'We do this all the time. . . .' Joyce, *Democratic Subjects*, p. 9.

CREATING A PEOPLE'S HISTORY:
POLITICAL IDENTITY AND HISTORY IN CHARTISM, 1832-1848

Robert G. Hall

'When the people of England are free, the people of the world will not be slaves. Men of France, Italy, and Germany-Liberty is a tree of long growth in England. It was planted at Runnymede; it was sunned by the fires of Smithfield; it was watered by the blood of Marston Moor, and the veins of Charles; it was fanned by the prayers of the Puritan, and dewed by the tears of the Exile--and now it is beginning to bloom beneath the fostering hand of the Charter.' [1]

This kind of attempt to place 'the people' at the centre of a historical narrative, that stretched from the Magna Carta, through medieval peasant revolts and the revolutions of the seventeenth century, to the present, pointed to some of the distinctive features of the Chartist approach to the past. Their version of history typically took an oral and public form, sometimes outdoors as part of a mass platform campaign, other times indoors as part of a Chartist dinner or lecture series. Ernest Jones' speech to a Tower Hamlets meeting, called to express solidarity with the Italian people, referred to specific episodes in English history; but, at the same time, he suggested that the history of 'the people of England' had broader, universal significance and meaning. There was also, in his account, a certain blending together of history and myth. After all, it was not 'the people,' in the usual Chartist sense of the phrase, that confronted King John at Runnymede in June 1215.

When Ernest Jones and the other people's historians tried to define their subject, they typically chose to associate 'the people' with 'the proletarian millions,' or the working classes. In his address, the anonymous author of *The People's Own History of England* made clear the subject, 'the people of England (comprehending in that term the great mass of the population),' of this historical work. 'The people,' the author charged, were excluded not only from citizenship but also from 'the HISTORY OF THEIR COUNTRY!'[2] This way of defining 'the people' was consistent with the Chartist tendency to regard 'the labouring classes' as 'the real 'people' and to denounce 'the middle class,' bankers, and 'cotton lords' as enemies of 'the people.'[3] And yet, despite this widely-accepted definition of 'the people,' the approach of these people's historians to their subject was shot through with ambiguities and contradictions. On the one hand, they readily included in their narratives the barons of Runnymede, Whig aristocrats, and gentlemen 'patriots'; however, they made few, if any, direct references to the contributions of two groups that made up together the majority of 'the labouring classes': women and children.[4]

Although Chartist activists and leaders not infrequently referred to statutes, documents, and printed authorities, they turned to history primarily out of the pursuit of democratic political power, not out of an impartial search for 'objective' historical truth. In other words, the creation of the people's history had and was put to a variety of political uses.[5] During the 1830s, the word 'democracy' still carried revolutionary overtones. In the minds of many, especially those of a conservative or loyalist cast, democracy was seen as foreign and alien and was closely associated with the violence and anarchy of the French Revolution and mob rule in the young American republic.[6] By tracing the historical origins of their movement and its programme through 1688 to the Magna Carta and the Anglo-Saxon past, the Chartists countered these negative associations and were able to claim constitutional sanction for their democratic vision, and the right of resistance, and the mass arming strategy.[7] Their radical interpretation of constitutional history represented, as well, a contribution to the moral pursuit of 'useful knowledge' and a potential source of inspiration and unity during the coming struggle. 'Upon the pages of the historian,' claimed William Aitken in a lecture, 'we see in bold relief, the daring spirits who have preceded us. The despot and the high-souled patriot are represented in their proper colours: the actions of the former are despised; the noblest feelings of our nature are lifted on behalf of the latter, - a desire to emulate him rises in our minds.'[8] Aitken's use of the pronoun 'him' to refer to 'the high-souled patriot' also points to another of the political ends to which Chartist representations of the past were put. Their versions of history, in effect, reinforced and, indeed, justified the Chartist emphasis on universal male suffrage and the link between citizenship and manhood.[9]

Though national, and often international, in perspective, the attempts of Aitken and others to create a people's history were ultimately refracted through, and were shaped by, the culture and traditions of the radical locality. A decentralized, loosely federated movement, Chartism drew its strength and numbers in the late 1830s and 1840s from hundreds of local associations and organizations. For over twenty years, one such thriving radical community had existed in Ashton-under-Lyne, a medium-sized mill town that was situated about seven miles east of Manchester.[10] Through speeches and toasts, rituals and symbolism, and songs and poetry, Aitken and his fellow Chartists there developed and publicly commemorated their own version of the history of 'the people'; they told stories about the Anglo-Saxon past, the French Revolution, Thomas Paine, Robert Emmet, the 'Ludding Times,' Peterloo, and other key episodes and personalities in the radical past; in doing so, they struggled to create a radical people's history, one that was primarily oral and visual in its form, as an alternative to Whig and Conservative interpretations of the past and to the expensive, text bound histories of the world of print.[11] The making of this alternative history served as a way of legitimizing their programme and strategy for winning political power, and as a way of dishing their opponents; it was also at the centre of Chartist efforts to construct a separate and distinct political identity and brand of democratic politics.

I

That the Chartists turned to history in their search for political power reflected the extent to which they were influenced by the historical and constitutionalist outlook of mid-nineteenth century society and political culture. In this period, celebrations of certain dramatic episodes, like the 1688 Revolution, and historically-based arguments that drew on constitutional and legal documents and precedents were, as James Epstein has pointed out, 'the very stuff of politics.'[12] The depth and intensity of contemporary political debates over the nature of the constitutionalist past underscored the lack of consensus about the meaning and trajectory of English history, and pointed to the role of partisan politics and the emerging party system in these historical controversies. This was hardly surprising; after all, political programmes and activities have typically involved, in the words of the Popular Memory Group, 'a process of historical argument and definition' and contention over interpretations of the past.[13]

For the Chartists, then, their efforts to create a clearly defined political identity almost inevitably led them to construct their own distinctive view of history as a counter-statement to the prevailing interpretations of the day. History was and is, to borrow Epstein's phrase, one way of defining 'the contested terrain between different social and political groups.'[14] In the 1830s, this was all the more the case, because at that point history was typically the province of members of the legal profession, clergymen, journalists, politicians, and men (and women) of letters, not of university-trained, 'professional' historians. Nor was archival research the universally accepted means of discovering and establishing historical truth. 'Scholarly editions of texts at one end of the spectrum and novels at the other,' as Bonnie Smith has pointed out, 'were both considered history.'[15]

Deeply rooted in partisan politics, the various Whig and Conservative interpretations of the past were crucial to the making of these different political identities. Looking back to their struggles with George III and to the Glorious Revolution and beyond, the Whigs chose to emphasize the unfolding of the cause of civil and religious liberty. In doing so, they upheld the right of resistance against corrupt and tyrannical governments, but they preferred to point to the role of moderate, incremental reform in dealing with what Lord Grey referred to as 'those abuses which have crept into the Constitution, and into the various institutions of the Country.'[16] From the perspective of most Conservatives, however, history demonstrated instead the need to conserve and protect 'the throne, the altar, and the constitution' from innovation and change and foreign influences: democracy, popery, and revolution. During the 1830s, speakers at Conservative dinners in Manchester and other towns of the cotton district embraced this historical outlook with a passion; through toasts and speeches they celebrated the military victories and heroes of the wars with revolutionary France and commemorated a version of the English past that was at once thoroughly Protestant (and Anglican) and monarchist in its sympathies.[17] There also emerged, in the decade or so after 1832, a trend in historical writing that cut across these kinds of partisan interpretations. This was the tendency to see the history of England, and other Western societies as well, in terms of the rise of what John Stuart Mill called 'the trading and manufacturing classes.'[18]

Sceptical about the historical reliability and truth of these interpretations, radicals and later Chartists knew only too well that the rich and powerful, and the victors, wrote history. 'If Washington had been defeated,' John Snowden told a Heyhead Green meeting, 'he would have been hung on Bunkers Hill as a rebel, but the tools of tyranny were defeated by him, and his name is one of the brightest spots in the History of Freedom.'[19] Chartists were also quick to point out how party biases shaped the writing of history. While acknowledging Thomas B. Macaulay's obvious talents, a notice in the *People's Paper* described his best seller, not as history, but as a partisan 'apology':

> Its purpose is unequivocal - being plainly an hypothesis of aristocratic liberalism - a deification of that base and cold blooded oppressor Prince of Orange - and a depreciation of anything that does not chime in with the existing political and social institutions of our country .... It is only the apology and defence of a party and a system.[20]

Radical critics countered this kind of 'apology and defence' in a variety of ways. By choosing to emphasize the role of 'the great mass of the population,' or the working classes, in history, they tried to move beyond the narrow definitions of historical causation and 'the people' in Whig and Conservative accounts. In a similar fashion they also challenged the tendency to reduce history to what William Cobbett dismissed as 'narrations relating to battles, negotiations, intrigues, contests between rival sovereignties, rival nobles, and to the character of kings, queens, mistresses, bishops, ministers, and the like.'[21]

One attempt to right these historical wrongs and to create an alternative, radical reading of the past took place in 1845 at London's City Chartist Hall, the setting for a series of twelve lectures by Thomas Cooper. In many ways, Cooper was uniquely suited to act as a people's historian. A plebeian intellectual, who had read widely in 'ancient and modern history,' he was a committed Chartist who self consciously cast himself as following in the footsteps of 'the glorious martyrs and fervent patriots of my fatherland.'[22] Interested as well in drama, especially Shakespeare, and poetry, Cooper the historian combined 'a dashing style of oratory' with dramatic readings, music, and some of his own 'People's Songs.'[23] Each of his lectures at the City Chartist Hall, promised a *Northern Star* advertisement, 'will be preceded and followed by the choral performance of one of these pieces, in which the audience will be invited to join.'[24]

Over the course of his weekly lecture series, Cooper outlined his own version of a people's history that ranged from the ancient world through the mists of the Anglo-Saxon past to 'Byron and modern literature.' After opening with lectures on 'priestcraft and despotism' in ancient Egypt and democracy and freedom in ancient Greece and republican Rome, he took up 'the Saxon period of English history' and 'our ancient democratic institutions,' and praised, in particular, the reign of 'the glorious Alfred.'[25] Cooper then gave a detailed and none too flattering account of the coming of William 'the Bastard' and his band of robbers; in the same lecture, he described 'the stern barons of Runnymede' and the insurrection of Wat Tyler and John Ball and 'their peasant compeers' and concluded with 'the so-called "Reformation" under the brutal Henry VIII.'[26] Turning to the revolutions of the seventeenth century, Cooper spared neither the 'tyrannical Charles I' nor 'the hypocrisy' of Oliver Cromwell; in contrast, however, 'the immortal patriots' John Hampden, John Pym, Henry Marten, Algernon Sidney, and 'the incorruptible Hutchinson,' the *Northern Star* noted, 'were energetically depictured.'[27] In subsequent lectures, Cooper discussed the revolutions in America and France (especially the latter) and traced the 'bloody persecutions of liberty which brought Brandreth, Despard, Thistlewood, and others, to the gallows.' He carried his radical history lesson through the 1832 Reform Bill and the origins of the demand for the People's Charter and concluded on an explicitly political note, with 'an impassioned exhortation to all who felt an interest in human progress to unite in an energetic struggle for the complete triumph of right.'[28]

Determined to expose the abuses of 'priestcraft and despotism' and to assert the right of resistance (and even revolution), Cooper was in line with other Chartist attempts to develop a distinctive interpretation of the past and to position the movement and 'the people' within the centuries-long struggle for liberty. What was unusual about Cooper, as a people's historian was that he left behind a detailed, autobiographical account of the intellectual and cultural influences that had shaped his historical perspective. In his early adolescence, he first came into contact with 'the spirit of Radicalism' through the journeymen who worked in a brushmaker shop near his home. The 'most determined politicians,' they lent young Cooper Hone's caricatures, read aloud radical newspapers, and engaged him in lively conversations about 'the "villanous rascals," Lord Castlereagh, and Lord Sidmouth, and Lord Eldon, and the Prince Regent.'[29] At about the same time, Cooper embarked on a more formal pursuit of knowledge through the world of books and the printed word. His plan of 'self-education' was a truly ambitious one:

> I thought it possible that by the time I reached the age of twenty-four I might be able to master the elements of Latin, Greek, Hebrew, and French; might get well through Euclid, and through a course of Algebra; might commit the entire 'Paradise Lost,' and seven of the best plays of Shakspeare, to memory; and might read a large and solid course of history, and of religious evidences; and be well acquainted also with the current literature of the day.[30]

The list of authors and titles that he mentioned in passing underscored the wide range and eclecticism of his reading in history: Julius Caesar, Plutarch, Tacitus, Edward Gibbon, 'Lingard's 'Anglo-Saxon Antiquities,' Foxe's Book of Martyrs, 'Neale's 'History of the Puritans,' historical works by Oliver Goldsmith and William Robertson, and 'Speed's and Rapin's folio histories of England.'[31] His reading of Shakespeare and Sir Walter

Scott, especially the Waverley novels, as well as the 'rational' writings of Volney and Elihu Palmer, also clearly informed and sharpened his approach to, and understanding of, the past. Drawing on these varied sources of historical knowledge, he entertained audiences in the Shakespearean Room of the Leicester Chartists with recitations and dramatic readings from Shakespeare, Milton, and Burns and on other evenings 'recited the history of England, and set the portraits of great Englishmen before young Chartists, who listened with intense interest.'[32]

II

For Cooper and the other autodidacts of the movement, history was crucial to the pursuit of 'useful knowledge.' In the late 1830s and 1840s, this meant, above all, political knowledge. This branch of knowledge, declared John Deegan, gave 'the people' insights into the far-reaching effects of 'class legislation' and 'the manoeuvres and contortions' of the Whigs and Tories; its acquisition marked a break with the apathy and defeatism of 'ignorance' and the first step towards winning political power.[33] 'If ever the people were instructed as he could wish them to be,' James Taylor remarked, 'they would not suffer oppression and insult as they had done.'[34] Historical knowledge was in turn a vital part of educating 'the people' about the uses and abuses of political power. History, claimed William Aitken in a lecture on Feargus O'Connor and democracy, 'was the light by which we could look upon past ages - the landmarks of what has gone before us; and by studying which with intentness, they would become wiser and more able to take part in the management of their country than they would be otherwise.'[35]

Drawing on speeches and toasts, commemorative rituals and ceremonies, music, songs, and drama, these leaders and activists of Ashton Chartism developed their own radical version of history, one that typically took a public form and relied, not on printed word, but on the spoken word. They turned to this kind of history as a way of instructing and inspiring 'the people' and as a way of forging a sense of unity and common struggle that cut across and broke down ethnic differences and animosities, divisions between the literate and illiterate, and between Chartists and old radicals 'from the school of Cartwright and Hunt.'[36] Creating a people's history was also at the centre of their attempt to build a distinct political identity and to distinguish themselves from the emerging 'liberal' and 'tory' political parties in Ashton.[37] Sympathetic to the American and French revolutions as well as to suffering Ireland, these people's historians tried to place English history within a broader, more universal history of liberty and challenged the portrayal of democracy as something foreign and alien and the loyalist emphasis on the relationship between monarchy, the Established Church, and the constitution in God's Elect Nation; their interpretation of the past stressed instead the historical roots of their democratic programme and the right of resistance and vigorously criticized, especially in the case of recent history, the Whigs and Tories for oppressing 'the people' and for, as Aitken put it, 'undermining the ancient foundations of British freedom.'[38]

Certainly since the days of the Blanketeers and Peterloo, Lancashire radicals had relied on the open air meeting as a way of defining a distinctive political style and programme; the mass meeting had also served as a dramatic way of asserting their right to participate in the public sphere and of communicating their message to ordinary men and women, many of whom remained, to a large extent, outside the print culture.[39] It was quite natural, then, for the Ashton Chartists to regard the hustings as the perfect forum for expounding their version of the past. Tracing many of the evils of the 1830s back to 'the aristocracy of the country, founded by that tyrant, William the Robber - or, if they would rather, William the Conqueror,' Charles Walker told a meeting in the marketplace that William had stolen the land from 'the people' and had abolished all the free institutions of the country; the only way to regain power from the aristocracy was through parliamentary reform.[40] In a similar fashion, John Deegan took up the theme of monarchical and aristocratic robbery and lost rights in his depiction of the Reformation; here he chose to underscore how members of the nobility, like the family of Lord John Russell, had benefitted, at the expense of the poor, from the plunder of the church during Henry VIII's reign.[41] Looking back into the distant past, he described universal suffrage as 'the birthright of Englishmen' and defiantly asserted the right of 'the people' to 'those constitutional rights which were gained for us not by moral but by physical force'; he also defended the right to bear arms and the calling of a National

Convention by pointing to specific historical precedents, like Magna Carta and the Glorious Revolution.[42] 'How was James compelled to abdicate--to resign his throne,' Deegan asked at a mass meeting in May 1839, 'and who called in the Prince of Orange? Why, it was what was termed in those days a National Convention, assembled in London.'[43]

In November 1839 a small band of radical veterans and activists gathered at the house of Mr Walker in Ashton to celebrate the birthday of Henry Hunt. Much had happened in the months since Deegan had delivered his militant history lessons to cheering crowds. In the aftermath of the three-day 'national holiday' in August, the mass platform campaign had collapsed amid a wave of arrests, confusion, and bitter self-recriminations. Under these trying circumstances, the Ashton Chartists met to reassert their political presence and beliefs in public and to begin the process of reviving and rebuilding the movement; in doing so, they turned to the conventions of elite political dining and modified them to their own political ends. The very setting for the dinner, as well as the songs that they sang and the speeches and toasts that they gave, placed the Chartist struggle within the historical context of 'the great and sacred cause of freedom.' Mrs Walker, 'the woman of the house,' had been wounded by a sabre 'on the blood-stained field of St. Peter.' Decorated with evergreens and portraits of radical heroes and patriots, the room itself where the dinner took place stirred up memories of past defeats and victories in the history of liberty. The evening's songs, like 'The Birth of Paine' and 'Peterloo,' and dramatic readings from the poetry of Robert Burns and 'Volney's New Age' likewise encouraged those who were present to try to understand recent events from a broad, historical point of view.[44] One of the many toasts that was given that evening explicitly underscored these kinds of associations:

> The immortal memory of Thomas Paine, William Cobbett, Major Cartwright, Robert Emmett, John Knight, Julian Hibbert, Hampden, Wat Tyler, Sidney, Thomas Hardy, Horne Tooke, Volney, Voltaire, Elihu Palmer, Mirabeau, Robespierre, William Tell, Andreas Hofer, Washington, Wallace, and all the illustrious dead

of every nation, who by their acts and deeds have contributed to the cause of liberty.[45]

This toast positioned Chartism within a radical tradition that stretched back to John Horne Tooke and Thomas Hardy in the 1790s and beyond to Major John Cartwright's *Take Your Choice* in 1776, a tradition that had survived many a setback and defeat. This historical roll call of England's contributions to 'the cause of liberty' also brought together local heroes, like Oldham's John Knight, and the well-known national figures John Hampden and Algernon Sidney as well as Wat Tyler, one of the leaders of the 1381 Peasant Revolt. By linking these English 'patriots' to the struggles of Scottish and Irish radicals and nationalists and to other European and American champions of liberty, the Ashton Chartists took an international perspective on the people's history; by including gentlemen and members of the landed classes, like Julian Hibbert and Hampden, they also chose, on this occasion, to expand their definition of 'the people.'

The evergreen-draped portraits, songs, and toasts at the 1839 dinner also demonstrated how 'invented traditions' and rituals, based on local history, contributed to the making of the Chartists' alternative history.[46] Of all the events that the Ashton Chartists chose to commemorate through the use of ceremony and symbolism, the one that cast the longest shadow was the fateful day of August 16, 1819. On that day, parties of men, women, and children marched, with flags and banners flying and the Stalybridge band playing, to Manchester for what Samuel Bamford called 'the most important meeting that had ever been held for Parliamentary Reform'; the Ashton contingent also proudly displayed a cap of liberty.[47] Soon after the meeting began, the Manchester magistrates ordered local yeomanry and troops to arrest Henry Hunt and the other radical leaders on the hustings. In the ensuing panic, at least eleven died, and around four hundred were wounded or injured in some way; at least eighteen men and women from Ashton and environs sustained injuries, some as the result of blows or sabre cuts, others as the result of being 'knocked down and trampled.'[48]

Outraged by the events of that day, James Higson and some of his friends organized in August 1820 an 'immense' crowd to commemorate the first anniversary of Peterloo. Bearing white wands, surmounted with black crepe, they gathered to sing Samuel Bamford's 'Song of the Slaughter' and later to march in procession through the town, 'headed with the well known black flag, as a symbol of mourning to the murdered ones.'[49] By turning upside down some of the conventions of elite politics, like the coronation parade, this ritual act of remembrance allowed radicals to assert the right of assembly and to critique and challenge local and national authorities.[50] Their practice of keeping 'sacred' the anniversary of 'the never-to-be-forgotten, never-to-be-forgiven, blood-stained 16th of August' placed Peterloo at the centre of their people's history and also reinforced the tendency to view the events of that day from a class perspective.[51] 'The bitter feeling which that brutal attack created amongst the operatives of Lancashire,' recalled Robert Cooper in 1868, 'is transmitted to this generation.'[52]

Over the course of the 1820s and 1830s, the Ashton radicals continued to hold dinners and processions to keep alive memories of Peterloo, until, as they put it, the 'authors and abettors of the deeds...are arraigned before a tribunal.'[53] For the young William Aitken, 'a Radical banquet of potato pies and home brewed ale' at 'Owd Nancy Clayton's' in Charlestown marked his initiation into radical culture in Ashton and its symbolic rendering of this crucial episode in the history of 'the people.' Wounded on 'that memorable day' at St. Peter's Field, Nancy Clayton, he recalled years later, had worn 'a black petticoat, which she afterwards transformed into a black flag, which, on the 16th of August, used to be hung out and a green cap of liberty attached thereto.'[54] The radical interpretation and memories of Peterloo also clearly influenced his belief in the historical right of Englishmen to bear arms and legitimized the Chartist strategy of mass arming. 'In 1819,' he told the jury at his trial, 'a peaceable meeting of the inhabitants of Manchester was held, when the people were attacked by the cavalry, and butchered in a most inhumane manner. This was the reason why the people went now to their meetings armed, and he contended that the people had a perfect right to do so.'[55]

Through the use of music and songs, the Ashton Chartists tried to dramatize these rituals of remembrance and their version of history and to draw in and include men and women who had, at best, a rather limited ability to read or to write. Early on, Samuel Bamford had recognized the potential gains of introducing music and the 'heart-inspiring song' to radical meetings. 'As it was a custom to sing hymns and psalms in the Church,' Samuel Bamford urged a Saddleworth crowd, 'he would advise the reformers to sing hymns to Liberty; & the French patriots at the dawn of Liberty in that country sung the Marseillois Hymn and so could the English Patriots with the same enthusiasm to rend the air with Hymns to Liberty.'[56] One such 'patriot' who composed and sang his own 'Hymns to Liberty' was the 'Charlestown poet' John Stafford, 'who, though he never had the opportunity of learning either to read or write, has composed songs that would do honor to a Southey.'[57] On special occasions, like radical dinners to commemorate Hunt's birthday or the Peterloo massacre, this 'village Hampden' made his contribution to the evening's proceedings by singing, to the tune of one of the popular airs of the day, 'The Life and Death of Henry Hunt,' 'Peterloo' or one of his other compositions.[58] Although *Northern Star* accounts always gave the title of the song that he sang, usually 'Peterloo,' they gave no details about the song itself or his performance. Stafford actually composed two different songs, one in standard English and the other in the vernacular, about what transpired on 'the plains of Peterloo.'[59] The first of these compositions, 'Peterloo,' was set to the tune of 'Green Upon the Cape,' a song that carried powerful political and indeed revolutionary associations. 'This song,' a Lees loyalist charged in 1819, 'was the instigation of the Irish rebellion 21 years ago.'[60]

'At the most urgent request of a large circle of Friends,' Stafford eventually crossed over into the world of print and published, with the help of the Chartist printer and bookseller John Williamson, a collection of some of his poems in 1840.[61] The preface to this slim volume emphasized the close relationship between his sense of history and his political beliefs: 'the following collection of his Songs [was] composed at various times during the last twenty years on occasions of Public excitement; when the author had no other object in view, but the advancement of the great and glorious cause of the People.'[62] Filled with critical and often caustic references to 'middle class people,' Whigs and Tories, 'parsons with lies,' and 'police men and vampires,' the printed versions of his songs recorded in verse the highlights of the history of Ashton's 'working people' from the 'Ludding Time' and Peterloo to the 1832 parliamentary election and the Ten Hours movement to 'The Welsh Patriots, Frost, Jones and Williams.'[63] Through his involvement in Chartist culture and its round of meetings, lectures, newspaper readings, and dinners, Stafford knew something about the key texts, the press, and national leaders of the movement and was well aware of the world beyond Manchester and the cotton district. In his collection of songs he mentioned by name William Cobbett, the *Black Dwarf*, Feargus O'Connor, and 'The Welsh Patriots' and in 'Miners,' a pro-trade union song, reminded his audience of the example of the French Revolution.[64]

At about the same time, a group of young Ashton Chartists with an artistic flair turned to theatre as a way of enacting a version of the people's history that appealed to those who 'never had the opportunity of learning either to read or write' and also placed the local struggle within an international context. Of considerable popularity was their theatrical presentation of the trial of the Irish revolutionary Robert Emmet.[65] Executed for high treason in 1803, the young Emmet was one of the most romantic of the martyrs of radicalism; during the 1830s, reprints of his famous speech from the dock circulated, O'Brien claimed, in the tens of thousands at least.[66] 'Among the many portraits that were given with the *Northern Star*,' recalled William Farish, 'none was more popular than that of Robert Emmet. The fervour of his youthful patriotism, and the poetic passion of his sweetheart, Miss Curran; immortalised in the touching verses of Tom Moore....throw a halo around a memory which is always attractive to sentimental and sympathetic natures.'[67] The young Chartist players, dressed in 'full' costume, clearly tried to appeal to these feelings in their public performances of the trial of Emmet in Charlestown and Hyde and at the Hall of Science in Manchester. The play, a notice in the *Northern Star* reported, had a 'striking effect' on members of the audience, some of whom wept during the performance.[68]

III

This kind of reaction to Emmet's fate provides some sense of the potential of the Chartist approach to history to transcend narrow national and ethnic boundaries and to create a sense of unity and shared aspirations that brought together, not only radicals of different generations and nationalities, but also passionate autodidacts and barely literate factory workers. Their radical version of the past also allowed the Chartists to counter the contemporary tendency to dismiss democracy as foreign and 'unEnglish' and to make a case for the historical foundations of their political strategy and democratic programme. Through references to historical and legal precedents, Chartist militants were able to assert the sovereignty of 'the people' and the right of 'a free people' to take up arms to protect 'their ancient liberties' against a tyrannical state; this was, the Ashton radicals asserted, 'the last and most solemn step, which the constitution requires them to take.'[69] In a similar way, the Chartists presented on occasion the People's Charter itself as an attempt to regain lost rights and looked back to the distant (and sometimes mythical) past to discover the origins of their decentralized, participatory approach to democracy. 'The more you dispose and subdivide legislative authority,' argued Bronterre O'Brien, 'the better and safer for public liberty. The great merit of our ancient Saxon institutions consisted in this:--that they allowed every parish, and every tithing and every county to legislate exclusively for its own internal affairs; alias for such matters as concerned only such parish, tithing, or county. This is genuine democracy.'[70]

For all their efforts to take a broad, inclusive approach to creating a people's history, the Chartists also marginalized or left out altogether certain groups. Although they displayed a far ranging interest in the contributions of 'patriots' of other lands, like Andreas Hofer, to history of liberty and regularly offered toasts to the memories of Emmet and Scottish radicals, the Chartists ultimately chose to emphasize England over the histories and traditions of the other nationalities.[71] On the other hand, Africans and women, rarely, if ever, appeared in Chartist narrations of the struggle of 'the people' for liberty and freedom. Two of the most dramatic reforms of the early nineteenth century, the abolition of the slave trade and slavery never figured very prominently in the attempts of the Ashton Chartists to create their version of the past. Nor did they refer to the well-known example of the Haitian revolutionary Francois Dominique Toussaint L'Ouverture or to the contributions of Robert Wedderburn, whose career was publicized in Richard Carlile's *Republican*, and the Spencean martyr William

Davidson to early nineteenth-century radicalism.[72] The absence of women from the people's history, in spite of the role of Nancy Clayton and others in its creation, represented yet another silent omission, one that the Ashton Female Political Union hoped to correct:

> We do not despair of yet seeing intelligence, the necessary qualification for voting, and then Sisters, we shall be placed in our proper position in society, and enjoy the elective franchise as well as our kinsmen. Remember, dear Sisters, what glorious auxiliaries the friends of the human race have had amongst our sex; ought we not to be proud, that we can point to Joan of Arc, Madam la Fayette, Margaret of Strafford, Charlotte Cordy, Flora M'Donald, and a host of others too numerous to name?[73]

With its emphasis on political and constitutional examples and precedents, the Chartist approach to history clearly failed to take up Cobbett's challenge to create a new kind of historical narrative and also ruled out certain political alternatives. It was difficult, as Thompson and Epstein have pointed out, to make historically-based arguments for women's rights, republicanism, or the redistribution of wealth.[74] Precisely because their people's history never really broke with the constitutionalist outlook of elite politics and continued to emphasize the roles of Whig aristocrats and 'patriots' of all classes, the Chartists' version of the past, and ultimately their political identity as well, were open to reinterpretation and expropriation. One place where this kind of shift in historical (and ideological) interpretation took place was within the narrow columns of the *Ashton Reporter*, a weekly newspaper that was owned by the radical Hobson family. While this radical-liberal weekly pushed, from the very beginning, an 'ultra'liberal reform agenda, the *Reporter* took equal care to graft the traditions and history of radicalism onto Liberalism.[75] By carefully selecting and reinterpreting key episodes, like Peterloo and the war of the unstamped, the paper began the process of rewriting history from a 'liberal' perspective:

Fifty years ago the charge of being a liberal was sufficient to consign a man to legal persecution and social ruin. Nay, within forty years the yeomanry of Lancashire rode down and sabred at Peterloo a meeting held to advocate the principles now so popular. A suffrage which should comprehend the masses; a ballot scheme which should protect the voter; and a curtailment of office which should restrain the representative, were then the cries only of men branded as revolutionaries or as dreamers of a political Utopia. What a change since then!.... Nothing short of ultraliberalism is now possible.[76]

Thus, by the late 1850s, one of the defining moments in the Chartist history of 'the people' was well on the way to becoming an episode in the unfolding of progress and the triumph of 'Liberal principles.'

NOTES

[1] *Northern Star*, 16 October 1847. At one point Jones apparently considered writing a more formal people's history. 'I have long intended,' he told a correspondent to the *People's Paper*, 'writing a *'History of the People of England,'* by 'people;' I mean the *veritable* nation--the great masses of the proletarian millions of our country. Such a history having never yet been written, it is high time it should be. The history proposed will begin with the Norman Conquest, and be carried down to the present day, dwelling at greatest length on the present social state of the people, and the Chartist movement, as the principal features in the English proletarian history.' See *People's Paper*, 10 February 1855.

[2] For a lengthy advertisement for this work, with an address from the author, see *Poor Man's Guardian*, 18 October 1834. The weekly numbers of this history were to commence on October 11, 1834; the price was 3d. See also, the *People's Paper*, 10 February 1855.

[3] *Northern Star*, 4 August 1838; *Bolton Free Press*, 22 June 1839; *Northern Star*, 24 November 1838.

[4] Dorothy Thompson, 'Who were "the People" in 1842?' in Malcolm Chase and Ian Dyck (eds.), *Living and Learning: Essays in Honour of J.F.C. Harrison*, Aldershot, Scolar Press, 1996, pp. 127-31.

[5] For recent attempts to assess the impact of different (and often highly partisan political) approaches to interpreting English history, especially 'popular constitutionalism,' during the nineteenth century, see John Belchem,

'Republicanism, Popular Constitutionalism and the Radical Platform in Early Nineteenth-Century England,' *Social History*, vol. 6, No. 1, January 1981, pp. 1-32; James Epstein, *Radical Expression: Political Language, Ritual, and Symbol in England, 1790-1850*, New York, Oxford University Press, 1994; James Vernon, *Politics and the People: A Study in English Political Culture, c. 1815-1867*, Cambridge, Cambridge University Press, 1993; *idem* (ed.), *Re-reading the Constitution: New Narratives in the Political History of England's Long Nineteenth Century*, Cambridge, Cambridge University Press, 1996.

[6.] Raymond Williams, *Keywords: A Vocabulary of Culture and Society*, revised ed., New York, Oxford University Press, 1985, pp. 93-98; Gregory Claeys, 'The Example of America a Warning to England? The Transformation of America in British Radicalism and Socialism, 1790-1850,' in Chase and Dyck (eds.), *Living and Learning*, pp. 68-69.

[7.] Epstein, *Radical Expression*, pp. 11-14.

[8.] William Aitken, *A Journey up the Mississippi River From its Mouth to Nauvoo, the City of the Latter Day Saints*, Ashton-under-Lyne, John Williamson, [1845], p. 29. For his sense of history, see also Robert G. Hall and Stephen Roberts (eds.), *William Aitken: The Writings of a Nineteenth Century Working Man*, Tameside, 1996.

[9.] For a discussion of the latter point, see Anna Clark, *The Struggle for the Breeches: Gender and the Making of British Working Class*, Berkeley, University of California Press, 1995, pp. 220-21, 232, 237, 267-68.

[10.] Paul Pickering, *Chartism and the Chartists in Manchester and Salford*, London, Macmillan Press, 1995, pp. 1-3, 34-35, 54-55; Eileen Yeo, 'Some Practices and Problems of Chartist Democracy' in James Epstein and Dorothy Thompson (eds.), *The Chartist Experience: Studies in Working-Class Radicalism and Culture, 1830-1860*, London, Macmillan Press, 1982, pp. 345-80; Dorothy Thompson, *The Chartists: Popular Politics in the Industrial Revolution*, New York, Pantheon Books, 1984, pp. 62, 106, 338, 341-68; Jon Lawrence, *Speaking for the People: Party, Language and Popular Politics in England, 1867-1914*, Cambridge, Cambridge University Press, 1998, pp. 3-6. For an overview of Chartism in the Ashton and Stalybridge area, see Robert G. Hall, 'Work, Class, and Politics in Ashton-under-Lyne, 1830-1860,' Vanderbilt University, Ph.D. dissertation, 1991.

[11.] For a provocative analysis of the relationship between the printed word and politics, see Vernon, *Politics and the People*, pp. 105-60. Even Bronterre O'Brien's short life of Robespierre was offered to the public in the late 1830s for the relatively high price of 6s. See Alfred Plummer, *Bronterre: A Political Biography of Bronterre O'Brien, 1804-1864*, London, George Allen and Unwin, 1971, p. 69.

[12.] Epstein, *Radical Expression*, p. 27. See also, Carl E. Schorske, *Thinking with History: Explorations in the Passage to Modernism*, Princeton, Princeton University Press, 1998.

[13.] The Popular Memory Group, 'Popular Memory: Theory, Politics, Method' in Richard Johnson et al. (eds.), *Making Histories: Studies in History-Writing and Politics*, Minneapolis, University of Minnesota Press, 1982, pp. 213-14; Vernon, *Politics and the People*, pp. 207-8. For a sampling of opinions on the rise of the party system during the 1830s, see T.A. Jenkins, *Parliament, Party and Politics in Victorian Britain*, Manchester, Manchester University Press, 1996, pp. 28-58;

Norman Gash, *Aristocracy and the People: Britain, 1815-1865*, Cambridge, Harvard University Press, 1979, pp. 156-86; Ian Newbould, *Whiggery and Reform, 1830-41: The Politics of Government*, Stanford, Stanford University Press, 1990; Miles Taylor, *The Decline of British Radicalism, 1847-1860*, Oxford, Clarendon Press, 1995.

[14.] Epstein, *Radical Expression*, p. 27.

[15.] Bonnie G. Smith, *The Gender of History: Men, Women, and Historical Practice*, Cambridge, Harvard University Press, 1998, pp. 19-20, 104-5, 117-18, 130.

[16.] *Hansard's Parliamentary Debates*, Third Series, 19 (1833): 752-53. Vernon, *Politics and the People*, pp. 304-05; Newbould, *Whiggery and Reform*, pp. 2-3; Epstein, *Radical Expression*, pp. 13-14, 177.

[17.] *Manchester and Salford Advertiser*, 29 July 1837. Vernon, *Politics and the People*, pp. 298-302; Epstein, *Radical Expression*, pp. 27, 152-53. For one such Manchester dinner to celebrate the king's birthday, see *Manchester and Salford Advertiser*, 3 June 1837. See also, Croker to Lord Hertford, 29 May 1839: For the last 150 years, the Whigs have been the 'violent and steady enemies of the Crown--the old leaven of Cromwell and the recent leaven of Tom Paine; the Scotch traitors, the Irish rebels, the British Jacobins.' Louis Jennings (ed.), *The Correspondence and Diaries of John Wilson Croker*, three volumes, London, John Murray, 1885, 2: 343-44.

[18.] J.M. Robson (ed.), *The Collected Works of John Stuart Mill*, Vol. 18: *Essays on Politics and Society*, Toronto, University of Toronto Press, 1977, p 121. For an insightful analysis of this approach, employed by Whigs and Conservatives alike, see Dror Wahrman, *Imagining the Middle Class: The Political Representation of Class in Britain, c. 1780-1840*, Cambridge, Cambridge University Press, 1995, pp. 352-61.

[19.] *People's Paper*, 30 August 1856. O'Brien made a similar point about existing histories of the French Revolution. See *McDouall's Chartist and Republican Journal*, 4 and 11 September 1841.

[20.] *People's Paper*, 22 December 1855.

[21.] William Cobbett, *Advice to Young Men*, reprint ed., Oxford, Oxford University Press, 1980, p. 301. For an important reassessment of Cobbett as a historian, see Ian Dyck, *William Cobbett and Rural Popular Culture*, Cambridge, Cambridge University Press, 1992, pp. 125-51.

[22.] Thomas Cooper, *The Life of Thomas Cooper*, reprint ed., New York, Humanities Press, 1971, p. 55; Thomas Cooper, *Address to the Jury*, Leicester, 1843, pp. 1-2. For an overview of Cooper's life and career, see Stephen Roberts, 'Thomas Cooper: Radical and Poet, c. 1830-1860,' Birmingham University, M.Litt. thesis, 1986.

[23.] Cooper, *Life*, pp. 34, 42-43, 163-70; R.G. Gammage, *History of the Chartist Movement, 1837-1854*, reprint ed., New York, Augustus M. Kelley, 1969, p. 202.

[24.] *Northern Star*, 5 July 1845.

[25.] *Ibid.*, 5 July and 6 September 1845.

[26.] *Ibid.*, 20 September 1845.

[27.] *Ibid.*, 4 October 1845.

[28.] *Ibid.*, 18 and 25 October and 1 November 1845.

[29.] Cooper, *Life*, pp. 35-36.

[30.] *Ibid.*, pp. 57, 55.

[31.] *Ibid.*, pp. 60, 33, 68, 62, 64, 51, 45.

[32.] *Ibid.*, pp. 169, 34, 43, 46, 65. In his 1845 lecture series, Cooper also blended together history and literature; along with historical topics, he discussed classical literature, Chaucer, Shakespeare, Milton, and Byron. See *Northern Star*, 5 July 1845.

[33.] *Northern Star*, 27 April 1839. William Benbow, *Grand National Holiday, and Congress of the Productive Classes*, London, [1832], p. 5.

[34.] *Northern Star*, 16 November 1839.

[35.] *Ashton Reporter*, 10 November 1855.

[36.] For this latter division in Ashton Chartism, see *Northern Star*, 30 September 1843 and 13 November 1841. In the early 1840s O'Brien also noted the division between the Chartists and 'all the old followers and disciples of Hunt and Cobbett, who have not hitherto enrolled themselves amongst the Chartists.' See *Poor Man's Guardian and Repealer's Friend*, no. 1. Sylvia Harrop discovered that during the years 1830 to 1836, between 83 and 96 percent of the grooms in Ashton signed the register of the Ashton parish church by making their marks; see Sylvia Harrop, 'Literacy and Educational Attitudes as Factors in the Industrialization of North-East Cheshire, 1760-1830,' in W.B. Stephens (ed.), *Studies in the History of Literacy: England and North America*, Leeds, Leeds University Press, 1983, pp. 48-50. Between 1841 and 1845 the percentage of grooms who made their mark in Ashton and other mill towns, however, was apparently somewhat lower: 49 to 61 percent. See W.B. Stephens, *Education, Literacy and Society, 1830-1870: The Geography of Diversity in Provincial England*, Manchester, Manchester University Press, 1987, pp. 94-95. For ethnic tensions in the Ashton and Stalybridge area before the mid-1840s, see Hall, 'Work, Class, and Politics,' pp. 66-72.

[37.] A letter from 'A Constant Reader' succinctly summed up political divisions in Rochdale and the other mill towns in the late 1830s: 'There are here, as in most other boroughs, three parties--the tories, the liberals, and the radicals.' *Manchester and Salford Advertiser*, 6 May 1837. See also, Hall, 'Work, Class, and Politics,' pp. 98-136.

[38.] *McDouall's Chartist and Republican Journal*, 31 July 1841.

[39.] John Belchem, 'Henry Hunt and the Evolution of the Mass Platform,' *English Historical Review*, Vol. 93, No. 4, October 1978, pp. 746-47, 772-73; James Epstein, *The Lion of Freedom: Feargus O'Connor and the Chartist Movement, 1832-1842*, London, Croom Helm, 1982, pp. 90-137; Susan Davis, *Parades and Power: Street Theatre in Nineteenth-Century Philadelphia*, Philadelphia, Temple University Press, 1986, pp. 3-6, 13-15, 114-15; Vernon, *Politics and the People*, pp. 208-14.

[40.] *Manchester Guardian and Manchester Times and Gazette*, 29 January 1831. At his trial Thomas Storah claimed: 'If we examine the history of the country--we will find that in the reign of King Ethelred, universal suffrage was the law of the land.' *The Trial of Feargus O'Connor and Fifty-Eight Others on a Charge of Sedition, Conspiracy, Tumult, and Riot*, reprint ed., New York, Augustus M. Kelley, 1970, p. 256.

[41.] *Manchester and Salford Advertiser*, 2 June and 22 September 1838.

42. Public Record Office, Home Office 40/47, Report of the Speeches Delivered at Public Meeting of the Chartists, held on Nottingham Forest, 22 May 1839; *Northern Star*, 1 June 1839.

43. *Northern Star*, 1 June 1839.

44. *Northern Star*, 16 November 1839. A later account of another Ashton dinner to commemorate Hunt's birthday dwelt at length on the significance of these portraits. At the head of the room was a full-length portrait of Hunt. 'Amongst the rest were to be found the portraits of those who have figured in the same school of politics as Mr. Hunt-- such as our undaunted champion and Hunt's successor, O'Connor, with Cobbett, Marvel, Emmett, Sydney, Frost, M'Douall, Hampden, Washington, Wallace, Tell, Hoffer, with a large oil painting of Peterloo.' See *Northern Star*, 16 November 1844.

45. *Northern Star*, 16 November 1839.

46. Epstein, *Radical Expression*, pp. 149-55; Eric Hobsbawm, 'Introduction: Inventing Traditions,' in Hobsbawm and Terence Ranger (eds.), *The Invention of Tradition*, Canto edition, Cambridge, Cambridge University Press, 1992, pp. 1-14; John R. Gillis, 'Memory and Identity: The History of a Relationship' in Gillis (ed.), *Commemorations: The Politics of National Identity*, Princeton, Princeton University Press, 1994, pp. 3-5, 7-11.

47. Nicholas Cotton, 'Popular Movements in Ashton-under-Lyne and Stalybridge before 1832,' Birmingham University, M.Litt. thesis, 1977, pp. 124-25; Epstein, *Radical Expression*, pp. 82-86; Samuel Bamford, *Passages in the Life of a Radical*, reprint ed., Oxford, Oxford University Press, 1984, p. 146.

48. John Rylands University Library, Peterloo Relief Fund, English Mss no. 172; Cotton, 'Popular Movements,' pp. 124-25. For general accounts of the Peterloo massacre, see Donald Read, *Peterloo: The 'Massacre' and Its Background*, Manchester, Manchester University Press, 1958; E.P. Thompson, *The Making of the English Working Class*, New York, Vintage Books, 1966, pp. 679-89; Joyce Marlow, *The Peterloo Massacre*, London, Rapp and Whiting, 1969; John K. Walton, *Lancashire: A Social History, 1558-1939*, Manchester, Manchester University Press, 1987, pp. 154-56.

49. For Higson's role, see his obituary in *Ashton Reporter*, 9 April 1859; see also, *Manchester Observer*, 19 August 1820.

50. In a letter to Henry Hunt, the Ashton radicals noted with pride that their Peterloo procession had attracted 'double' the attendance of the coronation procession in Ashton. Henry Hunt, *Memoirs of Henry Hunt*, three volumes, London, 1820-22, 2: 25. For loyalist opposition and attempts to prosecute Higson and others, see *Wooler's British Gazette and Manchester Observer*, 31 August 1822 and *Manchester Guardian*, 2 November 1822.

51. *Northern Star*, 22 August 1840 and 24 August 1844.

52. *National Reformer*, 14 June 1868. Born in 1819, near Manchester, Robert Cooper imbibed radical and freethinking principles at an early age, particularly from his father, who had attended the mass meeting at St. Peter's Field. 'My father,' Cooper added, 'only escaped being cut down by the drunken cavalry, by protecting himself with a stout stick, which is kept as a heirloom in the family. It was polished and inscribed with a motto commemorative of the event.'

53. Hunt, *Memoirs*, 2: 25.

54. *Ashton Reporter*, 30 January 1869.

55. *Northern Star*, 11 April 1840.

56. PRO, HO 42/177, Brother of No. 2 to Fletcher, 10 May 1818. Bamford, *Passages*, pp. 123-25.

57. *Northern Star*, 16 November 1839.

58. For examples of his public performances, see *Northern Star*, 16 November 1839; 14 November 1840; 16 November 1844; 13 November 1847. The phrase 'village Hampden' appeared in Thomas Gray's 'Elegy Written in a Country Church-Yard.' Several lines from this poem were reprinted on the title page of the printed collection of Stafford's poetry. John Stafford, *Songs Comic and Sentimental*, Ashton-under-Lyne, John Williamson, 1840.

59. Stafford, *Songs*, pp. 6-10. The details that Stafford mentioned in his two Peterloo songs suggests that he may have attended the meeting at St. Peter's Field. The Peterloo Relief Fund listed among the victims Samuel and William Stafford, both of Charlestown, near Ashton-under-Lyne. See Roy Palmer, *The Sound of History: Songs and Social Comment*, Oxford, Oxford University Press, 1988, pp. 260-62; John Rylands University Library, Peterloo Relief Fund, English Mss no. 172.

60. PRO, HO 42/191, Wrigley to Sidmouth, 11 August 1819. Among other things, Wrigley complained about the singing of 'that most vile and infamous of all songs, called Green upon the Cape' by radical crowds during the days leading up to the 16 August meeting. Lees was a small village near Ashton-under-Lyne.

61. Stafford, *Songs*, title page and preface, 'To The Public.'

62. *Ibid.*, 'To The Public.'

63. *Ibid.*, pp. 3-8, 15-17, 17-22.

64. *Ibid.*, pp. 6, 21-22, 15.

65. Elsewhere, during this period, other Chartist theatre groups performed Shakespeare and radical dramas about Emmet, William Tell, and John Frost. See Dorothy Thompson, *The Chartists*, pp. 117-18.

66. In the same issue O'Brien also argued that the enduring popularity of Emmet's speech contradicted 'the silly assumption that English working men have no sympathy for the wrongs endured by Irishmen.' See *Poor Man's Guardian and Repealer's Friend*, no. 4.

67. William Farish, *The Autobiography of William Farish: The Struggles of A Handloom Weaver*, reprint ed., London, Caliban Books, 1996, p. 50.

68. *Northern Star*, 31 October 1840. See also, *Ibid.*, 19 December 1840; 21 August 1841.

69. *Manchester and Salford Advertiser*, 30 June 1838.

70. *Poor Man's Guardian and Repealer's Friend*, no. 8. For insights into Chartist democracy, see Yeo, 'Some Practices and Problems,' in Epstein and Thompson (eds.), *The Chartist Experience*, pp. 345-80; Clive Behagg, *Politics and Production in the Early Nineteenth Century*, London, Routledge, 1990, pp. 1, 156-57, 224-26.

71. While in prison William Aitken wrote a short life of the Tyrolean patriot Andreas Hofer (1767-1810). See *Ashton Reporter*, 2 October 1869.

72. David Geggus, 'British Opinion and the Emergence of Haiti, 1791-1805' in James Walvin (ed.), *Slavery and British Society, 1776-1846*, Baton Rouge, Louisiana State University Press, 1982, pp. 123-49; for the radical careers of Wedderburn and Davidson, see Peter Fryer, *Staying Power: The History of Black*

People in Britain, Atlantic Highlands, Humanities Press, 1984, pp. 214-27; Iain McCalman (ed.), *The Horrors of Slavery and Other Writings by Robert Wedderburn*, Princeton, Markus Wiener, 1991, pp. 24, 28, 32-35. For an overview of the uneasy relationship between the abolitionists and Chartists, see Patricia Hollis, 'Anti-Slavery and British Working-Class Radicalism in the Years of Reform' in Christine Bolt and Seymour Drescher (eds.), *Anti-Slavery, Religion, and Reform*, Folkestone, William Dawson and Sons, 1980, pp. 294-315.

[73.] *Northern Star*, 2 February 1839. For the role of women in the commemoration of Peterloo, see *Ibid.*, 22 August 1840 and 19 August 1843; *Ashton Reporter*, 30 January 1869.

[74.] Thompson, *Making*, pp. 88-89; Epstein, *Radical Expression*, pp. 22-23. For one attempt to do so, see R.J. Richardson, *The Rights of Woman*, Edinburgh, 1840, pp. 12-13.

[75.] *Ashton Reporter*, 8 September 1860 and 26 December 1857. Founded in April 1855 the Reporter had as its senior proprietor Edward Hobson. Active in the war of the unstamped, Chartism, and the Land Company, Edward Hobson was present at Peterloo. After the death of brother Joshua, he took over the family's newsvending business and later started a series of short-lived local papers. See his 1867 obituary and that of William Hobson in the *Ashton Reporter*, 17 August 1867 and 1 October 1859.

[76.] *Ashton Reporter*, 26 December 1857. For the war of the unstamped as part of the struggle for 'Liberal principles,' see *Ibid.*, 5 October 1861. At the same time, however, a group of Ashton radicals contested this interpretation and struggled to keep alive the Chartist version of the past. For accounts of radical dinners to commemorate Henry Hunt's birthday and Peterloo, see *Ibid.*, 14 November 1857 and 20 August 1859.

COMMEMORATION, MEMORIALISATION AND POLITICAL MEMORY IN POST-CHARTIST RADICALISM: THE 1885 HALIFAX CHARTIST REUNION IN CONTEXT

Antony Taylor

In 1885 twenty-two former West Riding Chartists met for a reunion dinner at Maude's Temperance Hotel in Halifax. Here they sang the old songs, toasted the 1884 Reform Act, and celebrated the social and political progress that had transformed them from penniless outworkers into businessmen and civic leaders. Whereas in the past the radical dining tradition had been subversive of the existing political order, now it was resonant with images of mid-Victorian plenty; for the Liberal *Halifax Courier* the dinner confirmed the success of Gladstonian Liberalism and the era of stability it had ushered in.[1]

Unsurprisingly, historians have viewed the Halifax Chartist supper as an important footnote in the history of Chartism. Many of the older accounts of the movement conclude with it. David Jones and Edward Royle see it as a watershed moment, confirming the physical and spiritual end of the movement. Here it marks a full-stop in the history of a phase of Chartist-inspired popular radicalism.[2] For historians of the mid-Victorian period it provides testimony to the success of those movements that succeeded the Chartists. An oblique reference in the *Courier*'s account of the meeting shows that many of those present were co-operators; thus the event appears to confirm the shift away from political radicalism, to the social solutions to industrial problems evident in the manufacturing centres after 1850, and denotes a new-found class harmony.[3] For E. P. Thompson, the Halifax dinner is a misleading moment of calm, marking the apogee of a Liberalism that was about to be overtaken by the emergence of independent Labour politics after 1900.[4]

As Roland Quinault has demonstrated, a culture of commemoration was central to Victorian attempts to locate British institutions in the mainstream of the national past.[5] Popular politics was no exception to this. Moreover, by 1885 the concept of 'reunion' was already an established part of Liberal and temperance culture. Throughout the 1880s and 1890s numerous reunions brought together survivors of the early days of the temperance agitation to celebrate the health and longevity conferred by abstinence. In 1896 Chartist and Owenite veterans Benjamin Lucraft and William Campbell appeared on the platform at St. Martin's Hall, Charing Cross, alongside Dr. Frederic Lees, now an avowed Gladstonian, to celebrate lifetimes of sobriety.[6] At Halifax, as at Charing Cross, the Chartist veterans toasted their achievements in lemonade. Present in such episodes, and historians' interpretation of them, is the feeling that at some level meetings like the Halifax Chartist supper demonstrate the congruence of Chartism with Liberalism and illustrate the compatibility between the two movements on issues of temperance, co-operation, freedom of the press, and the Gladstonian programme of graduated parliamentary reform.

This article takes the Halifax dinner as a starting point in the discussion of post-Chartist continuities in nineteenth century radicalism. Confronting the currently fashionable argument that Liberalism is merely a late manifestation of the popular radical tradition,[7] it argues that the dinner provides a misleading image of the position occupied by former Chartists in the mid-Victorian consensus. In fact, Halifax Liberalism was far from united at this time. Four pages further on in the same edition of the *Courier* an account of a meeting to establish a Halifax Radical Association, in protest at the Liberal Party hierarchy, demonstrates the strong divisions that existed between radicals and middle-class Liberals on issues of labour representation, Ireland, compulsory vaccination, women's suffrage, and perceptions of the Chartist past. At this meeting, radicals too had long memories, and attempts by James Crossley to frustrate the return of independent working-men's candidates from the 1850s were recalled with bitterness.[8] A week before the dinner, Charles Bradlaugh had also visited Halifax to offer a rather different vision of the Liberal state to that propounded at the Chartist dinner. His speech highlighted excessive tax burdens, the expense of royalty, and the relics of 'Old Corruption' in parliament and the Civil Service - all long-standing Chartist concerns.[9] At a time of considerable divisions within Halifax Liberalism, there is therefore reason to suspect an element of stage management in the Halifax Chartist supper.

The Chartist dinner in Halifax has become better known than other events of this kind. It is most frequently encountered in discussions of the career of Benjamin Wilson, whose life history is usually seen as a classic 'Age of Equipoise' success story. His *Struggles of an Old Chartist* describes his transition from a physical force Chartist into a Liberal and co-operator who campaigned for Richard Cobden at Huddersfield in 1857 and died on the platform mid-way through a homily to Queen Victoria during the 1897 jubilee celebrations.[10] His memoirs apparently confirm the trajectory of the survivors of Chartism towards compromise with Liberalism. Wilson was not alone in the direction taken by his post-Chartist politics. The West Country Chartist leader Henry Vincent was also unabashed in his conflation of Chartism and Liberalism. In correspondence in 1878 towards the end of his life he described Liberalism as a natural continuation of 'the old flag of liberty'.[11] Nevertheless, recent work on the historical significance of 'memory' casts doubt on the reliability of reminiscences of the kind written by Wilson. Theorists of 'social memory' have demonstrated the degree to which memory can be characterised by structures of 'forgetting' as well as of remembering, and the elements of myth and collective memory that work their way into the first hand accounts presented as 'autobiography'.[12] In his important *Anzac Memories: Living with the Legend*, Alistair Thomson has shown that remembered life-histories are frequently contaminated by group myth to the extent that those aspects of an individual's past that fail to harmonise with this image can be subsumed or even repressed altogether. Hence Anzac veterans whose 'remembered' past failed to accord with national memories of the Australian experience in World War I privileged particular highlights of their experience over others to compose their memories in a way that made sense of their life-histories in the light of the nation's national epic.[13]

John Saville's research in a British context has made it clear that a related process is at work to reconcile the conflicting elements present in the memories of Chartist veterans who made the passage into Liberalism.[14] Elements that jar with the overriding image of a consensual mid-century Liberalism are very marked in Benjamin Wilson's reminiscences, but are never ordered in such a way as to provide an insight into the very considerable compromises involved in reconciling Wilson's past Chartism with a contemporary Gladstonian Liberalism in the West Riding. Wilson, for example, bought himself a gun in 1848 as part of a projected rising in Halifax; here the tone is apologetic, tempered by sadness – 'Those were times to make men desperate'.[15] Like other rank and file Chartists he also looked to the actions of the movement's leaders, particularly Ernest Jones who stood as a Liberal candidate in 1868, to legitimate his decision to campaign on a Liberal platform. Moreover, there are strong hints throughout the work that Wilson's course of action was not an easy one. He mentions in passing that he was accused of 'making a good thing out of politics' by selling out to the local Liberal Association and taking money from former political opponents.[16] This was a common slur that was frequently made against Jones in the 1860s, and no doubt reinforced Wilson's strong sense of identification with him. Nevertheless, the implications of such accusations for his relationship with Liberalism or any personal distress resulting from attacks by former comrades are never explored. Wilson's experience was not unique. Other former Chartists also experienced traumas in assimilating with Liberalism. At Chester the ex-Chartist mayor, William Farish, was boycotted by the civic elite for his attempts to tackle corruption in the borough.[17] For some Chartists, like Ernest Jones, alliance with the Liberal Party was a tactical measure only, leading him to suppress some of his earlier radical ideas. The same process is at work in the careers of radical veterans inspired by the Chartist tradition. The image of George Howell, for example, that emerges from his private correspondence is very different from the public face he presented in negotiations with wealthy Liberal backers of the Reform League. Writing to Professor Goldwin Smith in 1873 he showed that he was a cautious republican who looked forward to a future republic: 'The time will come when it will come to the front in the hands of good men and true'.[18] In 1889 he was active in campaigns to demand curbs on Civil List grants to royal offspring.[19] There is a residue here of an older radical tradition that overturns conventional views of Howell as a devout and willing Gladstonian.

    With these considerations in mind it is clear that memories of Chartism were more than just nostalgic reference points for both former Chartists and Liberals alike. Liberalism at mid-century sought to bring together the various strands of post-Napoleonic War radicalism, Chartism, and Gladstonianism in a shared celebration of the highpoints of mid-Victorian liberty. From the zenith of Liberal successes in 1868, middle-class Liberals were frequently in control of the physical survivals of Chartism and its precursors. Both Samuel Bamford and Ernest Jones were memorialised by monuments commissioned by Manchester's Liberal and literary elite.[20] Etched in the side of the granite memorial to Jones at Ardwick cemetery were lines from his speech 'Democracy Vindicated' in praise of suffrage reform in 1867. This highlighted the point of contact between the shade of Chartism, as exemplified by the Reform League, and Gladstonian state reformism.[21] Moreover, memories of the period 1837-1848 were frequently mediated through the eyes of a triumphant Liberalism. Obituaries in the Liberal press offered a selective reading of the careers of deceased Chartist leaders, which recalled their contribution to the Liberal consensus and advocacy of the correct Smilesian values. Repentant 'physical force' men like John Snowden of Halifax were especially embraced; some, notably William Grimshaw of Lancashire, became figureheads for the new permanent Liberal Clubs constructed in the 1870s and 1880s.[22] During these years the Chartists were often portrayed as participants in a joint battle for basic press freedoms in which radicals and Liberals stood side by side.[23] Many of these attitudes featured in Jane Cobden-Unwin's *The Hungry Forties: Life Under the Bread Tax*. Published in 1904 as a homily to the 'remembered' Liberal past, it reprised fading memories of the Anti-Corn Law League (ACLL) at a time of Liberal revival, whilst at the same time adding a new term to the political history of the nineteenth century. In this version of recent popular politics the League emerged as heroes, whose struggle against protectionism defused the potential for violent political protest and created the conditions for 'equipoise' at mid-century. The book's reading of Chartism reinforced this standard Liberal orthodoxy: 'The great Chartist movement was nothing more than a fierce revolt against low wages and dear food'.[24] Subsequently such values were re-asserted in cheap editions of biographies of both Cobden and Bright, published by her husband T. Fisher Unwin, which achieved a wide circulation during the celebrations surrounding the centenary of Cobden's birth in 1904.[25]

This vibrant Liberal populism found its strength in a fusion of plebeian folk memories of the violent actions undertaken by the Tory government at the time of Peterloo, and pure Cobdenite opposition to protectionism. The myths surrounding these themes showed a remarkable durability. As Peter Clarke has shown, they underpinned the New Liberalism in Lancashire, where a strong Toryism dictated the form of a compact between a weak Liberalism that had nothing to lose by co-operation with the Lib/Labs, and an enfeebled Labourism that was incapable of making gains on its own terms.[26] Such features are also evident in late Gladstonianism. In Manchester the protest against attempts by the House of Lords to amend Gladstone's 1884 reform bill coincided with the sixty-fifth anniversary of the Peterloo massacre. During this period the *Manchester Guardian* gave prominence to retrospective articles examining the event, and there was a reunion of all the remaining survivors around the commemoration.[27] At Bolton, the veterans were borne in procession under Liberal colours, and were photographed by an amateur photographer at a 'Peterloo' tea in Failsworth.[28] Events of this nature cemented the continuing links between older radical forms and Liberalism. ACLL symbols and memorabilia were very evident in he Liberal-led campaign for the Manchester Ship Canal, itself an emblem of the benefits of freedom of trade.[29] The Liberal myth of a tyrannical Toryism that caused low wages and high food prices was, however, always strongest at election time. This proved particularly the case in contests in which tariff reform, broader issues of protectionism, and other food-related issues became electoral concerns. The myth was especially potent in 1906, and in Lancashire was used as a weapon to oppose Chamberlainite Tariff Reform Proposals. In Manchester this election saw a renewed interest in Cobdenism and led to the re-printing of ACLL pamphlets and broadsides from the 1840s.[30] It also marked the final occasion on which elderly Chartist veterans such as G. J. Holyoake and William Henry Chadwick appeared on political platforms to espouse Liberal causes.[31] As late as 1923 the myth of the 'Hungry Forties' had still not lost its power; in an election that was also waged against Conservative protectionism, Liberals gained vitality from such rhetoric in a final demonstration of strength and unity. Speaking at Paisley at the height of the campaign, Asquith described conditions under Tory tariff reform proposals as leading inevitably to a rise in pauperism and high food prices as they had in the 1840s.[32]

As recent scholarship has demonstrated, there was a strong sense of continuity here that allowed former Chartists and Cobdenites to coalesce around issues of mutual concern. At the end of the century, imperial matters provided one such area of co-operation. Miles Taylor suggests that the political landscape of the 1890s was broadly similar to the decade of the 1850s. In both contexts, radicals opposed an unbridled militarism that imperilled the country's imperial position and raised concerns about the health and stability of democracy at home.[33] The Boer War in particular was seen as throwing the hitherto wise course of empire off track, by an arrogant display of imperial adventurism. Liberals were split by the Boer War, and all shades of opinion ranging from pro-Boer to pro-war were apparent in the party.[34] Nevertheless, the pro-Boer position was a strong one that gained the support of C. P. Scott and the organ of regional Liberal opinion - the *Manchester Guardian*. As in other aspects of Liberal opinion, the pro-Boer camp was sustained by memories of the ACLL. Recalling public hostility to Cobden and Bright for their opposition to the Crimean War, the secretary of the Liverpool Peace and Arbitration Society wrote in support of Scott: 'I can remember the Crimean War, the infinite passion of the multitude, the storming of the pulpits by the mob and the vindication, when the echoes of war had been driven away, of those who like John Bright (and) Richard Cobden had suffered, but had not flinched before the storm'.[35] C. P. Scott's postbag also contained correspondence from a former Chartist, signing himself 'a disciple of the late Ernest Jones,' who like those motivated by Cobdenite sympathies similarly declared his opposition to the war on the grounds that it was of a piece with British misrule he had witnessed elsewhere in the empire.[36] This comparison was an apposite one. In the 1850s radicals like Jones and J. M. Ludlow had also campaigned strongly against British policy in India after the Mutiny. For the Chartists there seemed to be clear predispositions to tyranny in far flung corners of the empire where Liberal political institutions were lacking and where there was no apparent will to import them from Britain. By the 1880s ex-Chartists like Thomas

Cooper and Joseph Cowen Jr. were supporters of imperial federation.[37] Federation projects held out the prospect of a devolved system of authority for former Chartists, and reduced imperial expenditure for Liberals. In the 1890s federation became the declared imperial governing principle of the Edwardian Liberal Party, and an important strut in the relationship with the Lib/Labs who were also much in evidence in the pro-Boer campaign.[38]

The strength of such sentiments of mutual attachment made it difficult for many members of the new Labour configurations of the 1890s to sever the intense psychological and emotional ties binding them to the image of a fused Cobdenite/Liberalism. In the 1890s John Trevor's Labour Churches newssheet, the *Labour Prophet*, still felt that support for independent labour representation was disloyal to the memory of Cobden and Bright. In an editorial, Trevor drew comparisons with the attitudes of an ungrateful son seeking to break away from familial bonds: 'Are we not like a son who having received a good education, despises his less cultured parents? Surely we are guilty of some ingratitude here'.[39] Like many other early Labourist papers in Lancashire, the *Labour Prophet* was heavily influenced by popular memories of the 1840s and the success of a broad popular Cobdenism; some editions carried pictures of prominent working-men supporters of a free trade platform, notably Ebenezer Elliot, 'The Corn Law Rhymer'.[40] There was often considerable trauma involved in the decision to organise apart from Liberalism for those steeped in this milieu in the former heartlands of the ACLL. Elsewhere former Chartists like Thomas Cooper, who were already disillusioned by the collapse of the popular platform agitations of the earlier part of the century, saw little room for any alternative Labourist organisations built around opposition to the Liberal Party. In his musings in later life Cooper opposed strikes in the London building trades and the U.S. and re-affirmed his adherence to 'The wisdom and beneficience of Richard Cobden's doctrines'.[41] Writing to Fred Pickles (who later became secretary to Keir Hardie) in 1885 he commented:

> How many years you, my sanguine friend, expect to live
> I cannot tell. But I must say to you frankly and without
> hesitation that if you could get a grant of life to the age
> of Methuselah you would not see the programme of

socialism marked out in the pamphlet you have sent me realised and established.[42]

For many mid-century radicals therefore the triumph of Gladstonian Liberalism seemed complete.

Nevertheless, although there was no organised focus of opposition to Liberalism during the highpoint of Liberal success, there were still strong anti-Liberal impulses that injected a profound note of dissonance into the relationship between the plebeian reform community and middle-class Liberalism. Memories of Chartism often provided a contentious area where tensions were generated during the festivals intended to celebrate the unity of Liberalism and the coherence of the Liberal vision of a radical and reforming past that paved the way for Gladstonianism. In this sense, the Liberal vision of recent political history was a profoundly 'Whig' one that excluded all those elements that did not fit easily into the mid-century political consensus. Despite his pessimism on the issue of independent Labour politics, Thomas Cooper acknowledged that as a former Chartist speaker he drew large crowds on his own merits in Yorkshire and Northumberland; two weeks after the Chartist reunion he was well received at a meeting in Halifax.[43] From the 1870s onwards a large number of memoirs and reminiscences about Chartism were also produced that revisited those aspects of the Chartist past that fitted less easily into a Liberal narrative of orderly progress and reform. Whilst all former Chartists protested their adherence to law and order in later life, much of this autobiographical writing was candid about the Chartist resort to illegality. Cooper's own account of the Potteries riots of 1842 was the most vivid sketch of the episode in print, sparing none of the details of violence, disorder and imprisonment.[44] The cult of martyrdom was especially developed in work of this sort. Chartists saw themselves as men who had suffered at the hands of an unjust state to achieve liberty for all. Interviewed in the *Bury Times* in 1894, William Chadwick commented: 'He was as strong a Chartist as when he started in the prison van, with fetters upon his ankles, for Kirkdale Gaol in 1848'. Although condemning unrest in the South Wales coalfield in the 1890s, Chadwick's reminiscences of the Oldham miners' march on Manchester in 1848 and threats of assassination against the queen

evoked strong echoes of the Jacobin tradition of revolt that had
been erased from Liberal historical memory and subsumed within
an anodyne vision of a Liberal 'reformist' past.[45] A photograph of
two elderly Chartist veterans dressed in their Sunday best and
holding Chartist pikes to attention in the *Oldham Liberal Bazaar
Souvenir* for 1913 captures the strong sense of incompatibility with
Liberalism that surrounded relics of physical force in Lancashire
and Yorkshire where the disturbances of 1839 and 1842 had been
especially severe.[46] In the West Riding, Liberals like Frank Peel,
writing at the time of the Eastern Question Agitation, sought to
tame memories of the violence connected with Luddism, which he
saw as a progenitor of Chartism, by portraying the movement as a
manifestation of a popular anti-war sentiment during the
Napoleonic Wars. The inference was that such agitations were
similar to those in progress in 1877-8 and also evident in
opposition to subsequent jingo frenzies in the 1890s when the work
was re-printed.[47] Such revisionism failed, however, to convince.
Historians of Co-operation in particular were uneasy about the
place of violence in the Chartist past. For them memories of
physical force seemed to jeopardise their position within
Liberalism. Following in the tradition of Holyoake's writings on
Co-operation, the many histories of local co-operative societies
produced at the turn of the century obfuscated their members'
Chartist connections, or denied outright Co-operation's roots in the
strike committees formed in the 1840s to help members of artisan
trades during industrial disputes.[48] On occasion Holyoake sought to
airbrush violence out of Chartist history altogether by blaming it on
erratic fellow-travellers or on the Irish. At a Chartist reunion in
Manchester in 1898 he condemned the 'accessories to the
movement,' 'the violences' and the 'eccentricities'.[49]

The Tories were acutely aware of the problems appeals to an
ambivalent Chartist tradition could pose for their Liberal
opponents, who were vulnerable on issues of physical force. The
Chartist connection with violence was sensitive ground, and by
invoking memories of the recent history of radical protest the
Liberals played into their hands on this issue. In the north-west,
from the 1860s, Tories used the slur of Liberalism's perceived
Chartist precedents to smear the Liberal Party with the taint of
sympathy for violence and extremism.[50] This frequently involved

tracing the links between Chartist memories, the Reform League, and Gladstonian sympathy for fairnesss and justice in Ireland. Behind the image of Liberalism revealed by these methods in the Tory press of the 1870s lurked the spectre of Fenianism and sometimes even the Commune.[51]

From the early 1880s onwards inconsistencies between the Chartist past and Liberalism are more apparent as Lib/Labs became steadily disillusioned with Liberalism in power and sought confirmation for their position from the recent radical tradition. Thus a 'remembered' Chartism became the focal point for reformers disappointed with Liberalism. In areas like the West Riding, where Toryism was weak and many working-class radicals were only partially integrated into Liberalism, Liberal versions of historical memory were now strongly contested.[52] Given the degree to which recent research has shown that the new Labourist organisations of the 1890s constituted a revival of an older radical tradition, it is natural that such memories should have played an influential part in the early psychology of Labour, the Social Democratic Federation (SDF), and the Socialist League.[53] There were, for example, strong resonances of Chartism and post-Napoleonic War radicalism in the Lib/Lab and SDF opposition to coercion in Ireland after 1881. This campaign brought former working-men Liberals like George Lansbury into independent Labour politics for the first time and reflected long-standing radical concern for justice in Ireland. *Reynolds's Newspaper* recalled the first Whig Coercion Act in Ireland in 1844 and derided Liberalism as increasingly in thrall to a despotic Whiggery opposed to all public liberties.[54] The emphasis on reform of the laws of property as they related to landownership, and land nationalisation proper, also evoked memories of Chartist and Owenite land-holding schemes of the 1840s. Issues like reform of entail and primogeniture straddled the fault line between Liberalism and Chartist-inspired radicalism. Nevertheless, this was perhaps the oldest radical demand of all and, as Roy Douglas has shown, was kept alive throughout the mid-century period by the pamphleteering work of former Chartists and radicals like A. A. Walton, who paved the way for Henry George's tours of 1881 and 1884.[55] At a time of *fin de siecle* existential panics there were elements of millenarian promise in the single-taxers' pledge to restore the value of the land to the people. Henry Hyndman reprinted the works of Thomas Spence as part of this tradition, whilst ancestral memories of the historical dispossession of the poor from the land by the Norman Conquest and later Tudor policy, figured as strongly in the propaganda of the Georgeite 'Red Vans' in the 1890s as they did in the work of the 'Norman Yoke' theorists of a century earlier.[56] Moreover, confrontations by the Labour pioneers over rights of access to public places also evoked memories of Chartist attempts to assert long-standing rights of assembly and public meeting in the face of opposition from the state, the police and local government. At meetings in Boggart Hole Clough, Manchester in 1897 to protest against the Corporation's decision to prevent Independent Labour Party (ILP) demonstrations in the park, reformers recalled these historic confrontations and located themselves in the tradition of the 'freeborn Englishman':

> Absolute freedom of public meeting is the greatest inheritance of the English people. Primitive law was debated, decreed, and carried out by and at free public meetings. Parliament and the judicature sprang from the free public meeting. When the Englishman founds a government in the wilderness, his constituent assembly is a free public meeting. When he has a grievance against his government at home, or any other grievance, his appeal is instinctively to free public meetings.[57]

Like the Chartists, the Labour pioneers also had an open spaces martyrology. SDF supporters interned after open space confrontations at Dod Street, Limehouse in 1885, were celebrated at public meetings on their release, and cheered for their endurance of 'plank beds' and prison food.[58] Such issues shaded into broader discontents with social and economic ills. As late as the 1920s opposition to the Poor Law and bad conditions in factories in the West Riding was still sustained by memories of Chartism and the attacks on 'Poor Law Bastilles' in 1838-39.[59] In addition, the differences between Liberalism and older radical traditions were compounded by the re-emergence of protectionism as a major political issue at the end of the century. With Chamberlain's proposals for tariff reform and imperial preference now openly debated, it became harder for Liberals to maintain the fiction that all Chartists had accepted the free trade agenda. At a meeting of Liverpool trade societies Joseph Chamberlain praised the Chartists for their opposition to the ACLL, and identified Cobden's opposition to trade unions and collectivist social reform as the reverse side of his support for free trade.[60] There was a certain amount of ambivalence in the Labour Representation Committee (LRC) about free trade, and many Labour supporters like Will Crooks (secretary of the Cobden Club) remained ardent free traders.[61] Nevertheless, Ernest Jones' most high-profile son, Llewellyn Atherley-Jones, was also able to argue that the support of a substantial minority of Labour MPs for protectionist legislation placed them in touch with Chartist opinions on this subject:

> It is remarkable that the attitude of the Chartists was on the whole favourable to protection, and in these latter days Keir Hardie, a whole hearted representative of the Chartist tradition, speaking in the House of Commons, said: "There is no member of this House who supports trade unionism (and) can claim to be a consistent free trader. Trade unionists of this country have no intention of allowing the sweated and under-paid labourers of continental nations to enter into competiton with them".[62]

In the West Riding the Labour press was highly critical of those Chartists who had accepted 'that pernicious doctrine about the half-loaf' a half-century earlier.[63]

From the 1880s most of the arguments arising from the different Liberal and Labourist interpretations of the Chartist past revolved around the career of Ernest Jones. The sheer spectacle of Ernest Jones' funeral in 1869 owed much to Liberal Party organisation. Under Liberal supervision the theatre surrounding the funeral procession emphasised the component elements of the Liberal electoral myth, providing a visual and emotional link between Gladstonianism, Chartism, the ACLL and post-Napoleonic War radicalism. The mutes who led the cortege had been present at Peterloo whilst amongst the pall-bearers were four veterans of 1848: Thomas Topping, Ben Whitely, John Bowers, and James

Cunliffe.[64] In his remarks at the graveside Edmond Beales, leader of the Reform League, emphasised the compatibility between popular radicalism and Liberalism, saying that Gladstone's ministry had completed the work begun by Jones in the 1840s: 'He was the same from the beginning to the end of his life with a beautiful consistency...Yet we must remember that while we survivors must deeply feel his loss, he had done his work'.[65] As part of this process subsequent commemorations at the cemetery emphasised the close proximity of Jones' grave to that of George Wilson, former chairman of the ACLL.[66] After Jones' death his sons carried on the tradition of political activism that was associated with his name under the banner of Liberalism. Two of his four sons became members of the progressive Liberal establishment. His eldest, Ernest Beaufort Annesley Jones, became a municipal health reformer in Manchester and campaigned strongly on the issue of contaminants in milk.[67] Llewellyn Archer Atherley-Jones, his youngest son, wrote precociously on female enfranchisement at an early age, entered parliament as the MP for North-West Durham in 1885, and is usually credited with coining the term the 'New Liberalism'.[68] This passage of Jones' sons into Liberalism softened the outlines of their father's Chartist career and made his name hostage to the Liberal tradition for many years. In later life Atherley-Jones unashamedly manipulated a sanitised version of his father's reputation to further his political ambitions within the Liberal Party. This reading of his father's past was overwhelmingly a Liberal one. It omitted his advocacy of physical force in 1848, his imprisonment, his profound Irish sympathies, and his many years of poverty. Instead Atherley-Jones highlighted his father's commitment to social justice, his legal work on behalf of the poor, and his appearance on Liberal platforms in Manchester in 1868. There was no room here for consideration of the elements within Chartism that failed to harmonise with Liberalism; at the Durham Miners' Gala ten years after Ernest Jones' death, Atherley-Jones commented: 'The working-classes of this country are Liberal to the backbone'.[69] Throughout Atherley-Jones' career there were tensions that arose from his obfuscations and denials about his father. At a constituency meeting in Dewsbury to choose an advanced Liberal candidate for the town in the general election of 1880, he was questioned closely about his commitment to radical causes, including anti-vaccination, triennial parliaments, and the Tichborne Claimant;[70] at North-West Durham in 1885 there was sufficent support for him from the miners' union to ensure his return, but some bad-tempered opposition for his renunciations of his father's Chartist past.[71] Nevertheless, Atherley-Jones' version of Ernest Jones' career became the orthodoxy for a whole generation of radical/Liberals. The souvenir programme of a celebration of Jones' life in Manchester in 1879, ten years after his death, spoke of the event as 'a red letter day in the history of English Liberalism'.[72] At commemorations in Halifax in 1891 Jones, like the ex-Chartists at the reunion supper, was portrayed as a premature Liberal. The Liberal *Halifax Courier* wrote: 'There was a good deal of prejudice against him but much of this went away in his lifetime. Since then Liberal politicians have learnt that he was far advanced, but in the right'.[73] The image of the 'Liberal' Ernest Jones created by Atherley-Jones also led eventually to his own advancement within the Liberal Party; speaking of him as a potential Judge Advocate General in Gladstone's 1892 ministry, Sir William Harcourt wrote: 'He is an able man, and a good Liberal, and his father's son has great claims on our party'.[74]

Despite the prevalence of the Liberal image of Jones, the SDF and the ILP sought to reclaim his memory from the middle 1880s onwards. Amongst the Labour pioneers he was remembered as the last Chartist leader and as a friend of Marx and Engels. Towards the end of the century there was a revival of interest in his poetry, and in areas like the West Riding, where direct memories of him were strong, there was a subversive Jones cult that contested the Liberal version of his history.[75] The longevity of his career into the 1860s, long after the other major figures in the movement were dead or had emigrated, meant that here there was a direct remembered exposure to Chartism, mediated through a source outside Liberalism, for radicals still living into the twentieth century. For the fathers of the generation who founded the Labour Party, meeting Jones or listening to his poetry was a formative experience that they recounted to their families. Benjamin Turner, the West Riding trade union leader, recalled:

> Right from my earliest days of political recollections I have known about Ernest Jones. My father was one of

an old body of radicals and Chartists in the Holmfirth area when I was a nipper...and there were in Holmfirth a little nest of men who may be termed the political "John the Baptists" of their day. They were radicals of a strong type and who were often looked upon as political outlaws by the Whigs of that day. My Uncle Jim, one of the founders of the Colne Valley Socialist League, was another of these men, and so strongly was he imbued with the faith in Ernest Jones that he called one of his sons Ernest Jones.[76]

This historical memory of Jones ran counter to the Liberal version of his career and drew upon the elements in his past that were omitted from the official version. Here aspects of his life were celebrated that were excluded from Liberal historiography. Most frequently mentioned were the privations he experienced on behalf of the Chartist cause and his poverty in later life. This inflection subverted the mid-century emphasis on improvement, self-help, and the correct Smilesian values. There is something Christ-like in the image of Jones that emerges from these accounts. The Reverend William Mitchell of Sale, writing in 1891, remembered him giving away his boots to a poor man in a story that recalled John Wesley or the medieval saints' cults:

Though it was raining hard he would set out to walk to a friend's house some five miles away that the poor man might be spared the paying of hotel expenses. For the same end, I have known him roll himself in a rag and sleep across the hearth of some poor man's home and vow in the morning that he had never been more comfortable. I have known him sit in his stockings whilst a cobbler friend mended his boots. One time a friend having observed that he had a poor shabby pair of boots on managed to get his measure and procure him a pair of new ones. When presented to him he declared that he had no need for two pairs and as he knew a poor man whose feet were just his size he would give him one pair of them.[77]

When the ILP ran parliamentary candidates in Halifax in 1895, Jones' name was frequently invoked as evidence of anti-Liberal feeling in the borough, prompting a sharp exchange with the elderly Benjamin Wilson who asserted that Jones had been in all essentials a Liberal. In an article in the *Halifax Courier* he disputed ILP claims that he was opposed to the Whig/Liberals of his day, suggesting that in the Manchester election of 1868, Jones had deliberately sacrificed himself by standing down early in the polling to ensure the return of Jacob Bright: 'What a noble deed of self-denial this was. What a pity the above generous action was not mentioned at the meeting of the ILP when one of their leaders said that a Liberal government put Ernest Jones into prison'.[78] Subsequently, however, Jones' career became a stand-by of anti-Liberal propaganda in Yorkshire that drew upon his well-documented hostility to both Whigs and Tories.[79] In 1921 the freethought lecturer Aurelius Basilio Wakefield was still giving lectures on his life that stressed his commitment to independent labour representation and bitter hostility to the Whig governments of his day.[80] Moreover, former Chartists were angered by Atherley-Jones' neglect of his step-mother, Mary, Jones' second wife. By the 1890s both she and Jones' daughter by his second marriage were destitute. This became a major cause in radical circles in the 1900s that did much to discredit Atherley-Jones' version of his father's career.[81] These non-Liberal accounts of his life forced a reappraisal of Jones' importance. Significantly, his monument in Ardwick cemetery was no longer maintained by local Liberals after the issue of Labour representation became an important one at the end of the century. Eventually it fell into disrepair until it was restored by a committee of trade unionists in 1913.[82]

For avowedly socialist groups like the SDF and the Socialist League, reference to past radical traditions was an important tactic that allowed them to refute accusations that they were importing alien and un-British ideas of continental socialism into the country.[83] Accordingly, Henry Hyndman and other SDF members located themselves very carefully in an older radical milieu, and drew upon a wide variety of examples to support the claim that they were the true heirs to the Chartist movement. Ernest Jones and Bronterre O'Brien featured significantly in this context. In 1906 Hyndman suggested that O'Brien had originally coined the term

'Social Democracy,' thus demonstrating the essential 'Englishness' of Marxist modes of thinking:

> Bronterre O'Brien, who for all that he was a Catholic and a soft-money man, invented the term social-democrat in 1838 which our ignorant hand-to-mouth hacks of capitalism imagine was imported from Germany, and with his fellows, preached vigorously the class war long before Marx and Engels.[84]

Similar claims were made for Jones; *Justice* wrote in 1884: 'Much as we appreciate the work done by foreign socialists and agitators, we have no need to look beyond the records of this island to find in Ernest Jones a man equal to Blanqui or Lassalle'.[85] Again it was overwhelmingly the swashbuckling, rambunctious element in popular radicalism that lived on in the SDF. It celebrated the 'glorious old physical-force Chartists'[86] and took from this tradition a strong sense of popular democracy and an urgent need for reform of state institutions. In 1884 Hyndman proposed the abolition of both houses of parliament, a National Convention elected annually on the Chartist model, and the sacking of the royal family 'in a polite manner'.[87] Recent re-assessments of the SDF have supported the organisation's own view of itself and seen the body as a manifestation of an older radical style that had deeper roots in London than in many other areas of the country.[88] Metropolitan socialists were especially sensitive to the Liberal annexation of the memories of Chartism, and sought to reclaim this radical pedigree for themselves. The *Christian Socialist* wrote:

> The other (accusation) is that we claim kinship with the Chartists of old times, with the heroes of a bygone age, whose memories are held in honour (for time, the great avenger, can give even a rebel honour in his own country), whereas it is your modern, sexless, opportunist radical who is the true descendant of the worthies of a manlier period.[89]

To a later generation of radicals, ageing Chartists embodied a level of radical commitment and dedication that demonstrated the shallowness and ephemeral nature of the media and mass entertainment culture of the 1890s.[90] Reformers like Edward Aveling spoke of a spiritual bond between the survivors of Chartism and a younger generation of socialists seeking to break away from the Liberal radicalism of their parents.[91] This sentiment was also evident in the regions. In 1888 Lancashire and Yorkshire branches of the SDF gathered ostentatiously at Blackstone Edge in conscious emulation of the Chartists.[92] Moreover, Chartism was celebrated primarily as a movement of radical, social, and political emancipation; and its survivors were looked on with awe as living links with a heroic past.[93] At SDF branch level this sense of continuity was cemented by lavish funerals for deceased Chartist veterans. The funeral of the Battersea branch's survivor of 1848, Thomas Halliday, was attended by all the members of the association bearing a red flag, and a wreath decorated with red flags was laid at the grave.[94] In 1898 *Reynolds's Newspaper* and SDF branches in London were also responsible for bringing together the last recorded reunion of Chartist veterans to honour the fiftieth anniversary of the Kennington Common meeting in 1848. The commemoration was an open-air event at Rye House, Essex, and was addressed by Tom Mann. Three Chartist veterans were on the platform and Chartist relics were on display, amongst them John Frost's sword, a plate commemorating Jane Carlile's imprisonment with her husband for publishing editions of Paine in the 1820s, and a copy of the *English Chartist Circular* from the 1840s.[95] One 88 year old veteran of 1848, W. Woodward, spoke dressed in 'the frilled shirt front and and buckled white tie of two generations ago'.[96] In such homilies Chartism was seen as symbolising a pure undiluted stream of working-class radicalism that refused all compromise with Liberalism. Former Chartists like G. J. Holyoake who were believed to have deserted the cause for Lib/Labism were reviled accordingly. *Justice*'s verdict at his death was: 'Unfortunately Mr Holyoake outlived his career of usefulness. He got so far stranded that he came to the conclusion that so long as the Tories could be kept from the reins of power the Liberal Party would emancipate the worker'.[97]

It is the persistence of negative images of Liberal icons like Cobden and Bright that surprises in radical memories of this nature. Attacks on Bright in particular were harvested from an authentic store of folk hostility to him over issues like his persistent opposition to the factory acts, his support for coercion in Ireland in the 1840s, and his refusal as Secretary of the Board of Trade to implement measures to prevent the adulteration of food.[98] Speeches from the 1840s illustrating these points were widely reprinted in radical journals. *Justice* wrote: 'nothing can pillory him so effectively as his own utterances' and 'he may yet have to see the Chartist heroes he vilified avenged'.[99] Similar sentiments were also noted by the radical press during the 1884 reform demonstrations in London when John Burns spoke out against Bright as an 'impostor' at a fringe meeting in Hyde Park.[100] These recollections are all the more remarkable for their failure to register within Liberalism, although their presence in 1884 indicates that much radical feeling had not been subsumed entirely within Liberalism but found free expression outside it. By the end of the century the New Liberalism's dismissal of the revived Cobdenism of 1906 as a retrograde creed that generated hostility to state action and empire, enabled anti-Bright sentiments to gain ground both inside and outside the Liberal Party. The pamphleteering work and dining activities of repositories of Cobdenite thinking like the Cobden Club now appeared increasingly irrelevant and out of date.[101] At the Colne Valley by-election of 1907, the first and last to be won by an independent socialist, the Liberal candidate, Philip Bright, suffered badly for his father's opposition to factory reform. He was repeatedly belittled on this issue, to the extent that the press was inclined to attribute the election of Victor Grayson to this hostility. The *Huddersfield Examiner* wrote: 'The unfair blows at him through his father's memory has been the one thing in connection with the election which has hurt the son of the great tribune of the people whom the Colne Valley has rejected'.[102] The presence of this strand of anti-Cobdenite feeling, linking the socialism of the 1880s with Chartism and the Reform League, thus exposes the fragility of the cultural leadership provided by figures like Bright, and forces a re-evaluation of the negative impressions of him that have been overlooked by recent work in this area.[103]

Chartist 'memories' in the wider context of the empire remain unresearched. Nevertheless, there is evidence that such remembrances were also of significance in the white settler colonies where, as in Britain, they formed a discourse of opposition to colonial elites, and were used to forge anti- (or post-) colonial identities. One example here may stand for many. The same features that made memories of Chartism a potent element in the re-configuration of Labourism outside the Liberal Party in Britain were also evident in Australia even before the foundation of the Australian Labour Party in 1891. Transportation and emigration meant that large numbers of former Chartists made their way to Australia; some Chartists, like H. R. Nicholls and David Buchanan, re-made their radical careers there.[104] Many of the ideas of English migrants to Australia, like William Lane and John Norton, who were involved in the creation of the Australian Labour Party were moulded through a direct exposure to Chartist history and traditions.[105] William Lane's commitment to communitarianism and utopianism, for example, was in part inspired by his reflections on Chartist and Owenite landholding schemes.[106] From the 1880s Chartist recollections were frequently used to undermine the formal structures of empire and to promote a cohesive Australian Labourist identity rooted in memories of British judicial tyranny at home. As a result, Chartist memorabilia circulated widely in Australia until the latter part of the century, and the movement was a regular point of reference in the early socialist press. In the 1880s, at a time of considerable disillusionment with the Crown in Australia, Chartist opposition to the monarchy was often cited as evidence of the injustices of British imperial rule. A correspondent in the secularist Melbourne *Liberator* recalled his radical father leaving England 'Because of the continued tax to support monarchy in profligacy' and that it had driven him 'into a wilderness'.[107] The large Irish presence in Australia also meant that measures like the Irish Coercion Bill of 1887 were bitterly opposed in the radical press. As in England, memories of Whig coercion in Ireland during the 1840s were invoked to support the view of a historical Whig/Liberal predisposition towards tyranny. To underline the point, verses entitled 'The Selfish, Tyrannical Whig' were re-printed from the *Chartist Circular* of 1840 in Henry and Louisa Lawson's paper the *Republican* in 1887.[108] Frequent notices of the careers of Chartist veterans like Gerald Massey also appeared in this paper, whilst events like Peterloo or the transportation of the Tolpuddle Martyrs in 1834 remained the touchstone of the Australian Labour experience for much of the nineteenth century.[109] On occasion, former Chartists like Sir Henry Parkes, who became Premier of New South Wales in the 1880s and a Liberal 'conservative' in later life, were berated for their betrayal of the Chartist faith in a similar manner to the attacks made upon figures like Holyoake in England.[110]

In April 1876 *The Times* noted that the twenty-fifth anniversary of 1848 had been forgotten in Britain, and suggested that there were no longer any Chartists for the reason that mid-century prosperity and democratic progress had put paid to the discontents that underpinned the movement. *Reynolds's Newspaper* challenged this viewpoint, asserting that the drive and energy that had once characterised Chartism was now evident in other political agitations, like republicanism, that owed much to their roots in the community of individuals and ideas Chartism had brought together.[111] *Reynolds's* was wrong about the strength of republicanism in Britain, but broadly correct in its assertion that many later movements of political progress could trace their ancestry back to the inspiration of Chartism. Accordingly, this debate touches an important issue. Chartism did not need to bequeath a legacy of individual personalities to be important to those who came after. As E. P. Thompson conceded, there was a sharp break in the radical tradition in the middle years of the nineteenth century, and as many departures as continuities evident in the history of Chartism's posthumous relationship with Labourism and socialism.[112] After 1880 no-one seriously advocated the revival of the movement. Only one risible attempt to re-activate it was made by William Thompson, editor of *Reynolds's Newspaper*, at the end of the century. His New Chartist Movement failed to mobilise any lasting support on the basis of a return to the Charter and a platform of moderate welfare reforms.[113] The failure of this campaign highlighted the differences that made Chartists like W.E. Adams feel uncomfortable with the new socialist currents of thinking, and the aspects of Chartism, and the older radical tradition that made them seem antiquated in the eyes of some Labourites.[114] Chartism, after all, had always distrusted the power of the state; socialism in contrast was reliant upon exactly the kind of state the Chartists despised to achieve its aims. Moreover, when Hyndman cited Bronterre O'Brien's opposition to the formation of trade unions as a reason for his own refusal to open negotiations with the trade union movement he showed that attempts to ape the political movements of the past could marginalise, as well as strengthen, political causes in the 1890s.[115] Thus the really important elements in the relationship between Chartism and Labour are the structures of remembrance and commemoration that made past radical endeavours seem relevant to most members of the L.R.C. even after the final surviving veterans were in their dotage. These alternative 'memories' undermined a Liberal vision that stressed the essentially unifying nature of the battles for English liberty at a time when an alternative, non-Liberal Labourism was becoming possible. As a result anti-Liberal commemorations of Chartism flourished in the years between 1880 and 1914 when socialism and Labourism were seeking to assert themselves against the Liberal Party machine. In 1919 there was a further renewal of interest in the movement following the passage of the 1918 Representation of the People Act, and to commemorate the centenaries of Peterloo and the birth of Ernest Jones.[116] This was a time of great uncertainty within Labourism when rank and file sought a new direction and finally scented the possibility of government. Against this background appeals to past certainties provided comfort.[117] Thereafter the natural wastage of Chartist veterans and the gradual ascendancy of Labour over Liberalism meant that there was no longer any need for the Labour Party to seek legitimation in the events of the early nineteenth century. A line could at last be drawn under the Chartist past with the knowledge that the movement's primary aim of parliamentary reform had been achieved.[118]

The Halifax Chartist reunion of 1885 has become a cliché that is in many ways untypical of the attitudes and expectations of a surviving generation of Chartist reformers. Scraping the surface of nineteenth century Liberalism, there is much underneath that cannot easily be accommodated within an image of an all-encompassing triumphant Gladstonian ascendancy. Many memories of the Chartist movement were quite simply too awkward to be subsumed as effectively as recent historiography has suggested. The Chartist tradition was never only a hostage to Liberalism, it also had an important part to play in the development of Labourism, and Chartist memories remained one of the most powerful demarcation lines between the two creeds. Ultimately this created a new Whig tradition that acted as an antidote to declining Liberal memories and provided the mythology for the onward march of Labour. In reality there were no stream-lined or fluid continuities between either Chartism and Liberalism on the one hand, or Chartism and Labourism on the other. Rather the issue of how memories of Chartism were constructed demonstrates the problematic nature of continuity arguments, and the open nature of many of the memories that have been described as the exclusive preserve of a triumphant mid-century Liberalism.

NOTES

My thanks to Owen Ashton, Peter Clarke, James Epstein, Martin Hewitt, Rohan McWilliam, and Mark Hampton for their helpful comments on earlier drafts of this article.

[1.] *Halifax Courier*, 11 July 1885, p. 3. For consideration of the role of the radical dining tradition see James Epstein, 'Radical Dining, Toasting and Symbolic Expression in Early Nineteenth Century Lancashire: Rituals of Solidarity,' *Albion*, Vol. 20, No. 2, July 1988, pp. 271-91 and *idem, Radical Expression: Political Language, Ritual and Symbol in England 1790-1850*, Oxford, Oxford University Press, 1994, pp 147-165.

[2.] See David Jones, *Chartism and the Chartists*, Harmondsworth, Penguin, 1975, p. 182 and Edward Royle, *Chartism*, London, Longman, 1980, p. 84.

[3.] See Neville Kirk, *The Growth of Working Class Reformism in Mid-Victorian England*, Basildon, Croom Helm, 1985, pp.148-68 and Peter Clarke, *A Question of Leadership: Gladstone to Thatcher*, London, Hamish Hamilton, 1991, p. 16.

[4.] Edward Thompson, 'Homage to Tom Maguire' in Asa Briggs and John Saville (eds), *Essays in Labour History*, London, Macmillan, 1960, pp. 276-316.

[5.] Roland Quinault, 'The Cult of the Centenary c.1782-1914,' *Historical Research*, Vol. 71, No. 176, October 1998, pp. 303-323.

[6.] Frederic Lees, *Dr. Frederic Richard Lees: A Biography*, H. J. Osborn, London, 1904, p. 261; for Lees' Gladstonianism see pp.200-203. Brian Harrison first noted the links between Chartist temperance and Liberal culture that have since become orthodoxy, in the 1970s; see Brian Harrison, *Drink and the Victorians: The Temperance Question in England 1815-1872*, London, Faber and Faber, 1971, pp. 367-87.

[7.] There is now a large literature on this subject, but see in particular Eugenio Biagini and Alistair Reid (eds.), *Currents of Radicalism: Popular Radicalism, Organised Labour and Party Politics in Britain 1850-1914*, Cambridge, Cambridge University Press, 1992, introduction; Eugenio Biagini, *Liberty, Retrenchment and Reform: Popular Liberalism in the Age of Gladstone 1860-1880*, Cambridge, Cambridge University Press, 1992, chs. 1-5; Patrick Joyce, *Democratic Subjects: The Self and the Social in Nineteenth Century England*, Cambridge, Cambridge University Press, 1994, pp. 85-136; and Margot Finn, *After*

Chartism: Class and Nation in English Radical Politics 1848-1874, Cambridge, Cambridge University Press, 1993, introduction and chs. 2, 3 and 4.

[8.] *Halifax Courier*, 11 July 1885, p. 7 and the *Halifax Guardian*, 11 July 1885, p. 7.

[9.] *Halifax Courier*, 4 July 1885, p. 6.

[10.] For notice of Wilson's death see the *Halifax Guardian*, 26 June 1897. Also see Benjamin Wilson, *Struggles of an Old Chartist*, Halifax, 1887; re-printed in David Vincent, (ed.) *Testaments of Radicalism: Memoirs of Working-Class Politicians*, London, Europa, 1977, pp. 195-242.

[11.] See a photocopy of a statement of faith by Henry Vincent dated November 1878 in the possession of Staffordshire University Library. My thanks to Owen Ashton for sight of this. Henry Vincent was a Chartist penitent who spent much of his later life seeking to atone for his part in provoking the Newport Rising, and re-casting his Chartist career as a Liberal one; see William Dorling, *Henry Vincent: A Biographical Sketch*, Manchester, Abel Heywood, 1879, chs. 8 and 9.

[12.] See Jacques Le Goff, *History and Memory*, English edn, New York, Columbia University Press, 1992, pp. 51-99. The most important work in this area has grown out of recent approaches to the Australian past; see Paula Hamilton, 'The Knife Edge: Debates about Memory and History' in Kate Darian-Smith and Paula Hamilton (eds.), *Memory and History in Twentieth-Century Australia*, Melbourne, Oxford University Press, 1994, pp. 9-32.

[13.] Alistair Thomson, *Anzac Memories: Living with the Legend*, Melbourne, Oxford University Press, 1995, especially chs. 2-3. Also see *idem*, 'The Anzac Legend: Exploring National Myth and Memory in Australia' in Raphael Samuel and Paul Thompson, (eds.) *The Myths We Live By*, London, Routledge, 1990, pp.73-82.

[14.] See John Saville, *1848: The British State and the Chartist Movement*, Cambridge, Cambridge University Press, 1987, pp.200-205.

[15.] Wilson, 'Struggles of an Old Chartist' in Vincent (ed.) *Testaments of Radicalism*, p. 210.

[16.] *Ibid*, pp. 218-20.

[17.] See William Farish, *The Autobiography of William Farish: The Struggles of a Hand-Loom Weaver*, 1889; re-printed, London, Caliban, 1995, pp. 154-5.

[18.] George Howell to L. Goldwin Smith, 12 December 1873, George Howell Collection, Bishopsgate Institute.

[19.] *Reynolds's Newspaper*, 21 July 1889, p. 3.

[20.] For Bamford's funeral and the construction of a memorial to him see the *Manchester Guardian*, 22 April 1871, p. 3 and the *Middleton Albion*, 13 October 1877, p. 2.

[21.] *Manchester Examiner and Times*, 10 April 1871, p. 4.

[22.] See John Snowden's obituary in the Liberal *Halifax Courier*, 6 September 1884, p. 3. A memorial was erected to Snowden by local Liberal dignitaries in Hillingdon parish church; see *ibid*, 28 February 1885, p. 4. William Grimshaw was a Lancashire Peterloo veteran who only narrowly avoided imprisonment during the 'war of the unstamped,' helped organise the first Chartist Kersal Moor meeting of 1838, and died in the 1880s a respected local Liberal and a pillar of the Prestwich Liberal Club. For his progress from outcast to patriarch of Liberalism in

East Lancashire see R. J. Broughton, 'William Grimshaw: The Chartist Hero of Prestwich,' *East Lancashire Review*, Vol. 2, 1891, pp. 178-83 and 217-20.

[23.] See Alexander Patterson, 'Feargus O'Connor and the *Northern Star*,' *Leeds Mercury*, supplement, 24 February 1900, p. 1.

[24.] Jane Cobden-Unwin, *The Hungry Forties: Life Under the Bread Tax*, London, T. Fisher Unwin, 1904, p. 243. Jane Cobden-Unwin made the same points in a public letter read to a free trade rally in opposition to tariff reform in the Free Trade Hall in 1902; see the *Manchester Guardian*, 16 May 1902, pp. 3-4.

[25.] For example John Morley, *Life of Richard Cobden*, London, T. Fisher Unwin, 1903 edn., pp. 648-9 and William Robertson, *The Life and Times of John Bright*, London, T. Fisher Unwin, 1912. For the thinking behind the 'Reformer's Bookshelf' see the biography of Unwin by his son; Stanley Unwin, *The Truth About a Publisher: An Autobiographical Record*, London, Allen and Unwin, 1960, p. 89. For the 1904 centenary celebrations of Cobden's birth at his former home in Sussex see *The Cobden Centenary: Programme Souvenir*, Midhurst, Sussex, June 1904 (Author's Collection). The persistence of the cult of Cobden is examined in Anthony Howe, 'Towards the "Hungry Forties": Free Trade in Britain c.1880-1906' in Eugenio Biagini (ed.), *Citizenship and Community: Liberals, Radicals and Collective Identities in the British Isles 1865-1931*, Cambridge, Cambridge University Press, 1996, pp. 193-218.

[26.] See Peter Clarke, *Lancashire and the New Liberalism*, Cambridge, Cambridge University Press, 1971.

[27.] *Manchester Guardian*, 16 August 1884, p. 8 and 18 August 1884, p. 5.

[28.] Sim Schofield, *Short Stories About Failsworth Folk*, Blackpool, Union Printers, 1905, pp. 63-66.

[29.] See Ian Harford, *Manchester and its Ship Canal Movement: Class, Work and Politics in Late Victorian England*, Staffordshire, Keele University Press, 1995, pp. 51-5 and 77-81.

[30.] See Election Materials and Ephemera, 1906 and 1910 (308 N6 V.108), Manchester Central Reference Library.

[31.] *Manchester Guardian*, 1 January 1906, p. 5 and 3 January 1906, p. 5.

[32.] *Ibid*, 3 December 1923, p. 11.

[33.] Miles Taylor, ' "Imperium et Libertas"? Rethinking the Radical Critique of Imperialism During the Nineteenth Century,' *Journal of Imperial and Commonwealth History*, Vol. 19, No. 1, January 1991, pp. 1-23. This point was first made in G. R. Searle, *The Quest for National Efficiency: A Study in British Politics and Political Thought 1899-1914*, London, Blackwell, 1971; new edition, London, Ashfield, 1991, pp. 87-89.

[34.] H. C. G. Matthew, *The Liberal Imperialists: The Ideas and Politics of a Post-Gladstonian Elite*, Oxford, Oxford University Press, 1973, ch. 5 and Martin Pugh, *The Making of Modern British Politics 1867-1939*, new edn., Oxford, Blackwell, 1993, pp. 103-108.

[35.] T. Suddely to C. P. Scott, 13 December 1899, Boer War Correspondence, *Manchester Guardian* Archive, John Rylands Library, Manchester University. My thanks to Mark Hampton for this reference.

[36.] A. W. Molesworth to C. P. Scott, n.d., *Manchester Guardian* Archive, John Rylands Library, Manchester University.

[37.] See Thomas Cooper, *Thoughts at Fourscore and Earlier: A Medley*, London, Hodder and Stoughton, 1885, p. 61 and Evan Rowland Jones, *The Life and Speeches of Joseph Cowen MP*, London, Sampson Low, 1885, pp. 259-79.

[38.] See an account of the foundation meeting of the anti-war Liberal League in the *Manchester Guardian*, 13 February 1900, p. 10 and for the Lib/Lab MP, William Randal Cremer's pro-Boer sympathies, Howard Evans, *Sir Randal Cremer: His Life and Work*, London, T. Fisher Unwin, 1909, pp. 216-23.

[39.] *Labour Prophet*, 1 November 1894, pp. 149-50.

[40.] *Ibid*, 1 November 1895, pp. 163-64.

[41.] Cooper, *Thoughts at Fourscore*, pp. 21 and 39-51.

[42.] Thomas Cooper to Fred Pickles, 7 July 1885, Labour Party Archive, National Museum of Labour History, Manchester.

[43.] Thomas Cooper, *The Life of Thomas Cooper*, London, Hodder and Stoughton, 1872, pp. 393-5 and the *Halifax Guardian*, 25 July 1885, p. 3.

[44.] Cooper, *Life of Thomas Cooper*, pp. 186-206. The offspring of Chartists also sometimes chronicled their relatives' excesses. Thomas Burt openly admitted his uncles' physical force tendencies; see Thomas Burt, *Thomas Burt: Pitman and Privy Councillor*, London, T. Fisher Unwin, 1924, pp. 24-5.

[45.] *Bury Times*, 24 February 1894, p. 2. Also see T. Palmer Newbould (ed.), *Pages From a Life of Strife: Being Some Recollections of William Henry Chadwick, The Last of the Manchester Chartists*, London, Frank Palmer, 1911, pp. 37-45; and for Chadwick's peripatetic lecturing activities the *English Labourers' Chronicle*, 26 February 1881, p. 3 and his obituary in the *Liberator*, Vol. 104, 7, 1908, p. 98.

[46.] The photograph is in Albert Marcroft, *Oldham Liberal Bazaar Souvenir: Landmarks of Local Liberalism*, Oldham, E. J. Wildgoose, 1913, p. 103.

[47.] See Frank Peel, *The Risings of the Luddites, Chartists and Plug-Drawers*, Brighouse, *Heckmondwike Herald*, 1880; new edition, London, Frank Cass, 1968, pp. 9-39. Also see *idem*, *Spen Valley: Past and Present*, Heckmondwike, Senior and Co., 1893, pp. 307-27.

[48.] See Peter Gurney, *Co-operative Culture and the Politics of Consumption in England 1870-1930*, Manchester, Manchester University Press, 1996, *passim*.

[49.] 'A Reunion of Old Chartists' in the *Locomotive Engineers' and Firemen's Journal*, Vols. 11-12, December 1898, pp. 547-49.

[50.] See Antony Taylor, ' "The Best Way to Get What He Wanted": Ernest Jones and the Boundaries of Liberalism in the Manchester Election of 1868,' *Parliamentary History*, Vol. 16, No. 2, September 1997, pp. 185-204.

[51.] See, for example, the *Manchester Courier*, 5 July 1872, p. 5 and p. 7.

[52.] The geographical strengths and weaknesses of later Liberalism are outlined in George L. Bernstein, *Liberalism and Liberal Politics in Edwardian England*, London, Allen and Unwin, 1986, pp. 1-5 and Keith Laybourn, 'The Rise of Labour and the Decline of Liberalism: The State of the Debate,' *History*, Vol. 80, No. 259, June 1995, pp. 207-26.

[53.] See on this theme David Howell, *British Workers and the Independent Labour Party 1888-1906*, Manchester, Manchester University Press, 1983, pp. 1-15; and

John Belchem, *Popular Radicalism in Nineteenth Century Britain*, London, Macmillan, 1995, chs. 8 and 9.

54. *Reynolds's Newspaper*, 30 January 1881, p. 2. *Reynolds's Newspaper* also celebrated the centenary of the 1798 rising; see *ibid*, 20 February 1898, p. 2.

55. Roy Douglas, ' "God Gave the Land to the People"' in A. J. A. Morris, (ed.), *Edwardian Radicalism 1900-1914: Some Aspects of British Radicalism*, London, Routledge and Kegan Paul, 1974, pp. 148-61.

56. See Charles Wicksteed, *Our Mother Earth: A Short Statement of the Case for Land Nationalisation*, (London, English Land Restoration League, n.d.), pp. 4-7; *Among the Suffolk Labourers with the Red Van*, (London, English Land Restoration League, 1891), pp. 6-14; and Joseph Hyder, *The Case for Land Nationalisation*, London, Simpkin, Marshall, Hamilton and Kent, 1913, chs. 3-4.

57. Howard C. Rowe, *The Boggart Hole Contest*, Manchester, Labour Press Society, 1897, p. 17.

58. *Justice*, 17 October 1885, p. 2.

59. See Charles A. Glyde, 'Thirty Years Recollections of the Socialist and Labour Movement: The Fight for the Factory Acts,' *Labour Pioneer and Yorkshire Factory Times*, 10 November 1921, p. 2; 24 November 1921, p. 2 and 1 December 1921, p. 2.

60. See Alan Sykes, *Tariff Reform in British Politics 1903-1913*, Oxford, Clarendon Press, 1979, pp. 56-7 and G. R. Searle, *Country Before Party: Coalition and the Idea of 'National Government' in Modern Britain*, London, Macmillan, 1995, p.48.

61. For a treatment of this subject see Frank Trentmann, 'The Strange Death of Free Trade: The Erosion of "Liberal Consensus" in Great Britain c.1903-1932' in Biagini (ed.), *Citizenship and Community*, pp. 219-50.

62. Llewellyn Atherley-Jones, *Looking Back: Reminiscences of a Political Career*, London, H. F. and G. Witherby, 1925, pp. 147-48.

63. *Labour Echo*, 6 July 1895, p. 1.

64. The fullest account of Ernest Jones' funeral is in the *Manchester Guardian*, 1 February 1869, p. 3.

65. *Manchester Examiner and Times*, 1 February 1869, p. 3.

66. See the account of the unveiling of a memorial to Jones in the *Manchester Examiner and Times*, 10 April 1871, p. 4.

67. W. Burnett Tracy and W. T. Pike, *Manchester and Salford at the End of the Nineteenth Century: Contemporary Biographies*, Brighton, W. T. Pike and Co., 1899, p. 256; and E. B. A. Jones, *The Present State of the Milk Trade and Suggestions for its Reform*, Manchester, Sale Urban District Council, n.d., pp. 1-5.

68. Llewellyn Atherley-Jones' statement on female suffrage is in the *Preston Guardian*, 20 April 1867. Also see Llewellyn Atherley-Jones, 'The New Liberalism,' *The Nineteenth Century*, Vol. 26, No. 150, August 1889, pp. 186-93.

69. *Newcastle Weekly Chronicle*, 21 July 1877, p. 8.

70. *Dewsbury Reporter*, 17 January 1880, p. 6.

71. See Atherley-Jones, *Looking Back*, pp. 20-21 and the *Newcastle Weekly Chronicle*, 25 July 1885, p. 8.

72. See J. Creuss (ed.), *In Memoriam Ernest Jones*, Manchester, Co-operative Printing Society, 1879, p. 4 and the *City Jackdaw*, 14 March 1879, p. 138.

73. *Halifax Courier*, 31 January 1891, p. 7.

74. Atherley-Jones, *Looking Back*, p. 66.

75. See for Jones' poetry *Justice*, 26 July 1884, p. 5. In the 1890s Jones became the patron saint of the Georgeite Single Tax organisations; see the *Single Tax*, 1 July 1897, p. 2.

76. Ben Turner, 'Ernest Jones' in the *Yorkshire Factory Times*, 23 January 1919, p. 3. Also see Ben Turner, *About Myself*, London, 1930, pp. 28-9.

77. W. Mitchell to A. B. Wakefield, 3 January 1891, Correspondence of the Ernest Jones Memorial Committee, Local Studies Section, Manchester Central Library.

78. Benjamin Wilson, 'The Independent Labour Party and Mr. Ernest Jones,' *Halifax Courier*, 16 March 1895.

79. See, for example, Charles A. Glyde, *Liberal and Tory Hypocrisy in the Nineteenth Century*, Pamphlet, Keighley, 1901; re-printed 1922, pp. 18-21.

80. Aurelius Wakefield was the son of a former Chartist. See the *National Reformer*, 5 June 1887, pp. 364-5; and his obituary in the *Halifax Courier and Guardian*, 30 November 1928, p. 5.

81. See correspondence in *Reynolds's Newspaper*, 3 September 1899, p. 5 and the *Co-operative News*, 22 November 1902, p. 1429. Ernest Jones' daughter by his second marriage, Mrs Clara Whittaker, lived on in poverty into the 1930s; see the *Liverpool Echo*, 15 September 1933.

82. See correspondence in the *Manchester City News*, 2 December 1911, p. 5; the *Daily Mail* 18 April 1913; and the *Trades Union Congress Official Souvenir 1913*, Manchester, Co-operative Printing Society, 1913, p. 17.

83. See Martin Crick, *The History of the Social Democratic Federation*, Staffordshire, Keele University Press, 1994, pp. 292-300.

84. *Justice*, 7 April 1906, p. 4.

85. *Ibid*, 26 July 1884, p. 1.

86. *Ibid*, 7 April 1906, p. 4.

87. Logie Barrow and Ian Bullock, *Democratic Ideas in the British Labour Movement 1880-1914*, Cambridge, Cambridge University Press, 1996.

88. See Jon Lawrence, 'Popular Radicalism and the Socialist Revival in Britain,' *Journal of British Studies*, Vol. 31, No. 2, April 1992, pp. 163-86; and Mark Bevir, 'The British Social Democratic Federation 1880-85: From O'Brienism to Marxism,' *International Review of Social History*, Vol. 37, No. 2, April 1992, pp. 207-29.

89. *Christian Socialist*, 1 July 1884, pp. 24-5.

90. See remarks by Herbert Burrows in *Justice*, 19 January 1901, p. 5. The broader ramifications of this argument for socialist culture are examined in Chris Waters, *British Socialists and the Politics of Popular Culture 1884-1914*, Manchester, Manchester University Press, 1990, chs. 1, 2 and 3.

91. Edward Aveling, 'George Julian Harney: A Straggler of 1848', *Social Democrat*, 1 January 1897, pp. 3-7.

92. *Justice*, 12 May 1888, p. 6.

93. See the description of an elderly SDF Chartist veteran as a 'survivor of the heroic age of working-class history' in William Stephen Sanders, *Early Socialist Days*, London, Hogarth Press, 1927, pp. 21-22.

[94.] *Ibid*, 5 September 1891, p. 3.

[95.] *Ibid*, 30 July 1898, p. 5. Also see for the background to the event *Reynolds's Newspaper*, 17 July 1898, p. 2.

[96.] *Ibid*, 24 July 1898, p. 8.

[97.] *Justice*, 27 January 1906, p. 1. In contrast Chartist survivors who remained aloof from Liberalism were lauded for their commitment to the faith; see the obituary of J. B. Leno in *ibid*, 17 November 1894, p. 3.

[98.] The main charges against Bright are outlined in Samuel Clarkson, *James Froude and John Bright MP: The Censor Censured*, Manchester, Tubbs and Brook, 1870, pp. 20-21.

[99.] *Justice*, 2 August 1884, p. 6; and 9 August 1884, p. 2. Also see *The Christian Socialist*, 1 September 1884, pp. 52-3.

[100.] See the *Newcastle Weekly Chronicle*, 26 July 1884, p. 3.

[101.] Matthew, *The Liberal Imperialists*, pp. 142 and 154.

[102.] *Huddersfield Examiner*, 20 July 1907, p. 6. Also see the editions for 8 July 1907, p. 4; and 19 July 1907, p. 2.

[103.] See especially Joyce, *Democratic Subjects*, pp. 85-136.

[104.] Paul Pickering, ' "Glimpses of Eternal Youth": Chartism, Poetry and the Young H. R. Nicholls,' *Labour History*, Vol. 70, No. 2, May 1996, pp. 53-70; and R. B. Walker, 'David Buchanan: Chartist, Radical, Republican,' *Journal of the Royal Australian Historical Society*, Vol. 53, No. 2, September 1967.

[105.] See Mark McKenna, *The Captive Republic: A History of Republicanism in Australia 1788-1996*, Melbourne, Cambridge University Press, 1996, chs. 6, 7 and 8.

[106.] See the entry on William Lane in the *Australian Dictionary of Biography*, Vol. 9, Canberra, Oxford University Press, 1983, pp. 658-9. I am also grateful to Andrew Mesner for information on Lane's Chartist connections.

[107.] *Liberator*, 29 May 1887, p. 10.

[108.] *Republican*, 7 January 1888, p. 5.

[109.] See for Massey *ibid*, 15 October 1887, p. 2 and p. 5, and for discussions of Peterloo and the Tolpuddle Martyrs the Melbourne *Liberator*, 20 September 1885, p. 6 and 29 August 1886, p. 3.

[110.] A. W. Martin, *Henry Parkes: A Biography*, Melbourne, Melbourne University Press, 1980, p. 367 and p. 421.

[111.] This debate is in *The Times*, 13 April 1876, p. 9 and *Reynolds's Newspaper*, 23 April 1876, p. 3.

[112.] Thompson, 'Homage to Tom Maguire,' pp. 287-9.

[113.] *Reynolds's Newspaper*, 6 August 1899, p. 4; and 17 September 1899, p. 4; and *Justice*, 19 January 1901, p. 5.

[114.] See Owen Ashton, *W. E. Adams: Chartist, Radical and Journalist 1832-1906*, Whitley Bay, Bewick Press, 1991, pp. 159-80.

[115.] Henry Hyndman, *Further Reminiscences*, London, Macmillan, 1912, pp. 336-7.

[116.] See Mark Hovell, *The Chartist Movement*, Manchester, Manchester University Press, 1918, pp. 300-12 and the *Manchester City News*, 18 January 1919.

[117.] See, for example, a flyer advertising A. B. Wakefield's lecture on Ernest Jones at the Chartist Rooms, Ripponden on 9 December 1921 in the Correspondence of the Ernest Jones Memorial Committee, Manchester Central Reference Library.

[118.] Even so, Chartist memories did not die out altogether. In the 1930s interest in the poverty and low wages commonly held to have provoked Chartism was revived by the depression, and featured in radical theatre. See Stephen Schofield, 'The Chartist' in J. W. Marriott, *The Best One Act Plays of 1936*, London, George F. Harrap, 1937, pp. 233-55.

INDEX

286

Also available from The Merlin Press:

IMAGES OF CHARTISM

Edited by Stephen Roberts
and Dorothy Thompson

Many books have told the story of Chartism. For the first time, this book draws together a pictorial record. Photography was in its infancy in the early Victorian period, and the only photographic record of a Chartist gathering is of the great meeting on Kennington Common in April 1848. Pictures of the Chartists themselves are all from wood or metal engravings, mostly published in the Chartist journals. *The Illustrated London News* published engravings of some of the more dramatic occasions, while *Punch* was always quick with a satirical comment. The editors have brought together these various representations of the Chartists, and an introduction provides a background to the pictures and their captions.

1998

ISBN   085036 475 2   Pbk   £12.95